The Younger John Winthrop

THE YOUNGER
JOHN
WINTHROP

BY

Robert C. Black III

1966

COLUMBIA UNIVERSITY PRESS

NEW YORK & LONDON

Robert C. Black III is Associate Professor of History
at Trinity College, Hartford, Connecticut.

Frontispiece:
The *Portrait of John Winthrop the Younger 1606–1676*,
artist unknown, is reproduced through the courtesy
of Harvard University.

Copyright © 1966 Columbia University Press
Library of Congress Catalog Card Number: 66-20493
Printed in the United States of America

For my friends of the fourteenth of May:
We can't be unhappy together.

Preface

T H E R E may somewhere exist an authentic historical or biographical "field" that is absolutely unworked; if so, I have yet to encounter it. Certainly the younger John Winthrop has long attracted a considerable notice: He has been sketched, subjected to medical criticism, and made the subject of copious footnotes; he has been presented as a builder of the Massachusetts Bay Colony, cited as the most significant influence in seventeenth-century Connecticut, and featured above all others in an admirable study of the Winthrop family. He even has served (in a widely read novel) as a noble-minded lover, frustrated by circumstance. Yet it may be ventured that he has not heretofore received full-scale biographical attention of the usual kind. That such treatment has been long overdue I am convinced.

To render appropriate thanks to all who have contributed to an effort of so many seasons is quite impossible. The cooperative nature of librarians and archivists is universally recognized, yet so unexceptionally cordial have been their efforts on my behalf that my feelings can only remain those of happy discovery. They have stood ready in many places, some of world-wide fame, others unpretentious: The Library of Congress; the Bodleian Library; the New London County Historical Society; the Connecticut Historical Society, whose director, Mr. Thompson R. Harlow, and his entire staff deserve special thanks; the British Museum; the Public Record Office of Great Britain; the American Antiquarian Society; the Massachusetts Historical Society, whose editor of publications, Mr. Malcolm Freiberg, has extended assistance far beyond the call of duty; the Connecticut State Library, where Mr. George Adams, legislative reference librarian, has proved especially helpful; the Long Island Historical Society; the New-York Historical Society; the New York Society Library; the Butler Library, Columbia University; the Museum of the City of New York; the Trinity College Library, Hartford, Connecticut, of which the librarian, Mr. Donald B. Engley and his long-suffering assistants must receive particular mention; the Watkinson Library, Hartford, over which presides the ever-cordial Mrs. Marian Clarke; and the Library of the Royal Society of London.

There are those who have rendered a less formal assistance: Mrs. Estelle J. Inch of Hartford, who performed, with an expert touch, most of the typing; Miss Phyllis Holbrook of the Columbia University Press, a master of the intricacies of editing; Professor Richard Dunn, now of the University of Pennsylvania; Professor Glenn Weaver of Trinity College, Hartford, Professor Philip Kintner, formerly of Trinity, now of Grinnell College, who reduced to understandable terms certain passages of archaic German; Professor George B. Cooper of Trinity, whose working knowledge of English historiographic byways is unsurpassed in America; and Professor D. G. Brinton Thompson of Trinity, whose admiration for Winthrop first suggested this effort; also R. W. Elliott, M.A., headmaster of King Edward VI School, Bury St. Edmunds, Suffolk; J. W. Hamilton-Jones of Streatham, London; and the Reverend A. B. Bird, rector of Groton and vicar of Edwardstone, Suffolk.

"They also serve who only stand and wait." Among these invaluable individuals must be cited the remainder of the author's colleagues on the faculty of Trinity College, but in particular Pro-

fessor Eugene W. Davis, who has endured literally years of mono-
logues about Winthrop. Furthermore, I must publicly commend my
wife, Regina M. Black, and my six children, for their acceptance of
long periods of silence and closed doors.

Most satisfying of all have been certain personal friendships, for
which the preparation of this book has been largely, or wholly, responsible. I have reference to P. E. Colston Pendock, Esq., whose
companionship so perfectly complimented a tour of autumnal East
Anglia; Bleddyn Griffith, Esq., who afforded educational shoptalk
and weekend relaxation in the Welsh hills; the Reverend and Mrs.
Frank Hughes, whose rectory provided so gracious a hospitality in
the midst of Winthrop's earliest landscapes; and Mr. Ronald S.
Wilkinson of Michigan State University, learned adept in the history of alchemy and esteemed friend, though we never have met.
Winthrop would have liked them.

ROBERT C. BLACK III

Trinity College,
Hartford, Connecticut,
January 3, 1966

Contents

Contents

The Younger John Winthrop

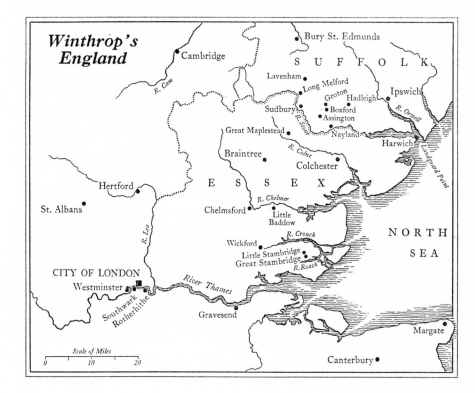

Winthrop's England

Cambridge

R. Cam

Bury St. Edmunds

S U F F O L K

Lavenham

Long Melford

Groton Hadleigh

Ipswich

Sudbury Boxford
Assington

R. Orwell

Great Maplestead

Nayland

R. Stour

Harwich

Landguard Point

R. Colne

Braintree

Colchester

Hertford

E S S E X

St. Albans

Chelmsford

R. Chelmer

Little
Baddow

R. Lea

Wickford

R. Crouch

NORTH

Little Stambridge

SEA

Great Stambridge

R. Roach

CITY OF LONDON

Westminster

River Thames

Southwark
Rotherhithe

Gravesend

Margate

Scale of Miles

0   10   20

Canterbury

CHAPTER I

The Backgrounds & the Beginning

THERE have been five John Winthrops of whom the world has taken special note.

The first enjoys the widest fame; it was he who became the principal figure in the establishment of Massachusetts Bay. The second was the eldest son of the first and came to dominate the affairs of early Connecticut. The third was the eldest son of the second and, in his own time, was likewise a significant influence in that colony. The fourth and fifth, less intimately connected, never became political leaders, but acquired transatlantic fame in matters of natural science.

It is the second of the notable John Winthrops with whom this study is concerned. Of the five, he was beyond doubt the most versatile; although distinguished in public life, his reputation in science was such that he has often been confused with John IV and John V. Very possibly he was the ablest. It is certain he was the most attractive—not only to the modern taste but to his contemporaries. Like his father, he became a part of American history, yet never ceased to be English. Nevertheless, except in basic physiognomy and in a notable personal vigor, he resembled his father hardly at all.

His roots were East Anglian, and his first impressions were of

effective things. There was a ceilinged room with sturdy timbering,[1] and there was a woman. She moved with an aristocratic rus-
tle, yet it was she who usually drew the curtains and brought him
his porridge. Her voice was quiet, but purposeful; it differed strikingly from the less modulated urgings and chidings of the nursery,
and it provided his first lesson in class distinction. Before long, he
knew the woman as his mother. But in the absence of a portrait he
found himself unable, when he was grown, to remember clearly
her face.[2]

He recalled in better detail his childhood landscapes. The Essex
countryside was substantial and useful. It rose in the gentlest of
undulations from the banks of little tidal rivers; behind labyrin-
thine hedges it bore clusters of sheep. There were lanes, rutted
and trampled, and acres of arable, whose clay-loam furrows presented a soggy geometry in the slanting sunlight. Across cloud-
scuddy horizons strode copses of elm, straight-boled and intricately
branched, and from one of them a church tower rose square-cut
against the sky. Up the tiny waterways the tides brought plump
little ships and left them careened upon the mud; they deposited
also a sturdy folk surnamed Brandt and Harlakenden, whose curiously gabled buildings had long been evident over these easterly
parts, for it was in Essex that the English estuaries faced most directly the delta lands across the narrow seas. And there were
closer, more intimate objects—the manor house, rather pretentious
in a homely fashion, stoutly framed, brick filled and plastered,
roofed with tiles, and an enormous barn with a cluster of satellite
buildings, heavily thatched. Close at hand, an island of woods
grew thick and beside the mansion a disciplined row of trees with
lower limbs carefully lopped.[3] Everywhere were odors, richly and
intimately agricultural.

These were the first abiding memories of a three-year-old boy in
the late autumn of 1609. To him, they represented only the beginning of all he would come to know; but to certain of his elders

they were a consummation of hopes long cherished. For a family did not dwell by chance in the mansion house of Great Stambridge, Essex. It took a bit of doing; such a residence meant comparative wealth; it was a measure of success; it conveyed prestige, indeed, rank. The Winthrops were not, in 1609, folk of the common sort.

But if they were clearly of the gentry, it is evident that they had not been so for a very long period. True, there were comfortable legends of a Robert *de* Winetorp who had dwelt in Yorkshire in 1200, and of an I. Winethorp in Lincolnshire in 1207. Another tradition, quite innocent of citation, maintained that a person of reasonably similar name had, at an ancient period unspecified, owned Marylebone Park, near London.[4] But the Winthrop record does not achieve confident documentation until 1498, and then it is the tale of a provincial lad who made good in the metropolis.

His name was Adam Winthrop, and he was born to obscure parents in the cloth-town of Lavenham, Suffolk, in October, 1498. A marked personal initiative carried him, by the age of seventeen, to London, where a nice balance of energy and good fortune insured his rise to the lofty eminence of a full master of the London Clothworkers Company. More satisfactory still were his financial rewards, which enabled him to marry well (twice), to marry his children better, and to acquire from the Crown, for £408/18/03, plus certain annuities of medieval origin, the Manor of Groton. Once the property of the deprived Abbot of Bury St. Edmunds, Groton lay not six miles from Adam's native Lavenham. Its acquisition was more than an investment; it was a symbol; and it was at Groton in November, 1562, that he died, full (by contemporary standards) of years and (by the standards of any period) of worldly success.[5]

Of his numerous offspring, the ablest was also called Adam. Born in 1548, he grew into an authentic squire's squire, and though not, strictly speaking, the proper heir was nevertheless invested with the lordship of the manor.[6] Like his father, he married effectively and twice.[7] Unlike his parent, but quite in harmony with accepted practice, he secured *part* of a university education.[8] Even when past thirty years of age, he undertook to read law at the Inner Temple, and in the winter of 1583/4 * was made barrister.[9] He was a prudent manager; he took particular pains with those portions of the Groton lands which were not in the permanent tenure of others, and before the end of the century his income from the sale of his own produce considerably exceeded that received from rents. He became in fact sufficiently wealthy to be regarded as a source of loan capital, and it is noteworthy that all of the moneys he extended were duly repaid, except in two melancholy instances that involved Her Majesty Queen Elizabeth.[10] He more than met his responsibilities in matters of public duty: His legal training was at the disposal not only of his own but of neighboring manors; he oversaw, *ex officio* and as a matter of course, the local poor; and he searched, on a like basis, the local cloth, but his sixteen-year stint as a kind of business manager for both Trinity and St. John's colleges, Cambridge, was clearly extracurricular.[11] It was quite in accord with squirely tradition, however, that he should devote himself—before queen, university, or country—to the interests of the Winthrop family.

His eldest son had been born, and baptized John, in January 1587/8, and the child was less than four and one-half years of age when his father undertook to secure verification of his gentility in the form of a "Confirmation of Arms." Issued under the authority of the Garter king-of-arms, this document proclaimed upon vellum that John Winthrop, "Sonne & heyre of Adam Wynthrop of

---

* THE dates provided herein are of the "Old Style" in common use among the English in the seventeenth century. They are *ten days* behind the more accurate dating of the Gregorian Calendar. It should also be borne in mind that the New Year ordinarily commenced on Lady Day (Annunciation to the Virgin Mary), which was March 25. Hence the divided year designations (that is, 1636/7) for dates in January, February, and the greater part of March.

Groton in Countie of Suff Gent," also "other the Children Issue & posteritie of the said Adam Wynthrope of Groton" should be invested with a "Shield or Cote of Arms" described as *"d'argent three Chevrerons Gules over all A Lyon rampant Sables, armed & langued, Azure.* . . . And for his Creast or Conizance *A hare proper, runninge on A mount Verte,* sett vppo A helmet in a wrethe of his Coullors with manbelles and Tasselles." [12]

Adam Winthrop was of course too much a realist to content himself with a mere certificate. The training of the heir of a country squire called for much more. To learn to ride, to apprehend proper husbandry, to understand the nature of responsibility, went without saying. To these, Adam was careful to add university training, and his son was not yet fifteen when, on December 8, 1602, he entered Trinity College, Cambridge.[13] But eclipsing everything, even the bachelor's degree, was the question of John's marriage. It was answered, in the fashion of the time and place, empirically.

That the fortunes of English families have been frequently and profitably advanced by way of the altar is too well known to require elaboration. But the effectiveness of the technique becomes particularly clear in the presence of a maiden like Mary Forth. Mary was a most unusual young lady in that she was the sole heir of profusely landed parents. It was in fact difficult to consider her otherwise than in terms of acreage. That her age exceeded by four years that of Adam Winthrop's son John was a matter of indifference.

Mary's father, John Forth, had been a younger son, but had nicely evaded the ordinary effects of primogeniture. In Suffolk, he held "messuages, lands and tenements, both freehold and copyhold," in the parishes of Kersey, Hadleigh, Layham, and Royden. In Essex, he was yet more handsomely possessed with "free messuages, lands, etc.," in Rochford, Hurwell, Assingdon, and (very conspicuously) in the Stambridges, Great and Little.[14] The

[5]

precise extent of his holdings is uncertain, but it was imperial. It is not known how he came by all of them, but a large proportion, including the Essex properties, he had acquired by virtue of a prudent marriage to the childless, but not landless, widow of two husbands. Her maiden name had been Thomasine Hilles; she dwelt at Great Stambridge, and there John Forth established his personal seat.[15] When, in good season, she died, she left to him the disposition of her acres and of their daughter.

If Mary Forth was thus richly endowed, she also was "well connected." Sixty years before, her paternal grandfather had been invested with Butley Abbey, and her uncle Robert Forth had served, in 1569, as high sheriff of Suffolk. Another uncle, William, had experienced the personal wrath of Queen Elizabeth. A cousin William enjoyed the prestige, but lamented the fees, of recent knighthood.[16] And if she was plain of face (we do not know this) and of not overly acquiescent temper (which seems rather more likely), she was manifestly a catch—such a catch as would justify the recall of one's son and heir from Cambridge.

And that is what Adam Winthrop seems to have done. It is not on record that John Winthrop was "sent down"; there is evidence neither of academic deficiency nor of any excess of spirits— youthful or alcoholic. There remains only Adam Winthrop's diary, and its meaning is sufficiently plain:

> [January 12, 1604/5]—. . . Mr. John Foorth came to my house.
> [March 14, 1604/5]—I and my soonne viewed over Mr. John Foorthes land at Carsey [Kersey] and Hadley.
> [March 26, 1605]—I and my Soone did ride to Mr. John Foorthes of Great Stambridge in Essex.
> [March 28, 1605]—My soonne was sollemly contracted to Mary Foorth by Mr. Culverwell minister of greate Stambridge in Essex cum consentu parentum.
> [April 16, 1605]—He was maryed to her at Stambridge in Essex by Mr. Culverwell.[17]

But though this union between a young woman of twenty-one and a half-mature boy of seventeen clearly reflected a landed, rather than a romantic, interest, it quickly produced offspring. It was not ten months after Mary had repeated her vows before the Reverend Mr. Culverwell when, in the dark of the morning of February 12, 1605/6, she was delivered of a son at the manor house of Groton.[18] Adam Winthrop must have been particularly pleased that the infant was a boy. Eleven days later, beside the font in Groton Parish Church, he was given his father's name, John.[19]

If Mary thus early confronted her youthful spouse with the responsibilities of parenthood, she continued to increase them at rather frequent intervals. Henry Winthrop was born at Groton in January, 1607/08; Mary appeared, at Great Stambridge, in February, 1611/12; and again in Groton she gave birth to two infant daughters named Anna, one in late July of 1614, and the other in June, 1615. Neither Anna survived, and the mother died in childbed with the second.[20]

Marriage likewise imposed upon John Winthrop a particularly demanding schedule of estate management. As the heir of *two* families, he was obliged to master the intricate details of *two* aggregations of property—how intricate can be appreciated only by one who is learned in the technology of late-medieval land tenure. There were constant passages, on horseback, from Groton to Stambridge, from Essex to Suffolk, from Suffolk to London. In the beginning, Mary and her infants were established chiefly at Groton, but in the autumn of 1608 they were moved to her father's house at Great Stambridge.[21] The reason is not entirely clear. But the removal, into the parish of the Reverend Mr. Culverwell, was momentous. Indeed, from the viewpoint of North American posterity, Mary Forth provided John Winthrop with but two things of lasting importance: his first-born son and namesake and his friendship with Ezekial Culverwell. Beside these, her acres scarcely mattered.

It was Ezekial Culverwell who made a Puritan of the elder John Winthrop—not Adam Winthrop, who plainly was not the reforming sort, nor Trinity College, wherein John later admitted himself to have been "lewdly disposed." [22] John's sudden and heavy responsibilities no doubt played some part, but Ezekial Culverwell remained always the major influence.[23]

When the Reverend Mr. Culverwell had joined John Winthrop and Mary Forth in marriage in the spring of 1605, he already had been rector of Great Stambridge for fourteen years. The son of a London haberdasher and a graduate of Emmanuel College, Cambridge (an institution *par excellence* of the ecclesiastical left), he long had been notable for tendencies of the reforming—and nonconforming—kind. To John Winthrop's first born, he could present but the vaguest image, for the child was not yet four when Mr. Culverwell quitted Stambridge forever, the unhappy victim of the episcopal axe.[24] But with the father it was another story: The young squire was fascinated. The chaste arrangements in the little church, the grave sincerity of its pastor, his provocative sermons, the earnest discussions before the mansionhouse fire, all these aroused in John Winthrop a profound response. He presently embarked upon an intensive program of self-examination, whereof he kept copious notes, or "experiencia." He fretted over self-indulgence; he abandoned (apparently with success) the use of profanity, playing cards, and sporting firearms; he strove to reduce his enjoyment of food and to improve his attention to sermons, even of the inferior kind that were rendered by Mr. Nicholson, the rector of Groton.[25] Through the remainder of his life, he never neglected these moral exercises, and as the "experiencia" lengthened so—in a fashion not always comfortable—did the character of John Winthrop.

Ezekial Culverwell was deprived of his Great Stambridge living in 1609. It can hardly have been at the request of his parishioners; if he was "Puritan," so, to a degree, were they. For the plump ships that penetrated the Essex estuaries carried ideas as well as goods, notions which stuck fast in the heavy soil. But no one lamented Mr. Culverwell's ejection more bitterly than John Winthrop; he who had given meaning to Stambridge was gone, and all that remained were an unexciting wife, who forbore to vex herself with theological questions, and a dominating father-in-law, who still was lord of the manor and let the heir know it.[26] John Winthrop soon was driven in upon himself; he became morose, indeed ill, and turned more frequently to prayer.[27]

All this the eldest child observed—and failed to comprehend. Of the gentle countryside, with its sheep and its elms and its lanes, he grasped the importance. Of the services at the ancient little church, he sensed the inevitability. Even for his distracted father he felt respect and affection. But for the things his father prized most, he developed little understanding.[28] John Winthrop had become a dedicated Puritan. John Winthrop, Jr., never did.

THE YOUNGER John Winthrop was seven years old when he last saw his maternal grandfather; it was on May 15, 1613, that John Forth died at Great Stambridge—*vir pietate clarus* was the final and respectful pronouncement of the other grandfather at Groton.[29] But though John Forth may have been notable for his devotion to religion, his passing was a deep relief to his son-in-law. Scarcely had his remains been laid to rest within the Great Stambridge Parish Church when John Winthrop admitted (in his "experiencia") his profound thanks.[30]

But if Mr. Forth ever had been aware of his son-in-law's feelings, his last will and testament failed to reveal it. The marriage agreement of 1605 seems to have been scrupulously honored. The core of his holdings at Great Stambridge went jointly to John Winthrop and to John the younger; his other properties (scattered over two counties and seven parishes) he transmitted to his other grandsons; his daughter and son-in-law were to serve as executors and guardians. Adam Winthrop himself had witnessed the document, and no one made any difficulty when it was submitted to probate at Ingatestone on the fourth of June following.[31]

There had been a period when John Winthrop had happily turned from threadbare old Groton to the more stimulating neighborhood of the Stambridges and the Reverend Mr. Culverwell. But now, though John Forth's will was a cause for satisfaction, he longed to exchange Stambridge for Groton again. A principal motive was the presence at Boxford, close to Groton, of Mr. Henry Sands, for some time the "reader" at Boxford Church and a master of theological discourse—a veritable Culverwell. Indeed, as early as September, 1613, John Winthrop was meeting with a cluster of kindred spirits at Mr. Sands's house to organize a discussion group of plainly reformist flavor.[32]

This was decisive, and it was not long before John Winthrop, Jr., was taken with his mother, his brothers, and his infant sister to dwell once more at his native village.[33] Though he can hardly have remembered the place, the change cannot have been very disrupting, for the essentials of Groton did not differ conspicuously from those of Stambridge. To be sure, the tidal creeks and their chunky little ships were absent, and the plateau upon which Groton stood sloped away rather more steeply into deeper valleys, and the parish church was of a stubbier aspect. But there was the same kind of manor house, the same array of outbuildings, the copses of elm, the intricate hedges, and an identical geometry of furrows beneath the autumn sun.

Groton did require two adjustments of a personal kind. The first proved happy: At the new manor house lived the child's other grandfather, Adam Winthrop, still the complete squire, vigorous and competent, conformist rather than enthusiast, in no sense other-worldly, but worldly with restraint. People noticed that he and the grandson at once developed a mutual understanding.[34] The second brought dreadful, if ephemeral, grief: The boy was at the beginning of his tenth summer, when the family found itself suspended once again among the tensions of childbirth. But this time they were not to find release in a spate of announcement and congratulation; instead they interred Mary Forth Winthrop and the second infant Anna beneath the chancel of Groton Church. Childhood's sorrow is brief, but as the younger John gazed upward at the oddly wrought timbers above the nave and listened to the halting intonations of the Reverend Thomas Nicholson, he knew at least the pain of deprivation.[35]

To his father—still only twenty-seven—the passing of the wife of his youth must have been a blow, but it is noteworthy that it evoked no theological speculations in his "experiencia"; moreover, he lost little time in providing his children with a new mother. Indeed, the details were perfected within two months and four days of the burial of her predecessor, and the formal ceremony seems to have been delayed for three months more solely by the unexpected demise of the bride's father.[36]

Her name was Thomasine Clopton, and she was five, not merely four, years older than John Winthrop. She was of one of Suffolk's first families (the noble parish church at Long Melford was conspicuously adorned with Clopton tombs and brasses), and she came to marry John Winthrop from Castleins Hall, a compact little mansion within the bounds of Groton itself. It furthermore is clear that the Cloptons were distinctly of the Puritan persuasion and that Thomasine herself held religious views of a kind calculated to delight her husband.[37]

To John Winthrop's children she proved an admirable mother —for one year. Then, on November 30, 1616, she gave birth to a daughter. On December 2 the infant expired, and a day or two later it became obvious that Thomasine, too, was ebbing away. It was a hideous proceeding; for close to seventy-two hours the dying woman, trussed up appallingly in a tight "waystcote" and gloves, held macabre court to her family and a long procession of servants and tenants. The younger John, now nearly eleven and already impressionable, was naturally distressed; his father was inconsolable. He paced and he prayed, and when, in the afternoon dusk of December 8, his wife breathed her last, he was careful to crowd every detail into his record of godly experiences.[38]

Yet life at Groton Manor provided a growing boy with more than emotional crises. There were occasions of a less personal kind —the arrival of new tenants, the departure of others, and the births of other people's infants. Of still greater interest were a game of "footebal," wherein a neighborhood youth broke his leg, and the appearance, on the third of May, 1617, of Aunt Anne (Winthrop) Fones with a small bevy of London cousins, including two little girls named Elizabeth and Martha. They lingered long at Groton; Uncle Thomas Fones arrived in the middle of July, and they did not depart until August 25, in thunder and rain.[39]

Young John Winthrop's formal education had, of course, been undertaken some time before—precisely where and in what fashion we cannot be certain. The essentials of reading and writing were dispensed with a fine informality in seventeenth-century England—by one's parents (if literate) or by some happily unregulated village schoolmaster or by a convenient clergyman. But at about the age of eight, the proceedings stiffened abruptly—for privileged or selected boys—with their entry into "grammar school." Here they were subjected for perhaps seven years to a classical curriculum that meant business. When it was done, the survivors were competent in *Latin*—to the practical exclusion of anything else—and were deemed ready for work at a university. As intellectual training, it was intense; in terms of achieved results, it must command our respect.[40]

Of the grammar school years of John Winthrop, Jr., we do not know a great deal. Down the highroad from Groton Manor House, close to a turning before a lovely flintwork church, stood the Boxford Free Grammar School. This establishment was currently a matter for considerable regional pride; its thirty-seven "governors" were a catalogue of neighborhood consequence, and from 1616 to 1623 its principal master was one Hoogan, whose superior pedagogy was recognized even at Cambridge. But Boxford resembled most English schools of the period in its lackadaisical record keeping, and if John Winthrop, Jr., actually attended, the fact cannot be authenticated. We can only be sure that he did not complete his secondary education so close to home. For this he was sent twenty miles across High Suffolk to the King Edward VI School at Bury St. Edmunds.[41]

The reason is obscure. It was not the motherless situation of his family, for the elder John, with all his lamentations, permitted himself to remain Thomasine's widower for only a year and a quarter. In fact, the prescribed negotiations for another wife were well under way in little more than nine months.[42]

It proved a difficult business, but Margaret Tyndal was worth it. She was three years younger than her suitor, she possessed a "lovely" countenance, and her toleration of the religious anxieties of others was pronounced. Her lineage surpassed even that of the Cloptons; the Tyndals were, in truth, so impressive that they plainly were loath to bestow a daughter upon the elder John Winthrop. His suit was ultimately successful, but there were many rides across the Stour to the Tyndal seat in Essex before he and Margaret were married in the curious little brick and flintwork church at Great Maplestead in April, 1618. The groom's eldest child was already past his twelfth birthday, but it was not long before he was conscious of a deep affection for this newest stepparent. Years after her death John Winthrop, Jr., declared that Margaret Tyndal Winthrop had been "as deare to my selfe" as if she had been his actual mother.[43]

Precisely when the boy was sent to Bury St. Edmunds is uncertain, but of the town and of the King Edward VI School we know a good deal. Bury had been from an ancient period a center of religion and learning. Thanks to the widely advertised relics of St. Edmund and to the executive vigor of a succession of mitred abbots, there had arisen at Bury a remarkable complex of monastic buildings, in particular an abbey church, of which the west front was 250 feet wide and the nave and choir close to 500 feet long; in terms of simple grandeur it was unsurpassed in Western Christendom. But it also had been envied, and when Henry VIII's dissolution came in 1539, the townspeople had turned upon the great church as a hated symbol. With pick and gunpowder they had torn it to pieces, and when, some eighty years later, the younger John Winthrop arrived from Groton, Bury St. Edmunds rose dominantly secular beside some of Europe's most profound ruins.[44]

But if the old order was gone, the learning it had patronized continued to flourish. Though not the largest of English grammar schools, King Edward VI was reckoned one of the best. Its endowment (chiefly in lands) was handsome; its curriculum was unusually broad; Greek was prescribed, and the suitably motivated could undertake additional work in French, Italian, or Spanish. The training offered was in truth of such quality that an unusual proportion of the student body came—like young Winthrop—from a distance and were placed about the town in private lodgings under the care of selected "hosts and hostesses." The school itself stood (until 1660) close beside the River Lark; its latest generation of students delights in the legend that it occupied a building which currently serves as a public house. In any case, the situation was picturesque; the little stream was arched by willows and a medieval bridge, swans paddled in the quiet current, and in the autumn gloaming the ruins of the abbey church rose huge and soft against the sky.[45]

Here at Bury, John Winthrop, Jr., enjoyed what modern educators would call a "successful experience." A primary factor in this happy development was the high master, John Dickenson, a man of extraordinary talents, whom the governors of King Edward VI were careful to keep at his post with repeated increases in salary. But another element was the youthful John himself. He was by no means handsome; his complexion was too dark, his eyebrows too arched, and his nose was more than fulfilling the well-known Winthrop standard of length. Nor does he seem to have been, in the usual sense, an outstanding scholar; though King Edward VI resembled Boxford in the informality of its records, we may assume, on the basis of facts later to become evident, that John Winthrop the Younger was not notable for the steadiness of his efforts. Yet, he was not an ordinary lad, for he clearly was blessed with the priceless trait called "personality." His fellow students may not have been greatly impressed, but his elders were. His host and hostess (their names have not survived) and his masters (the remarkable Mr. Dickenson in particular) never quite got over him. So early in his career did John Winthrop, Jr., discover his capacity to enchant! [46]

CHAPTER 2

Maturity Deferred

BUT always there was the problem of Puritanism. The boy could hardly avoid it, just as he scarcely could elude the seventeenth century, East Anglia, or his father.

Puritanism was, and remains, many things to many men. It was etymologically a nickname. It was ethnically English. It sought further to de-Romanize, from within, the Anglican Church. It set lofty standards of personal excellence. It emphasized the Old Testament. It endeavored to reduce the unthinking pursuit of earthly pleasures. Most of all, it was an intellectual movement, and its leaders were intellectuals. But, as intellectuals are wont, they disagreed as to details and with such vigor that they presently debated them into competing fundamentals. So Puritanism became a thing of multifarious facets—spiritual, temporal, scholarly, and passionate.[1]

It is indeed rather easier to declare what Puritanism was not than to assert what it was. Though English, it was by no means wholly of English origin, nor did it appeal in any one of its aspects to every Englishman. Though it endowed the papal curia with collective incarnation as the Whore of Babylon, it studiously refrained from rejecting the learning of medieval Christendom.[2] It was no simple engine of repression; it did not denounce as such sex, alcohol, or the new tobacco, all of which it permitted (in moderation) as entirely consistent with the glory of God. Very significantly avoided was the preaching of any nonsense as to the virtues of religious toleration; the English Puritans were as one with the enormous majority of seventeenth-century Europeans who believed in the exclusive and universal application of God's will as they happened to perceive it.

It cannot be denied that Puritanism strove to emphasize the role of religion in the conscious life of the individual. But the results were far from monastic; the things of the spirit were always to be pondered over in the midst of worldly concerns. The Puritan shoemaker remained a shoemaker. The Puritan squire (the elder John Winthrop is a typical example) remained a squire. And a very real squire he had become.

Already the heir to certain of the Forth properties and trustee for the others, he personally had taken over, before 1620, the greater part of the Groton lands as well.³ As early as the summer of 1617, he was expanding his holdings by purchase in the fruitful region beyond Boxford, close to Nayland and the Stour Valley. That he was by 1622 indubitably lord of Groton is proved by his "grant," on June 25, of a coroner's commission to his own father. It was no light responsibility; his acres, a large proportion whereof were a-blat with grazing sheep, exceeded 500; he was responsible for petty neighborhood justice; four times annually he had to attend the Quarter Sessions at Bury St. Edmunds; and his was the disposition, not only of the living of Groton Church but of waifs, strays, felons' goods, and "free warren." ⁴

It was an expansive life, but John Winthrop endeavored to proceed with a godly prudence. This was, however, no guarantee of success, for precisely as the young squire was organizing, and even extending, his domain, the very props were being pulled from beneath the economy of East Anglia. From olden times, the regional specialty had been woolen cloth, its principal market the Netherlands, its exclusive agents the celebrated Merchant Adventurers. Then, in 1613, the impecunious James I had bestowed, for a consideration, a new monopoly of the traffic upon a mercantile combination headed by one William Cockayne. From the start, Cockayne and his associates conducted things with a conspicuous dearth of wisdom; the Dutch refused to deal with them, and the entire trade became swiftly disrupted. By 1617, Cockayne's company was finished, and the traditional commerce of East Anglia never wholly recovered. Indeed, the 1620s are remembered there still as a time of catastrophe, and Puritan precepts of estate management quite failed to spare the Winthrops from its effects. They did not, to be sure, go bankrupt; they did become, increasingly and comparatively, land poor.[5]

THE ELDER John already was wrestling with these economic woes when his son and heir was pronounced, at Bury St. Edmunds, fit for admission to a university. This meant additional expense, but there apparently was no thought that the boy should on this account abandon his education. The sole question seems to have been the selection of a college, and the choice (a little unexpectedly in view of family tradition) fell not upon Trinity, Cambridge, but upon Trinity, Dublin.

One reason was religious. Though certain Cambridge colleges had served for a considerable period as forcing frames for advanced Protestantism, the episcopal influence had recently imposed upon their undergraduates a formal assent to the Thirty-nine Articles. Such a requirement was of course anathema to many Puritans—and to many Puritan parents. But nonconformists quickly discovered a promising refuge in Trinity, Dublin, of which the staff and atmosphere were at once Cantabrigian and unorthodox. It was a situation, moreover, that the royal advisers appear to have overlooked, and there consequently were, at Dublin, no oaths or other undertakings which a Puritan could not in good conscience accept.[6]

Another factor was the younger John's Aunt Lucy. This young lady had become espoused to Emmanuel Downing, a lawyer of acknowledged parts and expectations, whose religious convictions were suitably Puritan; furthermore he was a widower, and the affairs of his deceased wife required his early presence in Dublin. His marriage to Lucy Winthrop had been announced for April 10, 1622, at Rotherhithe, the well-known maritime suburb of London, and he intended for Ireland, with his bride, shortly thereafter.[7]

John Winthrop, Jr., was sixteen years of age when he departed for Trinity, Dublin. It was his first extensive journey; indeed, it may have been his initial penetration of the world beyond Suffolk and Essex. It is likely that he proceeded first to Lucy Winthrop's wedding and that he thereafter accompanied the bride and groom to Dublin in the manner (one suspects) of excess baggage. If this be so, he visited London—clamorous, crowded, and noisome, athrill with new conceptions, but as yet more than half-medieval. Very probably, also, he experienced for the first time the discouraging passage down the English Channel, with its days' long beat into the wind, for it was summer before he reached Ireland.[8]

If the London of 1622 smacked still of the Middle Ages, Dublin seemed altogether a medieval town. Its venerable ramparts remained nearly intact, and the great majority of its citizens still dwelt within them, packed among the quaint deficiencies of a thousand years.[9] But Trinity College shared little in the flavor of its city. It lay well to the east of the aging walls, amid fields and meadows which, though prolific in swine and vagrants, were intensely and eternally green. Save for an antique bell tower, the relic of a defunct monastery, its buildings were comparatively new and distinctly attractive in their combination of timbering and Dutch brick. Trinity was organized in the Cambridge fashion, with a complicated hierarchy of provosts, deans, fellows, tutors, scholars, fellow commoners, pensioners, and sizars. Its curriculum seemed equally traditional; theology remained the central discipline; Greek, Hebrew, logic, natural and moral philosophy, physics, metaphysics, rhetoric, and ethics were all subordinate. A knowledge of Latin was assumed, and lectures were customarily delivered in that tongue. In lieu of formal examinations, there were declamations and disputations conducted verbally in Latin.[10]

Nevertheless, Trinity, Dublin, offered its students rather more than an unseasoned rehash of medieval scholasticism. Since 1609, the provost had been the extraordinary William Temple, one of the most brilliant of living Cambridge graduates. Temple was of such ability that he had become, at the age of thirty, secretary to Sir Philip Sidney, and that celebrated man actually had died in Temple's arms. Far more significant, alike for Trinity, and for the youthful Winthrop, was his enthusiasm for the ideas of the French philosopher, Peter Ramus, in particular a suspicion of uncritical scholarship and a faith in natural reason. Temple recently had been knighted by the lord deputy for Ireland, but he was by no means a spokesman for Jacobean policy. His leanings were Puritan; at the college chapel services he refused to wear a surplice—on the logical, though specious, grounds that he was not in holy orders.[11]

Like other universities of the period, Trinity provided neither playing fields nor formal opportunity for physical exercise. It consequently was quite inevitable that the hundred undergraduates should erupt into a variety of picturesque misdeeds, running the gamut from roof scaling to hooting at the local maidenry, and it is small wonder that young Winthrop was confronted upon his arrival with a prodigious array of regulations or that his father's first letter admonished him to work hard, remember God, and avoid temptation.[12]

John did work hard—in the beginning. He adequately remembered God, though not with the introspection of his parent.[13] Temptation he rather effectively side-stepped; he appears not to have been involved in any major roisterings, and he most often was to be found in his study gown, hunched in a pew in the college library. Here he found books beyond previous experience. Here was a table with globes and an unusual collection of maps, while in a corner hung a human "sceliton," thoughtfully clothed in "taffety hangings." Winthrop was enchanted, and shortly after his arrival penned an enthusiastic letter to his brother Forth, recommending that he, too, "goe on in the corse of learning." [14]

Trinity, Dublin, resembled other universities of the period in its emphasis upon tutors. These learned and dedicated individuals fulfilled a triune purpose: as professors, they lectured; as advisers, they stood watch over the progress (and the behavior) of particular students; and as financial functionaries, they saw to the payment of tuition and other fees.[15] It is more than probable that Winthrop's tutor was the excellent Joshua Hoyle, an earnest, yet understanding, Yorkshireman, who later became a member of the Westminster Assembly of Divines.[16] Under his supervision, the youth exhibited—for a time—unusual promise, and as late as June, 1623, his father could commend him for having "profited even beyond my expectations. . . . No distance of place, or length of absence, can abate the affection of a loving father towards a dutiful, well deserving child." [17]

Unfortunately, these happy circumstances did not long endure; the first hint of trouble appeared in the autumn of 1623, when the boy abruptly expressed a desire to return home. "Think not of seeing England," replied the senior Winthrop, "till you may bring a hood at your back." But this and other encouragements proved unavailing, and by the following spring, the son's morale had so deteriorated that his father was driven to point out that, without a degree, "this time wilbe lost." Nevertheless, before winter had come again, John Winthrop, Jr., was back in England, hoodless and empty handed.[18]

It is possible at least to surmise the reasons. One seems to have been simple homesickness. At the time of John's entry into Trinity, Dublin, there had been a good deal of family discussion as to the feasibility of establishing a Puritan colony overseas—in Ireland. The newly wedded Downings, Emmanuel and Lucy, had, of course, actually gone. And in April of 1623, the elder John Winthrop himself had expressed a serious interest. "I wish oft," he had written his son, that "God would open a waye to settle me in Ireland, if it might be for his glory." But God made no decisive move. There was saddening news of the death of the well-loved grandfather Adam Winthrop. And it presently became evident that Emmanuel Downing, his wife, and their infant son would themselves return permanently to England. Even an interesting coterie of university friends—a graduate student named Robert Worrall, a certain Will Usher, and a variety of Hoyles, all of whom John had charmed—failed to overcome his loneliness.[19]

Another and more cogent reason was a simple lack of staying power. His studies required persistence, but the young man lacked the capacity (or the willingness) to persist. So pronounced was this form of immaturity that it was already in the way of becoming a character defect. Indeed, it would linger for years, until the generally remarkable career of John Winthrop, Jr., became uncomfortably littered with unfinished tasks and abandoned designs. It too often was the distant grass that grew greenest. And on this occasion, despite the emerald fields about Trinity College, it grew on the English side of the Irish Sea.

T o b e s u r e, he was quite devoid of ideas for his own future. At Groton (where his stepmother already had filled the manor house with a generation of younger brothers) he hung listlessly about for weeks, and when an occasion took him close to Bury St. Edmunds, he neglected even to call upon his still-adoring host and hostess. Yet he did not wholly lose the ability to captivate. Though his behavior was such as to alienate his father, no parental explosion came. On the contrary, when the son suggested, in a Macawber spirit, that he might cast about London for a time, the elder Winthrop appears only to have recommended that he call en route upon his most distinguished uncle and aunt, Sir Henry and Lady Mildmay. This the youth took pains to avoid. But upon his arrival in the metropolis, he was quick to take advantage once more of the avuncular hospitality of the Downings.[20]

The rising young couple currently had lodgings in Cornhill, "at the signe of the Cocke, nere the Exchange." It was a convenient spot from which to sample the cramped delights of London, but young Winthrop remained, insofar as a career was concerned, quite without impulse. To select, by oneself, a future, requires a certain stature, and it was the father in the country, not the son in the city, who discovered a suitable opportunity. "I am now offered a place in the Temple with Mr. Gurdons soone," he wrote on February 22, "where you may have a chamber freely for the most part of the yeare. . . . I shall thinke long to heare somewhat of your settlednesse." There was no need to "thinke long"; the son seized upon the suggestion with alacrity; it not only promised an honorable situation but avoided the necessity for a dreadful, personal decision. Where there is such a will, there is a way, and with lawyer uncle Emmanuel Downing further to smooth it, John Winthrop, Jr., was admitted, on February 28, 1624/5, to the mysteries of the Inner Temple.[21]

At the limit of the western "Liberties" of London stood the famous Temple Bar, which in 1625 consisted of a narrow gateway beneath a timbered house that sagged. A few yards to the east a subsidiary passage opened laterally; it, too, carried a house, but this structure, being a tavern of aristocratic patronage, rose four-square. The passage itself was of yet greater consequence; it afforded a principal access to the Inner Temple, and beyond it the centuries had laid down a labyrinth of buildings, and a concept of life, that surpassed in complexity anything in the kingdom. It was an extraordinary environment. The law student of 1625 still could take note of the passings of Sir Edward Coke to and from his chambers; he was able, nay, obliged, to worship in a church of singular plan and dignity; and at every turn he was exposed to the notions, exquisitely refined, of the finest minds his island had produced. But the notions were presented with a perplexing imprecision; the church was decayed and oppressed by incongruous outbuildings; and beside the principal gateway itself the Fleet Street prostitutes plucked at the gown of even the aging Coke. It was not a place wherein a restless youth could handily acquire steady habits.[22]

The junior Winthrop did not do so. Granted, there is nothing to indicate an undue patronage of ale houses or any patronage at all of the light ladies of the neighborhood; he always was to be alien to coarseness. We hear nothing of intramural carousings or even of his participation in the semiofficial—and frankly bibulous— Christmas revels that refreshed the legal atmosphere at the appropriate season.[23]

Nevertheless, he did not take kindly to what little there was of academic discipline. The Inner Temple encouraged residence within its precincts, two to a chamber, a policy which was heartily endorsed by his father.[24] But he contrived not to share quarters with young Robert Gurdon[25] very long, and by autumn was again living with uncles and aunts. Emmanuel and Lucy Downing played him host repeatedly; they still were rising in the world and now dwelt off Fleet Street in Peterborough Court, the former residence of a prince of the Church. Though claustrophobic, it was in many respects convenient; it lay but a few rods from the Inner Temple; a public water supply splashed from a nearby "conduit";

and a creaking sign, depicting a bishop, directed the steps of visitors.[26] But even more than the Downings, Winthrop sought the hospitality of Thomas and Priscilla Fones.[27] Uncle Thomas lived less elegantly than Uncle Emmanuel; his house was in the Old Bailey, at no great distance from Fleet Street, but distinctly beneath it, topographically and socially. Nor did his profession of apothecary convey the kind of status enjoyed by Downing as an attorney of the Court of Wards and Liveries.[28] Yet John felt strangely drawn by his bourgeois uncle's calling—its substances, apparatus, and odors—even its superstitions. Moreover, there were his uncle's daughters, now young girls in their teens, who understandably afforded more stimulating company than George Downing (whose current age was two). Elizabeth Fones had grown into a precocious and lively maiden, possibly at odds already with the precepts of her time and place. Martha was younger, only fifteen in 1625, but clearly a more passive personality. Of Elizabeth he became fond; Martha, six years later, he married. But neither was a determining factor in his present preference for lodgings at the sign (erected for the convenience of his uncle's more illiterate customers) of the three fawns.[29]

For though Winthrop was becoming aware of suitable young women, his sphere of admiration appears not to have extended just then to the Fones girls. In circumstances no longer clear, but certainly in the course of 1626, he had become enamoured of the younger daughter of Edward Waldegrave, Jr., of Lawford, Essex. Her Christian name eludes us, but it is obvious that the senior Winthrop did not take to her at all. He did proceed so far as "some speech" with the lady's father, and he conceded the Waldegraves to be "a Religious and worshipfull familye."[30] But he considered the girl impossible; she seemed to him dangerously unstable—"crooked" was the colloquial term he used in a long letter to his son—and he concluded with an admonition (rendered, for greater emphasis, in Latin) to consider well any irrevocable decision.[31] The son considered so well that the affair was safely ended within a fortnight, and when a Miss Pettual attracted his fancy the following month, the elder Winthrop had only to counsel prudence.[32]

Of enormously greater significance were the comments of his parent with respect to an unhappy trend of events in East Anglia, where there had arisen difficulties of a distinctly political character. Before the end of 1626, the letters from Groton were openly hinting of unrest throughout the eastern counties over King Charles's notorious forced loans. The position of the Winthrops in the matter is suggested by their close association with Sir Nathaniel Barnardiston, a Puritan worthy, whose response to the royal policy threatened him with early confinement, while in December the younger John was requested to present his father's "love and service" to Sir Francis Barrington, a kindred spirit who already had been locked up for a month in Marshallsea Prison. "Acquaint him how thinges have gone in our Countrye," the father directed, "but you must doe it in private." [33]

Yet the senior Winthrop himself was hardly disposed to play the martyr. He trimmed a little; perhaps he could ill afford to do otherwise. Several months previously, he had sent Forth, a younger son, not to Trinity, Dublin, but to Emanuel, Cambridge, where presumably the youth rendered the prescribed homage to the Thirty-nine Articles. Nor was he above accepting an office under the Stuarts; in fact, he sought one. Furthermore, he got it, thanks to certain discreet manipulations engineered by his eldest son with the advice and counsel of the sophisticated Downing. The appointment (as one of three attorneys authorized to practice before the "Court of Wards and Liveries") promised handsome fees. It also was the sole early and obvious fruit of the legal studies of John Winthrop, Jr.[34]

We must, in fact, conclude that the young man was once again intellectually adrift and oppressed with ennui. He appears never to have reached even the second level of a lawyer's apprenticeship, that of mootman, or inner barrister. His sole intimate at the Inner Temple was a fellow student nearly as uncommitted as himself, an unusual young man named Edward Howes. Of obscure origins (possibly he came from Groton; certainly he was without money), Howes was less a lawyer than a born intellectual. He could discourse convincingly upon almost anything, but his strongest bents lay in the direction of alchemy and mysticism. John Winthrop, Jr., was entranced by him, and the evenings he devoted to Howes (in lieu of the prescribed digests) were the beginning of a permanent friendship. In fact, it was Howes who, in combination with Thomas Fones's apothecary shop, was responsible for the curious fact that John Winthrop, Jr., quitted the Inner Temple no barrister—either "inner" or "utter"—but an enthusiastic alchemist.[35]

For there was as yet little maturity in him. Its absence was sufficiently indicated by numerous and somewhat pointless visits to Groton, and nervous changes of lodging from the Foneses to the Downings and back to the Foneses again, until his brother Forth wrote from Cambridge that he was "as hard to be found of me as in a Labyrinth." Indeed, his abandonment of the law was only a matter of time. It came in April, 1627, when he confronted his father (doubtless in the latter's new attorney's chamber in Temple Lane) and informed him he could stick it no longer. It was vital, he declared, that he should see the world.[36]

And so plausible seemed this latest pronouncement of John Winthrop, Jr., that his father quite agreed.

CHAPTER 3

Two Voyages to Manhood

TO a restless young Englishman of the seventeenth century the great world meant inevitably the sea. For more than a hundred years the national instinct had been turning outward, and young John Winthrop himself could sniff salt among the passages of the Inner Temple. To even his father, the sea seemed an acceptable substitute for interrupted learning.

There was, to be sure, a difficulty. Winthrop was not only restless but well born. To hang about the nearest quay until taken into the forecastle of a wineship or to await, in a promising taproom, the arrival of the press gang was out of the question. He perforce fell back again upon the resources of nepotism, and again the magic uncle was Emmanuel Downing. Never at a loss for a suitable arrangement, the redoubtable attorney had only to send down the Thames to Chatham dockyard, where his brother Joshua enjoyed exalted office as a commissioner of the Royal Navy. Even so, Winthrop did not secure quite the "place" he had in mind, which was a purser's berth aboard a vessel "for Turkie"; such indeed was hardly in Joshua Downing's gift. But when it came to a naval expedition, the commissioner could do something handsome, and it happened that a major enterprise was in the immediate offing.[1]

Amid the bewildering alarms and excursions which passed

among the early Stuarts for foreign policy, England had recently stumbled, without quite intending to do so, into war with France. It is a little difficult to disentangle the motives; one was religious and related to the contemporary distresses of the French Huguenots, while another sprang from the hapless intrigues of King Charles's favorite, George Villiers, first Duke of Buckingham. A third (possible) influence was the German war, now in the tenth of its thirty tragic years and already productive of monumental confusion in the minds of all but the most astute.[2]

In any case, it was currently the English plan to dispatch an elaborate amphibious force to the relief of La Rochelle, a French Atlantic seaport renowned for Protestantism, autonomy, and volume of trade. That the city was not yet under siege and that the *Rochellais* were themselves loath to receive an English garrison seem not to have concerned anyone unduly. Neither did the fact that the command of the enterprise was bestowed upon the inept Buckingham. But the circumstances enabled Joshua Downing to offer Winthrop as attractive a position as a young gentleman of his age and station could desire. He accepted it at once, and early in May, 1627, was off down the Thames to report aboard the man-of-war *Due Repulse* in the capacity of captain's secretary.[3]

He discovered his ship in a thicket of masts at Gravesend and quickly found himself in circumstances exciting beyond previous experience. *Due Repulse* had been selected for the rear admiral's flag, and this fact put him in the company of the two possibly most salty individuals in the Royal Navy. William Hervey (recently created Lord Hervey) was not only rear admiral but a living legend, whose record stretched back to the Armada. Captain Thomas Best was of comparable reputation: A former merchant skipper, he had done business at the cannon's mouth from Surat to Bali. The circumstances of rank and protocol naturally permitted close association with Best only, but merely to be aboard the same vessel with two such personalities was an education. Moreover, it was clear from the start that Captain Best liked the cut of John Winthrop, Jr.[4]

Due Repulse was likewise a veteran. She had been launched in 1596 for the Cadiz adventure of the Earl of Essex; rebuilt, and probably somewhat modified, in 1610, she still could be listed among the dozen or so most powerful vessels in the king's service. She was about 100 feet in length; her beam was 37 feet; and she normally drew 15 feet of water. She carried 1,638 square yards of canvas; her armament totaled 40 guns, light and heavy. If statistics meant anything, she was a respectable ship, and her immediate command was of unquestioned dedication. However, we may be suspicious of the state of her maintenance and of the quality of some of her company.[5]

Winthrop liked everything about his duties, which were honorable yet exclusively clerical. In all that was required of him he proved himself proficient. He even enjoyed a certain leisure, which he promptly and characteristically devoted to intelligent observation.

Events developed rapidly. The thicket of masts moved quickly into the Medway and became a grove; before the end of May the grove had passed around the Kentish bulge to Portsmouth to become a forest. On June 11, the word spread that the king himself would visit the fleet; there was a great dipping of oars and pealing of ordnance, and even Winthrop was awed as a bearded and agreeable young man stepped aboard *Due Repulse* to the formal genuflections of officers and men. There followed rumors of a conference on shore and of decisions taken, and clusters of uncouth fellows who called themselves soldiers stumbled over the bulwarks. It is likely that Hervey and Best looked at them askance. But young Winthrop's eyes shone as the English fleet, nearly one hundred sail in all, stood out to sea in the summer dawn of June 27, 1627.[6]

It was, from the beginning, rather more than a lark. To hold such an armada together, up wind and down channel, called for unremitting attention, and *Due Repulse*'s log steadily lengthened. Nor was Winthrop unaware that war could be dangerous; he carefully preserved a final letter from his father, a quiet splendid thing, wherein the Calvinist position was expressed in a style from which the Elizabethan touch had not wholly departed: "Be not rash upon ostentation of valor, to adventure yourself to unnecessary dangers; but if you be lawfully called, let it appear, that you hold your life for Him, who gave it you, and will preserve it unto the farthest period of His holy decree." [7]

No hostile vessel challenged them, but the impetuous Buckingham so forgot his primary objective as to order a chase of some Dunkirk privateers. This accomplished nothing; it merely scattered his ships, and while they awkwardly regathered, a Dutchman out of Portsmouth spread accurate word of the English design over the entire French coast, not forgetting the Île de Ré, the key to the approaches of La Rochelle. When, therefore, on the tenth of July, Buckingham appeared with the English vanguard, he found the island garrison unsurprised and in a mood to fight.[8]

Still in *Due Repulse*, with the second division, John Winthrop, Jr., had his first view of war on the following day. It was not without grandeur: two emerging lines of coast, dotted with villages and tufted trees, and in the channel between rolling thunder and tall ships darting flame. But a full day of broadsides produced no visible effect, and Buckingham threw his infantry hastily ashore on the Île de Ré. The operation came close to disaster; though the troops at last made good a lodgment, their ineptitude was manifest to those who, like Winthrop, watched from the ships.[9]

The French continued stubborn, and the English effort subsided into siege and blockade. The days passed endlessly; on the island was an indecisive popping of musketry, on the ships, boredom and a good deal of sickness. Late in August an elaborate army, Royal and Catholic, appeared before La Rochelle, whereupon, wrote

Winthrop, "they began to fall out with some store of great shott on both sides." But Buckingham would not be distracted from his original design, and in truth there was little immediate cause for the English to join in the direct defense of the city. Even Winthrop sensed the reason: "They feare not the [French] kings' forces so long as our fleet keepe the sea open to them," he wrote his father. "When I had well viewed the towne I marveiled not that it holds out . . . , for I think it almost impossible to take it by force if they be not shutt up at sea as well as by land." [10]

But the English effort was doomed and so, though not until many months more, was La Rochelle. Buckingham, in fact, was dogged by the ill fortune that so often accompanies incompetence. Late in September, the French on the island were unexpectedly reinforced, and thereafter the posture of the English deteriorated steadily. An attempt, on October 27, to storm the island defenses at St. Martin was repelled with frightful losses; someone had neglected to provide scaling ladders high enough for the walls. Moreover, when the surviving English attempted to withdraw to the islet of Loix, they were caught upon an open causeway and slaughtered in masses; forty of their flags hung that Christmas in Notre Dame. The islet was held, thanks to a burnable bridge, but the remnants which reached the ships were pitiable to behold—squalid, speechless, and caked with old blood. That Buckingham had sustained a major disaster was obvious, and Winthrop could hardly conceal his relief when the sails cracked full of dank November wind and the English fleet slipped in defeat from the Île de Ré.[11]

He had emerged without a scratch, nor had he suffered any illness.[12] But he had seen war at short range—and had been fairly sickened. To thunder salutes to a king, to empty impersonal broadsides at an island, were stirring enough. But with actual combat there was something dreadfully wrong; the Elizabethan ardor had gone out of it; it was the English who had lost. The time would come when he would have to consider the war question from a place of decision, and indeed he never ceased to realize that a capacity for force must ever be a capital element among men. But always he was to seek alternatives to bloodshed: the confident pose, the effective alliance, the reasonable compromise. He might even proceed so far as to issue threats. Yet from war itself he would shrink as from an evil beyond calculation.

Buckingham reached Plymouth after a passage of less than four days. He brought with him less than half his troops, and his fleet, though physically intact, experienced early disintegration from lack of funds. The royal ships naturally continued longest on active service, and Winthrop kept Captain Best's papers in order until *Due Repulse* was berthed in the Thames for the winter. Moreover, a renewed tour of duty seemed a possibility for some time thereafter.[13]

His return to Groton, though in defeat, was happy enough; his parents had worried much for his safety, particularly when they first had learned of the "bad sucsese" of the expedition.[14] Nor was winter jollity wholly proscribed, even in so Puritan a village, and he found he could pass the leaden afternoons as an authentic center of interest. Though hardly a sailor, he was home from the sea, and not without honor.

B u t t h e time soon came when he found himself again at loose ends. If he hoped that his place with Captain Best would once more become available, he was to be disappointed. If he spoke of a return to the Inner Temple, he made no positive move to do so. His formal education, in fact, was at an end, and he continued to think irresponsibly of another voyage, perhaps this time "for Turkye," perhaps for destinations more distant still.

He was now of age and the eldest son of a landed gentleman, and there were neighborhood formalities requiring his attention: a boundary to adjust, a quit-claim deed to sign. But after the middle of February he was back in London, "casting about," occupying a chamber above the apothecary shop and enchanting the Misses Fones with his talk. At Groton, his father still nursed the delusion that he would resume his legal studies; indeed, the judicial processes of Westminster yielded so much more certain an income than the rents of East Anglia that he had begun seriously to consider abandoning the country for good, and near the end of February, he wrote to John at the Foneses, asking that he inquire for a house, preferably in an "open place," in or adjacent to the city.[15]

We do not know if John ever investigated any suburban real estate, but it is clear that his father could not quite bring himself to such a decision. In March, Charles I opened his third Parliament, and that historic body hastened to raise the political issues which soon were expanded into the Petition of Right. If the elder Winthrop's "office" depended upon the Crown, his sympathies lay with the squirearchy and their cousins of the City, and he was never the man to deny his friends for more pelf. He therefore refrained from committing himself wholly to the Court of Wards, and he partially relieved his financial difficulties by the sale of the freehold and copyhold lands at Great Stambridge. Herein he received some plainly generous cooperation from his son, for whom the properties had originally been intended. Together they sold them, an acreage no longer of record, but embracing much of the gentle countryside the younger man had known as a child. The purchaser was Henry Fetherston, a stationer of Blackfriars; the price was £590; the bargaining had been hard. Father and son signed the indenture together on May 14, 1628.[16]

Behind the celebrated issues of the day—divine right, statute law, tunnage and poundage—England was undergoing fermentation. Like the growth of a major wine, it was no simple process, nor was it related solely to the contest between Parliament and the Crown. It most particularly was not a "trend," transcendental beyond the control of man (no politico-social phenomenon can ever be), but it left numerous individuals confused and disturbed and subject to outwardly illogical responses. For it is abundantly plain that the majority of contemporary Englishmen had no accurate notion of where they were going; thus, even so intelligent a person as the senior John Winthrop could devote himself to an outmoded law court in 1628 and in 1630 supervise the establishment of a legally questionable colony thousands of miles beyond the seas.

It was through this electric atmosphere that John Winthrop, Jr., moved in the spring of 1628. Aged twenty-two, and as disarming as ever, he nevertheless had not quite put aside childish things. He took obvious care not to return to the self-discipline of the law and wandered airily about London in search of activity that would better suit his tastes. For a moment, he thought he had found it in a new venture which just then was attracting interest in mercantile circles. It proposed a settlement upon the northern coasts of America in a region called New England; its tone was strongly Puritan, and its executive director was an intense and humorless gentleman from the west country named John Endecott. But to John Winthrop, Jr., it was important only that its object was vague and far away, and it is interesting to note that he was restrained from joining the enterprise by his father.[17] (Before the next year was out, the older Winthrop was to find himself at the head of the same undertaking in reorganized form.) But the parent nevertheless perceived that the spell of the sea was upon him yet. Emmanuel Downing, who could contrive anything for this nephew, was again called upon, and by June another "place" had been found, this time aboard the *London*, a Levant Company merchantman intending shortly for Leghorn and Constantinople. In the interim, the nephew continued to wander carefree about the metropolis, observing, listening, and sending off to Groton some very discerning comments upon the current and epic struggle between Parliament and king.[18]

London, carrying an unremembered cargo and John Winthrop, Jr., dropped down the Thames early in June. Through most of the summer she threaded the placid Mediterranean (the call at Leghorn occupied nearly a fortnight), and it was September 13 before she entered the Golden Horn. For Winthrop, everything was quite up to specification. His "place," in terms of the ship's hierarchy, was lofty; he was subject to no responsibilities other than money, and this his father had undertaken, through Downing, to provide. Winthrop, in fact, was a pioneer cruise passenger. But his impressions were not ordinary. Behind Leghorn, the architectural splendors of Tuscany awaited his inspection in matchless sunshine, but of these he had little to say. Instead, he was taken with botanical gardens, one at Pisa and another at Florence; two decades later, he still remembered them as extraordinary. Upon the ancient wonders of Constantinople he commented not at all, remarking instead upon this morning's arrival of a legate from the contemporary "Holy Roman" Emperor and the problems incident to a recent fire which had consumed 12,000 houses. Yet he differed little from the average sightseer in the matter of tourist economics. "It may be thought I am a very ill husband," he wrote Emmanuel Downing, "but none can believe the charges in these Countries but he that hath experienced them." [19]

He further perfected his ability to make friends: Judah Throckmorton was a pleasant young gentleman from Warwickshire, voyaging to the Levant in pursuit of "prospects"; John Freeman was a leader of Constantinople's mercantile colony; Sir Peter Wyche was the English envoy to the Ottoman "Porte." Winthrop got on particularly well with Wyche, who was a remarkable person, renowned for his diplomatic abilities and with the Privy Council in his future. There even is evidence that their relationship approached the semiofficial. [20]

Yet when *London* sailed from the Golden Horn just before Christmas, John Winthrop, Jr., departed with her. He had toyed with the idea of an excursion to Jerusalem,[21] but (like many trippers before and since) had held back in the face of rumored disturbances. With him went the genial Throckmorton, whose Levantine prospects had somehow paled, and neither appears to have felt much regret as the noble Byzantine skyline faded into the Propontine mists.

Favorable winds carried them swiftly from the straits; within a week Captain Maplesden was making his first intended call at the Venetian outpost of Zante. But when *London* set course for Venice itself, the fickle Mediterranean winter turned against her. Frustrated by head winds, driven repeatedly behind cloud-hung Dalmatian headlands, the ship did not reach the littoral of Malamocco until January 31.[22] Nor was this the worst. Hardly had *London* paused for inspection when she was pronounced a health hazard, and her entire company was confined for a month upon the tiny islet of Lazaretto. The amenties were nil (Winthrop thought the place a "purgatory"), and it was small comfort that the narrow windows opened upon a vision—of a fairy city that walked upon the waters and beyond it, ethereal with distance and snow, the Alps.[23]

Like Constantinople and the Tuscan towns, the Venice of 1629 stood near the pinnacle of its outward splendor. Yet, when at last he could enter the city, Winthrop demonstrated little interest in its usual curiosities. His surviving letters are characteristically devoid of lions and mosaics and concerned with political intelligence and the heartlessness of money changers. He devoted himself chiefly to the thing he did best, which was meeting people. As usual, he delighted everyone, including—once more—the English ambassador. This was inevitable; Sir Isaac Wake was a man of the world, a consummate diplomat, an orator of distinction, and a master of political theory and practice, precisely the sort to appreciate this kind of young man.[24]

Yet Winthrop's most interesting Venetian companion was not

Sir Isaac but a Dutch scholar who had joined the ship at Constantinople. Jacobus Golius was without doubt the most exceptional man whom Winthrop encountered upon the Mediterranean journey. His field was oriental languages, particularly Arabic and Persian; he had just completed a tour of the greater part of the Ottoman dominions; and he brought with him a collection of manuscripts without equal in Western Europe. Each proved a boon to the other through the deadly weeks on Lazaretto, and they were constantly together during the remainder of Winthrop's stay in Venice. Ten years later, he still remembered their friendship as "most agreeable." [25]

He was nevertheless in no mood to linger. He might charm diplomats, but not money lenders. He did perform some routine errands for Freeman, one of which took him as far as Padua and produced a meeting with the eminent antiquary John Price. But he abandoned *London* in favor of an earlier sailing in a Dutch vessel, whose master could not promise to land him in England at all. [26]

The remainder of his tour was an exercise in frustration; for weeks his ship dared not proceed beyond Zante, thanks to dangers unspecified but doubtless of a political character. It was full summer before she entered the English Channel, and there the "too favorable winds" condemned him to gaze helplessly from the bulwarks at the passing cliffs of home. Further and tedious navigation brought them at last to Amsterdam, where, on July 27, 1629, Winthrop stepped ashore, still on foreign soil and nearly devoid of money. He could only send off additional letters requesting further advances and make his way among the dikes and water courses to Flushing, whence ships were apt to depart most frequently for England. [27]

He secured a fortuitous passage on August 10 and reached London three days later. He disembarked with little else than the clothes he wore; in Holland he left a debt for 80 guilders and his trunk as security. Since his departure, fourteen months before, he had not received one word from home.[28]

That such a journey should serve to season a young man is a little curious, for he had been throughout no more than an intelligent and rather privileged observer. Yet it soon would become plain that the southern sun had baked away certain of his immaturities; never again would he display so striking a lack of persistence, so slight a capacity for concentration. Manhood had come late, and it had not altogether suppressed his deficiencies. But it had arrived.

It was well that it had. For as his little vessel glided up the Thames to London, John Winthrop, Jr., faced personal revolution.

CHAPTER 4

The Governor & Company
of the Massachusetts Bay
in New England

H E received the accumulated news at Peterborough Court
from his Aunt Lucy Downing; all of it was startling.[1]
Most lurid was the intelligence concerning his brother Henry,
who had exhibited as restless a disposition as his own and had left
England in December, 1626, to join a "plantation" upon the West
Indian island of Barbados. There he had accumulated great expectations and greater debts; he had returned that spring, quite unabashed, to London and had become promptly and improperly involved with his first cousin Elizabeth Fones. The enraptured
lovers had hastened to marry, but the episode allegedly had contributed to the death of Uncle Thomas Fones on the fifteenth of
April preceding.[2]

Four days later John's paternal grandmother, Anne Browne
Winthrop, had passed away at Groton.[3]

In mid-June, his father had given up his office in the Court of
Wards and Liveries.[4]

And there was talk of the removal of the entire family overseas
to a part of America called New England.

Lucy Downing could not elaborate upon this last stupefaction.
But John's uncertainty was brief; explanations came from his father in less than a fortnight. The rumors were far from baseless;

indeed, the overseas design was already well advanced. Moreover, his participation therein was earnestly solicited.

His response was prompt and affirmative—and reflected a precise understanding of his parent:

> For the business of New England, I can say no other thing, but that I believe confidently, that the whole disposition thereof is of the Lord, who disposeth all alterations, by his blessed will, to his own glory and the good of his; and, therefore, do assure myself, that all things shall work together for the best therein. And for myself, I have seen so much of the vanity of the world, that I esteem no more of the diversities of countries, than as so many inns, whereof the traveller that hath lodged in the best, or in the worst, findeth no difference, when he cometh to his journey's end; and I shall call that my country, where I may most glorify God, and enjoy the presence of my dearest friends. Therefore herein I submit myself to God's will and yours, and, with your leave, do dedicate myself . . . to the service of God and the Company herein, with the whole endeavors both of body and mind.[5]

This time, he perceived that his parent (and perhaps his parent's Jehovah) meant business. Nor would he ever thereafter struggle against what he knew to be inevitable; on the contrary, he became notable for the ease with which he could estimate, and accompany, any major current. Most especially would he be careful, in a community of Puritan associates, to give the Puritan God his prescribed due.

Of the organization to which he had committed himself, he learned the details only gradually. The Governor and Company of the Massachusetts Bay in New England [6] was already, by the autumn of 1629, an elaborate undertaking, with a conspicuously complicated background. Its beginnings could be traced back to 1606 when, with a plain disregard for historical simplicity, the secretariat of James I had authorized, by means of a single charter and under the common style of "Virginia," *two* separate transatlantic enterprises. One of these "Virginia" companies maintained headquarters in London and gave unprofitable birth to the famous colony of the same name. The other, established at Plymouth, could produce no more than an abandoned townsite beside the Gulf of Maine and a collection of paper projects wherein an itch for empire was inextricably entangled with traditional conceptions of land tenure.

As is customary with bankrupt corporations, both "Virginias" underwent reorganization. London's colony suffered, in 1624, public seizure and became royal ground. The Plymouth enterprise experienced, in 1620, private resuscitation with all that goes with it—the infusion of fresh capital, the politely concealed extinction of the old, the exciting new management, the promising new concepts. There was even a fresh corporate title, "Council for New England," and a new and distinct royal patent, complete with political rights of a medieval sort.

Unhappily, the Council for New England fell prey to common lethargy. Its domain was imperial—all of North America between the fortieth and forty-eighth parallels—but it made no use of it other than to allocate lavish parcels of land to its individual members and even, for a consideration, to outsiders. Most of these grants, moreover, were carelessly defined; they frequently overlapped and failed to square with geography. They invited much trespassing; indeed, the first effective settlement of New England was to a great extent the work of interlopers.

One association of council grantees resided in Dorsetshire and called themselves the Dorchester Company. They had commenced overseas operations in 1624 and had not been conspicuously successful, but certain of them were willing to give the thing a further try. Strengthened by new associates and new capital, and under the new style of "New England Company," they acquired from the Council for New England a band of territory extending from a point three miles north of the Merrimac to a point three miles south of the Charles and (as was usual in that century) westward to the Pacific Ocean. This was the enterprise which had so in-

[42]

trigued John Winthrop, Jr., in the spring of 1628. It was also the immediate ancestor of Massachusetts Bay.

Only one more corporate reorganization was required, and the principal New England story could begin. It was plainly a slippery proceeding, engineered perhaps by the Earl of Warwick. It was done without further reference to the Council for New England; it produced a final change of name; it elicited yet another royal charter; and it involved (the Council for New England to the contrary notwithstanding) political powers. It attracted the serious notice of the elder John Winthrop in the spring of 1629, just as his son was struggling to get home from Venice.[7]

The royal patent of the Governor and Company of the Massachusetts Bay in New England had passed the seals on March 4, 1628/9. This famous document[8] was to be so strong an influence in the career of John Winthrop, Jr.—and has served as a basis for so much that is significant in American history—that it warrants careful examination. It was not, in one sense, an extraordinary instrument; it furnished a legal framework for a private corporation and as such its structure differed little from other royal charters of its time and place. The principal officer of the company was denominated "governor"; his modern designation would be "chairman of the board and president." There was a "deputy governor," or vice-chairman. There also was a board of directors, which was called, in the fashion of the day, a "council"; its members (they numbered eighteen beside the governor and deputy governor) were known as "assistants." The stockholders, whose initial status resembled that of modern equity investors, bore the curious title of "freemen." The council, like a twentieth-century directorate, met frequently, the entire company rather seldom—four times a year in the case of Massachusetts Bay. The assemblies of the whole body—governor, deputy, assistants, and freemen—were referred to as "General Courts."

But if the Massachusetts charter varied little from the normal, it did exhibit one peculiarity with a capacity for revolution. *The location of the company's principal office was nowhere specified.* There was nothing to require that the enterprise should be managed from London or Plymouth or indeed from England at all. Less extraordinary, in the seventeenth century, was its feudal quality: Massachusetts Bay was to be legally a fief, held of the Crown by the company in "free and common soccage as of his Majesty's Manor of East Greenwich." This was more than a picturesque theory; a fief was liable to resumption for cause.

Yet the company's financial affairs were conducted with a sophistication that smacked of a later period. Two classes of stock were offered in the beginning, and later there were three. The device of the subsidiary company was employed and so was the idea of varying liens on profits. Finally, a clear, though unofficial, distinction was made between shareholders who emigrated to America and those who did not. The seventeenth-century Englishman spoke of the first "planters," a term meaning *settlers,* not necessarily agricultural. The second he called "adventurers," a word that may seem inappropriate—until the risks involved are considered.[9]

On Tuesday, July 28, 1629, the freemen of the Massachusetts Bay Company picked their way through the London lanes to a "General Court" of supreme consequence; it was upon this occasion that a removal of the entire undertaking, including the patent and the greater part of the shareholders, from England to America was seriously considered for the first time. The thing had been in the air, of course; weeks earlier, one of the more influential freemen, Mr. Isaac Johnson, had broached the matter to Emmanuel Downing and, very likely, to the senior John Winthrop, though neither seems yet to have become associated with the enterprise. Johnson possessed broad acres and Puritan sympathies, and on the very day of the company court aforementioned, John Winthrop and Emmanuel Downing were riding across the Lin-

colnshire fens to his seat at Tattersall, where they remained clos-
eted for a fortnight with other worthies, also landed and Puritan.
They subsequently adjourned to Cambridge, where, on August 26,
the elder Winthrop and eleven others signed the famous agreement to emigrate to New England—lock, stock, and Massachusetts Bay charter.[10]

In London the Bay Company met repeatedly (and probably in
violation of the letter of its own patent) in General Court. On August 28 and 29, the removal policy received formal endorsement.
Subsequent sessions were called for September 19 and October 15,
and, on October 20, still another meeting chose John Winthrop
governor of the corporation. He had been preferred to men such
as Isaac Johnson and Sir Richard Saltonstall, and was clearly surprised.[11]

John Winthrop, Jr., had offered himself "to the service of God
and the Company" on August 21, but he did not take horse for
Groton until late in September. Of the details of his homecoming,
there is no record, not even of the first meeting with his father.
Yet the latter must have noticed the sea change—the more purposeful step, the greater stability, the lesser impatience. The
sturdy frame had acquired a mature set, the homely features a
look of confidence. Only the charm was unaltered; it quickly set
village and manor by the ears, and when presently the elder Winthrop was called to London, he left the younger behind to influence, for God and company, the entire neighborhood.[12]

This was no problem. A respectable proportion of the countryside was persuaded already though it is difficult to understand
why. North America could scarcely, in 1629, be certified a land of
promise, save by those who would suppress the facts. The East
Anglian gentry were politically restless, but their memorable contest with Charles I was hardly well begun. But of the itch to emigrate there is no question. Nor is it possible to deny the strength of

the religious motive, which already had set the Puritan mind to dreaming of a community whose affairs should be ordered not to the king's taste nor to any man's but to God's.[13]

Thus, the immediate interests of the Massachusetts Bay Company required less proselyting than administration, and in truth its management proved able and vigorous. The colonial purpose was never for a moment forgotten. The participation of artisans was especially solicited; there was an obvious effort to balance personnel with shipping space; and supplies were provided on contract, let well in advance. John Winthrop, Jr., soon found himself involved in a variety of situations: At London, behind the sign of the bishop, were earnest discussions. At Colchester, set within walls upon a hill, was a certain "Mr. Heath the Kinges Workman," who afforded instruction in the design of forts. Beneath Colchester, the estuary of the Colne pinched out between littered quays, and here was trouble; so much freight for Massachusetts Bay was accumulating that the local customs officers had to be quieted with a special Lord Chancellor's warrant. Near Harwich was an actual fort of Mr. Heath's construction; young Winthrop was directed to sketch it. Back once more at Groton Manor, he encountered family turmoil—and also the Fones girls. Elizabeth—his sister-in-law since the preceding April—was big with child; her younger sister, probably to his own surprise, caught his eye. Martha Fones may indeed have been fetching; her economic advantages were clearly limited.[14]

He already had been of assistance to Elizabeth. Her new husband was of debonair instincts, oriented toward dogs, horses, and the pursuit of happiness, and when he had spoken of an unencumbered return to the West Indies, John had taken steps to keep him in England. But to Martha he was more than helpful; he fairly overwhelmed her, and by midwinter there appears to have been an "understanding" between them.[15]

Martha Fones played a singular role in the life of John Winthrop, Jr. For one thing, she was his first cousin, and marriage with so close a relative was not customary. There also are hints of other difficulties, perhaps deliberately concealed—questions of property and clashes of personality. In any case, the prospective groom thought it judicious to procure an extraordinary marriage license and from no less an authority than the Archbishop of Canterbury. It was dated February 20, 1629/30; doubtless he took advantage of a London visit to cross to Lambeth and charm it out of the archiepiscopal assistants who governed such things. Rendered in official Latin, it permitted the wedding (without further publication of banns) either in the parish church of Groton or in the parish church of St. Lawrence, Ipswich. It cited the approval of parents and guardians and implied a desire for an early solemnization. It also set aside any objections incident to consanguinity. However, if young Winthrop's application were found to contain any misrepresentations, it was forthwith to be void.[16]

It has been asserted that this document was indeed secured upon subterfuge and that the marriage of John Winthrop, Jr., and Martha Fones was unlawful. The truth of this cannot be proven. Yet the known facts are peculiar. There was no speedy solemnization; the ceremony was delayed for nearly a year. Moreover, there was later trouble, equally obscure, which will be considered in due course.[17]

Meanwhile, the business of New England was proceeding apace. On February 10, 1629/30, there met in London the final General Court of the Massachusetts Bay Company to be held in the Old World. Later in the same month, the senior Winthrop visited Groton for the last time; by the twenty-sixth, he had left it forever, taking with him two of his younger sons—Stephen (who was not quite eleven) and Adam (not quite ten). Behind him he left his wife, stalwart amid agony of soul and already far gone in her sixth pregnancy.[18]

John Winthrop, Jr., was in London, his thoughts of Martha

Fones totally eclipsed by the fascinations of company affairs. Such dedication to business may have seemed out of character; the shrewd John Freeman had once taken his measure at Constantinople and observed that "the affayres of Marchants . . . doe not Comply with your Dispositione." [19] But the Massachusetts Bay Company involved no ordinary trafficking; its essence was political and its future embraced dreams that transcended any Levantine concept of profit. It was a cause wherein the younger Winthrop was moved, for the first time in his life, to genuine effort, and in his enthusiasm—and in his disposition to minimize pitfalls—he already was exhibiting a temper that was nicely attuned to the New World.

His father left London on March 10; with the younger boys, and also Henry, he proceeded overland to the company fleet at Southampton. There, on April 7, 1630, he joined in the well-known declaration that the undertaking should not be construed as secession from the Church of England. On April 8 he sailed.[20]

Nearly a year and a half separated the departures of the two John Winthrops; and it was probably the most trying period in the experience of either. The burdens of the elder can be imagined; the reality was worse. He might write that New England was "exceeding good, and the climate very like our own," but the initial statistics of the colony of Massachusetts Bay tell an appalling story: 200 of the original Winthrop fleet were dead before the spring of 1631, and 80 more had returned to England before the end of the same year. The son, of course, faced no such horror, but his undertakings were sufficiently difficult. Though without specific office, he served as one of the two or three most active agents of the Massachusetts Bay Company still in England; he undertook to manage the multifarious concerns of the Winthrop family; and he contracted a difficult marriage. That each parcel of problems was rather intimately related to the others made things no easier.[21]

His company duties were perhaps the least perplexing. They included the selling of shares, the collection of debts, the solicitation of gifts, financial clearings, traffic management, and the release of (meticulously doctored) New England news.[22] They required constant travel, chiefly over the familiar roads between London and Suffolk, but one occasion took him deep into the west country, to Bristol, where a sturdy merchantman, the *Lion*, was taking on emergency cargo for Massachusetts and an earnest and youthful clergyman named Roger Williams was waiting to embark. Everything about the *Lion* seemed in confusion, and Winthrop was recalled to London before it could fully be settled, but he and Williams liked the look of each other.[23]

His penchant for people continued undiminished, and in the course of these months he found himself in the company of nearly every sort and condition of man. Emmanuel Downing exhibited prodigious energy; though a convinced Puritan, he remained throughout a man of affairs, little given to scriptural quotation and privately loath to face a wilderness with frigid winters. John Humphrey, chosen deputy when the elder Winthrop was raised to the governorship, was connected, by marriage, with the peerage and for some time had dabbled in long distance "adventures" overseas. Though fond of the spice of profit, he was a walking concordance—and earnestly concerned for the sanctity of others. Thomas Goffe, though only yesterday the deputy himself, chose, when the pinch was on, to evade his financial promises. Matthew Cradock behaved better; indeed, he was a financial magician, and if company debts did not turn exactly liquid beneath his touch, they at least remained unquestioned. Sir Nathaniel Barnardiston was one of the knights of the shire for Suffolk and typified its discontented and Puritan gentry, except that he was immensely rich. He was inevitably approached for a donation, but the results are unknown. William Peirce was master of the *Lion* and an expert mariner; though sympathetic to the disaffected, he left religious theories to others. Francis Kirby was the sort of merchant whose activities presumably did not conform to Winthrop's "disposition"; though a man of liberal education, his life was bounded by warehouses—he was enormously useful. At Braintree was a nameless smith, whose axes and augers were so highly regarded that the senior Winthrop wrote from "Charlton in N: England" to get a supply, "whatever they cost." [24]

At Groton remained the greater part of the Winthrops and a variety of subsidiary persons, including Martha Fones, for whom John had such embarrassingly little time, and an uncle, Thomas Gostling, who was oddly indefatigable in his disapproval of New England.[25] All were inclined to lamentation. In fact, the atmosphere of home was such that Winthrop was happiest when the company's interest called him away, especially in the direction of London, for it presented an opportunity to tarry en route with his most impressive—and most comfortably situated—relatives.

John Winthrop, Jr., once had avoided calling upon Sir Henry and Lady Mildmay, but that had been from the mysterious motives of youth; nowadays he sought them eagerly. The Mildmays lived in handsome style at Graces, an estate of impressive proportions in the Essex parishes of Little Baddow and Danbury. Its mansion stood on the slope of the region's loftiest hill; built solidly of brick, with gable ends in the Dutch fashion, it afforded gracious living of the kind that Winthrop could best appreciate. Sir Henry (who was his father's first cousin) was thoroughly civilized; though of military background and Puritan leanings, he took greatest delight in a collection of maps and pictures. He was the principal patron of the parish church of Little Baddow, wherein the old religion had left a vigorous wall painting of St. Christopher, and he permitted no reformist nonsense about erasing it. How frequently Winthrop paused with the Mildmays we cannot say. But there is evidence that his visits may have tempted him to regret his commitment to Massachusetts Bay.[26]

Such feelings were fleeting; he continued to thrive upon the activities of this kind of company. To be sure, he was deficient—as humanists are wont—in the matter of accounting; he kept elaborate jottings, but they were assembled in shocking disarray. (They even were interspersed with data of a family nature.) Yet he gave much satisfaction. "Among many of the sweet mercies of my God towards me in this strange land," wrote his father in the spring of 1631, ". . . this is not the least, . . . that he hath given me a loving and dutiful son. God all-sufficient reward thee abundantly for all thy care and pains in my affairs." [27]

His family responsibilities were less happy, thanks in part to a pair of tragedies. In New England, his brother Henry had hardly set foot upon land when, on July 2, 1630, he fell into a tidal creek and was drowned. At Groton, his brother Forth (who, in an immature performance much like his own, had abandoned his studies) took suddenly ill in November; before many days he, too, was dead. For John, these melancholy events meant more than personal grief. Henry left his wife and an infant daughter, and Forth a fiancée; all three posed vexations of a legal and administrative nature.[28]

More complicated still was the disposition of the Winthrop lands. The data are incomplete, but at the time of the decision to emigrate, Groton Manor and its dependencies possessed a minimum of 545 acres; a complex of tracts in the parish of Lavenham (Suffolk) embraced 83 more; while a residuum of scattered properties near the Stambridges (Essex) totaled 98. The last appear to have been disposed of prior to the governor's departure for America. But Groton proved something else again. For one thing, it was desirable that it should serve as a temporary home for Margaret Winthrop and her younger children. For another, it seemed wise to retain the core of the family possessions as insurance against disaster. The elder Winthrop could therefore risk only tentative negotiations before sailing, and by the time it was clear that Massachusetts would survive, the price of grain (no one mentioned the already depressed wool) had dropped in East Anglia from 15 to 11 shillings and had carried the value of land with it.[29]

Before its completion, the sale of Groton Manor became a labor of the first magnitude. In the beginning, it was hoped that the purchaser would be Brampton Gurdon, lord of the manor at nearby Assington, a personal friend and a Puritan, but too elderly for anything like Massachusetts. But Gurdon, though an earthy sort and indeed not perfectly literate, was no one's fool; he consulted attorneys, who discovered difficulties. Another promising buyer was Lawrence Wright, a widely known physician, who had expressed sympathy with Massachusetts, but Dr. Wright insisted that another manor be accepted in part payment. Groton finally was disposed of—in the late spring of 1631—to one Warren, a London grocer in search of prestige; the price was £4,200, which hardly fulfilled the senior Winthrop's estimate a year before of £5,760. (The 83 acres at Lavenham appear not to have been sold at all.) [30]

Finally, through all these months of decision is woven the question of Martha Fones. It is a problem quite impossible wholly to resolve; for Winthrop himself there seems never to have been a fully satisfactory solution. Lambeth Palace had issued its extraordinary license on February 20, 1629/30, but it was not until February 8, 1630/31 that he and Martha stood together in Groton parish church to be united in marriage. Why the ceremony was so delayed we do not know. But surviving evidence makes it clear that the young couple faced serious difficulties as they turned down the dank little nave as man and wife.[31]

For one thing, the necessities of Massachusetts Bay quickly called Winthrop back to London again. For another, he departed with a strong suspicion that he had married a young woman who did not love him. The trouble, indeed, was so intimate that both resorted, in their letters, to a crude (and easily broken!) cipher.[32]

"Bee perswaded of my love to thee," entreated Martha early in

April, "notwithstanding my pasions and weaknes which formerly haue caused thee to thinke the contrary."

"My dere," he replied, "thou needest not feare but I am fully perswaded of thy love, nor thought the contrary, although thy clouding of thy loue sometime hath suddenly darkened my mind with greife and sadnes: but my deare let us beare with one an other's weaknesses an seeke to cherish loue by al menes, for that wil make our condition sweete houever."

It appears that his stepmother presently sensed that all was not well, and it was at her urging that Martha rode up to London about the middle of April. This produced an improvement, and when, toward the end of May, she returned to Groton, he wrote her in the style of a lovesick boy, concluding with "a hundred and twenty kisses an[d] as many more."[33]

However, their distresses were by no means at an end. Martha had claims to certain properties, but they were in "jointure" and so entangled with the rights of others that they could not be made good. Moreover, while she was in London that spring, the Groton neighborhood was shaken by the rumor that their marriage had been pronounced a scandal and that the groom had been taken to court and given a proper dressing down. The good wives of the parish whispered that the young people were too nearly akin, that they had wed without consent, and that Martha was under age. It was all discussed with a healthy relish, and Uncle Thomas Gostling went so far as to prophesy legal repercussions so awful that further departures for America would be out of the question.[34]

Gossip of this kind frequently enjoys a basis in fact, yet acquires, in the spreading, much baseless elaboration. John and Martha were indeed first cousins, but that had been put right by Canterbury's license. The ceremony as performed in Groton Church was hardly an elopement. Moreover, the bride had passed her twenty-first birthday.[35] Yet the marriage, if lawful, was nevertheless cited as not altogether proper—by what authority, in what court, and upon what grounds no one can with entire confidence say. But there survives a letter (once more in an elementary cipher) in which Winthrop warned his wife not to disclose to anyone that he did not intend to pay a certain fine of five marks. "I feare," he explained, "it may by the same tatling tonges be spread abroad and come to some of the aldermans ears with additions." [36]

It is therefore probable that something unbecoming had occurred. It even is conceivable that Winthrop had taken liberties with the truth when he had assured the Lambeth secretaries that his proposed marriage enjoyed the blessing of parent and guardian. It is possibly significant that he was taken to court shortly after the unhappy issue of Martha's "jointure." But we should above all take cognizance of his willingness to get what he regarded as properly his own—even by means which a purist might not think perfectly seemly. Unfriendly critics will discount the charm and call him slippery; the more understanding will recognize at once that his was the stuff from which diplomats are made.

Finally, there is the problem of Martha Fones herself. She left no portrait; she appears at best like a shadow between controversial lines. We may venture to think of her as physically attractive; otherwise, and in the absence of an assured dowry, why should Winthrop have sought the hand of a first cousin? We may confidently assert her unusual education—else how could she cope with a cipher containing Greek letters? But equally plain was her emotional instability, which an ingenuous code can reveal to us yet.

Most significant of all, Martha Fones was never to become a major influence in the life of John Winthrop, Jr. She and their only child became casualties of the American frontier. Thereafter the record is silent, save that he would name a later daughter Martha. But for history it is important, not that he plighted his troth to Martha Fones, but that he gave his support to the Governor and Company of Massachusetts Bay in New England.

CHAPTER 5

Massachusetts Bay in New England

FROM the edge of America, where a cluster of hastily erected buildings had been christened Boston, John's father wrote to recommend that they cross on the *Lion;* Captain Peirce, he said, was a mariner of exceptional skill and particularly concerned for the comfort of his passengers. Peirce himself sought their patronage, but there was a period during the spring of 1631 when the younger Winthrop feared that his affairs could not be settled until too late for a sailing that season. The distractions incident to Groton and Martha were complicated by a shortage of money; and his stepmother reported that the tenants were disposed to "complayne of the hardnesse of the times, and would be glad to be foreborne." But funds at last were found, and for three weeks, beginning July 15, *Lion* lay at her London berth, taking on cargo, much of it consigned to New England in the Winthrop name. There were rather few household goods; the emphasis was on foodstuffs, harness, seeds, rope, and suits of sails. But Winthrop nonetheless contrived to include a "barrell of bookes," chiefly "chimical."

The workaday pressures of the past two years had in no way stifled his interest in natural phenomena. In the midst of his most exacting responsibilities, there always was time for discourse with the remarkable Edward Howes, who currently and conveniently was employed at Peterborough Court by Emmanuel Downing. Closer to Groton, he discovered still another fascinating intellectual in the person of Henry Jacie, a young clergyman who served the many-acred Brampton Gurdon in the capacity of personal chaplain. Jacie was a walking concordance, and distinctly reformist, but he was likewise an enthusiastic observer of the Lord's physical world, and he and Winthrop held much happy conference beneath the oaks of Assington.[1] When the latter at last could sail, he left instructions with the youthful cleric to note, day by day, the direction of the wind, a chore which Winthrop undertook to perform simultaneously at sea. Whether Jacie's results (they were duly dispatched to Massachusetts) proved significant in comparison with his own is unremembered, but the very nature of the experiment indicates a sophistication of weather theory greatly in advance of the age.[2]

Unlike his father, John Winthrop, Jr., rarely kept a journal, and we therefore know comparatively little of his first transatlantic voyage. However, it is certain that he was accompanied by his wife, his half-brother Adam, his stepmother and her infant daughter, Anne; and almost certain that his sister Mary and his sister-in-law Elizabeth (with her child) were likewise of the party.[3] That they embarked at the Downs, the famous roadstead off the extremity of Kent, may seem peculiar, but it was a common practice and served to reduce somewhat the period on shipboard.

They were escorted to Sandwich by John Humphrey, deputy governor of the Massachusetts Bay Company. Humphrey was a born manager and therefore helpful; but he was no master of the *bon voyage,* and Winthrop was doubtless relieved when he was called unexpectedly back to London. Even so, Humphrey contrived to get off a final letter, in which he exhorted the young man to place himself without reservation at the Lord's disposal. Significant of the variation possible among Puritans was a postscript appended by Uncle Emmanuel Downing, who advised "by al meanes you should carrie good store of garlicke to physicke your cowes." [4]

Where the livestock was taken on is not known, nor is the day of *Lion*'s sailing. It must have been near the end of August, 1631.[5] Of *Lion* herself, there are convenient estimates; she was possibly of 250 tons, which made her rather larger than the Pilgrim Fathers' *Mayflower*. Her passengers numbered, on this particular voyage, about 60; aside from the governor's family, the most notable personage aboard was a scholarly young Essex clergyman named John Eliot. So comparatively sparse a company at least assured a minimum of crowding.[6]

Yet no Atlantic crossing of the seventeenth century could be warranted pleasant. The ships of the period were designed for cargo and not for creature comforts. A kind of first-class cabin, of temporary partitions, might be thrown up between decks, and possibly was for the Winthrops. The cuisine, thanks to limitations of space and the danger of fire, was inferior from the beginning, and after a ship was a week at sea, became a daily and deadly sequence of dried or salt meat, flour biscuits, oatmeal porridge, and dried pea soup. The great "tuns" of beer which were carried fulfilled a serious purpose; properly casked, a malted beverage did not, like water, go easily bad. But the worst feature was the absence of ventilation, especially in foul weather, when the hatches were closed over seasick passengers and physicked cattle alike.[7]

The details of the voyage can only be surmised. England reached after them for a while, but presently the last of Cornwall and the Scillies faded away, and the ship burrowed southwest into the open Atlantic, quite alone except for the volplaning shearwaters and the marching sequence of the weather. The Old World had vanished astern for less than a week when they lost their first passenger; it was the tiny Anne Winthrop. Yet it was a singularly merciful crossing; there was but one additional death, a second child of unremembered identity.[8]

Lion made her landfall on November 2. America appeared before them without majesty; a long sandspit to larboard; ahead, beneath a slow cyclone of gulls, a bay, with islands of undistinguished profile. But the wind blew toward them from the land; how they savored it cannot easily be imagined. Beside one of the islands, *Lion*'s anchor went down. Their Atlantic crossing had taken more than two months; to traverse the continent ahead would require, of their descendants, more than two centuries.[9]

"The wind being contrary, the ship stayed at Long Island," noted the elder John Winthrop in his journal, "but the governor's son came on shore, and that night [Thursday, November 3] the governor went to the ship and lay aboard all night; and the next morning, the wind coming fair, she came to an anchor before Boston." [10]

Their debarkation inspired quaint formalities. As the Winthrops drew away from *Lion* in Captain Peirce's boat, the ship's guns boomed in salute, while at the landing place an array of militiamen delivered "divers vollies," and a ridiculous little cannon spat fire. Beside them waited the principal officers of the colony, gravely bowing, and clusters of ordinary folk. More significant than the solemnities, however, were the fresh provisions which had been collected for the occasion: "fat hogs, kids, venison, poultry, geese, partridges, etc." Already the newcomer to Massachusetts Bay might reasonably hope to survive.[11]

Behind the drifting powder smoke, the New England Boston had just entered its second year of existence. Here, upon an oddly shaped peninsula, the company's artisans had produced a village, as English as they could make it: gabled, chimneyed, and thatched. (They had experienced little sea change, and they knew nothing of log cabins.) Yet even the prejudices of East Anglian craftsmen could not assure a perfect reproduction of Groton or Little Baddow. For it had been quickly discovered that this part of the New World afforded neither lime nor stone that could be readily shaped. Hence New England rose wooden from the wilderness and remained so for centuries.[12]

In this marginal village upon its curious promontory, John Winthrop, Jr., passed his first American winter. We know few of the details. He underwent a period of illness, possibly severe, but for recent immigrants this was not unusual. If he was impressed by the un-English intensity of the season, he chose—as a man concerned for the future of Massachusetts—not to emphasize the point. Like the others, he endured it; famine, at least, was no longer a problem, and there was sufficient companionship—and responsibility—to preclude a dangerous tedium.[13]

Early Massachusetts was conducted upon five major premises: farming, fishing, commerce, politics, and religion. With farming and fishing the Winthrops concerned themselves only indirectly; even the pressures of the American environment did not demand that a Suffolk squire or his principal heir should personally attend to plows and nets. Nor was the heir to exhibit much aptitude for commerce; the years were abundantly to certify what the merchant John Freeman had recognized in Constantinople: John Winthrop, Jr., had little inclination toward trade. However, there is a nice distinction between commerce and enterprise, and for the latter he would disclose a lifelong penchant. For the untried, the speculative, the romantically grandiose, he had an insatiable appetite. It was a characteristic by no means of American derivation, but it went far to explain his rise as a leader upon an American frontier.

For a period, beginning that spring, he regarded the fur traffic as an "enterprise" and was delighted when the company requested that he undertake its management. Yet it failed to flourish. Perhaps it never could in New England; the Charles was not the

[59]

Mohawk nor the Merrimac the Ottawa. But it is equally plain that Winthrop, over the long pull, was no merchant. The fur trade, for all its glamor, required ledgers. It was, he discovered, a business.[14]

On the other hand, he appears to have acquired a distinct, if temporary, reputation as an importer. Acting in behalf of the company, his family, and himself—the three interests can be regarded as nearly coterminous—he superintended a number of heavy shipments, embracing such diversities as glass, deal boards, brimstone, canary seed, and indentured servants. He dealt chiefly through Francis Kirby, which was one reason for his success. Moreover, amid the paraphernalia of subsistence were additional consignments of personal books, including an Archimedes, an English grammar, an almanac, and the catalog of the latest Frankfurt book fair. He in fact was gathering one of the outstanding libraries of colonial North America, and he discovered in Kirby and, especially, in Edward Howes an effective pair of purchasing agents.[15]

For all its quasi-independent posture, Massachusetts never sought total isolation, and as one of the better educated men in the colony, Winthrop maintained, from the beginning, an extensive overseas correspondence. Such letters performed the function of newspapers and were filled with public concerns; eastward went assurances of survival and growth, westward, intelligence of Archbishop Laud and King Gustavus Adolphus. They were likewise conveyors of vital statistics, with elaborate data upon births, health, illnesses, and deaths. But Winthrop's letters were also notable for their emphasis upon scientific matters; his discussions with Howes and Jacie were continued, at even so great a distance, with enthusiasm. Howes had a flair for the practical, writing variously of silk culture, the northwest passage, the medical arts, and a "necessary instrument for great ordnance." In Jacie the goodly tendency of the English clergy to contemplate the wonders of nature continued unabated; among his denunciations of Anglican policy we find a discussion of Tycho's Star (the famous nova of 1572), and in June of 1632, he requested Winthrop to watch, on October 3, for "a fearful Ecclipse of the Sun." The eclipse letter was delivered with time to spare, and Winthrop stood ready on the day indicated, but the weather turned hopelessly cloudy, and there was no appreciable dimming of the light. The region of totality lay, in fact, 3,000 miles from Boston.[16]

Though born with an instinct for the scientific, John Winthrop, Jr., never made a *profession* of "natural philosophy"; for an Englishman of the seventeenth century, this was quite unheard of. Indeed, it is difficult to associate him with any single calling. His aptitudes, though pronounced, were strikingly various. Yet, if required to place him in a category, we should be obliged to cite the political. Given his quality of charm, his ability to distill satisfaction from the unsatisfactory, it could not be otherwise. It is particularly revealing that his father, who, for all their dissimilarities, appreciated his merits, lost no time in introducing him to the politics of Massachusetts Bay.

The government of the infant colony was in a condition calculated to delight a political scientist—a body corporate and private in the process of conversion into a body corporate and public. That which had been strongly commercial was turning chiefly political. To be sure, there existed considerable precedent for this kind of thing; Virginia and New Plymouth, each in its fashion, had experienced the same transition. But the case of Massachusetts remains classic.

This metamorphosis of the Bay Colony has long thrown students into confusion. But if the essentials are borne in mind, things become clear enough: (1) A royal charter had empowered a private corporation to colonize a specified portion of North America. (2) With the approval of the stockholders, called freemen, the headquarters of the company had been moved overseas, and, lest anyone should become awkward in the future, the charter itself was taken along. (3) The original freemen had invested money, and rather few of them actually crossed the Atlantic as planters. (4) At the first General Court of the company to be held in America, October 19, 1630, it seemed reasonable, in a time of crisis, to so violate the charter as to bestow plenary powers upon the chairman and directors (that is, governor and assistants). It also appeared desirable to extend freeman's status to 109 colonists actually resident, regardless of their financial contribution. (5) By the spring of 1631 and with the possibility of mass extinction apparently at an end, the company management (that is, government) felt it appropriate to unveil before the General Court a further and deeply cherished conception of freemanship, whereby an individual's competence for the place should be determined, not solely by residence, but by *membership in a church.* To this the court assented on April 17. (6) By the spring of 1632, the first subsistance crisis was so obviously over that certain of the more thoughtful residents could risk the luxury of criticizing the management (government) of Massachusetts, especially for its assumption of powers not authorized in the company's charter.[17]

Rather curiously, John Winthrop, Jr., for all his labors in England, had not yet become a freeman of Massachusetts Bay. But no one was now disposed to make difficulties, either over his membership in the Boston church (the precise date escapes us) or over his admission to freemanship on April 3, 1632. Nor was there any recorded opposition when the General Court of Elections elevated him on May 9 to the office of assistant.[18]

One would give a good deal to know all that went on in and behind the scenes of that spring election meeting of 1632, for much that was decisive came from it. But it is clear that the administration of the elder Winthrop fell under attack in two particulars: (1) The practice whereby the governor was chosen from and *by* the assistants; and (2) the habit of the governor and assistants of issuing orders of a general, or *legislative,* character, including the levy of taxes.[19]

[62]

None of the unpleasantness, only the final decision, was spread upon the company minutes of May 9. Management plainly had to give way. The selection of the governor from among the assistants was retained, but the choice thereafter was to be made by the "whole Court," freemen included. Moreover, the "raiseing of a publique stock" (taxation) was to be the responsibility not only of the chief executive and his aides but also of a special committee of freemen composed of "two of every plantation." Under the circumstances, the election of the younger John as an assistant remained the principal consolation of the Winthrop interest. And if the freemen refrained from murmurs of nepotism, they had exhibited an instinctive touchiness upon the more vital questions. It is most of all to be observed that the outcome rather closely conformed to the written requirements of the Massachusetts Charter.[20]

Having sworn, as an assistant, "true faith and allegiance to our Sovereign Lord King Charles" and to "do equal right and justice to all," [21] John Winthrop, Jr., at once found himself in close association with an unusual coterie of magistrates. Of his father, re-elected governor, enough has been said to indicate the stature. Thomas Dudley, once again deputy governor, was of mature years, varied gifts, and unimpeachable integrity, but he suffered from a vast inflexibility and a propensity to take offense. Roger Ludlow, a west-country man in his early forties, was a lawyer of established reputation; his New England career would presently certify to the catholicity of his tastes—and his roving disposition. William Pynchon reflected, like the Winthrops, the vigor of a family whose gentility was less than ancient; his wealth was considerable, and his personal talents embraced public service, private enterprise, and religious controversy. Simon Bradstreet was a young man of many abilities, whose personal and political longevity would one day prove monumental; his ultimate eclipse by his gifted first wife was by no means an indication of weakness. He was of moderate personal temper, and we may safely assume the younger Winthrop was drawn to him forthwith. We may also suppose that Winthrop enjoyed less rapport with Increase Nowell, who was elderly and subject to intense personal opinions, and that he was drawn scarcely at all to John Endecott, whose reputation for rigid commitment to programs has survived three centuries. The remaining two assistants were temporarily in England and had been elected *in absentia;* this may well have been an advantage, for one was the reproachful John Humphrey, the other a Lincolnshire Puritan named William Coddington, whose personal instabilities would one day become a particular thorn in the younger Winthrop's side.[22]

It already was the custom to hold a meeting of governor, deputy, and assistants in the first week of every month, except in winter, and it was on these occasions that Winthrop made his first acquaintance with the politico-judicial processes of Massachusetts Bay. Dignified neither by tradition nor by obvious potency, these little assistants' courts carried on their business with a formality that was as vital as it was quaint. Most of their concerns were minor: the determination of fence lines, the enforcement of labor contracts, and the restraint of woodlot fornications. Yet these represented the very roots of New England politics, and John Winthrop, Jr., though he may have played at first a minor role, did not miss a meeting for nearly a year. Nor could he fail to take note of something else—the granting of land. Two hundred acres went that June to Dudley (deputy governor). Three hundred acres were received by Endecott (assistant) in July. Ludlow (assistant) got 100 acres, and the senior Winthrop (governor) 50 particularly desirable acres in November. Only a single allotment appears to have been made that year to a person who was not a member of the Court of Assistants.[23]

More absorbing still was the famous quarrel between governor and deputy governor, which continued, with lulls, from the spring of 1632 through the autumn of 1633. It sprang from causes both private and public, from the fact that Winthrop, not Dudley, was governor, and the fear that Boston, not Newtown (Cambridge), was becoming the capital of Massachusetts. Dudley produced nearly all the uproar, but if the younger Winthrop did not often participate, he at least could witness the business at close range. It was more than a teapot disturbance, for it involved authentic interests. It was enormously instructive.[24]

Another area of difficulty was the external; 3,200 miles of Atlantic Ocean were already less a barrier than an avenue of communication. Not all the letters that came to Boston conveyed routine news; certain of them demanded crucial decisions. As early as 1632, it was obvious that the colony was provoking displeasure in high places, and even the younger Winthrop began to receive warnings. From Edward Howes he learned that "an egregious knave . . . would give none of you a good word but the governor he was a good man and kept a good table but al the rest were Heriticks." "I know," wrote Francis Kirby, "I shall not need to advise you that the prayeing for our kinge be not neglected in any of your publique meetings, and I desire that you differ no more from us in Church government then you shall find that we differ from the prescript rule of gods word, and further I meddle not." From a new living in Yorkshire, Henry Jacie spoke of rampant "Popery" and warned that he and Winthrop might have to cease corresponding through ordinary channels. There also were rumors of a new standing committee of the Privy Council (the first of a considerable spawn) to "settle the affairs of New England," and Howes presently sent word that unfavorable gossip concerning the Bay Company was running unchecked through London.[25]

Winthrop must have passed on this intelligence to his father, but whether he played a significant part in the response of Massachusetts is uncertain. Yet it was such as to command his approval. To England went respectful assurances; [26] in America there was no change whatever. It was precisely his kind of policy, and one is tempted to wonder if he did not charm it through the Court of Assistants past the stiff necks of Nowell and Endecott. But if he did not suggest the technique, he obviously took it to heart. Moreover, it is instructive to recall that Massachusetts, so long as she could employ the arts of courteous evasion, experienced little difficulty in maintaining an unauthorized, but virtual, independence.

CHAPTER 6

Enterprise at Agawam

A CERTAIN Thomas Dexter, though a freeman, had pronounced the government of Massachusetts "captious." For
this, the Court of Assistants, gathered at Boston on March 4,
1632/3, ordered that he be put in bilbows, disfranchised, and fined
£40.[1]

There is nothing to suggest that John Winthrop, Jr., thought
these penalties too severe or that he took a particularly active part
in the meeting. He had, in fact, other and more engrossing problems to consider. For he was about to lead a colonial enterprise of
his own.

The thing had developed during the winter. In mid-January,
the governor had learned that Acadia, the great continental pro-
jection which flanked New England's sea lanes to Europe, had
ceased to be questionably Scottish and had become rather less ob-
scurely French. The elder Winthrop reacted instantly: All available assistants were called into emergency session, and on the seventeenth it was decided not only to fortify the Bay itself but also to
undertake a new settlement at Agawam, "least an enemy, finding
it void, should possess and take it from us." [2] It was the first of an
historic series of Bostonian responses to danger from the maritime
east.

Agawam (it has long since been renamed Ipswich) lay beyond
the granite elbow of Cape Ann and faced the Isles of Shoals across
waters renowned for cod. But it afforded more than fishing; unlike
much of New England, the region had never served as a glacial
dumping ground, and it already was reputed "the best place"[3] on
the coast for agriculture. It had, wrote Edward Johnson two decades later, "very good land for husbandry, where rocks hinder not
the course of the plow."[4] Aside from its comparative remoteness
(it lay 30 miles from the head of Massachusetts Bay), Agawam's
sole disadvantage was an awkward bar at its river mouth.

Even so, Massachusetts would have preferred not to have
reached for Agawam so early as the spring of 1633. Her population was as yet insufficient for even so modest an expansion, and
the emergency character of the occupation was evident in the limitation of the pioneer party to thirteen, most of them men of a
practical turn. Of the entire group, only Winthrop was of special
distinction.[5]

They departed on their mission before the beginning of April,
1633; almost certainly they proceeded by water. They did not encounter any French or unfriendly Indians or any genuinely disastrous acts of God. But even with abundant raw materials, and in
the mild half of the year, the creation, with a dozen men, of a village was no sinecure. To what extent Winthrop participated in the
sweaty side of the business is unspecified; presumably it was little;
his role was to plan, oversee, and encourage. He was a natural en-
visioner, and his remarkable personality possessed an infinite capacity for morale. But there is strong evidence that he found it
irksome—day after day—to administer, and in the course of the
first crucial months he withdrew himself to Boston, not once but
five times. That he should attend, on May 29, the General Court
of Elections, is understandable, but his presence at the assistants'
meetings for June, July, August, and September is a matter for
wonder. (They dealt chiefly with alcoholic excesses, sexual misbe-

havior, and the wanderings of domestic livestock.) Only a single transaction that summer was in any way significant—the permission which was granted, on September 3, "to Mr. John Winthrop Junr. . . . to sett up a trucking howse upp Merrymak Ryver." (Another enterprise—envisaged.) [6]

Meanwhile Agawam languished dangerously. His own dwelling—a modest enough affair of two stories and four rooms—remained unready for occupancy as late as October.[7] Winthrop, in fact, was exhibiting in this, his first independent command, a weakness which would become painfully characteristic. He was long on planning, but short on execution. He knew how to organize, but not to supervise. He was deficient still in the ability to persist. From his own undertakings, he too often walked away.

Too often—but not invariably, and seldom at a fatal time. The fact remains that he established Agawam so firmly that a decade later it had become the second largest settlement in Massachusetts Bay Colony. At the decisive moment, he managed to give his artisans the kind of leadership the situation demanded. Through the remainder of 1633, and until April of 1634, the Court of Assistants saw him no more. Presently he was bombarding his father with requisitions for livestock, clothing, additional personnel, lead, grain, and a suitable clergyman. By the end of October, it was evident that he intended not only to see through the founding of Agawam but to settle there himself.[8]

Aside from his susceptibility to distraction, his greatest problem was his wife. Martha Winthrop frankly did not relish the prospect of life in a peripheral village over against savages and Frenchmen, and she took to expressing her dissatisfactions in the querulous cipher of her bridal days, until her husband was driven to point out in similar code that such melancholy was a device of Satan. Thereupon Martha turned to practical argument: She supposed their house at Agawam would be in its unfinished state quite unsuitable for winter habitation; besides, there was no likelihood of the settlement's obtaining a minister. Yet she abandoned the struggle at last and early in November she arrived, shivering beneath a red cloak and accompanied by servants and several chests of household belongings.[9]

Though hers was hardly the stuff of which pioneer women are made, Martha's fears were not without foundation. Her new abode was located attractively enough upon a sunny slope, with an outlook down a widening estuary toward spacious marshes and a hint of the sea. But even with the additional furnishings, its four rooms could afford but a sparse existence.[10] Winthrop himself found the winter weeks depressing enough: His father burdened him with unsolicited advice of a religious nature; the afternoons had just begun to lengthen when Martha discovered herself—apparently for the first time and very likely to her horror—with child; and at least one observer was moved to exhort them, from the sanctuary of Boston, to endure for the sake of divine reward.[11]

Yet Winthrop was not the sort to abandon himself to gloomy introspection. His wife might brood, but he appears to have been content to make the best of a temporarily dismal business. Nor was he wholly cut off from the world; down the raw coast came occasional letters, not only from the governor at Boston but from Emmanuel Downing and (most happily of all) from Edward Howes, overseas. Howes was as stimulating as ever, but at times too prolific with unrealistic suggestions, and he never could bring himself to experience "want and penurie" in New England. Yet he was a capital purchasing agent, especially of books, and his shipments other than books, which included such diversities as wolf dogs and codling apple slips, may have been useful.[12] Moreover, there were occasional visitors, of whom a certain William Hilton was perhaps the most interesting. Hilton had once been a resident of Plymouth Colony, but since 1627 had dwelt at Piscataqua, a region already renowned for its rude plenty. He examined Winthrop's Agawam with a practiced eye, and in a subsequent letter, penned about the beginning of May, 1634,[13] suggested that the settlement might place less emphasis upon clams and more upon swine—*fattened upon Indian corn.* Such hogs were, he declared, a most satisfactory source of food. That Winthrop ever acted upon this advice we cannot say; in any case, the clams of Little Neck have long since gained the local argument. Yet Hilton's views were significant for America, and it is perhaps not too much to regard this letter of 1634, written in the chill of a down-East spring, as an early major document in the history of Iowa.

But if Agawam never became a Sioux City,[14] it should not be assumed that Winthrop's leadership was lacking in imagination. If ever he developed an *idée fixe* for New England, it was a belief in the merits of a diverse economy, and his efforts in this direction would soon become a major preoccupation. The concept was, of course, fundamentally sound, but—like many another enthusiast in an undeveloped land—he too often strove to force matters into a desired pattern before their appointed time and in consequence suffered successive frustrations. For Agawam, he thought in terms of codfish, animal husbandry, beaver pelts, and the Indian traffic, and his London correspondence with the versatile Mr. Kirby reveals a plan of operations, both public and private, of impressive dimensions. Agawam did afford substantial advantages; its association of cow and cod was by no means an impractical economics for seventeenth-century New England, and if, late that spring, Mr. Kirby reminded Winthrop of an unfavorable personal balance of £29/6/0, the sum was less than catastrophic. Only the beaver and the Indians failed absolutely to pay.[15]

His zeal for the place continued, through bleakness of season and the lamentations of Martha, for nearly a year. In sound English fashion he took care to acquire—for himself—rather extensive parcels of land: One, which he called Argilla, lay two miles southeast of the settlement; another, still further removed, was centered upon an elevated promontory called Castle Hill, beside the river mouth. Each embraced about three hundred acres; both promised much, either because of superior soil or because of the native marsh grass, a homely growth esteemed as cattle fodder. Another property lay closer to the village; doubtless he thought here in terms of house lots, for its extent was no more than six acres. On none of these tracts, however, does he appear to have erected buildings of consequence, and his use of them was confined to haying and grazing.[16]

In fact, the horizons of John Winthrop, Jr., could not long remain so parochial. His own background and inclinations ordained otherwise. By spring, he already was restless, and on the first day of April, 1634, he once more took his seat at the regular assistants' meeting at Boston, an act of truancy which was, by this time, entirely excusable.[17]

It also marked the beginning of another, and very instructive, stage in his political training. For Massachusetts stood once again on the verge of an explosion. Briefly (and at the risk of oversimplification) it may be said that the officials of the Bay Company had fallen into the attitude of many another corporate management, namely, that the adequate performance of their duties should be rewarded with something like permanent tenure of office. They still did not realize that Massachusetts had become less a land and trading venture and more a public body with distinctively political concerns. Perhaps the rank and file of the freemen did not altogether perceive this, either, but they increasingly behaved as if they did—until the petty upheaval which shook the colony that spring resembled less a corporate proxy fight than the overthrow of a public administration.

As early as the April assistants' meeting, there were signs that Governor Winthrop's regime faced serious difficulties. To be sure, a good deal of time was spent upon ordinary matters; there were peculations to punish, and there was much land-granting to the right people. But the assistants—the younger John Winthrop

among them—were also moved to issue four significant orders:
(1) Land grants which remained unimproved for three years were
to revert to the colony, (2) all land-holdings were to be more precisely surveyed, (3) the price of grain was "lefte at liberty to be
solde as men can agree," and (4) a formal loyalty oath (wherein
the king remained unmentioned) was imposed upon all permanent
residents of Massachusetts Bay. It is obvious that the first three
were tailored to meet existing criticism, the last to minimize its
effects in the future.[18]

John Winthrop, Jr., failed to attend the famous Court of Elections which met at Boston on May 14. We do not know why, but it
was unfortunate. Admittedly, he could not have stemmed—for all
his personal magnetism—the revolt of freemen and freemen's
deputies, who seized the occasion to topple his father's government. But he deserved to experience the process in person—not
merely to hear about it from prejudiced lips. It was an exciting
contest. The elder Winthrop himself was not unaware of what was
coming, and the official party endeavored to neutralize the assault
with the eloquence of the Reverend John Cotton, who, in a passionate "election sermon," declared that an officeholder should not
be turned out without specific cause, any more than "a private man
out of his freehold." It availed them nothing. The freemen, by secret ballot, chose as governor not Winthrop but his political bête
noire, Thomas Dudley. As deputy governor they selected Roger
Ludlow, a recent apostate from the Winthrop faith and doubtless
equally offensive. They demanded, and got, a view of the company charter, on the strength of which they demanded, and got, a
revision of policy whereby all rights of basic legislation were
vested, not in the governor and assistants only but in the entire
General Court. They demanded, and presently got, an investigation of and report upon the Winthrop regime. Though the elder
John was elected, and his son remained, an assistant, the rout
could hardly have been more complete.[19]

But if John Winthrop, Jr., missed the immediate furor, he appears not to have been blind to its significance. Never was he to fall into the particular error of his father, the assumption that a governor's commission somehow conferred the vague and paternal rights of a country squire. Though scarcely a liberal, he never would confuse his personal status with the public good, and he never would be charged, as his parent had been, with a clear misappropriation of power.

A contributing factor in the little revolution had been the mutual jealousy of two villages, each of which desired to become the seat of government of Massachusetts Bay. And because the "popular" party had won, the next assistants' meeting (it was called for June 3, 1634) was held not at Boston, which was Winthrop's place of residence, but at Newtown, which was Dudley's. This time the younger Winthrop did appear, took the prescribed oath of office, and sat through a drowsy session devoted to swine and uncontested wills. At the meetings for July and August, however, he was once more absent, and again we do not know the reason. It probably was not the advanced stage of Martha's pregnancy; it was not the habit of seventeenth-century husbands to interrupt the conduct of public business to attend the confinements of their wives. Moreover, he seems not to have been unduly concerned by her condition; in a letter of July 20 to his father, he included, without special comment, appropriate greetings from Martha.[20]

Then came tragedy. The principal historian of Ipswich has asserted, unfortunately without citation, that Martha Fones Winthrop died in childbirth, probably in late August or in early September of 1634, together with an infant daughter.[21] Of the death of both, however, we can be confident: Martha's pregnancy is adequately documented; her husband's remarriage the following summer is fully established; and during the interim there is no surviving reference either to a child or to Martha. Indeed, John

Winthrop, Jr., seems never to have mentioned her in writing again.

One at least can sense something utterly pathetic. Perhaps it is a tale of a fragile doll, once profoundly loved, bright-faced when new, but quite incompatible with anything so difficult as New England, and thus loved steadily less. Or else it is of a lovely young woman, equally delicate, equally unsuited to the wilderness, but deeply cherished to the end.[22] For the sake of John Winthrop, Jr., one would wish for the latter.

They must have laid mother and infant to rest, beneath towering maples, on the raw, new slope which one day would be called the Old Burying Ground. From it, toward the east, was still a hint of the sea which Martha had crossed, and westward, the American hills, beyond which her descendants now never could pass.

Martha was part of the price of Agawam, and so was the dismal homestead to which her young widower returned. But the reckoning was nearly complete: Agawam would survive; the place at last had acquired a minister, the Reverend Nathaniel Ward, a man of many talents, not the least of which was the ability to combine a Puritan orthodoxy with a wry sense of humor. Moreover, during the coming winter, Mr. Ward would enjoy the assistance of Thomas Parker, a theologian of acknowledged parts, around whose person the winds of major controversy already had swirled. Agawam, indeed, now felt so confident of its future that it had sought, and received, from the Bay authorities the right to rechristen itself—in respectable English fashion—Ipswich.[23]

Though John Winthrop, Jr., remained the town's leading resident, he was no longer indispensable to its welfare. Throughout his last summer with Martha, his municipal responsibilities had lessened, and now he could discover no reason why he should linger in the company of his long-faced domestics, daily confronted with the memorabilia of the deceased. He still was an officer of the

Massachusetts Bay Colony, and it was quite in order that he should minimize his bereavement with absence upon public business.

He had missed the two General Court sessions which were held in September, meetings at which the echoes of the springtime crisis had reverberated away, but he sat again upon the assistants' court on October 6. Once more the formal agenda posed nothing of importance; the principal recorded business was the misbehavior of one John Lee, whom the court fined for enticing a maiden of the governor's household "to goe with him into the cornfeild." [24] The real concerns of the session were kept carefully unofficial and out of the journal. They quite transcended individual peccadilloes; in fact, they involved considerations of transatlantic scope. Moreover, they served to remove John Winthrop the Younger from the distresses of Ipswich for nearly a year. Within a month he found himself on the high seas, aboard an unremembered vessel, plunging toward England upon errands which were at once public, private, and confidential.

CHAPTER 7

The First Return to Britain

THE public occasions were paramount. It was less a journey in the family interest, still less in his own behalf. For at stake was the integrity of Massachusetts. In prospect, the colony had provoked little opposition; as a reality, it had given offense to three major interests: (1) the Council for New England, whose prerogatives had been so nicely overlooked, (2) the Crown, whose officers the charter had deceived and whose dignity the Bay government was affronting by inattention, and (3) the Church of England, whose episcopal emphasis the whole Massachusetts community was denying by open nonconformity. Counter moves were quite inevitable. The first had come as early as December, 1632, when the complaints of Sir Ferdinando Gorges and others of the New England Council had inspired a temporary committee of the Privy Council, charged with an investigation of Massachusetts. The elevation, the following summer, of the high churchman William Laud, as Archbishop of Canterbury, lent vigor to the proceedings; and a full-fledged "Commission for Foreign Plantations" (of which Laud was chairman) appeared at the end of April, 1634. Already the complex evolution was under way which one day would produce the celebrated Lords (and Boards) of Trade.[1]

It was not long before Whitehall began to issue specific direc-

tives. Certain of them merely sought to tighten, with particular reference to New England, existing regulations for the departure of
persons overseas. But another, dated February 21, 1633/4, ordered
Matthew Cradock, as the principal company representative in London, to obtain possession of the Massachusetts charter and turn it
over to the Privy Council, pending final disposition.[2]

Massachusetts was fully aware of this peril by the middle of
1634. Its response was typical: No formal reply was attempted,
only a program of evasion—and of military preparedness, wherein
the enemy remained carefully unspecified. A temporary advocate
was discovered in the person of Edward Winslow, who was about
to embark for England, but his mission was vague, and he was a
freeman, not of Massachusetts but of Plymouth Colony. Significantly, when the magistrates came to dispatch a pair of their own
agents, it was done so quietly that neither their appointment nor
their departure was given public notice. But the subsequent record
makes plain that John Winthrop, Jr., was one of them.[3]

His instructions likely were verbal. He might, should the occasion offer, engage in political conversations, but his particular concern was to encourage a heavier emigration—of a correct godliness
—to New England. Though he still was only in his twenty-ninth
year, the Bay already had enough experience of his personality to
realize that here was the perfect salesman. Also worthy of notice
was the continuing concern, even in the midst of political crisis, for
manpower.

Winthrop's colleague was in many respects his antithesis, the
very personification of systematic Puritanism. The Reverend John
Wilson was sixteen years his senior. A theologian of unusual at-
tainments, he had become the first "Teacher" of the First Church
of Boston and quickly had been recognized as a leading dispenser
of orthodoxy. But there is no evidence that friction developed between them; Wilson was, for all his granite commitments, of an

affable disposition, and if ever a man drew breath who knew how to avoid quarrels, it was John Winthrop, Jr.[4]

They traveled practically incognito; Wilson, in fact, appears to have assumed the name "Warner." They sailed sometime between October 6 and November 7, 1634; probably it was later than earlier, for Winthrop had ample time to settle his affairs in Ipswich. His house and his household servants were placed at the disposal of the Reverend Nathaniel Ward; his other possessions were left in charge of an old Agawam associate, William Clarke. In a "long great chest" he laid away the last reminders of Martha, a black woolen dress, a sea-green gown, and her red cloak; into a trunk marked A.W.F. (the initials of Martha's mother) went a piteously complete baby's layette. No doubt Winthrop was relieved to find himself at last on shipboard, though the vessel was tiny and the season late.[5]

It was not a pleasant crossing. Their intended port was Barnstable, in Devon, but the Atlantic gales carried them not into Bristol Channel but among the savage fingers of Ireland. In the circumstances the ship could venture no farther, and her passengers were put ashore at Galway.[6]

There was nothing for it but to slog overland along execrable pony tracks. Yet Winthrop contrived to improve the occasion; amid bogs and an uncouth peasantry, he discovered a West Country Englishman of initiative and derring-do named Sir Charles Coote. How this gentleman impressed the strait-laced Wilson we do not know, but he entranced young Winthrop, who pumped him dry of information concerning the Irish iron industry.[7] After Sir Charles came further morasses and an encounter with a band of disorderly kerns,[8] but by mid-December they were safe in Dublin, discoursing happily at the fireside of the excellent Joshua Hoyle, professor of Divinity at Trinity College and Winthrop's former tutor.[9]

The diversion to Ireland was not wholly an inconvenience; after

[79]

all, Winthrop's primary mission was to encourage immigration into Massachusetts, and he must have been aware that large numbers of the right people—restless, antipapal, and nonconforming —dwelt in nearby Ulster. In any case, the latter part of December saw him pressing toward the hulking wet hills of Northern Ireland. He traveled alone (Wilson made directly for England),[10] and well before the end of the month, he was at Antrim, locked in earnest negotiation with an enthusiastic Presbyterian and engrosser of land named Sir John Clotworthy. Sir John was an entrepreneur of major importance; his enterprises embraced the whole of the British Isles, and his connections were everywhere varied and influential. Indeed, he would one day sit in the Long Parliament and would chide (in person) Archbishop Laud upon the scaffold. But now, as he and Winthrop conferred together through the dim afternoons beside Lough Neagh, he dwelt with enthusiasm upon New England; not only should there be a "transmission of yonge children" thither, it should become renowned for cattle and sheep, preferably his own.[11]

Their discussions attracted a cluster of regional worthies, and it is plain that Winthrop made an impression, in particular upon Ulster's leading eccentric, a congenitally rebellious Scot named John Livingstone, who for the time being (and despite an irregular ordination) was minister of Killinchy in County Down. Livingstone was fascinated by Winthrop's portrayal and hurried back to his congregation full of enthusiasm for Massachusetts. That he never saw the New World was due chiefly to an unexpected act of God, but years later his grandson would marry, in America, one of Winthrop's granddaughters.[12]

Winthrop quitted Ireland early in January, 1634/5, bearing with him elaborate plans and an awkward code with which to keep them confidential. His movements thereafter are difficult to follow; probably he crossed to Scotland and possibly made use there of three letters of introduction—to suitably "godly" persons—

which Livingstone had provided. There is even some evidence that he visited Edinburgh and Leith.[13] But he cannot be located with confidence again until February, when he appeared in the East Riding of Yorkshire, in the company of his old friend, the learned Puritan cleric, Henry Jacie.

Poor Jacie had fallen upon evil days. He had been appointed, in 1633, vicar of Aughton—a quiet country village, complete with castle, beside the River Derwent. But it had afforded little immunity from Anglican discipline, and within a year he had been summarily removed from his living. Jacie had been rescued from destitution only by the timely patronage of Sir Matthew Boynton, a baronet of more than local consequence, whose sheep dotted the Yorkshire Wolds and whose religious convictions deviated markedly from the official.[14]

Whether Winthrop encountered Sir Matthew through Jacie, or Jacie through Sir Matthew, is uncertain, but it is obvious that the three conferred at length, talks which further developed the notion of New England as a Puritan sheep run. The Winthrop personality was again at its best; long before Winthrop was done, both Boynton and Jacie had become enthusiastic converts, and, when presently he moved on to the city of York, their emigration to Massachusetts was already in the planning stage.[15]

Of Winthrop's transactions at York, we know next to nothing. Apparently he ventured in Jacie's behalf into the very shadow of the great archiepiscopal minster, for Jacie later expressed appreciation for his "great paines and love." [16] But Winthrop cannot have tarried there long; by the beginning of March, he had traversed the remaining leagues of the Great North Road and was entering the familiar precincts of London.

H i s   m i s s i o n was but half completed. Nevertheless, he appears to have felt that his public responsibilities had been met, at least for the time being, and his activities now turned private, if not personal. As of old, he lodged with the Downings, not, to be sure, among the cramped respectabilities of Peterborough Court, but at a spacious new residence beside Lincoln's Inn Fields, where London was spawning a rather splendid new suburb. Here, in comfortable association with his uncle, Winthrop commenced the discharge of an accumulation of family business, in particular the purchase of supplies, of which he had brought with him elaborate lists. He also could initiate formal, albeit fruitless, inquiries as to Martha's dowry. But of greatest consequence, personally, was the receipt of a letter from John Endecott, written at Salem, Massachusetts, the eighth of the previous December.[17]

Mr. Endecott desired to sell his English house and hoped that Winthrop would be so good as to act as his agent. To expedite things, he also had written to his old friend the Reverend Hugh Peter, then in Holland, and to Peter's stepson, a certain Thomas Reade, said to be in England. Would Winthrop kindly seek out and consult with the latter? [18]

Winthrop probably knew nothing of Reade, but he must certainly have heard of Hugh Peter. This celebrated man was possibly the most notable nonconforming divine of his century. Though still rather young (he was then no more than thirty-seven), Peter already had found it necessary to seek refuge from the Laudian wrath beyond the narrow seas. His future was great with controversy, lofty station—and the gallows. Of greatest significance to Winthrop, however, was his marriage, a decade previously, to Mrs. Elizabeth Cooke Reade, the widow of a representative country squire, whereby the young theologian had acquired three stepsons and three stepdaughters.[19]

One can only surmise how these disparate elements—John Endecott, his English house, Hugh Peter, and the stepchildren—fell so nicely into place within the destiny of the younger John Winthrop. It was hardly the doing of Thomas Reade, who seems to have been in Rotterdam.[20] Very likely the catalyst was Emmanuel Downing, who knew the comings and goings of Puritans as did no one else and who certainly was aware that *Mrs.* Peter was then in London. At any rate, we may suppose that it was he who directed Winthrop to her door.

It is intriguing to consider what happened next. With Mrs. Peter lived her youngest daughter, Elizabeth Reade, aged eighteen,[21] and it is likely that a single look at her was enough to cause John Winthrop, Jr., to forget Endecott's house and Martha's dowry and even the forlorn grave on its Massachusetts hillside. Within an astonishingly few days he had asked for her hand in marriage. Her favorable response was, of course, inevitable; seldom has so young a maiden been courted by so irresistible a suitor.

There remained certain formalities, especially the investigations into respective prospects and stations. These imposed a considerable interval. John and Elizabeth were wed in the Church of St. Matthew in Friday Street on July 6, 1635. No doubt the marriage office was performed by the rector, the Reverend Henry Burton, an irrepressible Puritan of advanced opinions, highly regarded by the bride's stepfather, but less so by the Anglican Establishment. Yet the church itself spoke for the past; it stood crowded by rooftops beneath gothic St. Paul's; and as Winthrop and his bride emerged to face their American future, the countenance of medieval London confronted them still.[22]

Of this young woman whom he had made his wife rather little is known. Like Martha, she left no portrait. She may have been *petite*,[23] but her complexion, dark or fair, is unrecalled. It is obvious, however, that her origins, which had little to do with the ebullient Mr. Peter, were solid. Her father had been Edmund Reade of Wickford, Essex, a gentleman of substance in a substantial countryside; her mother, whose roots could be traced to the neighborhood of Groton, seems to have been of a country stock fast becoming a county family. Her own childhood had been equally wholesome; it had comprehended some of the fairest landscapes in England. Her own generation had by no means lost its vigor: Of her three brothers, one became a physician, another a respected country squire, and the third (it was Thomas Reade) achieved a colonelcy in the parliamentary army. It was a rather cultivated family; Elizabeth herself seems to have spoken— though in East Country accents—a singularly graceful English. Against such a background it is curious to record that she could write only with difficulty.[24]

Her intimates called her Betty. She was, in a conventional manner, a Puritan and was fluent in the idiom of Scripture. She was a genteel and accomplished housekeeper. Unlike Martha, she was admirably fitted for life in seventeenth-century New England.[25]

B ETWEEN courtship and marriage there had been no round of gaiety; such was not the Puritan habit, nor did it specially accord with the bridegroom's disposition. But he cannot have been idle. His purchases, on family account, continued heavy. There also was business to transact in behalf of his stepmother, at Great Maplestead and elsewhere, and hardly had he won the hand of Elizabeth Reade when he was jogging over the familiar highroads into the eastern counties. His exact movements are unknown, but he proceeded at least as far as Groton; and one may speculate upon his feelings as he looked once more upon the goodly Suffolk countryside.[26]

Meanwhile, at Whitehall, the royal and ecclesiastical disenchantment with Massachusetts was approaching a climax; quo warranto papers, soon to be laid before the Court of King's Bench, were demanding that the Bay Company show cause why its charter should not be revoked; there even was talk of an early confiscation, and Winthrop was warned, while at Groton, to "walk warily." Yet it proved unnecessary that he should play the martyr for Massachusetts. If anyone was competent in the procedures required to neutralize such an attack, it was Emmanuel Downing, and Downing appears, as the principal Bay attorney, to have accomplished just that. Moreover, the prosecution was peculiarly liable to distraction; the offenses of a cluster of villages, 3,000 miles away, could hardly hold the official attention in the face of an increasing opposition in England itself, and in the end Massachusetts would be forgotten in the midst of a far greater constitutional struggle at home.[27]

But the episode was nevertheless a part of Winthrop's education. We cannot say that he contributed to Downing's strategy, or even that he followed his uncle, bearing briefs, among the Whitehall courtyards. Yet his presence in London, indeed, at Downing's house, during the initial maneuvers is certain, and his nimble intelligence cannot have failed to digest the technique—the contrived encounters, the gentle nuances, the deft applications of influence. It must enormously have confirmed his natural understanding of the facts of political life.

He furthermore found himself in the middle of developments that went rather beyond the question of Massachusetts. The dissatisfactions which were shaking the realm had bred a host of additional enterprises in the image of the Bay Company. Though most proved abortive, and none quite fulfilled the whispered expectations, a few yielded tangible results, and it was with one of these that Winthrop became concerned. It was a venture of some magnitude. Its beginnings went back several years, to March 19, 1631/2, when Robert Rich, the second Earl of Warwick, had prepared, in the name of the Council for New England, and in favor of an association of Puritan bigwigs, the rough draft of an American charter. Its provisions were as generous as they were imprecise: There was the inevitable land grant, commencing from a "river there called Narraganset river" and extending "the space of forty leagues upon a straight line near the sea shore towards the southwest, west and by south, or west, as the coast lieth towards Virginia." Additional and equally obscure clauses could be construed

[85]

to authorize a de luxe extension to and across the Pacific Ocean. Within this parchment imperium, the beneficiaries were vested with all the rights which the Earl of Warwick "now hath," though what these were the patent did not specify.[28]

Equally devoid of precision is the record of the "patent" itself. That Warwick was sympathetic to the Puritan movement and that he was, as of March 19, 1631/32, president of the Council for New England are known. That his proposal, perhaps redrafted, was submitted, on June 21, 1632, to a select committee of the council is likewise certain. It is furthermore of record that he was, a few months thereafter, removed from his presidency. Beyond this, however, all is confusion. It is perhaps reasonable to suppose that the earl's scheme was turned down by the other New England councilors and that his "patent" never achieved legal existence at all.[29]

But the reality of the patentees was another matter. They were widely known: Many were wealthy; all, or nearly all, were of gentle birth; two were peers. Among them we find the names of Pym and Hampden; included were men who already had "adventured" in the Massachusetts Company. But the dominant individuals, both in rank and enthusiasm, were William Fiennes, first Viscount Saye and Sele, and Robert Greville, second Baron Brooke.[30]

The English Puritans thoroughly understood the workings of interlocking corporations, and it was inevitable that the bright young agent from Massachusetts should be presented to the Warwick patentees. We may safely reconstruct the details: the private meetings in paneled chambers, the careful queries of the mature and worldly Saye and Sele, the excited interjections of the youthful Brooke, the quick responses of Winthrop. The outcome was also inevitable; he captivated them, and it was not long before he was tendered an extraordinary proposal, no less than the provisional governorship of their American domain. His response was

[86]

prompt and favorable. For here was indubitably an enterprise, perhaps of transcontinental extent. That it involved at least a temporary abdication of his commitments to Ipswich and to Massachusetts seems not to have occurred to him. He accepted their commission on Tuesday, July 7, 1635.[31] It was the day following his wedding.

If the so-called Warwick patent was cloudy, Winthrop's instructions were sufficiently plain. He was to govern not the indeterminate reaches of the whole grant but "the River Connecticut in New England and . . . the harbors and places ajoining." He was charged with the construction of buildings and fortifications "at the River," while a particular effort was to be made to provide suitable dwellings for "men of qualitie." He would recruit sufficient labor (fifty men at least) at Massachusetts Bay. His authority was to continue for a full year following his arrival at his post—to which he undertook to proceed "with all convenient speede." The document bore signatures which read like an abbreviated *Who's Who* of Puritanism: Saye and Sele, Sir Arthur Hesilrige, Henry Lawrence, Sir Richard Saltonstall, George Fenwick, and Henry Darley. If an outstanding sponsorship could guarantee a colony, the future of this was assured.[32]

The concerns of Massachusetts, of his family, and now of the "Puritan Lords and Gentlemen," imposed quantities of administrative detail. Nevertheless, Winthrop contrived to find time for intellectual diversion. He was much in the company of the many-talented Henry Howes; we hear of discussions with a mysterious Dr. Euer, who may have been a Rosicrucian; and it even has been suggested that Winthrop became an initiate of that occult order. Yet he derived his greatest satisfaction from an acquaintance with a pair of Germanic brothers, Abraham and Johann Sibert Kuffler, both doctors of medicine, but whose real love was alchemy. Abraham is said to have accompanied the Duke of Buckingham's La Rochelle expedition as an explosives expert; he had married a daughter of the Dutch "philosopher and naturalist" Cornelius Dribbel and had worked upon such diverse problems as dyestuffs and submarines. He thought so highly of Winthrop that he presented the young visitor with a favorite alchemical volume, the property of his late father-in-law; on the flyleaf, Winthrop proudly inscribed the circumstances of the gift and significantly underlined certain portions of the German text which dealt with the treatment of metalliferous ores.[33]

For all his distractions, Winthrop got under way for America in an astonishingly short time. This was not wholly consequent upon his executive skills: The "Lords and Gentlemen" were a large organization and—for the time being—of dedicated purpose. All the multifarious arrangements—the purchase of supplies, the procurement of personnel, and the charter of ships—appear to have been placed under the general supervision of a vigorous young "Turkey merchant" named Edward Hopkins—a man whom Winthrop would come to know, under later and curiously different circumstances, very well indeed. Hopkins enjoyed the assistance of numerous others, among them the Reverend Philip Nye, a fugitive divine with an entrepreneurial flair, whose presence in England was shielded so meticulously from the authorities that it has since escaped the notice of many historians. Nye scoured the countryside for "servants"; Hopkins concentrated upon his special talents, which were merchandise and shipping. Winthrop, in fact, was left comparatively free to devote himself to his other concerns, which were complicated enough, embracing the hire of personal servants, the travel arrangements of his half-brother Deane (whom he was taking to New England for the first time), and the final letters (dispatched in code from a goldsmith's shop in Fleet Street) to Sir John Clotworthy.[34]

It was still high summer when he handed Betty Winthrop up the ladder of the London merchantman *Abigail;* she was pale from recent illness and perhaps from apprehension. The vessel was crammed; her passengers numbered more than two hundred. There was rather little "quality"; the bulk of the company was of the plain folk so necessary to the New World—husbandmen, glovers, a tanner, a baker, a starchmaker, a blacksmith, a shoemaker, and yet more husbandmen, plus at least a score of undifferentiated young people. *Abigail* carried them all in impersonal squalor, which a supplementary cargo of livestock strongly emphasized.[35]

We do not know to what extent Winthrop was able to ease the tedium with intellectual discourse. *Abigail* was accompanied by a second vessel, named *Defence,* and precisely who traveled on which is not in every case clear. The uncertainty was perhaps deliberate: The well-born and learned who sailed for New England that season were likely objects of suspicion, and this would have been especially true of a remarkable group of clergymen, of which John Wilson, Hugh Peter, John Norton, John Jones, and Thomas Shepard were the principals. Together they must have transformed one of the ships into a floating ark of the covenant, but which one we cannot say. They traveled under assumed names, and indeed there is evidence that Mr. Peter was smuggled aboard only hours ahead of the king's officers. In any case, Winthrop must soon have wearied of so theological a company, and he likely sought solace in the person of young Henry Vane, who, though himself incognito, is known to have traveled in *Abigail.* Vane was a Puritan, but no cleric; his alias had been assumed primarily to avoid embarrassing his father, who was Comptroller of the King's Household. He was a man of considerable sparkle—perhaps in this respect the equal of Winthrop—and deeply ambitious, yet his American experience would establish a tendency to political misfortune that would carry him, decades later, to his public execution on Tower Hill.[36]

Their circuit of the English coast was unusually swift; they were in and out of Plymouth before the end of July. The Atlantic crossing was something else; it required ten weeks, and several on board contracted smallpox. Once again Winthrop kept no diary. He may, like his father, have marveled that they suffered no deaths. But he preserved from this voyage only his business papers, including a final and mysterious packet which a special bearer placed in his hands at Plymouth.[37]

Abigail and *Defence* entered Massachusetts Bay together. It was the first week of October, and the New England autumn already had touched the monotonous shores with splendor.[38]

CHAPTER 8

The Fitful Years

"CONVENIENT speede" had carried John Winthrop, Jr., back to Massachusetts in less than three months. Yet he failed to traverse the remaining 150 miles to the Connecticut River in less than five. Hardly had *Abigail* cast anchor when he was confronted with a situation as tortuous as the Boston lanes.

It was to an extent his own fault. He had departed as an agent of Massachusetts Bay and had returned as the governor pro tem of quite another—and possibly competitive—enterprise. He had not been perfectly circumspect. But the controlling element was the otherwise happy circumstance that the Connecticut afforded a navigable approach to the finest agricultural land in New England. Word of this was spreading, and numbers of the coastal English already were falling into a fundamental North American pattern and turning their faces westward.

The first had gone out from Plymouth, the "Old Colony" which the Pilgrim Fathers had founded nearly a decade before Massachusetts Bay. Their leader was Edward Winslow; they had ascended the Connecticut to the site of Windsor as early as the summer of 1632. This had provoked swift reaction from the Dutch, whose Adriaen Block had been the first European to explore the river, and who now dispatched thither an emergency garrison to establish, beside the mouth of a minor tributary, an outpost called "House of Hope." Plymouth responded with a "great new barke," which cruised triumphantly past the Hollanders to the head of navigation; Plymouth, in turn, was overawed by yet greater numbers from Massachusetts. It was, by this time, the summer of 1635, and in England the "Lords and Gentlemen" were laboring to translate their dubious patent into yet another plantation, based upon the same favored region.[1]

For Winthrop, the Dutch proved the easiest to neutralize: They were comparatively weak; they were not Englishmen, and he already commanded the means to render them harmless. He had brought with him—chiefly in *Abigail*—£2,000, a sum calculated to inspire wonders of cooperation at Boston; *Abigail* (and possibly *Defence* as well) was unloading a consignment of ammunition; and a good proportion of their passengers had come in the service of the "Lords and Gentlemen." He furthermore could expect additional ships, similarly laden. Thus, when rumors drifted in that the Dutch director at Fort Amsterdam intended further occupation of the lower Connecticut, Winthrop acted at once. On November 3, 1635, he sent an advance party to Long Island Sound, and the Netherlanders found them there, in a posture of defense, beside the river's mouth.[2]

His Massachusetts competitors were another matter. Though without evidence of ownership (they could exhibit not even a spurious patent) they were nevertheless vested with rights of a peculiarly effective kind—possession and superior numbers. Already there had occurred an unpleasant confrontation between reconnaissance agents of the Warwick interest and a party from Dorchester, Massachusetts. Moreover, young Henry Vane nearly destroyed any hope of an accommodation. Impatient, presumptuous, and endowed with a profound instinct for indiscretion, he adopted the role of Warwick advocate and informed the Boston magistrates to their faces that the Bay settlers in the Connecticut

Valley should "make room" or the Lords and Gentlemen "would divert their thoughts and preparations some other ways." The reaction of a Thomas Dudley, or even of the elder John Winthrop, can be imagined. How the situation was quieted is nowhere specifically set forth, but it is highly probable that it was the younger Winthrop who suggested how the court might deal with this irrepressible young man. Vane was, before everything, *vain,* and the procedures adopted bear the Winthrop touch: 1) On November 1, 1635, Vane was admitted as a member of the church of Boston; 2) on March 3, 1635/6, he was made freeman of Massachusetts Bay; and 3) on May 25, 1636, he was chosen (at the age of twenty-three) governor of the Massachusetts Bay Colony. Niccolò Machiavelli, whose works are still to be found in Winthrop's personal library, would have understood.[3]

Yet no entire resolution of the Connecticut impasse was achieved until the beginning of March. When at last it came, it made considerable sense: The Massachusetts squatters recognized the claims of the Lords and Gentlemen—and Winthrop as governor—while Winthrop and his colleagues accepted the squatters. In addition, the Bay magistrates were inspired to issue a "commission," good for a year, wherein the positions of Winthrop and the Massachusetts people were reasserted and a frame of government recommended. That the Bay had no positive right to do this made little difference; the principal contending parties were for the moment satisfied.[4]

Transactions of such length and delicacy kept Winthrop almost continually in Boston; in any case, he still awaited the arrival there of additional men and equipment. Of manpower, he acquired little more; gossip over the enterprise had so alerted the English authorities that even Lord Brooke was obliged to abandon his recruiting. But Winthrop did receive further supplies. On November 28, a diminutive North Sea coaster of 25 tons, named *Bachelor,* sailed into Boston harbor and shortly was followed by a second vessel of unrecalled proportions called *True Love*. Both carried quantities of Connecticut freight; a little incredibly, *Bachelor* brought also fourteen passengers, among them a bluff professional soldier named Lion Gardiner and his Dutch bride. Their appearance occasioned much administrative labor, and it is apparent that Winthrop could not even visit Ipswich that season. "Your absence hath bredd us much sorrowe," was the mournful comment of the Reverend Nathaniel Ward. "I feare your tye or obligation to this state and in special to this towne is more than yow did well consider when yow ingaged your self another way." [5]

Winthrop was particularly heartened by the arrival of Gardiner. This sturdy man, then thirty-six years of age, brought with him a military reputation of substance. No pike-wielding boor, his specialty was the design of fortifications, and his most recent service, under the Prince of Orange, had been as an engineer. While on duty at Rotterdam, he had become acquainted with Hugh Peter, and this shortly had led to his employment by the Lords and Gentlemen. His commission specified that he should direct the defense of the Connecticut River for a period of four years, at an annual salary of £100. Gardiner was of Scottish origin, but, unlike certain of his countrymen, was little given to pointless heroics. [6]

Perhaps Winthrop still remembered the "convenient speede"; at any rate, when he got away at last for the Connecticut, he rejected the usual circuit of Nantucket Shoals in favor of a more direct passage, in part overland and scarcely yet perfectly known, via Narragansett Bay. He departed shortly after March 20, 1635/6. Behind him at Boston, he left Elizabeth, already grown thick with child. Gardiner set out almost simultaneously, though probably by sea; his wife, who accompanied him, was closer still to her first confinement. [7]

Winthrop's was a journey which constant repetition would etch into a classic route of intercolonial travel. Past Boston Neck and the last huts of Roxbury, the way led southwestward through 25 miles of wilderness, which an unsuspected glacial epoch had cluttered with boulders, bogs, and sandy plains. Though astir with spring, it seems to have repelled his East Anglian tastes, and when, after two days, the track suddenly gave upon a finger of tidewater, he noted with relief that the land had turned more fertile. In the estuary, a tiny ship awaited him, the *Blessing of the Bay*, pioneer product of maritime Massachusetts. Thereafter his progress was more comfortable; the inlet broadened magnificently; it was sufficient, he supposed, for shipping of 500 tons. (One wonders if he did not already associate it with the "Narragansett River" of his charter.) On its western shore, he paused at the village of the sachem Canonicus; though represented in advance as a "great Citty," it proved but a scattering of hovels. It was not his initial encounter with Indians, but likely his first with Narragansets. Winthrop was unimpressed; in common with most seventeenth-century Europeans, he was little disposed to admire aboriginal cultures.[8]

On the morning of April 1, they emerged from the bay and steered westward toward an array of low-strung points and islands. Among them the channels were tricky, but the wind held fair, and before many hours, *Blessing* was furrowing the spacious corridor of Long Island Sound. It was daylight still when she brought Winthrop past marshes and sandy peninsulas into the mouth of the Connecticut River.

They called the place Pasbeshauke, an English rendering of a Dutch corruption of Algonkian sounds, the significance of which has been lost. It would be some months before one of the Gentlemen would honor the Lords by renaming it Saybrook.[9] But meanwhile, regardless of nomenclature, Winthrop was governor, and the governor of an infant settlement must proceed in the expectation of trouble. Winthrop's derived from five principal sources: his employers, his employees, the upriver settlers from Massachusetts

Bay, the Pequot Indians, and his own lack of pertinacity. Of the five, we must regard the last as the most serious. Yet the others afforded sufficient discouragement.

It is obvious, for example, that the Puritan Lords and Gentlemen already had expended the greater part of their dedication; only one, George Fenwick, ever appeared at Pasbeshauke to establish a serious residence. "The gentlemen seem to be discouraged," noted the elder Winthrop as early as June, 1636. Grave interruptions developed in the flow of company supplies; foodstuffs failed to arrive at all. Yet Saybrook experienced no real starving time. Massachusetts Bay, not to mention Plymouth Colony, had long since overcome its initial food crisis; the older plantations in fact were burdened that year with a "great glut" of provisions. On the other hand, the cargoes of pease and beef which the Bay coasters brought to Saybrook were accompanied by stiff invoices (some of them drawn up by Winthrop's own father), and it was not long before the youthful governor abandoned all pretense of an exact accounting in favor of an empirical—and frequently private— traffic. Herein he was quick to take advantage of Saybrook's natural endowments as a place of transshipment between river craft and ocean-going vessels, and, as Gardiner sweated over his fortifications, Winthrop kept the little colony going with a lively exchange of prunes, textiles, maize, furs, and (for the aboriginal taste) looking glasses and jew's-harps.[10]

It is curious to discover that Winthrop, for all his personality and instinct for leadership, was vexed at Saybrook with labor difficulties—most of which were routine. The housing was crude; the food was monotonous; there was insufficient beer; the company failed to issue enough clothing. But the principal grievance was unusual, even in Puritan New England: Winthrop had failed to make adequate provision for divine worship. This was a deficiency so grave that his laborers placed it at the head of a written catalogue of dissatisfactions and indicated that there must be a quickening of the religious pace ere the Lord could restore their "hartes and afactiones." It was an obvious tribute to the screening to which the Puritan patentees had subjected their personnel.[11]

Nor did the Winthrop charm suffice to reduce a still more serious discord upriver, where the Massachusetts majority had undertaken to dislodge the Plymouth minority from its holdings. There was no question of bloodshed; the disappropriation was carried through with all the paraphernalia of frontier legality—Indian cessions, nonexistent charters, and references to the Holy Bible. There even was held, on April 26, a "General Court," the first proceeding under this style in the history of Connecticut. Though Winthrop was not a stated delegate, it is likely that he used the occasion to make his initial ascent of the river to the raw meadowland village called Newtown, later Hartford.[12] There he did his best for the Plymouth interest, not as an advocate but in the extension of good offices. His efforts "tooke little effect"; the Massachusetts squatters made good their uninterrupted possession of the choicest portion of the Connecticut Valley. "'Tis pitty," wrote Edward Winslow from New Plymouth, "religion should be a cloake for such spirits." [13] It also was painfully evident that Winthrop's writ ran no further than a cannon shot from Saybrook fort.

To his own associates, the Pequot Indian problem appeared the most critical of all. Such terror did these few hundred savages inspire, that they demand at least cursory comment. Like the other natives of southern New England, they were of Algonkian speech, and their manner of living conformed to the corn and hunting pattern characteristic of eastern North America. Unlike their neighbors, however, they were comparative newcomers (from the upper Hudson) and were conspicuously competent in warfare and the levy of tribute. Indeed, some of the earliest English to enter the Connecticut Valley had come in response to the appeals of the Indian victims of Pequot aggression.[14]

Because the whites did in fact interfere with their wilderness imperialism, the Pequots developed an early hostility to the advance of the Puritan frontier. More than any other Indians, they became addicted to "outrages," chiefly pillagings, but there also had been selective murders, notably of the captain and crew of a small Virginia ketch. Though Massachusetts entertained little love for Virginians (so early is evident a famous American dichotomy!) the victims *were* English, and that had been enough to produce rumblings at Boston. The Pequots responded with an embassy, bearing gifts and excuses. These the Bay received with reluctance; the magistrates had expected something more substantial, such as the surrender of the murderers.[15]

The Pequots inhabited the mainland shore of Long Island Sound, not far to the east of Saybrook, and it was perhaps natural that Massachusetts should turn at this juncture to John Winthrop, Jr. Though governor of a separate plantation, he recently had been reelected an assistant at Boston, and the Bay saw nothing anomalous in employing him as its Indian agent. A formal commission to this effect was drawn up on July 4, authorizing him to reopen negotiations with the Pequots, to demand the delivery of the murderers, and—in case of refusal—to inform the Indians that the English proposed to "revenge the blood of our countrymen as occasion shall serve." [16]

Winthrop seems to have been apprised of these new responsibilities by George Fenwick and Hugh Peter, who appeared at Saybrook a week or so later in the company of an intelligent young Londoner named Thomas Stanton. That Winthrop was bound to undertake such a chore is not clear; Lion Gardiner, who little relished unnecessary warfare, advised him strongly against it. Winthrop was perhaps equally averse to violence, but he had small respect for Indians, while Fenwick (who represented his employers) and Peter (who was his father-in-law) urged action. In any case, the confrontation was held, the demands made and rejected, and the threats issued. Stanton, who had a flair for

Algonkian syntax, made the English position brutally plain. Gardiner, who could put no more than a score of fighting men into the field, not unnaturally protested to the end.[17]

Thereupon Winthrop committed the most ungenerous act of his life. Having flung down the gauntlet before the Pequots, he abruptly quitted Saybrook and returned to Boston with Fenwick and Peter. Gardiner, left behind with his twenty soldiers (to say nothing of a wife and infant child), came close to taunting him with cowardice. It was indeed behavior which the most charitable observer would be hard pressed to excuse. To be sure, Winthrop had learned that Elizabeth had given birth to a daughter; true, he assured Gardiner that he would recommend caution at the Bay; granted, the future would demonstrate that Saybrook was not quite in mortal danger. He even spoke of an early return. Possibly it was merely another instance of the Winthrop disposition to superintend the launching of an enterprise and then to leave its administration to others. If this be so, it was carrying a question-able policy too far.[18]

One naturally shrinks from charges of pusilanimity. In the absence of data it is perhaps fairest to cite him as irresponsible. The Lords and Gentlemen appear to have thought him so; they with-held part of his salary, and it required two years and repeated representations by Emmanuel Downing before his "reputation and fidelity" were reestablished with all of them.[19]

W I N T H R O P returned to Boston in leisurely fashion; he appears even to have risked en route a reconnaissance of the Pequot coast. But it is likely that he already had privately written off Saybrook —and the patentees. Though time would prove that his true and ultimate interest lay in Connecticut, he now proposed to reconcen-trate his talents and energies at the Bay. That this was the case was demonstrated by his appearance, on September 6, at a meeting of the Boston court of assistants. A magistrate in good standing since his initial election in 1632, he had scrupulously refrained, while governor under the Warwick Patent, from direct participation in the affairs of Massachusetts, and his sudden reappearance sufficiently attested to his renewed allegiance. It hardly was necessary that he should write Gardiner several weeks later that he was "not like to returne." [20]

Though the September docket (largely dealing with alcoholic excesses, over-vivacious young women, and too careless references to the Lord) was humdrum, Winthrop's arrival at Boston was coincident with weighty developments. It was a period of controversy. It saw more of the uncomfortable transactions necessary to insure that a corporation should become a commonwealth, and it witnessed the "antinomian" contest and the religious martyrdom of Anne Hutchinson. Through the political proceedings, John Winthrop, Jr., played a cautious, though by no means ineffective, role. The religious troubles he quietly evaded.

We should like to know more of the details, but the years 1636/41 yield comparatively little concerning John Winthrop, Jr. There is evidence that he reestablished his residence at Ipswich and that he was living there with Elizabeth and his new "Little Betty" before the end of 1636.[21] It also is obvious that he derived no more satisfaction from the place now than in the past. All too revealing are a nervous sequence of land acquisitions and sales, a persistent interest in external undertakings, and the fear, repeatedly expressed, of his fellow townsmen that he might once again depart from their midst. Their worry was far from groundless; as early as 1637, Winthrop was fascinated by a rumor that he would be placed in command of the "castle" in Boston harbor, and for three years, beginning in 1636, he became absorbed in the development (another enterprise!) of a saltworks beside the estuaries of Salem. The latter not only elicited the hopeful endorsement of the General Court, but demanded Winthrop's personal supervision over considerable periods. Its product, if meager, at least enjoyed an authentic demand in a farm and fish economy.[22]

Meanwhile, at Ipswich, Elizabeth fretted through a succession of pregnancies. She bore her first son on March 14, 1637/8; they called him Fitz-John.[23] Lucy appeared near the end of January, 1639/40, while a year later there seems to have been a stillbirth.[24] She could hardly, by contemporary standards, have hoped for happier results, but she grew to hate the winds that blew over the marshes and the crude homestead with its drafts and agues. She furthermore experienced servant problems, with which she did not scruple to harass her husband and even, on one occasion, her father-in-law. Indeed, she made use of every opportunity to abandon Ipswich in favor of Boston and the less primitive "mansion house" of the elder Winthrops.[25]

Though faintly irritated by his wife's preference for creature comforts, Winthrop could not wholly blame her. He remained himself more than a little bored by Ipswich, whose special concern, after the labors of frontier living, was religious controversy. Nor was the village deficient in the talents necessary: In the late winter of 1637/8, the ailing Mr. Ward resigned his pulpit to the care of Nathaniel Rogers and John Norton, battlers both for a systematic theology.[26] Their thunderings were scarcely to Winthrop's taste, and he appears to have countered the tedium with a steady and systematic expansion of his personal library. It already was probably the most notable collection in English America, and for this he could thank not only himself and Edward Howes but the efforts and advice of an important new acquaintance.

Dr. Robert Child (1613–53) is best remembered as the "remonstrant" in a later, and particularly violent, doctrinal disputation. He deserves a better fame. He was that comparative rarity of the seventeenth century, a physician with a medical degree. Young, energetic, and full of ideas, he was in many ways similar to Winthrop himself, especially in the remarkable catholicity of his interests. He did not settle in New England until 1641, but his existing friendship with Winthrop suggests an earlier visit. Moreover, it is likely that Child was the influence most responsible for converting Winthrop's predilection toward alchemy into an active commitment to medicine.[27]

As a buyer of books, Dr. Child was fully qualified. When Winthrop requested that he purchase the alchemical writings of Pierre Jean Fabre and a copy of Franciscus Georgius, *de Harmonia Mundi,* Child demurred, declaring that he would not spend Winthrop's good money upon such inferiorities. In their stead he suggested Angelus Burgravius and dispatched—gratis—certain titles from his own library, including three volumes descriptive of the French Jesuit voyages into Canada, "that you may see how they proceede in the conversion of those Heathen and how little the Lord hath blessed them in there proceeding." [28]

By 1641, Winthrop possessed a library of authentic distinction. The number of titles cannot be stated with precision; it may have surpassed a thousand. A large proportion of its considerable remains bear imprints earlier than 1640, but the dates of acquisition are, save in a handful of cases, impossible to determine. Two volumes of Tycho Brahe appear to have belonged to his father. Of special significance is a copy of Paracelsus, *Das Buch Meteororum,* with German text, which Winthrop signed and dated July 25, 1640, and which he particularly prized because it contained the autograph and personal notations of the brilliant John Dee. It can be assumed, however, that the collection was by this time of singular breadth, embracing the works of intellectual giants like Machiavelli, Kepler, Bodin, Pascal, More, and Erasmus, together with more pedestrian dictionaries of alchemy, treatises on rose culture, and a discussion (in Flemish) of gunshot wounds. Reminiscent of his discourses with Edward Howes were several studies upon the Rosicrucians.[29]

Yet John Winthrop, Jr., would never become, in a perfect sense, a scholar; his nervous temperament forbade it. He was far better attuned to the politics of man, and it was to this kind of activity that he now was chiefly drawn.

H E W A s fortunate in the ability to indulge his penchant. It already has been noted that this was a period of controversy in the development of Massachusetts, and Winthrop found himself—on the whole, happily—in the thick of it. At stake were questions of war, religion, empire, and what we should nowadays call—with considerable imprecision—democracy. The last had already, by the middle of 1636, come to a head; the others were imminent.

Winthrop's notions concerning free government are nowhere officially set forth; the records of New England colonial governments are singularly reticent about such things. The famous argument over a "standing council" was approaching its height, but his position therein is obscure. When, in October of 1636, John Cotton presented to the General Court his curious "Model of Moses his Judicials," Winthrop seems not to have expressed his opinion of it. (We do not even know whether, on the twenty-eighth of the same month, he voted for or against the establishment of Harvard College.) [30] Yet, for all the dearth of premises, we may venture to assert that he already regarded politics as less a matter of principle than of possibility. That he enjoyed an infinite capacity for being elected to office is certain; not once in the course of his career was John Winthrop, Jr., to be removed, against his will and by political action, from public responsibilities.

The war question nearly placed him on active duty in the field. The late autumn of 1636 had produced a gloomy correspondence with Saybrook over the "insolent" behavior of the Pequot Indians, and it was partially in response to this that the General Court, sitting in adjourned session at Boston on December 13, reorganized the colony's militia into three regiments, of which Winthrop was commissioned lieutenant colonel of the Third. English blood was finally spilled on February 22 (within view of the Saybrook palisade), and in a letter to Winthrop a month later, Gardiner broadly hinted that aid from Massachusetts would be gratefully received. The Bay responded with speed and imprecision. By the middle of April, an advance detachment, under the immediate command of the efficient and controversial John Underhill, already was gathering; on the eighteenth, a special session of the General Court endorsed plans for a total commitment of 160 men; while the regular Court of Elections, meeting at Newtown (Cambridge) on May 17, saw fit further to adjust the command structure: "Mr. John Winthrope Junior, Mr. Symon Bradstreete & Capt. Israel Stoughton, being put to lot, which should go fourth in the expedition against the Pecoits & Capt. Stoughton was chosen." Whether Winthrop lamented this loss of military opportunity is questionable; in any case, Stoughton's role would be that of a pursuer of remnants.[31]

Much worse was the so-called "antinomian" crisis, for it threatened the whole theory and practice of Puritan Massachusetts. The question has provoked a vast and complicated literature, and he who will but read a small part of it will quickly realize that a thorough grasp of the subject can be achieved only in the seventeenth-century fashion—by living with it. Yet it may be said that the "Antinomians" emphasized a private relation between God and the individual and therefore could be regarded as threats to any prescribed ecclesiastical system. To be sure, the official New England Way was heavily influenced by Calvinism, and Calvinism underscored the omnipotence of God with its famous doctrine of predestination—which in turn asserted that the salvation or damnation of every person had long since been fixed, quite regardless of his performance in this life. One might suppose that this would render any ecclesiastical organization unnecessary, yet the notion had been laboriously rationalized into a disciplined Church—or a collection of disciplined Churches—complete with a clerical interest. Moreover, this religious establishment was so dominant a feature of the community that any serious criticism of it became, automatically and at once, a political question.[32]

The magistrates, being politicians, endeavored first to attack the problem by indirection. They postponed any crude assault upon Antinomianism and instead organized a quiet campaign against young Governor Vane, whose tendencies were antinomian. At a General Court, held on December 7, 1636, in Boston Meeting House, it was announced (with every indication of regret) that Vane was considering an early departure for England. At a subsequent session on March 9, 1636/7, were passed certain provisional votes of censure, though not against Vane. Then on Wednesday, May 17, 1637, the General Court of Elections gathered beneath the riverside elms at Newtown to administer the *coup de grâce:* Not only was Vane replaced as governor by the elder John Winthrop; he was not even granted the courtesy of a lesser office. Moreover, when Vane sailed away for England eleven weeks later, the official honors were minimal.[33]

The decision had in fact been made, and with little unpleasantness, yet the Antinomians (in particular the Reverend John Wheelwright and his remarkable sister-in-law Mrs. Anne Hutchinson) chose not to respect the handwriting on the wall. Whereupon the magistrates, politicians still, sought to get the difficulty out of politics altogether by referring it to a "synod" of the clergy, an ancient device with a record, over the centuries, of only moderate success. Though the reverend pastors assembled (again, at Newtown) from points as distant as the Connecticut Valley, and though, on September 7, they issued an overwhelming endorsement of the official position,[34] the Antinomians threw up theological entrenchments on the opposite bank of the Charles and dared the establishment to do its worst. The question therefore remained political and squarely beneath the noses of both John Winthrops. Their respective responses proved significantly divergent.

John the Elder pulled out all the stops, legal and (it must be added) extralegal. The affair reached a memorable climax at Newtown in November, when a packed and pitiless General Court cut short the antinomian argument and ordered the deportation of Wheelwright, Mrs. Hutchinson, and a sympathetic Boston deputy.[35]

John the Younger simply faded from view. He failed to attend any of the November sessions. Indeed, he appeared at no public assembly until the General Court of March 12, 1637/8 and thereafter resumed his truancy through the Court of Elections (at which he was notwithstanding reelected!) until the assistants' meeting on the fourth of the following September. (It is of interest that his absence from a General Court of June 8 provoked a fine of five shillings.)[36]

Winthrop's neglect is certain; the reason for it is not. Through the fall and winter, he appears to have been no farther afield than Ipswich; and though part of the season was unusually severe and though he was wretchedly ill for a period with dysentery, neither of these disruptions coincided with his unfulfilled responsibilities. Of his activities during the spring and summer we are less positive; he was presumably at Ipswich for a part of the time; possibly, on other occasions, he was engrossed with the saltmaking at Salem. But there seems to have been nothing that should absolutely have precluded his presence at court,[37] and one is tempted to wonder if his abstentions did not proceed from a private disapproval of the behavior of his father and the official coterie. His personal opinions in the antinomian crisis are not documented, but with respect to certain later and similar episodes they are. Indeed, there is nothing more conspicuous in the character of John Winthrop, Jr., than his *disinterest* in theological questions. If his orthodoxy was unimpeachable, it was also routine. That religious abstractions should be permitted to threaten the peace of an entire community quite offended his sense of the rational. He did not, it must be admitted, often say so; as an eminently practical being, he had no instinct for unprofitable crusades.

By the autumn of 1638, the antinomian furor had largely died away, and its victims had departed from Massachusetts to their several destinies. The triumph of the official party appeared complete. Many of the traditional personalities were again assembled in the council: Winthrop the Elder as governor, Dudley as deputy governor, Humphrey, Nowell, Endecott, Bradstreet, and Winthrop the Younger as assistants. Of lesser experience, but equally canonical, were Richard Saltonstall, son of the respected Sir Richard; Israel Stoughton, once of the left wing, but now safely reconverted, a person of "substance," honorably returned from the Pequot war; and Roger Harlakenden, a promising young gentleman of noble lineage and solid connections, whom the governor thought "very godly," but who faced an early and unanticipated death.[38] All, or nearly all, might reasonably have expected a permanent tenure of office in the most perfect of Puritan environments. This was not quite to be, and the upshot would nicely supplement the political education of John Winthrop, Jr.

Seventeenth-century Massachusetts has long since been pronounced oligarchic, a label which no less than the senior Winthrop would cordially have endorsed. But oligarchies are relative things, and the Massachusetts example proved not to be so rigid as certain of its proponents would have liked. It is true that the conservative regime of 1637 survived practically intact through two elections. But by 1640 the deputies were again in a mood for a change. There was no question of revolution; the identical individuals were again returned to office. But there occurred a wholesome reshuffling of the offices themselves; Dudley was elevated to the governorship and Bellingham made deputy. There were similar adjustments the following year, and there developed, in and out of public, the discussions and hard labor which led, before the end of 1641, to the adoption of the Massachusetts Body of Liberties. There was nothing revolutionary in this either; it was essentially a reconstruction, in conformity with practical experience, of the original Bay charter. Yet it clearly reinforced the New World tendency toward *written* frames of government.[39]

If John Winthrop, Jr., played a significant part in the drawing up of the Body of Liberties, the fact cannot be authenticated. However, his old friend, and Ipswich neighbor, the Reverend Nathaniel Ward is known to have produced the final draft, and, though Winthrop was not in America at the time of its adoption, it is difficult to imagine that he did not act as an intermediary between Ward and the magistrates. That Ward seriously sought his advice seems less probable, though by no means impossible. In any case, the episode could not help but reinforce his understanding of the New England way of government.

There were two additional and major difficulties which Winthrop was called upon, as an assistant, to consider.

The first represented nothing new; it was in fact a recurrence of the threat which Emmanuel Downing had worked so hard to stifle in the spring of 1635. Two years later it emerged once more into the open; on May 3, 1637, the Privy Council, sitting appropriately in the Inner Star Chamber at Whitehall, instructed the attorney general to call in the charter of the Massachusetts Bay Company; while on July 23 the king himself declared his intention of appointing Sir Ferdinando Gorges—guiding genius of the late defunct Council for New England—governor general of all the New England settlements. It was a disturbing prospect; it was at precisely this moment that most dust was being raised by the proponents of the gospel according to Archbishop Laud, and the horrid details, together with a lengthy commentary from the nonconformist point of view, were hurried off to Winthrop by his friend Henry Jacie.[40]

Though the mills, royal and Anglican, ground slowly, they did not grind particularly fine. No order addressed specifically to Massachusetts came from Whitehall until April 4, 1638, and it did not reach Boston until late in the summer. Its language was sufficiently blunt: Following a quo warranto process, judgment had been rendered against the patent of Massachusetts, and the document was forthwith to be returned to England into the hands of the Lords Commissioners for Plantations. A refusal to comply would produce summary action of foreclosure upon the whole colony.[41]

The magistrates refused to panic. They did, on September 7, exhibit the order to the General Court, but it was evident to anyone who glanced at Boston harbor that the royal words had no teeth. Back to the Lords Commissioners was sent not the patent but a "humble petition" of extraordinary verbosity. To what extent the younger Winthrop may have inspired this particular response is unknown, but it is reasonable to assume that it received his unqualified endorsement. Moreover, as in the past, it worked. No repercussions arrived until the following June (1639), when the elder Winthrop learned, in a strictly private letter, that the Lords Commissioners "did now again peremptorily require" the charter. But not a frigate appeared to train its guns at Boston. Already the royal displeasure had been diverted by other and more immediate concerns.[42]

This did not mean, however, that Massachusetts could relax into an uninterrupted enjoyment of its special virtues. Rather incredibly the embarrassments of Charles I served to plunge the colony into a major economic depression. So long as altar and throne were able to govern the mother country without effective opposition, numerous Englishmen could regard the Bay as a beacon of hope, a newer and more righteous England. This concept guaranteed a steady immigration (there were 3,000 arrivals in the summer of 1637 alone), and many of the newcomers debarked with full purses. But once the Stuart fortunes began to ebb, Massachusetts quickly assumed a different and more accurate image and the immigrant stream—and the flow of its specie—shrank to a trickle.[43]

It was the dearth of hard money which posed the most serious hardship. Massachusetts possessed little (not excepting the beatified cod) that was capable of producing an overseas trade balance. It was a condition shared by the American colonies of more than one power and has been in fact characteristic of almost any "underdeveloped" region one can name. The situation had become acute by the latter part of 1640. It quickly produced admonitions (never a difficulty in a Puritan colony) against "living above one's station." It inspired an attempt at a managed economy: In October, the General Court declared that payments in kind were to be regarded as legal tender and offered handsome subsidies for the local manufacture of textiles. In June of 1641, it endeavored to stimulate the harvest of wild hemp. More significant still was a program for the encouragement of prospecting, whereby those "at charge for the discovery" of mines would enjoy exemption from public levies for twenty-one years.[44]

It is safe to assume that the younger John Winthrop had much to do with these transactions, in particular the last. Like so many who dedicate themselves to private enterprise, he was seldom loath to encourage a public favor. Most important of all, he soon was caught fairly up in the effervescence of a new "adventure," his first conspicuous enthusiasm since the empire of the Lords and Gentlemen. Transatlantic, rather than transcontinental, it promised power, pelf, and the official gratitude of Massachusetts Bay Colony. Its central idea was the production, in America, of iron and ironmongery, and it put John Winthrop, Jr., on shipboard, bound for England, before the summer was out.

CHAPTER 9

Adventure in Iron—with Diversions

TH E first century and a half of American history are crowded with references to colonial agents—some posted permanently in the mother country, others dispatched to the Old World on specified errands. John Winthrop, Jr., served in the latter capacity on three different occasions, of which his journey in 1641 was the second, and his last in behalf of Massachusetts Bay. He departed in midsummer, one of a small company of representatives.

The mission had been under consideration as early as February, but it did not receive formal approval until the June meeting of the General Court, and even then the decision was taken without publicity. Nevertheless, as in 1634, Massachusetts did not stint in the quality of her agents. Hugh Peter (drafted from his Salem pulpit over the vociferous objections of his congregation) was one. Another was the Reverend Thomas Weld, pastor at Roxbury, a more rigid personality than Peter and with a reputation for unfelicitous controversy, yet acknowledged one of the ablest of Puritan divines. The third (and least remembered) was William Hibbins of Boston, a "substantial merchant." Fourth, and apparently last to be appointed, was John Winthrop, Jr.[1]

Their purposes were varied. They were to render, as conditions permitted, aid and comfort to the parliamentary interest. They were not openly to solicit aid, but they should discreetly urge the creditors of the Bay Company to soften their demands. They should beat a constant, yet cautious, tattoo for New England and the New England Way. In addition, Winthrop undertook a special assignment, which was the promotion of a company for the manufacture, in America, of iron and iron implements.[2]

He established his family at his father's farm at Ten Hills on the Mystic, conveniently close to relatives; Elizabeth was already three months into another pregnancy.[3] He embarked with the others on August 3. He carried with him a number of mineral specimens, chiefly of bog iron; Peter went armed with a commentary from the pen of Emmanuel Downing as to the most effective subterfuges to be adopted in the event of further attacks upon the patent.[4]

Their vessel was a mere coasting bark, stinking of fish. It also was crowded; there were forty-four passengers altogether. And they were not taken directly to England; all were put ashore a fortnight later on the bleak shingle of Newfoundland, where Peter and Weld attempted to improve the situation by preaching to transient fishermen. Their ship for England, when at last it appeared, was almost equally small—60 tons—and fully as odorous. Their passage was miserable: For twenty days the little vessel shuddered and plunged through almost uninterrupted storms. This time, however, they were not driven into Galway, which was a better fortune than they realized—1641 was for Ireland a year of slaughter and rapine (chiefly at Protestant expense) almost without parallel. By September 27, they were already in Bristol Channel and the following day ascended the Avon to the quays of Bristol city. Winthrop was still there on October 8 when he learned of a ship for New England and sat down near midnight to write Elizabeth: "Remember me to all my deare freinds brothers sisters cozens, and specially to thy deare selfe with my blessing to my children. God keepe you all. Thy affectionate Husband John Winthrop." [5]

Essentially nothing is known of the activities of the Massachusetts agents for more than six months thereafter. Presumably they established their headquarters in London. But they quickly discovered that England was for the time being in no mood to listen to colonial publicity. Already Crown and Parliament had crossed political swords; within less than a year they would clang openly on the field of battle; meanwhile, the situation was such that proposals for American ironworks or the refinancing of Massachusetts could hardly hope for a hearing. For a time even Winthrop was reduced to the performance of shopping chores for female relatives at home.[6]

Hibbins presently threw up the business and returned to America. Peter, Weld, and (almost certainly) Winthrop were thereupon invited to participate in a semiofficial campaign of retaliation, organized by a "Society of Adventurers," against the Catholic Irish. Peter and Weld accepted at once and were duly enrolled as chaplains; Winthrop took the measure of the officer in charge, a tough and humorless Scottish baron named Alexander Forbes with a background of religious warfare, and politely declined. It was a characteristic response and much to his credit: The expedition devoted the summer of 1642 to the sack of coastal Munster and Connaught, a quite pitiless performance in the spirit of Israel smitting the Canaanites. It was not his sort of proceeding.[7]

IN LIEU of this pious violence, he chose to undertake a private journey to the Continent, a tour neither for sentiment nor for the contemplation of routine wonders but in quest of stimulating acquaintances. One would like to know more of the details. The trip may have been suggested by his old friends Abraham and Johann Sibert Kuffler, or even by the renowned linguist Johannes Comenius, who was just then in England.[8] Whoever the inspira-

[113]

tion, Winthrop visited Hamburg, Amsterdam, and The Hague—and almost certainly Brussels. Everywhere he sought out individuals of education and imagination, men like himself, though in many instances more profound than he.

Northwestern Germany and the Low Countries were crowded that year with scholars and intellectuals, refugees from the final disasters of the Thirty Years' War. A favorite rendezvous was Hamburg—a city of obvious distinction, Hanseatic and imperial, still wealthy, and physically untouched by conflict. Among its twisting "fleets," so reminiscent of the canals of Amsterdam, Winthrop made the acquaintance of a fascinating group of savants with a bent toward medicine, among whom he became particularly intimate with a certain Doctor Johannes Tanckmarus. Like so many physicians of his era, Tanckmarus had pronounced "philosophical" tendencies—backward drawn toward the mystical, forward searching toward the inductive. It is likely that their friendship played an important part in awakening Winthrop's interest in the healing arts, and there is no doubt at all that Tanckmarus and his wife became fond of this unusual Englishman.[9]

Winthrop departed Hamburg early in September, 1642, bound for Amsterdam. He journeyed overland, carefully skirting the fringes of the war; his heavier belongings he packed in a chest and placed aboard a Dutch merchantman. This was unfortunate; the ship was captured in the North Sea by a Dunkirk privateer and taken as booty to Nieuport in the Spanish Netherlands. Arrived in Amsterdam, Winthrop could at first secure no satisfaction beyond a judicially certified deposition as to the facts. Yet his visit to the Low Countries proved a happy interlude. Thanks to the comparative unconcern of the Hollanders with other people's orthodoxies, the United Provinces were the scene of more erudite speculation and good conversation than any other spot in Europe. For Winthrop it was an intellectual feast. At Amsterdam he encountered the brothers Kuffler and a fascinating philosopher-alchemist who called himself Augustinus Petraeus. He was introduced to the already famous Johann Rudolf Glauber. Their discussions—carried on in a composite of German, English, and university Latin—were eminently satisfying and were supplemented with semiprofessional conferences with practitioners of pharmacy. They no doubt confirmed Winthrop's inclination toward the medicine of Paracelsus, with its belief in the merits of internal commotion, chemically induced.[10]

Even the search for his chest yielded unexpected dividends. When, early in November, he sought the help of the English resident at The Hague, he encountered yet another kindred spirit. Sir William Boswell was of royalist sympathies (Winthrop spoke of him, with perfect accuracy, as "the King's agent"), and they both must have been aware that the tensions at home already had resolved themselves into a thunder of cavalry. But Boswell was before all else a man of cultivation, and he had the good sense not to probe Winthrop too deeply. In a letter of introduction, written in Winthrop's behalf to the English representative at Brussels, he avoided all reference to Massachusetts and described his petitioner as a gentleman of Suffolk and a "student in Physique." [11]

Winthrop penetrated the Spanish Netherlands to the dunes of Dunkirk. The resident at Brussels, Sir Henry de Vic, was a university-educated Channel islander, fluent in French, but seems not to have been effective in recovering Winthrop's pirated chest; even Dunkirk yielded only a single book of his manuscript notes. Brussels, however, was the kind of place Winthrop loved; wealthy, refined, and generously adorned in exquisite Gothic, it was at this period one of the greatest cities of the Continent. But best of all the Duchy of Brabant was renowned for the sophistication of its iron industry, and it is significant that Winthrop later endeavored to introduce in America an "indirect" refining process in every essential similar to the practice of the Spanish Netherlands.[12]

More stimulating still was an encounter with Johannes Amos Comenius. This "brave old man" (he was actually a clear-eyed and vigorous fifty) was possibly the most distinguished displaced intellectual in Europe. The last bishop of the Moravian Brethren, he is better remembered as the first scholar to apply systematic methods to the teaching of languages. Whether Winthrop met him in England or in the Low Countries no one can say, but there is reason to believe that he almost succeeded in recruiting Comenius for the faculty, if not the presidency, of Harvard College. Winthrop, of course, had no special commission to undertake such a thing. Yet it appears to have required the intervention of the powerful Chancellor Oxienstern, plus a liberal array of fringe benefits, to get the scholarly Moravian safely past the Winthrop personality to a university appointment in Sweden.[13]

H I S   R E T U R N to England can be traced with greater confidence: A nameless vessel carried him to Ipswich, in his native Suffolk, before the beginning of January, and by February he had reached London, where he established lodgings at the house of a Mrs. Goff in Philpot Lane. He found the City a-murmur with rumor; only a few weeks had passed since the latest—although bloodless—confrontation of Cavalier and Roundhead at Turnham Green. Yet the appeal to arms seemed somehow to have dissipated the worst of the public anxieties; even the chaffinches sang earlier than usual that year; and it was not long before Winthrop discovered that the right people were at last in a humor to consider projects for ironworks—particularly in New England.[14]

The idea, under the circumstances, made a good deal of sense. Iron was obviously a strategic material; its output, in England, was as yet assured neither to king nor Parliament; the English business community had a civil war on its hands; and the market was swiftly rising. If Winthrop had not appeared with his plan, someone else would have done so.[15]

His peculiar talents for salesmanship cannot, of course, have come amiss. Neither could his "connections." Together they assembled a quite unusual muster of capitalists, in whom public spirit and private appetite were nicely combined. It was a very fair sample of the great, inchoate, but commercially oriented group which presently financed (and sometimes ventured to lead) the regiments of the New Model. They ranged from clergymen to brewers; they included drapers, merchant tailors, and contractors for military supplies. There were at least two public officers of rank: Nicholas Bond and Cornelius Holland, respectively charged (by Parliament) with the administration of the households of the Duke of Gloucester and the Prince of Wales. There was John Becx, a Hollander of little refinement, but of limitless wealth. There was the physician, Robert Child, a polished jewel, intellectual, speculative, and of less than princely estate. There even were those of professional experience in ironmaking, of whom Thomas Foley, Joshua Foote, and Lionel Copley were representative. The whole proceeding must have been much to Winthrop's taste, and from it there quickly emerged a distinctive association of entrepreneurs, who called themselves "The Company of Undertakers of the Ironworks in New England." It was not, properly speaking, a corporation; charters and patents were not obtainable simply for the asking, and none appears to have been contemplated. But shares in the enterprise were offered and placed in a corporate fashion: A single unit was priced at a surprising £50; most subscriptions involved more than one; the redoubtable Becx took forty. Things developed so favorably that Winthrop began looking for shipping space as early as the fifth of May.[16]

The raising of capital is one thing; the recruiting and equipping of an enterprise can be quite another. The professionals, in particular Joshua Foote, tried to be helpful, but it was at this point that the undertaking first came close to miscarrying. Foote was presumably competent; he was a member of the Company of Ironmongers and indeed valued his own services very highly. Yet he found it nearly impossible to hire, and keep hired, a minimum cadre of experienced laborers. They were disposed to "much grombell," he told Winthrop. "You ware best to gitt som new England man and give him 5s to acompeny these men tell thay be settled aship bord." No bloomery man was available at all, and Foote finally admitted that he would have to be "bred upe" in New England. Nor were "stones" suitable for furnace linings easily to be found; a shipment of these did not get away for Massachusetts until September.[17]

Yet even these considerable difficulties failed to engross all of Winthrop's time. His instinct for erudite interchange continued irrepressible, and if the City yielded no bloomery man, it continued to afford handsome opportunities for philosophical contacts. It was doubtless during this period that he first encountered the elder Samuel Hartlib, an ex-Prussian of great virtuosity, patron of scholars, protégé of Comenius, and intimate of Milton; his liking for Winthrop was immediate and would lead one day to important consequences. It also is probable that Winthrop was presented to the fabulous Sir Kenelm Digby, freebooter, experimenter, and suspected espionage agent; if so, it was in jail, to which Digby had been committed by order of the House of Commons. The prisoner's well-known Roman Catholicism was of course regarded by Winthrop as inconsequential. Digby, as one might expect, thought Winthrop magnificent.[18]

Nor was this all. Scarcely had he settled himself at Mrs. Goff's when he was "importunately desired" by the Messrs. Peter and Weld to lend a hand with their "agitations" for Massachusetts. The reverend pair had returned safely from supplying the religious needs of Forbes's pillagers and were currently and quietly abandoning the cause of New England in favor of more promising opportunities. If Winthrop grasped their real intentions, he seems to have said nothing; he devoted, as he later declared, his "best indeavour to assist them, in all their negotiations . . . with many expensive travailes therein." Among other things, he combed the market for indentured servants and covered a debt, previously incurred in the name of the colony for a supply of linen cloth, with £50 of his own money. In addition, he probably saw something of St. Stephen's Chapel, Westminster, for the Long Parliament of King Pym was moved to proclaim its approval of Massachusetts, and on March 10, 1642/3, the Commons passed a bill removing all export duties from merchandise shipped to New England.[19]

He even found time to consider his personal affairs. Months'-old letters informed him that he was the father of another son (who had been baptized with the singular but significant name of Wait-Still); Elizabeth, he learned, bore his absence "verey well before company," but prayed often and tearfully for his return. Though distinctly of tougher fiber than Martha, she found Ten Hills and —especially—Ipswich depressing. So, at a transatlantic distance, did he; though obliged to accept a dubious bill of exchange, he was delighted to dispose of 300 acres in the Topsfield district to a London tailor. He did not, however, consider quitting New England; on May 10, he expended nearly £10 upon an assortment of bed-clothes, which he forwarded overseas, and on the nineteenth he engaged, upon indenture and in the service of his family in America, a girl named Mary Gore. Her contract survives; it forbade in sturdy phrases all the basic dissipations, from alehouses to promiscuity.[20]

Still without a bloomery man or sufficient lining stones, Winthrop loaded what equipment and personnel he had aboard the London merchantman *An Cleeve*, toward the end of May. He was in a hopeful mood; he possessed about £1,000 in working capital and the unexpected company of Emmanuel Downing; and he had reason to hope he could establish at least the rudiments of an American ironworks before the end of summer. He reckoned without the bureaucratic mind: Though presumably conformable to Parliament and, by implication, to Puritan New England, the port control officers proved inexplicably loath to issue clearances. Day upon frustrating day *An Cleeve* swung helplessly on her cables beneath the rooftops of Gravesend, and when the official obstinacy finally eased, a persistent east wind kept them in the Thames for several additional days.[21]

Their fortunes continued outrageous. Just as *An Cleeve* was fairly clear of the Kentish forelands, the wind shifted decisively to the southwest and blew steadily from that quarter (and into their faces) for a month or more. They did not attain the open Atlantic for six weeks, and it was eight weeks additional, and the beginning of September, before they made Boston. By this time, the greater part of Winthrop's company was in scarecrow condition from scurvy; even he admitted to illness "in some measure." [22] Already it was obvious that no iron would be drawn from an American furnace for the remainder of that season.

B u t h e did not lose his enthusiasm—yet. He faced two immediate problems: the selection of a works site and the solicitation of local support, both private and public. He lost little time in attacking the first; scarcely had he begun to recover from the voyage when he set out upon a reconnaissance of every major bog between Marshfield in Plymouth Colony and Cape Elizabeth in the present state of Maine. He suspected from the beginning that his ultimate choice would fall upon a tract of swamp and brook, close beneath the Blue Hills and within the limits of Braintree, but he nevertheless took care to investigate every prospector's rumor over the whole extent of coast, digging into marshes, picking over glacial hillocks, and critically assessing their respective merits. He managed to complete the survey before winter, and Braintree was indeed his selection. Bog ore was concentrated there in a large "veine"; there was a little stream to dam and, to English eyes, nearly limitless timber for the manufacture of charcoal. Moreover, the district did not lie remote from established plantations.[23]

There was only one thing wrong with Braintree: The most favorable sites for furnace and forge were already in private hands and would have to be purchased. Winthrop had studied the question with care: Should he spend his precious funds upon land that lay close to a settlement, or should he negotiate for a free tract so isolated that he would be obliged to create an entire village? He went so far as to set forth the problem at length in a written "discourse" for the consideration of the London adventurers.[24] But the decision was really his; he could not expect to receive overseas directives for nearly a year. Winthrop chose Braintree and the expensive land. It was, so far as an intelligent estimate could make it, the right choice. It was not entirely his fault that a trial at practical ironmaking would prove him wrong.

His efforts to attract local capital were no happier. There was precious little in Massachusetts; the whole ironworks idea had itself been brought forward in response to a chronic deficit in overseas balances. In the course of two years, Winthrop was able to extract investment capital from exactly *six* Massachusetts residents, and to one of these (it was his uncle Emmanuel Downing!) he was obliged to lend the money. The others provided a total of £173 1s. 2d., but though they were numbered among the most substantial citizens of three towns, it is doubtful whether the funds they invested were of the sort receivable in London without discount.[25]

As might be expected, Winthrop enjoyed better success with public favors. It was no small advantage that he was still an assistant [26] and could exert his considerable talents for persuasion from within the General Court. On March 7, 1643/4, he submitted a petition of ten articles, asking, among other things, for rights of monopoly, freedom from taxation, and the privilege to acquire, without cost to the Undertakers, suitable mineral reserves within the public domain. The response of the court was generally favorable; it offered to prohibit the establishment of any competing enterprise for a period of twenty-one years, and further negotiations elicited not only the desired land grants and tax exemption but freedom from militia duty for both stockholders and employees. But the magistrates nevertheless were careful to stipulate that these advantages should be consequent upon the development of complete facilities—furnaces, forges, and mills—and that none of the company's output should be shipped outside the colony until local needs had fully been met.[27]

Winthrop probably felt no serious personal objection to these provisions. Yet they reflected, as between the London investors and the Boston magistrates, a serious divergence of viewpoint. The former thought in terms of an exportable production, smelted and wrought at transoceanic distances from Prince Rupert's horse and (always assuming the permanence of parliamentary control of the sea) salable to patriotic buyers for the kind of money which London merchants were willing to accept without a fuss. The magistrates, on the other hand, sought a domestic supply of a necessary commodity which they could not pay for in England. Neither purpose was compatible with the other, and even John Winthrop, Jr., could not straddle the divergence of interest.[28]

More unfortunate still was the experience at Braintree. The owner of the necessary land, Edward Hutchinson, was willing to convey it for £100; Winthrop suggested an equivalent share in the company, but this economical idea appears not to have been well received.[29] The wages of his workers were no better than a fixed charge, nor could the men be efficiently employed until there were furnaces and bloomeries and forges for them to operate. Moreover, construction costs exceeded estimates in a manner all too familiar upon colonial frontiers. How heavy the deficits really became cannot be determined with accuracy; Winthrop's clerk, one

William Osborne, was not a man of pronounced literacy. Nevertheless, even he could set forth the basic facts: Only a single furnace was ready by December of 1644, yet expenses already had surpassed invested capital (there could be as yet no question of an operating income) by perhaps £40.[30] In his letters to London, Winthrop could only report less progress, and heavier liabilities, than had been anticipated—and ask for additional money.

The reaction of the English shareholders, when it came, was less than enthusiastic: They bluntly disallowed a large proportion of Winthrop's expenditures—in particular the purchase of land—and they nearly as bluntly relieved Winthrop of his duties. It required the efforts of Emmanuel Downing, who was in London on another of his visits, to convince them that they still owed him a salary. It is indeed a matter for wonder that their dissatisfactions were presently and gracefully quieted; perhaps only Downing, and the recollection of the Winthrop personality, could have done it. In any case, when the Undertakers came, on June 4, 1645, to write their formal notice of dismissal, they were genuinely cordial.[31]

Winthrop was himself quite ready to be rid of his responsibilities. Like the beaver trade, like Ipswich, like Saybrook, the direction of an ironworks was after all an unexciting thing. Though he was to get on famously with his successor, Richard Leader; though he would follow the subsequent fortunes of the enterprise with a polite interest and even, on occasion, lend it a helping hand; though he would concern himself with other ironworks, actual and imaginary, his real association with the Company of Undertakers was at an end. Once more the time had come for a change.[32]

Brilliant, persuasive, and marvelously attuned to his fellow men, John Winthrop, Jr., had yet, at the age of thirty-nine, to discover himself.

CHAPTER 10

Journey Home—with Deviations

SUCCESSFUL men frequently are endowed with striking powers of concentration. (It is an aptitude which has served mercifully to simplify the labors of hundreds of biographers.) But it was not a characteristic of John Winthrop, Jr. His penchant for distraction, so marked in his youth, decreased but slowly with age and indeed remained noticeable to the day of his death.

He literally found it difficult to keep a single iron in the fire. In June of 1644, just as his Braintree project was approaching its most critical stage, he took time to petition the Massachusetts court for "leave to make a plantation at Pequot," of which a principal advantage was said to be its suitability for an ironworks![1] He moreover was unable to focus his attention solely upon iron. Long before Braintree, and well before the organization of the English "Undertakers," another, and still more elusive, mineral had captured his fancy.

Among the specimens which Winthrop had exhibited in London were certain darkish fragments of a substance called "black lead." In an age as yet unacquainted with the versatility of the carbon atom, few suspected that it might not be a metal at all. It was known, however, to be useful in the manufacture of writing implements and as a pigment, and there were those who too readily believed it might contain a profitable proportion of silver. (Its modern name is graphite.)

Exactly how these fragments had come into Winthrop's possession no one knows, but they attracted the interest of a number of his English acquaintances, in particular Dr. Robert Child. Winthrop and his ironworkers were less than a month out of Gravesend when, on June 27, 1643, Child wrote of his continued interest in the New England "black lead mines" and requested additional samples. Winthrop, too, was anxious to pursue the matter; and by the early autumn of 1644 he already had put a reconnaissance party into the field. A vigorous trio—Thomas King, Stephen Day, and Richard Smith—they quickly located the deposits among certain ledges 60 miles west of Boston in a region whose Algonkian name was "Tantousq" or "Tantiusque." They furthermore secured the signs manual of two resident Indians upon a provisional bill of sale, whereby approximately 10 square miles of the locality were transferred to Winthrop's ownership. This was confirmed on November 11 by a more formal instrument, drawn up in Winthrop's own hand and certified with the marks of two additional natives. Still other deeds were executed as prudence and the notoriously fluid nature of native relationships might require; one was dated as late as November 16, 1658.[2]

Winthrop also took care to secure the official blessing of the Massachusetts General Court, whereupon he commenced operations in a fashion which the proprietor of any speculative mineral property would at once understand: He left the actual work to another. This he achieved by means of a mildly complicated lease, of which the second party was Thomas King.[3]

Like many North American mining ventures of a later era, Tantiusque occasioned a flurry of excitement. Fresh samples of the black lead were carried to England by the peripatetic Emmanuel Downing in the winter of 1644/5 and there subjected to assay; at least two of the reports indicated a handsome percentage of silver, which was not only encouraging but an interesting commentary on the contemporary state of the metallurgical arts. Only Robert Child appears to have suspected the truth; to him the latest specimens resembled "earths or chalks" rather than metals, and though he hesitated to add a sour note, he advised Winthrop to proceed with caution.[4]

The remainder of the tale is reminiscent of numerous later and greater speculations in environments more spacious than the hills of Tantiusque. There were other leases—two in 1657 and one in 1658. But there is no evidence of a net income—only of transportation difficulties and technical problems and the indisposition of workmen to submit to isolation. Though he never fully abandoned his predilection for black lead, Winthrop would ultimately describe his Tantiusque experiment as discouraging. "It may be," he added with the pathos of a true promoter, "God reserves such of his bounties to future generations." [5]

I F J O H N Winthrop the Younger fancied himself a mineralogist, he seldom had much to say of his political ambitions. Nevertheless, it was in the latter area, not the former, that he achieved his clearest distinction.

Through two visits to England he had been reelected, *in absentia* and as a matter of course, to his place among the assistants. It cannot have been solely because of his father; to be the eldest child of the elder John Winthrop was not always an avenue to preferment. Indeed, he had returned from England in 1643 to find his father the target of heavy criticism. Much had transpired in the course of the preceding two years—unexpected things like a war between two Acadian beaver barons and the litigation inspired by an obscure woman's sow.

The Acadian business had been strikingly picturesque. It involved a contest, across the Bay of Fundy, between Charles de Saint Étienne de la Tour and his principal competitor, Charles d'Aulnay-Charnisay, and in June of 1643, not long before the younger John came ashore with his emaciated ironworkers, the Seigneur de la Tour had appeared at Boston with a shipload of armed retainers. He was accorded a friendly reception; his men were even permitted to land and to practice their evolutions upon the neighborhood training ground; moreover, the governor permitted him to charter five additional vessels. It is likely that the senior Winthrop sought thereby to promote a down-East balance of power to the advantage of Massachusetts, yet there were those at the Bay who thought the policy ill-advised, and they criticized it openly.[6]

The pig affair was of greater moment. Its origins were as homely as a wandering brute in the lanes of Boston, yet Mrs. Sherman's sow was to be of much consequence for America. Certain contributory elements, in particular the lowly station of Mrs. Sherman and the open intimacy of her opponent, Captain Keayne, with the magistrates, converted a minor bickering into a contest of constitutional significance. While the younger Winthrop was yet in England, the whole dispute had been brought before the General Court, wherein the governor and assistants had sustained Captain Keayne, while the deputies—rather unexpectedly and emotionally —had endorsed Mrs. Sherman. By the time Winthrop had debarked from *An Cleeve,* both factions, official and popular, were scarcely on speaking terms.[7]

As a duly reelected assistant, John Winthrop, Jr., was privileged to witness firsthand the outcome of both controversies. Whether he endeavored, at the May elections of 1644, to prevent his father's unseating we cannot say. But he did involve himself in the Acadian situation: There are hints of a speculation on the Penobscot —presumably to be made possible by the distraction of the French. Yet power balances between fur companies are precarious things; in any case the younger Winthrop began presently to wonder if the French might not be eliminated entirely and suggested, as a suitable instrument for the purpose, the redoubtable Scottish Protestant Baron Forbes. In December, he wrote Forbes directly, asserting that "the English colonies heere would be grat to have their brethren of Scotland to be their neighbours." It was plainly an invitation to intervention, approved in advance by his colleagues. But, though the letter was entrusted to Emmanuel Downing, there was no response; perhaps Forbes already had quitted Britain to pass his numerous declining years on the Continent.[8]

The extent of Winthrop's participation in the sow case is not so clear. But it is known that he was present at the memorable session of the General Court at Boston, beginning on March 7, 1643/4, at which the worst of the existing dissatisfactions were quieted. (It was the occasion of his first solicitation of favors for the Braintree Ironworks.) Gathered in the sparsely fitted meetinghouse were his father (for the moment still governor), Endecott (still deputy governor), eight of the assistants, and forty deputies. The atmosphere was hardly improved by the arrival of a cluster of Indian sachems, and it is possible that their presence contributed signficantly to the famous decision that magistrates and deputies should thereafter *meet separately*. The solution was, in the circumstances, reasonable, but none of those involved—the younger Winthrop included—seems to have realized he was setting a precedent of capital importance. Nevertheless, what had once been the general meeting of the management and stockholders of a private corporation had now been converted to a public legislature of two houses, and this would one day become a habit of transcontinental scope.[9]

And there was a further straw in the wind—the tendency, even among these English colonists of the first generation, to seek common ends not in disciplined unity but as confederates. This too would establish a transcontinental pattern. Its initial manifestation was the New England Confederation, or United Colonies.

It must never be forgotten that Massachusetts was not coterminous with New England—though this often was implied at Boston and assumed in London. Disregarding the genuinely debatable regions to the north and east, there were by now no less than five New England jurisdictions: Plymouth, Massachusetts Bay, the "notoriously heretickal" Rhode Island and Providence Plantations, the more orthodox river towns of Connecticut, and—in shreds and patches beside Long Island Sound—New Haven Colony, the most intensely Puritan of the lot.[10] All save Rhode Island were on reasonably cordial terms; all including Rhode Island were subject to an identical parcel of difficulties. It is precisely from such situations that Anglo-American federations are derived.

There had been intercolonial negotiations as early as 1637, but nothing substantial was achieved until the spring of 1643, when intelligence of the civil war in England abruptly underscored the possibility of external attack—Dutch, French, or aboriginal. Under these circumstances, a species of union was achieved within weeks, and before the younger Winthrop returned from London, the United Colonies of New England was an official, though untested, reality.

It was an arrangement of the most provisional kind. The participating jurisdictions included the four "Puritan" colonies of Massachusetts, Plymouth, Connecticut, and New Haven. (Rhode Island, always deemed beyond the pale, was never permitted to join.) Each was authorized to send a pair of "commissioners" to an annual meeting—of which two were to be held in Boston for every one held at Plymouth, Hartford, or New Haven. The commissioners were vested with generous powers of speech—and little more. To what extent such an organization would prove effective in coping with practical problems only experience could reveal. Moreover, the financing of any collective undertaking—military or otherwise—was left conspicuously unresolved.[11]

With the creation of the "United Colonies" John Winthrop, Jr., had obviously nothing to do. Nevertheless, it was to remain a feature of the New England scene throughout the remainder of his life, and his last public duties would be performed as a United Colonies commissioner from Connecticut in a season of awful crisis.

I T W A S now 1645. Winthrop long since had completed his political apprenticeship. Yet comparatively few of the fruits of his maturity were to be plucked by Massachusetts Bay; already he was on the point of casting his lot with another, and younger, plantation. But before his departure he was confronted with one more of the politico-religious crises which at intervals rocked the Boston court, and once again his response would be scarcely what would normally be expected of a Puritan magistrate.

The episode concerned none other than his gifted friend Dr. Robert Child. Child had, early in 1645, reappeared at the Bay, apparently to establish a permanent residence. One of his motives was Winthrop himself, and, for all his doubts as to the nature of black lead, he exhibited a continued interest in Tantiusque.[12] Child closely resembled Winthrop in the variety of his interests and, like Winthrop, had developed certain personal views which did not fully square with orthodox New England conceptions. Unlike Winthrop, however, he was unable to keep his opinions to himself; on the contrary, he undertook an open crusade, wherein he revealed himself to Massachusetts as a public danger and, to posterity, as a poor politician.

Child brought with him from England a curious baggage of beliefs. He reckoned himself a Presbyterian and endorsed the notion of a centralized Church, controlled by its clergy through representative synods, but with comparatively easy conditions of membership. He appears at the same time to have subscribed to the new and revolutionary ideas of religious toleration and the separation of Church and state. Finally, he was an incipient imperialist and wondered if the current and virtual independence of Massachusetts were really a desirable condition. It at once will be obvious that every one of these positions violated the most fundamental doctrines of the New England Way.[13]

The issue came quickly to a head; Child was not one to leave a reform to time and evolution. He failed to attract many disciples (he was in this respect a lesser politician than even Anne Hutchinson). But he set his ideas down, in authentic Roundhead form, in a written "Remonstrance" and presented it, subscribed with about twenty signatures, to the General Court on May 16, 1646. Though the remonstrance was also denoted a "humble Petition," it threatened, failing early satisfaction, a direct appeal to the English Parliament.[14]

The reaction of the General Court was approximately what might, in the premises, have been expected. There was a period of expostulation, increasingly ill-tempered, and the inevitable referral to the clergy. Then, beginning in November of 1646, the magistrates cracked down. Fines of varying severity were levied (twice in the case of Child), and the principal offenders, Child in particular, were forcibly restrained from departing for England with their appeals. Although the official attitude was later moderated, it was obvious that Massachusetts would brook little deviation from the prescribed.[15]

Such were the issues, and the consequences. They all are abundantly documented. Yet the position therein of John Winthrop, Jr., is difficult to discover. That he sat among the magistrates when Dr. Child submitted his remonstrance is probable. But in the minutes of the subsequent sessions, and until the elections court of 1647, his name simply fails to appear, and that he chose, as in the Hutchinson case, not to take part in the dispensation of vengeance is clear beyond a reasonable doubt. The court was not ready with its fines and denunciations until November 4; weeks earlier Winthrop had departed the jurisdiction to take up a provisional residence 100 miles away upon Fishers Island in Long Island Sound.[16]

It was typical behavior. Many would decry it upon ethical

grounds. They would forget his political nature and that politics are the art of the possible. The decision against his friend was already certain. No knightly importunity would have altered the outcome; such a performance could only have rendered him unavailable, for years to come, for leadership in any Puritan colony. Furthermore, he did not reject Dr. Child. The crisis in no way affected their friendship; from his place of restraint at the house of George Munnings in Boston, the doctor continued to correspond with him and at length. Child, to be sure, long remained angry with Massachusetts and in the spring of 1648 wrote from England that he would not have "any thing to doe with that Country hereafter . . . unless my fines be restored." But at no point was there the slightest evidence of disenchantment with the younger Winthrop.[17]

It was another revealing episode. If John Winthrop, Jr., ever developed a maxim for public office, it was the unwisdom of too uncompromising an opposition to facts. The world, of course, requires idealists. It has an equal need for practical politicians. Winthrop sympathized with the former as did few men of his day. But it is among the latter that he must always be counted.

S I N C E H I S return from England in the late summer of 1643, he had altogether abandoned Ipswich in favor of Ten Hills, beside the tidal Mystic. The change had been made for reasons of convenience (the place was scarcely an hour's sail from Boston) and also because of the house, which was a superior structure, built partly of stone. Moreover, the core of the property, wholly enclosed and comprising above 30 acres, had passed unexpectedly into his own control within a month of his arrival—a development related to certain financial difficulties of his father.[18] Here, in September, 1644, Betty gave birth to another daughter, who was baptized Mary at the Boston church.[19] In terms of physical comfort, Ten Hills greatly surpassed Ipswich, and it lay so near the center of activity in New England that Winthrop might logically have made it his permanent home. This he did not do; his removal, in the autumn of 1646, to Long Island Sound has been noted. But, as with so many of his decisions, it is difficult to find the reason. We may cite his nervous temperament. Furthermore, for all their unfeigned and mutual esteem, he may have questioned the wisdom of establishing a fixed residence so close to his father. They were not genuinely compatible; their respective viewpoints lay an interplanetary distance apart. Even the elder Winthrop was aware of this, and there were times when he tried earnestly to reduce the gulf between them—by urging the younger man to change. "Study well, my son," he wrote on one occasion, "the saying of the Apostle, Knowledge puffeth up. It is a good Gift of God, but when it lifts up the mind above the Cross of Christ, it is the Pride of Life and the High-way to Apostacy. . . ." [20] But even such Jacobean phrases availed him little; to mold this son into the Massachusetts pattern would have required no less than divine intervention. Failing this, a too constant and intimate association must have become an embarrassment to them both.

Yet considerations such as these can have been only contributory. The vital factor was that John Winthrop, Jr., once again had caught the urge to "plant." Nor was it a sudden, or even a recent, fancy; it antedated by many months the Undertakers of the iron-works. This time he coveted an island, called Fishers, at the eastern entrance of Long Island Sound, close by the coast of the Pequot country. Though its jurisdiction had been claimed by three public authorities, he long since had come to an understanding with all of them—Massachusetts Bay in October, 1640, Connecticut in April, 1641, and George Fenwick (who administered what remained of the Saybrook interest) the succeeding May. He had begun even to think in terms of not only the island but the mainland adjacent. [21]

Winthrop nevertheless committed himself very gradually and

with conscious prudence. In June of 1644, he discussed the project at length with his colleagues of the Massachusetts council (it was the occasion on which he proposed an additional ironworks), and on the twenty-eighth the entire court, deputies included, endorsed the design, though with the stipulation that "fit men" should join the plantation within three years. In the spring of 1645, he invited the participation of suitable private persons; thanks to his genius for promotion, the response was encouraging. At Boston, Major Edward Gibbons joined him in an arrangement whereby a competent husbandman named William Bartlett would tend a concourse of hogs and goats on Fishers Island. To the adjacent mainland— still of unproved fertility, but rived with promising estuaries—he attracted a number of prospective settlers, in particular Cary Latham of Cambridge and, from an increasingly moribund Saybrook, the Reverend Thomas Peter, a younger brother of his father-in-law, whom Winthrop placed in immediate charge. (No doubt he recalled the pious dissatisfactions which had marred his own Saybrook experience.) He also took care to lend the stimulation of his own presence. Indeed, the settlement might have been safely founded before the end of that summer, had not certain Indians of the neighborhood fallen into a complicated woodland imbroglio.[22]

This particular portion of southern New England had always been coveted by the natives, chiefly because of its protected waters and superior fishing. It had in consequence been the object of much aboriginal aggression, of which the recent occupation by the Pequots was the best remembered. But the Indians, as empire builders, were notably unsophisticated; even the Pequots were unable to preserve their unity, and some time prior to their ruin beneath the muskets of the English, they had been weakened by the secession of a certain Uncas, who had founded a competing tribe called "Mohegan." In due season, Uncas and his followers associated themselves with the English in the Pequot war, wherein they performed the functions of jackals. Yet Uncas was plainly more than a scavenger. Grasping, ambitious, and thoroughly amoral, he was a master of wilderness intrigue. His apparent support of the English, and the invention two centuries later of a fictional descendant, have endowed him with a reputation for nobility which is substantially undeserved. (It is significant that John Winthrop, Jr., distrusted him cordially.) Uncas was, in 1645, already approaching his sixtieth year (he was destined to live past his ninetieth). He usually dwelt close to the great estuary called Pequot River, near the limit of tide. His name, not inappropriately, signified a fox.[23]

Certain of the surviving Pequots had, following their defeat, been placed under the suzerainty of Uncas, whose harshness toward them remained unrelieved by any administrative benefits. However, their prospects for rebellion were, barring English intervention, quite hopeless; Uncas's sole serious Indian rivals were the Narragansets, that rather large, but inchoate and ordinarily not very warlike, tribe which occupied the western mainland of present Rhode Island, and it was a difficulty between Uncas and the Narragansets which upset Winthrop's program in the summer of 1645. The unpleasant details may be dispensed with. It is sufficient to say that an overmotivated young Narraganset sachem, whose name the English rendered as "Miantonomo," had mounted a raid into Mohegan territory and had been unexpectedly captured. Uncas was sly enough to deliver his prisoner into the custody of the Connecticut magistrates at Hartford, and there followed an episode of frontier diplomacy of the kind in which Uncas excelled. Involved were Connecticut, Massachusetts, and the United Colonies; ultimately Miantonomo was released, but in such a manner that Uncas could arrange his murder without having to face judicial consequences.[24]

Among the Narragansets there was understandable wrath; by the spring of 1645 it even was rumored that a part of their revenge might be wreaked upon the English. This, plus a vigorous bush skirmish between the Indians concerned, provoked an extraordinary meeting of the United Colonies commissioners at Boston, beginning on July 28, and sent Winthrop scurrying back to the Bay, possibly at some personal risk, to press for intervention. The official response was more than adequate: It was announced that three hundred men should take the field forthwith. Winthrop may not have subscribed to the official sympathy that was expressed for Uncas, but at least a termination of the hostilities was achieved. No English blood was spilled, and on August 27, an embassy of Narragansets and tributary Niantics, all voluble with promises, scrawled their marks upon a peace pact.[25]

Winthrop's plans had been delayed for months. He did not, however, lose interest. Otherwise he would not have ventured, late that autumn, upon an overland return to Pequot by way of a little known and highly experimental route. He must indeed have regarded it as a special undertaking, for he so departed from his ordinary habits as to keep a daily journal, written for the most part in Latin.[26] Very possibly he had in mind a variant track which should pass close to the black lead of Tantiusque and at the same time avoid travel through the Narragansett country.

If so, the effort was a failure. He rode from Boston on the afternoon of November 11, accompanied by a packhorse and an unremembered companion. Their initial progress was without incident, but by noon of the following day a blast of snow rattled the dead leaves of the trailside oaks, and the weather turned so severe that they missed Tantiusque entirely. In the circumstances Winthrop deemed it prudent to abandon his reconnaissance in favor of the circuitous but well-marked trail through Springfield, Hartford, and Saybrook. It was a wise decision; the storms continued for days, and even the Connecticut River became choked with early ice. (This appears to have been his closest approach to his black lead deposits; there is no evidence that he ever thereafter penetrated the region.)

Winthrop found Saybrook half-derelict. Fenwick had quite thrown up the enterprise: The previous year—and following much obscure and complicated bargaining—he had taken it upon himself to convey the entire plantation, transcontinental presumptions possibly included, to the colony of Connecticut. Indeed, it is unlikely that Fenwick was still in residence; his wife had recently died, and he appears not to have rested thereafter on the order of his going, for England and for good.[27]

But if Fenwick was no longer at Saybrook, the Reverend Thomas Peter was. Peter had felt it wise to withdraw from Pequot River at the time of summer troubles, but it was not difficult, thanks to the recent Indian treaty, to reawaken his interest. And when, after four additional days of storm, Winthrop continued toward Pequot, Peter went with him and so, apparently, did a number of his congregation. They reached their destination promptly and at once resumed their examination of plantation sites. There Winthrop presently left them and continued toward the Bay in the company of one "Jonathan R." [28] Significantly, he no longer tried to force a passage by way of Tantiusque; the weather again deteriorated, and in the Narragansett country he abandoned his Latin notations for the convenience of hasty English. But when, on December 5, he came at last to Boston and Ten Hills, he concluded his journal with a suitably formal *"Deo Gratias."*

Winthrop was by this time entirely committed to Pequot. There would be further distractions, including learned correspondence with England and the acquisition of a paper domain on Long Island.[29] Nor was there yet any question of abandoning Ten Hills, whose management he placed in the hands of three "trustie and beloved frends." But the last of his Ipswich holdings was gone; in March, Thomas Peter came to the Bay for further conference; and on May 20 the Massachusetts court was pleased to extend to Winthrop, Peter, and their associates the right to transfer any inconvenient natives from the better Pequot tracts to the equivalent of reservations. The irrepressible Uncas contrived again to be troublesome, but by the middle of October, 1646, Winthrop at last was ready to depart for Fishers Island. With him went Elizabeth and their eldest son, Fitz-John; little Betty and the younger children remained for the time being at Boston in the care of their grandparents. With him also went Elizabeth's older sister Mrs. Margaret Lake, a lady of uncertain, but apparently unexceptionable, past, of whom they both were deeply fond. (She would continue for a number of years as a member of their household.)[30]

Their departure cannot be fixed precisely, but it preceded October 26. It is known that they traveled entirely by water and that they paid a friendly call en route at Newport, the Rhode Island plantation of the eccentric William Coddington. They were becalmed for a day off Block Island, but reached their destination in time to settle themselves ashore before the whole of southeastern New England was stricken by what was obviously a tropical hurricane.[31]

Fishers Island must have been even less desirable a place in which to weather such a tempest than it is today, but they suffered no reportable losses. Moreover, Winthrop had at last, at the age of forty, and following so many deviations, established himself on the doorstep of the nearest thing to a home he was ever to know.

CHAPTER I I

New London, Connecticut

THE hurricane of November, 1646, wreaked small havoc upon southernmost New England. There in fact was little which it could have destroyed. Yet the region promised much. It surpassed even Massachusetts in the matter of protected waterways: To the east, Narragansett Bay afforded an entire complex of estuaries; westward, a full three-quarters of the coast lay enclosed by Long and Fishers islands. Into the interior, the Connecticut River could be ascended by average vessels for 50 miles; even Winthrop's Pequot was sufficiently navigable for 10.

With the exception of Saybrook, the earliest English settlements had been established not along the shore but considerably inland at the river towns of Springfield, Windsor, Hartford, and Wethersfield, and of these the last three had combined to form the political entity known as Connecticut. They furthermore had helped fix another American tradition: Quite without external sanction, they had created—for their local purposes—a government. Adopted in 1639, the Fundamental Orders of Connecticut [1] differed in no major respect from the practices of Massachusetts Bay—to which, of course, its authors had been most recently accustomed.

Though placed at the head of a natural seaway, primitive Connecticut was, in a relative sense, little disposed toward trade. Its primary concern was, and long would remain, agriculture, an interest fortified by a combination of goodly soil and squirearchal memories. Yet Connecticut quickly showed evidence of the kind of nervous expansionism for which American agrarians would one day become famous. Already the colony had acquired—or thought it had acquired—the extraordinary patent which the Puritan Lords and Gentlemen had received—or thought they had received—from the Council for New England (had its whole substance been realized, Connecticut might ultimately have been unrolled into a ribbon 3,000 miles long). For the moment, of course, the patent yielded only Saybrook, but the Hartford magistrates were not slow to pursue alternative opportunities. Even before Winthrop encamped upon Fishers Island in 1646, Connecticut claimed jurisdiction over a number of outlying possessions: Stratford and Fairfield up the coast to the westward and, on eastern Long Island, Easthampton and Southampton.[2]

Somewhat younger than Connecticut, but quite as extralegal, was the colony of New Haven. It was also in certain respects the most remarkable of the Puritan plantations in North America. New Haven represented New England at its most meticulous. The flavor of the place is nicely suggested by its original leadership, which lay, for practical purposes and for twenty years, in the hands of two men: Theophilus Eaton, a mercantile and Puritan Londoner of striking wealth and religious intensity, and the Reverend John Davenport, one of the most effective reforming divines ever to serve the City business community. The details (occasionally colorful, almost always obscure) need not concern us. But it should be noticed that New Haven—like Connecticut—was a kind of half-acknowledged child of Massachusetts, that—like Connecticut—it bore evidence of its maternity in the fundamental structure of its government, and that—like Connecticut—it early revealed an Anglo-American instinct to expand. Though never much more than a republic in microcosm, New Haven had, by

1646, spawned, and proudly acknowledged, the towns of Milford, Guilford, Stamford, Greenwich, and Branford, plus, on Long Island, a beachhead at Southold and a judicial claim to Southampton.[3]

Indeed, among the settlements of southern New England, the sole striking deviation from the ordinary was to be found in the colony of Rhode Island and Providence Plantations. That the earliest Rhode Islanders were regarded by their fellow New Englanders as dangerous pariahs is of course well known. But it is instructive to recall the special reason. Actually, the Rhode Islanders resembled the other colonials in almost every respect: They were, in their beginnings, extralegal; they displayed expansionist characteristics; and they developed, albeit with certain local frictions, a government of authentic corporate form. (The government even acquired a measure of authenticity when, in March, 1643/4, Roger Williams extracted a "charter" from the Long Parliament.) What set Rhode Island apart, what kept it in a condition of political segregation, and to the end outside the Puritan system, was its religious posture; for the colony already was generally committed to the new and, to most Europeans, still unacceptable notion of religious toleration. It was a difference which seventeenth-century New England proved unable to transcend, and it endowed certain ordinary difficulties with an intensity which was unfortunate for all concerned.[4]

It was into the midst of this unstable southern New England milieu that John Winthrop, Jr., sought in November of 1646 to introduce himself, his family, and his Pequot plantation. He arrived with the somewhat timeworn authorizations of Massachusetts (October, 1640), of Connecticut (April, 1641), and of the now defunct Saybrook (May, 1641), plus the renewed endorsement of Massachusetts dated June 28, 1644.[5] But it is obvious that he was in no hurry to assert his political affiliation—or to experiment with a declared independence. Like many another pioneer settlement, Winthrop's Pequot received practical implementation first.

Winthrop's immediate problems appeared in five forms, of which four were common to almost any English contact with the New World and the last was of special consequence in New England: 1) A site for the settlement, or at least for its core, had to be selected. 2) A government—if only rudimentary—must be provided. 3) A means for economic survival must be discovered. 4) The regional Indians had to be dealt with. And 5) the religious needs of the community had to be met, especially in the person of an acceptable clergyman.

For Winthrop, the first problem proved one of the least. It may be doubted that he ever seriously considered fixing his permanent headquarters on Fishers Island. Nine miles in length, of slender dimensions, and for much of its extent at least 4 miles from the mainland, the place was better suited to the sequestration of livestock than to the administration of a colony. Winthrop remained there, under what must have been uncomfortably primitive conditions, for less than six months, and the spring winds of 1647 still were roaring through the island oaks when he moved his family across the water to a stubby peninsula on the western bank of the Pequot estuary. Its Indian name was Nameaug, which may have referred to its superior fishing; from the European point of view, it was attractive in terms of a sheltered anchorage and patches of arable land. Already it carried a scattering of English huts, and here, atop a ledge of rock, with a view of his river between the trees, he established his personal seat. How adequate it may have been by the end of that summer we cannot tell; ultimately it would become, by contemporary standards, a show place, with a dwelling house of stone, set within a garden and an orchard and surrounded by carefully delineated fields and pastures.[6]

The creation of a local government was even less troublesome. Winthrop thoroughly dominated the early stages of his Pequot settlement; no North American tendencies toward "democracy" could seriously offset his unique combination of prestige, ability, and personality, and what he conceived the administration of his plantation should be, it was. As an Englishman of political good sense, he wasted no time upon experimental absurdities, and Pequot—or Nameaug—was organized like almost any other early New England town, with a semimedieval land pattern of house lots, plowing lots, wood lots, and commons, and an unexceptional muster of local officials, including a constable, five "townsmen" (that is, selectmen), two fence viewers, two clearers of highways, and two overseers of weirs. There was perhaps an American quality in the regulations which sought to insure that grants and allotments should actually be taken up within six months, and provision was made for a town meeting on the last Thursday of every February. But there was no nonsense about social, or even political, equality. Winthrop was chosen a townsman as a matter of course until—in 1651—he sought release from the position, and it is obvious that no gathering, either of townsmen or of the town at large, desired or dared to thwart him. It is suggestive, moreover, that the early records of the place refer to but four individuals under the style of "Mr."—Jonathan Brewster, Robert Parke, Deane Winthrop, and John Winthrop, Jr.[7]

If the initial politics of Pequot were thus no more than a routine application of Winthrop's ideas, its economics were quite another matter. There to be sure was no "starving time." But the plantation experienced to the full the universal New England difficulty in developing a salable export. Winthrop thought chiefly in terms of beef, mutton, and pork, and he offered no apology when he solicited both hayseed and breeding stock from heretical Rhode Island. The sale of his output, however, was easier imagined than fulfilled. From London, his brother Stephen suggested the shipment of *beaver*. From Massachusetts, his father wrote that beef and pork were fetching no more than threepence a pound, and a

New London, Connecticut

leading Boston merchant, Amos Richardson, advised against sending a single animal to such a market. In the autumn of 1648, an
experimental overland cattle drive nearly ended in disaster, thanks
to the wilderness terrain and Indian pilferage. Furthermore,
Pequot proved deficient in meadow and marsh, and, to expand its
hay production, Winthrop was driven to occupy additional territory to the west of the Niantic River. (This he rationalized on the
grounds of a half-remembered, and clearly unofficial, Indian purchase of 1636.) A respectable traffic in livestock was ultimately
achieved. But in the beginning it was hardly sufficient to pay a portion of his own debts, not to mention the obligations of his associates, and, to the end of his life, Winthrop's correspondence would
be peppered with the kind of woes with which a modern rancher is
all too familiar.[8]

Pequot was in fact a rather typical infant plantation. If it encountered trouble in finding something which it could sell, it experienced absolute frustration when it sought to attract fresh infu-
sions of capital. A variety of circumstances, in particular the
parliamentary victory in England and the unsatisfactory proof of
Winthrop's previous puddings, combined to make 1648 a year of
special discouragement. Overseas, only the generous personal
intervention—with convertible funds—of Emmanuel Downing
appears to have saved Winthrop from fiscal ruin, and it quickly became clear that there was nowhere else in England the slightest
hope for additional support. Yet Pequot, like so many American
communities which have been denied external capital, contrived to
carry on, albeit upon a reduced scale, without it.[9]

Pequot's financial dilemmas, being hopeless, were quietly evaded. Its Indian problems were by comparison merely intricate—and
therefore of public concern. The English nature enjoys an astonishing capacity to endure economic adversity, but it is seldom so
patient in the presence of an alien race. Threepenny meat prices

never so disturbed Winthrop's plantation as did the conflicting brushland aspirations of the Mohegans, Niantics, Narragansets, and residual Pequots.

It was characteristic of Winthrop that he should seek to minimize his Indian difficulties by establishing a regional balance of power. He proposed, in essence, to avoid bloodshed by matching capabilities for violence. A principal element in his system would be, of course, his own English settlers. Another was the possibility —which he seldom permitted the natives to forget—of collective action by the United Colonies. Among the Indians themselves, the greatest potential lay with the Narragansets, who were by far the most numerous, though of indefinite organization, and with the Mohegans, of whom the personification was always the precious Uncas.

In theory, still widely certified by memories of the Pequot war, Uncas was a "friend" of the English. Indeed, he and his Mohegans had for some time enjoyed the open patronage of Connecticut Colony. Yet it was Uncas who posed the most immediate threat to any system of Anglo-aboriginal checks and balances, and Winthrop was not slow to adopt an anti-Uncas policy. Though a born intriguer, the Mohegan sachem was not quite subtle enough to deprive Winthrop of reasonable grounds for action against him. The Indian's capacity for patience was not unlimited, and he reached his boiling point over the question of his Nameaug-Pequot underlings. These unfortunate creatures had greeted Winthrop's settlement with delight, and they quite naturally took advantage of the opportunity to bewail their lot. Nor were their lamentations without effect, for by the summer of 1646 Uncas and his Mohegans were already so provoked as to assail an Anglo-Nameaug hunting party. In the course of the following winter, moreover, a brother of Uncas, by name Nowequa, undertook to land on Fishers Island and parade insolently about in the presence of Winthrop's own household. Other "sinful miscarriages" followed, which served further to arouse the plantation—against Uncas and in favor of the Nameaugs.[10]

Winthrop deplored bloodshed. He also thoroughly appreciated the merits of force. He therefore undertook to confront the Mohegans not directly with his own muskets but with the displeasure of the United Colonies. It was a tactic which came close to failure. Despite Uncas's lapses, his pro-English reputation died hard. At New Haven, in September, 1646, the commissioners of the United Colonies were willing to accord him no more than a slap on the wrist. At their next meeting (held at Boston the following July), Winthrop appeared in person, and on this occasion a moderate fine was imposed, but the commissioners still could see no reason why the Nameaug Pequots should be relieved of their vassalage. Twice (the second time literally upon his deathbed) the elder John Winthrop himself urged a *rapprochement* with Uncas, and for all the support of the Pequot planters, the Nameaugs received no formal relief until 1654.[11]

Winthrop of course realized that the United Colonies were not the sole means by which he might reduce Uncas to size. This fundamental aim was in fact achieved as early as February 24, 1646/7, thanks to certain informal negotiations at Saybrook, at which Winthrop and John Mason (the latter speaking for Connecticut) induced Uncas and the Nameaug sachem, Cassasinamon, to accept a sensible arrangement, whereby the Mohegans would refrain from "molesting" their satellites in return for a reasonable and regular tribute. Nor did Winthrop so violate the principles of diplomacy as to try to destroy Uncas. The decline of the latter was hardly under way when there appeared at Nameaug the Niantic sachem, Ninigret, bursting with speech and obviously bent upon filling the anticipated vacuum. Winthrop gave him short shrift: He informed Ninigret he must consult the United Colonies and "attend their orders"; this, he warned, would be "the only way to attaine . . . peace with the English." When the ebb of Uncas continued to inspire other groups of Narragansets with similar aspirations, Winthrop made it clear—quietly but with precision—that the English on Pequot River would go to his defense in case of attack.[12]

Complicated though his Indian difficulties may have been, it is likely that Winthrop's final problem, the acquisition of a clergyman, caused him the greatest personal vexation. He was admirably endowed for the conduct of a sensitive diplomacy; but for the creation of a religious establishment he was distinctly less gifted. When Pequot first was envisaged, he had reason to hope he might be spared this particular responsibility; it will be recalled that an early and conspicuously active associate was the Reverend Thomas Peter. But Mr. Peter had a wife and family in England, while Marston Moor and Naseby suddenly had reopened to him a thousand English pulpits. Moreover, in the summer of 1646, he was stricken with a severe illness. This appears to have settled the matter; Peter departed for England in December. He did try to arrange for a suitable successor, and he served generously (though without success) as a transatlantic spokesman for Winthrop's colony. But the pastor problem was once again in Winthrop's lap.[13]

It was to plague him for four years more. A special friend of Peter, the Reverend John Jones, declined to exchange an uncertain post at Fairfield for a firm call (with supplementary benefits) at Pequot—"for several reasons," he informed Winthrop, "which I will not now trouble you with." Friends and relatives at the Bay endeavored to be helpful; at least four names were brought to Winthrop's attention in the course of 1648, but without result, and the three masters of arts created by the latest Harvard commencement hurried to secure positions elsewhere. Toward the end of 1649, Winthrop went so far as to offer the post to the Reverend Marmaduke Matthews, although the latter was in public disrepute for alleged deviationism, but even Matthews preferred not to chance Pequot and, following further doctrinal unpleasantness at Malden, Massachusetts, returned to his native Wales. Indeed, Winthrop failed to discover an interested candidate until late in 1650, when at last he obtained the services of the Reverend Richard Blinman, for eight years minister at Gloucester. Mr. Blinman brought a number of his congregation with him, but he drove a rather stiff personal bargain, including a brand new dwelling on a 6 acre plot and a starting salary of £60 per year.[14]

Thus pequot survived—English, Puritan, and arricultural. Yet there remained the problem of political affiliation—not only for the settlement but for Winthrop himself.

In practical terms, it was a choice between Massachusetts and Connecticut. There was never a question of Rhode Island or of New Haven. Nor was independence a serious alternative; there is no evidence that Winthrop ever considered it. The essential decision was reached by 1650: Pequot—regardless, perhaps, of the views of its inhabitants—went to Connecticut. The geographic merits of the choice are obvious. It also is probable that certain legal considerations played a part. Only the role of Winthrop remains obscure. Possibly he intended it so.

Both Massachusetts and Connecticut could, as former associates in the destruction of the Pequots, lay claim to the region by virtue of military conquest. Connecticut, furthermore, could cite the imperial, though uncertain, rights conveyed by the "Warwick Patent." A provisional accommodation between the two had been worked out as early as 1638,[15] but it had not been ratified and was not discussed seriously again until 1646, when Winthrop's settlement brought everything to a head. There was, of course, little possibility of an armed collision. It was precisely the sort of problem for which the United Colonies had been established, and the dispute was formally taken up at the meeting of the United Colonies commissioners held early in September at New Haven.

It might be supposed that John Winthrop, Jr., would espouse the cause of Massachusetts as a matter of course. He was still legally a resident of that colony; his father was its very symbol; while the sympathies of his own settlers were dominantly with the Bay. Yet he refrained from taking a precise stand. Neither, it should be noted, did Massachusetts. As early as June, 1646, the elder Winthrop had noted in his journal that "it mattered not much" to which jurisdiction Pequot should belong, since the United Colonies had "made all as one"—a rather incredible expression of faith. Later in the summer, Samuel Symonds urged from Ipswich that the Pequot enterprise not be abandoned, even at the price of annexation by Connecticut. The younger Winthrop continued noncommittal; he had repaired not to the New Haven meeting but privately to Boston. "I cannot direct at such a distance," he wrote Thomas Peter on September 3, "but you know what is to be done: and whats best for our plantation." [16]

Though the commissioners from the first inclined toward Connecticut, they arrived at no decision that year. But prior to their next meeting, which was held at Boston the following summer, Winthrop was much in the company of Connecticut personalities, in particular the deputy governor for 1647–48, Mr. Edward Hopkins. There was no rigid agreement; such was seldom Winthrop's way. Yet it is known that he dispensed medical advice in behalf of Mrs. Hopkins (who was sinking into a long and melancholy insanity) and that he and Hopkins arranged to travel to the Boston meeting together. It furthermore is recorded that Winthrop, in a personal appearance before the commissioners, indicated that he was "indifferent" to the assignment of his settlement and that the commissioners thereupon decided for Connecticut. Insofar as can be determined, Massachusetts accepted the award with good grace.

Connecticut proceeded at once to acts of sovereignty: On September 9, 1647, the Hartford General Court voted to commission Winthrop as Connecticut's principal magistrate for Pequot, with powers "to execute justice according to our lawes and the rule of righteousness." Early in November, Mr. Hopkins appeared at Nameaug to deliver the commission in person; he found that Winthrop had not yet returned from Massachusetts, but he "harboured" at Winthrop's house and swore in a constable (Cary Latham). Winthrop's appointment was confirmed by further act of the General Court on May 18, 1648.[17]

There could now be little doubt that Pequot was a part of Connecticut. Yet the precise status of the plantation remained to a degree uncertain until May 17, 1649, when the Hartford court issued a series of directives, which established what we should call an incorporated town. One of these provided for a permanent local judiciary, of whom Winthrop naturally was one; another described the municipal boundaries; still another recommended the name "Faire Harbour." [18] All these prescriptions appear to have been well received at Pequot—except for the name. This was unexpected; the substitution of an English for an Indian designation was a recognition of permanence. The inhabitants, however, were partial to "London" or "New London" and had so declared in town meeting on February 22, 1648/9. Winthrop himself wondered if so ambitious a name might not give offense, and in fact the Connecticut General Court refused to approve it for more than eight years thereafter.[19]

The annexation of Winthrop's plantation—call it Pequot, Nameaug, or New London—did not mean the immediate assimilation of Winthrop himself. For a considerable period, he chose to maintain a curious bicolonial relationship, wherein Connecticut regarded him a local magistrate, while Massachusetts retained him as an assistant. He had held the latter position without official interruption since 1632, and he permitted his routine reelections to continue through the spring of 1649. His motives are not altogether plain. It is apparent that his interest in public affairs at the Bay was on the decline; there is no evidence that he attended more than a single session of the court of 1647–48, and his most significant appearance thereafter was coincident with an official favor—the grant, in May, 1648, of *3,000* acres near the mouth of the Pawcatuck River, to be used as the basis of another salt works. His participation in the election meeting of 1649 was no more disinterested.[20]

That he clung so long to Massachusetts may have sprung from an indisposition to weaken the ties with his parents. But his stepmother, the estimable Margaret, died suddenly in 1647, and in the final days of March, 1649, an exhausted dispatch rider appeared at Pequot with word of the passing of his father. Winthrop contrived, by water and by horse, to reach Boston in time for the funeral on April 3 and walked with the casket in solemn procession amid the thud of the minute guns. It was the end of an era—as much, perhaps, for John Winthrop, Jr., as for Massachusetts Bay.[21]

Thereafter his emphasis lay always with Connecticut. He already had the Hartford magistrates, in particular Edward Hopkins, spellbound; and though they must have been aware of his residual loyalty to Massachusetts, they urged him—even prior to the death of his father—to attend their next Court of Election; and they went so far, on March 14, 1648/9, as to place his name in nomination for magistrate—not merely of Nameaug but of Connecticut. This appears the more extraordinary when one considers that Winthrop had not yet been admitted a freeman of the colony.[22]

It has been said, unfortunately without citation, that Winthrop in 1649 gave formal notice of his retirement from the Massachusetts Court of Assistants. This may have been so; his subsequent moves to fix his residence at Pequot would make such a resignation reasonable. Furthermore, the Boston court in October, 1649, ordered that the assistants should thereafter be nominated by the freemen of the several towns (thus removing the choice to some extent from the control of the "establishment"), and it also is true that Winthrop on May 22, 1650, for the first time was not re-elected. But any supposition that he was eliminated against his will is scarcely tenable. Nearly a week previous, on May 16, he had been made, by action of the General Court at Hartford, and almost certainly at his own request, a Connecticut freeman.[23]

One additional formality was necessary to complete his transfer. On July 23, 1650, the First Church of Boston recommended, over the signatures of John Cotton, John Wilson, and Thomas Oliver, that Winthrop and his wife be received into the Church of Christ at Saybrook.[24] Puritan New England could afford no more valid proof of a change of residence!

W I N T H R O P was never so naïve as to confuse public service with unintelligent self-sacrifice. When leadership yielded rewards, he was disposed to receive them without painful self-evaluation. Already his New Londoners had tendered him one of the most generous assortments of rights and privileges ever seen in New England. He had spoken of glassmaking; therefore, the "great white sandy beach over against Bachelor's cove" would be his; indeed, he could take "sand, earth, or stones" of any kind from any source within the town. He was extended the ferry monopoly. He was given all the "little islands of Rocks" within the harbors. He might erect a mill wherever he chose. A princely tract beside the Mystic was reserved in his name. He was given the sole right to quarry the "White Stones on the great West Neck." The siting and construction of any public building was made subject to his approval. He and his heirs were to possess a "casting vote" in the disposition of unalienated land or other public property. Moreover, Winthrop's own land was to remain tax free "for the time to come." It was an extraordinary parcel of privileges, nor does Winthrop appear to have stood upon the order of their acceptance.[25]

There were, in fact, times when New London seemed little more than his personal domain. His nervous energy continued irrepressible and infectious; the town meeting continued, practically on call, to invest him with almost anything, from fishing rights to a mill site and additional islands. The mill and its appertaining dam were erected at public charge, yet Winthrop and his heirs enjoyed—free of competition—their entire revenues. (The town recorder, Obadiah Bruen, noted in July, 1651, that forty-two individuals—among whom no Winthrop is evident!—had "wrought" at the dam.) He steadily increased his herds; from Lion Gardiner, since 1639 settled upon an island domain across the Sound, he received repeated shipments of sheep and cattle. On Fishers Island, his goats throve so exceedingly that a casual Narraganset raiding party was able, in 1654, to slay 200 of them. His mansion house, slowly taking shape on its rock ledge, already commanded an imperial prospect: Beyond garden and orchard and a grove of monumental oaks, his river ran like a corridor toward the Sound and the islands beyond. Winthrop typically reacted with dreams, always expansive, yet never quite so grandiose as to be wholly implausible. Pequot River would become a major channel of the Indian traffic: "My heart is with you," wrote Thomas Stanton, by this time one of the leading traders in New England, and requested Winthrop to set aside a residence lot. A bellicose world cried for saltpeter; Winthrop would supply it, and off to a selected list of Boston merchants went a prospectus in manuscript, urging the creation of a stock company, whereof the capital should be at least £3,000. Insolvent or no, he was by now a recognized entrepreneur, and, like many a later executive of impressive indebtedness, was presently solicited to contribute "towards the welfare and prosperity" of Harvard College.[26]

Nor could such a man fail to attract invitations to special public service. Roger Williams's patent of 1644 for a combined "Rhode Island and Providence Plantations" had drawn vigorous fire from William Coddington, who fancied himself the guiding spirit of an autonomous Rhode Island and secured, in 1651, an antithetical commission from the English Council of State to prove it. Neither side was prepared for formal violence; both sought the intervention of Winthrop, which, in view of the religious question, was significant and, in view of his later behavior, a little foolhardy. The Williams faction even attempted to expand his assistance into the political annexation of Pequot. (Winthrop's good offices, if any, were entirely informal.) A leading Hartford resident, Mr. Edward Elmer, a man of much misplaced energy, sought him in 1649 as governor of an hypothetical settlement on the banks of the Delaware.[27]

River and Sound gave New London a distinctly southwesterly orientation, and if the Delaware was as yet too distant to attract Winthrop's interest, an early intimacy with the Dutch West Indian Company at Fort Amsterdam was quite inevitable. We do not know when or in what circumstances he first looked upon the remarkable environment of Manhattan Island or became acquainted with the tiny, yet already cosmopolitan, municipality which occupied its southern tip. It is likely, however, that the initial encounter occurred nearer New London, whose horizons were constantly interrupted by Dutch topsails, and the meeting no doubt was hastened by the company's "director," the famous Petrus Stuyvesant, whose policy it was to seek out the English in quest of commerce and, if possible, of political accommodation. Stuyvesant's own New Netherlands possessed a sizable, if not dangerous, English minority; moreover, his principal secretary, George Baxter, was an Englishman.[28] Stuyvesant was, for all his reputation for vanity and ill temper, a man of much good will and good sense, and it was not long before he was on the best of terms with John Winthrop, Jr. Their friendship would continue unbroken, except upon a single famous occasion, to the day of Stuyvesant's death, and as early as the winter of 1649/50, the Dutch director had so fallen under the Winthrop influence that he offered "large and ample priviledge and accommodation" if the latter would only come to reside in New Netherlands.[29]

N e v e r t h e l e s s, Winthrop could enjoy a still broader and, to him, infinitely more satisfying popularity. Nothing at New London —neither Uncas nor the deficits nor the absence of the greater part of his personal library [30]—was permitted wholly to interfere with his intellectual pursuits. Even the discouragements of 1648 were to a degree mitigated in the person of William Berkeley, an imaginative Bermuda merchant who dabbled in alchemy. Two years later came a letter from his old mentor at Hamburg, Dr. Tanckmarus, enclosing supplementary correspondence from Dr. Paul Marquart Schlegel, a German of astonishing parts—physician, biologist, and pioneer in obstetrics—who sought North American specimens, intelligently collected. Winthrop was genuinely distressed when his replies—with or without the specimens—went astray.[31] But he probably derived greatest satisfaction from his encouragement of George Stirk, a young Harvard alumnus with a special penchant for alchemy.

Stirk (his name is frequently rendered Starkey) occupies a more than incidental place in the record of the younger John Winthrop. He appears to have been born the son of a clergyman in Bermuda in 1627; his graduation, in 1646, from Harvard College is fully documented. His later career, chiefly in England, as a physician and savant is clouded with controversy, not all of it favorable to his personal reputation, yet he died gallantly among his patients in the midst of the London Plague of 1665.[32] His direct acquaintance with Winthrop seems to have been rather brief, yet it is through Stirk that the true importance of Winthrop's alchemical activities emerges most clearly.

Anyone who would consider this matter must bear always in mind that "science" in the seventeenth century was hardly, in its modern, inductive sense, yet born. There was still much commitment to the notions of the past—to the reality of the supernatural, to considerations of religion, to the advantages of secret cults—and in no area was this more conspicuous than in alchemy. Even so late as Winthrop's day its literature was marked by an unabashed occultism and its practitioners typically sought anonymity through the use of pseudonyms. Of particular prominence among the latter was a certain "Eirenaeus Philalethes" (Peaceful Lover of Truth), said to be a man of English nationality and New World residence, the identity of whom has since become a favorite problem for devotees of alchemical history. Their suggestions have been widely various; it is interesting to find that two principal candidates have been Robert Child and George Stirk.[33] Furthermore, a later and meticulously careful investigation has produced impressive evidence that Philalethes was Winthrop himself.[34] This thesis moreover has subsequently been strengthened by the discovery of an anagram within *Introitus Apertus,* or *Secrets Reveal'd,* a principal work of Philalethes, by which the author is identified as Winthrop.[35]

That Winthrop was in fact Philalethes may not be universally accepted as proven; *Secrets Reveal'd* contains elements—especially of chronology—which do not square with the record. Yet the claim must be regarded as likely. Identity does not necessarily demand the identical; alchemists, especially, were shadowy figures, often promoted into fabulous proportions, and it is hardly too much to conceive that Winthrop, writing under a pseudonym (which incidentally fitted him to perfection), should later be so manipulated and perhaps plagiarized as to become, in this aspect of his career, a legend beyond historical recall. (There are reasons to suspect that Stirk, who is known to have been concerned with the Philalethes tracts, was a principal manipulator.) Most intriguing of all is the possibility that Winthrop, as Philalethes, is to be numbered among the half-dozen leading alchemists of his era, an accepted "adept" within a proud and jealously restricted brotherhood.

Yet it must also be pointed out that Winthrop failed to maintain a permanent enthusiasm for alchemy, in its ordinary sense. Even before his association with Stirk it was already on the wane; his alchemical library must have been one of the finest in the world, yet their correspondence indicates that the greater portion of it lay unused at Ten Hills. To assume that he rejected the art as a fraud would, of course, be unwarranted. Rather, it is probable that his original penchant had evolved naturally into a commitment to medicine, in particular a medicine in which the elusive "Stone" played an important role. The Stone, moreover, was no deceit; it was in Winthrop's time a widely sought agent of purification, physical and even spiritual.

OVERSEAS, his brother Stephen had been unexpectedly converted to the new cause of religious toleration and wholly divorced from the official New England Way. "God declares . . . perticularly agt. that spirite," he wrote Winthrop in the winter of 1650/1, "The Lord in mercye keepe it from . . . [your settlement] or else it will spoyle yor farmers, shipp and iron works." Stephen might have saved his paper and ink: Winthrop was more than willing to support such views—provided they were acceptable to the greater part of the community. His disposition to theological partisanship continued nil; with Roger Williams he discussed, privately, proscribed books, and on one occasion carried to Providence a volume of Jesuit maxims.[36] Indeed, his natural moderation presently got him into difficulties with the Hartford authorities. When his cousin and former sister-in-law, Elizabeth Fones, a woman of pronounced energy and numerous questionable marriages, sought refuge at Pequot from the official displeasure of both Connecticut and New Haven, Winthrop had no compunction about taking her in; he even offered employment to her consort of the moment, William Hallett. From New Haven, Theophilus Eaton wrote to suggest that the fugitives be sent into exile, but the Connecticut court, in tones of righteous indignation, ordered their immediate arrest. Winthrop was unwilling openly to defy such a directive, but he saw to it that Hallett and Elizabeth were gotten safely away to New Netherlands ahead of the inevitable warrant.[37] Nor was this the only occasion upon which he quietly interposed himself between the magistracy and an alleged adulterer; a young New London spinster was similarly charged that very spring, while six months later the axe was brandished over the head of Winthrop's miller, Thomas Newton. But there is nothing to indicate that either was brought to trial, and Winthrop's efforts in behalf of Newton are amply documented.[38] Though personally free from sexual immorality, he would never lose his easy tolerance for those who were not.

There were additional distresses. Winthrop's plantation was lacking in competent blacksmiths; Hallett seems to have been one; while another, William Cheesebrooke, had hardly established himself in the neighborhood before he was charged, from Hartford, with illegal sales of firearms to the Indians. Cheesebrooke was of bumptuous disposition, and it would appear that Winthrop had personally to intervene before he could be induced—following two years of ill-tempered interchange—to make his peace with the authorities. (As late as 1652, New London was obliged to offer lavish inducements to secure the services of a farrier in Roxbury, Massachusetts.)[39] The Indian troubles were interminable. In the spring of 1649, the ubiquitous Uncas involved himself in personal combat with a Narraganset upon the deck of a trading ketch in Winthrop's own river; there followed a Mohegan raid upon a Narraganset village, which achieved the murder of an ancient squaw. Rumors of fearful complexity filled the woods and, before things were quieted, had engaged the attention of Rhode Island,

Connecticut, and the commissioners of the United Colonies. Winthrop, of course, found himself fairly in the middle. Never the sort to admire Indians, he remained especially irritated with the uncouth aspirations of the Mohegans. "I seriously lament the Issue," he wrote Governor Haynes of Connecticut, ". . . of setting up new monarkes of the treacherous hethon and such as have beene already by the mighty hand of the lord subdued to the English." The year 1650 was equally one of alarms; there even was talk in English circles of a "preventive" war—presumably against the Narragansets. Land hunger was this time an obvious factor, and Winthrop's own lust for real estate remained pronounced as ever. Yet he undertook, in the circumstances, to counsel prudence, and when Humphrey Atherton, newly commissioned captain of the Boston artillery company and a man with the instincts of a nineteenth-century filibusterer, suggested an early assault, Winthrop begged for moderation. "Sir," he wrote on November 10, "I hope your wisdome will lead you rather to accept of any reasonable termes of peace then beginne a warre of such doubtfull hazard." [40]

New London continued depressingly unprosperous. Amos Richardson, the Boston merchant, tried to be helpful, but bills of exchange were practically unobtainable. Winthrop was driven, late in 1649, to seek credits through his father's widow Martha, and when these were held up by legal technicalities, he was so brazen as to suggest that he be "loaned" the £200 which the Massachusetts General Court recently had appropriated in behalf of her infant son.[41] In December, 1648, a large Dutch merchantman, called *Golden Morning Star*, was driven off course amid floating ice and piled onto some rocks near the mouth of the Pequot. The vessel was salvaged, but the incident gave rise to an awkward legal tangle—and a worse reputation for Winthrop's river. Most discouraging of all, New London was, as late as May of 1652, not yet self-sufficient in terms even of foodstuffs.[42]

[159]

It is small wonder that he sometimes turned in despair from the noble prospect that spread before his uncompleted mansion, small wonder that he should consider throwing up the whole wretched business. Through the winter of 1649/50 he dabbled with half-serious plans for a return to England, and when George Baxter wrote of the residential advantages of Gravesend, Long Island, he indicated a half-willingness to remove there. Up the Sound at Guilford, within the jurisdiction of New Haven, rose the stone mansion of the Reverend Henry Whitfield, long since completed and perhaps the finest private seat in English America; when Whitfield returned overseas in the spring of 1650, Winthrop made informal inquiries as to its purchase.[43]

Yet New London contrived, after a fashion, to retain him. His bouts of melancholy invariably were succeeded by reconstituted American dreams. If the soils of Pequot were thin, there would be alternative riches within its rocks. "There hath been earnest motions to me . . . to make some search and trial for metals in this country," he wrote John Haynes in May of 1651, and he thereupon "made bold to propound" that the Connecticut General Court should endow him with an appropriate license, the suggested text of which he was kind enough to furnish. The court's response was favorable—perhaps more favorable than he had intended. Two days later, on May 15, it vested him with all the lead, copper, and other metals he might discover within the public domain. It furthermore elected him "magistrate" (that is, assistant) of Connecticut Colony.[44]

Like it or no, Winthrop had developed roots. He would never be able to free himself of them all.

CHAPTER 12

Life & Politics
in a Wilderness Colony

WINTHROP did not witness his elevation to the Connecticut magistracy; he was at the moment en route to Boston on business incident to the hire of the Reverend Mr. Blinman. Nor does he appear in the beginning to have taken his new responsibility very seriously; there is evidence that he visited Hartford, on a medical mission, during the following autumn, yet he failed to attend a meeting of the court for two full years. One can only speculate upon the considerations, public and personal, which assured his reelection in May, 1652, and in May, 1653.[1]

He did go up to Hartford for the spring court of 1653, and thereafter the magistrates saw him rather more frequently. He cannot have found the sessions unpleasant. Hartford was only a village (it contained less than 200 ratepayers), but it occupied an attractive site behind its river meadows, and during court periods the spacious yard surrounding its meetinghouse bustled with activity.[2] Moreover, Winthrop's colleagues, whom the freemen, following the Massachusetts habit, tended repeatedly to reelect, were generally persons of background and competence. Edward Hopkins was a businessman of imagination, whom Winthrop had known since the beginnings of the Ironworks Undertakers. He had been acquainted with John Haynes even longer (it will be recalled that

Haynes had been governor of Massachusetts Bay from 1635 to 1636), and their friendship had grown closer still when Winthrop undertook the treatment of Haynes's second wife, who had become subject to "violent fits" of a mental nature. Matthew Allyn was perhaps the first citizen of Windsor, willing always to assume public responsibilities; equally vigorous was his son John whose solid intelligence and exquisite calligraphy would eventually make him, for decades, secretary of the colony. Of similar stature was John Talcott, a native of Braintree, England, and a veteran of Massachusetts politics, who had been a public personality at Hartford since 1637; both he and his son of the same name would serve uninterrupted years as Connecticut treasurer.[3]

Winthrop quickly absorbed the notions and practices of Connecticut politics. Their fundamental resemblance to those of Massachusetts has been noted, yet a number of significant differences deserve emphasis.

The first involved the suffrage: A Connecticut "freeman" was not required to be a member of a recognized Church. This by no means should be taken to indicate an extraordinary "liberalism"; no person might be a freeman who had not first become an "admitted inhabitant" of a town, a junior grade of citizenship much dependent upon the quality the Puritans called "godly conversation." Furthermore, as the years went by, the General Court thought proper to impose additional requirements; by 1659, the candidate had to be at least twenty-one years of age, to possess an estate (for practical purposes real estate) worth £30 or more, to have "borne office" in his town, and to present a certificate of character endorsed by the major part of its deputies. The system was therefore little more liberal (in practice) than that of Massachusetts or (in theory) than that of England. It has been estimated that, between 1639 and 1662, fewer than 230 Connecticut residents actually achieved freeman's status.

Secondly, the General Court of Connecticut did not, during

Winthrop's lifetime, divide into two houses. Nonetheless, a noticeable tension had developed between magistrates and deputies, and the court had plainly followed its English instinct when, in February, 1644/5, it ordered that a majority of the magistrates *or* of the deputies present would be sufficient to disapprove any legislation. This provided the substance, if not the full paraphernalia, of separate chambers.

Thirdly, no Connecticut governor was permitted, following his year in office, immediately to succeed himself. This long since had produced an amiable reciprocity between John Haynes and Edward Hopkins, commencing in 1640 and continuing to the death of the former in January, 1653/4.

Finally, it should be remembered that Connecticut's frame of government, the celebrated Fundamental Orders, did not share the *legal* character of the Massachusetts Bay charter. This was not wholly a disadvantage. Unlike Massachusetts, early Connecticut could revise its Orders whenever it appeared desirable—and repeatedly did so.[4]

In common with practically any English plantation one may care to mention, Connecticut remained for long uncertain as to its territorial limits. Thanks to protracted negotiations and a promise to pay, in installments and in kind, the sum of £1,800, the colony had secured in 1644 an uncertain and partial title to the dubious "Warwick Patent." The conveyance had embraced the patent lands at least as far west as Saybrook; moreover, George Fenwick had undertaken, in the name of the proprietary Lords and Gentlemen, to provide more tangible proof of ownership "if it come into his power." But the transaction could create an ocean-to-ocean Connecticut only in the imagination of the most optimistic.[5]

This Warwick Patent would continue a chimera always. That the Hartford magistrates ever laid eyes upon a genuine copy may be doubted. Even had the patent existed in law, it could hardly under prevailing circumstances have been fulfilled in fact. In three directions, south, east, and west, a trio of external interests held claim—by physical occupation—to vital segments of the Warwick territories.

One of these was the colony of New Haven. Its inconsistency with the Warwick claims was self-evident.

Another was the Dutch West India Company. This had become, since the defeat of the Pequots, Connecticut's principal bête noire. Its territorial pretensions were as vague as they were hostile to those of the English, and it still maintained, squarely in the face of Hartford, its post on the Connecticut River. That neither party had resorted to violence was, in fact, a measure of the weakness of both. Negotiations, conducted with the protocol and subtilty of a European princeling, were at last gotten under way at Hartford on September 11, 1650. Eight days later there was agreement: A line—possibly the first international boundary in American history —was traced across an imperfect map, northward from the west side of Greenwich harbor and southward, across Long Island, from the west side of Oyster Bay. To the east would be English ground, to the west, Dutch. The pact was entirely provisional, pending ratification in England and the Netherlands. Winthrop, still half-autonomous at Pequot, had no hand in it.[6]

The other principal competition came from Rhode Island. It was a contest which, on the basis of authorities cited, was quite impossible to resolve. The Rhode Islanders or the greater part of them founded their case upon the charter of March 14, 1643/4, which described a region extending west from the boundary of Plymouth Colony "about twenty-five English miles to the Pequod River and country." [7] This simply did not square with geography, even had Plymouth been blessed with an established frontier, which it had not. Connecticut grounded its claims upon the gossamer Warwick Patent, which placed its eastern limits at the "Narragansett River," a geographic expression which might or might not be identified with Narragansett Bay. The imbroglio, in fine, was hopeless and was destined to continue for many years beyond the deaths of the original contestants.

Less aggravating were the uncertainties with Massachusetts. Thanks to the incompetence or laziness of the first surveyors, these too would persist for many years. But the principal issue, the affiliation of Springfield, had already been determined; the village appertained to Massachusetts. Controversies over the right of Connecticut to impose duties on Springfield's goods continued for some time, but had largely died away before Winthrop came to Hartford as magistrate.[8]

By mid-century, it was apparent that Connecticut would survive for an indefinite period. Ill-defined geographically and by no means unimpeachably legal, the colony nevertheless enjoyed a functioning government and was developing slowly, but steadily. Its towns continued to proliferate; by 1652, they numbered at least eleven. Its statutes had been reduced to codified form.[9] Its internal politics were distracted by neither a Hutchinson nor a Child, and the knotty question called the "Half-Way Covenant" did not yet demand a categorical answer. Winthrop probably was relieved that so much of the business of the General Court dealt with homely things like surveys, fences, and venial sin; he never would be disposed to thrust his considerable feet [10] into unnecessary controversy. His attendance at the sessions continued somewhat fitful. But he did make an effort to appear at the election meetings in May, and this was sufficient to insure his retention as an assistant; "once a magistrate, always a magistrate," remained more than a catch phrase. Yet one must suppose that his quiet good humor and his obvious gift for leadership were the controlling factors.[11] Inevitably, Hartford would seek him not only as an officer of the colony but as a fellow townsman. A letter of August, 1654, signed by half the village quality, cited "the state and frame

of our conditions in severall & varius respects together with our
confidence of yr willingness to advantage us in whatever may con-
duce to our wellfare . . . ," offered a "convenient house" and
ventured to hope that offers from "others else wher may not
divert yr thoughts from us who stand in soe much need of
you." [12]

In the Connecticut border lands, affairs were less happily
ordered. The year 1654 was one of particular troubles: A number
of the English aspired to selected tracts of Mohegan land; Uncas
not unnaturally objected; and the incident required the intervention not only of Winthrop but of Major John Mason and Matthew Griswold of Saybrook, whom the Hartford magistrates
ordered to New London for the purpose. Further to the east, the
Narragansets got out of hand; before it could be disposed of, the
situation required the armed intervention of the United Colonies.
And the sticky problem of Uncas and his Pequot helots was not yet
fully quieted.[13]

But if the Indians were a vexation, the Dutch seemed a positive
menace. The provisional Treaty of Hartford was never fully ratified; furthermore, conflicting interpretations, overseas, of maritime rights led to the outbreak, in July of 1652, of the first of a trio
of Anglo-Dutch wars. What New England should undertake in
the premises was at first left wholly to local option. Its response
was less than wholehearted: The more westerly settlements were
frantic with rumors that the Dutch director meant to unloose the
Indians upon them, and at a meeting of the United Colonies in
April, 1653, Connecticut and New Haven pressed urgently for an
offensive effort. But Massachusetts, unquestionably safe and moreover sensitive for the maintenance of a profitable Manhattan
trade, demurred, and the "United Colonies" could manage no
more than a committee to visit (and bluster at) Petrus Stuyvesant.
The two border colonies thus were thrown back upon their own
limited resources. For the moment, they could do little more than

place a ridiculous little cruiser in Long Island Sound, take defensive precautions on land, and appeal overseas to the great Oliver Cromwell.[14]

Cromwell, who already was a sovereign in everything but name, doubted the usefulness of North America; his own "western design" laid emphasis upon the tropical Antilles. But the magistrates of Connecticut and New Haven were careful to forward their address through an influential channel,[15] and the Protector's response, when it came, proved comparatively sympathetic. Two armed ships, bearing plans and proclamations, appeared at Boston in June of 1654, and there might have been an assault upon New Netherlands after all had not tidings of the Anglo-Dutch peace of April 5 arrived a short time later.

Winthrop played, amid this bellicosity, an inconspicuous role. He had nothing to do with the first demands for offensive war; his attendance at meetings of the Connecticut court remained curiously irregular; and the public records mention only his appointment, "if at home," to a committee for organizing the defense of New London. Yet his private correspondence reveals enough more to suggest that he consistently opposed any hostilities. His views moreover were shared by Petrus Stuyvesant. In February, 1652/3, as notice of the outbreak of war still crept westward from Europe, the Dutch director sniffed trouble and sent off to Governor Endecott of Massachusetts, via *Winthrop at Pequot,* a proposal that trade should continue as usual so far as North America was concerned. Stuyvesant was marvelously candid; in a supplementary letter to Winthrop he concealed literally nothing, either as to his fears or as to his intentions. Winthrop's reaction was prompt and hearty: He hurried the Dutch note to Boston by special Indian messenger and forwarded Endecott's answer (which proved to be only slightly equivocal) to Manhattan with the observation that Stuyvesant's attitude should have a happy effect. Late in June, 1654, as half of New England spat upon its hands and considered offensive operations anew, we discover him at Saybrook, attending an illness of Mrs. John Mason. No war! No war—unless the balance of capability were so weighted on the English side that bloodshed would be negligible.[16]

I T S H O U L D not be assumed, however, that his repeated absences from the Hartford sessions [17] reflected a simple dissatisfaction with the colony's external policy. Winthrop had fallen into a position—mercifully less common in the seventeenth century than in the twentieth—wherein he must watch too many pots. His major concerns were still at New London, but even there they had gotten, for the time being, out of hand. His sawmill commanded unexcelled timber resources, but its operations were continually interrupted by shortages of labor. He nonetheless envisaged a second sawmill and toyed with the notion of a supplementary goat herd on the mainland, midway between New London and Hartford. He wondered if indigo, a contemporary and profitable growth of Barbados, might not also be found suitable for Pequot River. He continued to fuss with plans for a saltworks. Upstream, well beyond New London's limits, he began the acquisition of additional land. In Massachusetts, in the district soon to be incorporated as Billerica, he held a large parcel for a rise—and was plagued, inevitably, by trespassers. In New London, he was no longer a "townsman," but his public responsibilities continued numerous and, if we may believe the data, rather petty. Typical was his concern with the trial, on March 24, 1653/4, of a certain "Will Bratlitt" (that is, Bartlett—a hint, so early, of a Yankee twang!), whose late winter frustrations had exploded into a cloud of peccadilloes, including drunkenness contrary to law (fine, 10 shillings), unnecessary labor on the Sabbath (10 s.), selling powder and lead to the Indians (10 s.), and dispensing strong waters without a license (another 10 s.). In 1654, New London was so tardy in remitting its share of the colony rates that Treas-

urer Talcott threatened from Hartford to send down "the mar-
tiall" to collect them; it was Winthrop who had personally to
intervene. On June 13, 1655, Will Bartlett once again was in
difficulties over strong waters, but this time his case was obscured
beneath a prodigious overburden of displaced animals, leaky
houses, and last wills and testaments. The medical needs of the
community grew apace, and it was Winthrop who had to search,
without success, for a regular physician, and who had in the
meantime to fill the role himself.[18]

T H E   E A R L Y New Londoners conceived themselves fortunate in
the possession, as a "physician," of John Winthrop, Jr., and if the
sickroom influence of a vibrant and kindly man is indeed of thera-
peutic value, they were right. As to the beneficent effects of his
remedies, however, one may venture to hesitate. It is true that, in
his emphasis upon chemical specifics, Winthrop stood well to the
fore of the medical thinking of his day, and it is undeniable that
the chemical road to healing has since yielded dramatic results.
Winthrop was furthermore disposed to experiment; though occasionally he resorted to ancient Galenist remedies like wormwood
and anise, his prescriptions more often were compounded of ingredients like saltpeter, antimony, mercury, tartar, copperas, white
vitriol, sulphur, iron, and red coral. We also discover powdered
ivory, rosin, saffron, sassafras, aloes, balsam, and rhubarb—
perhaps a less terrifying complex.[19]
    Winthrop of course must be evaluated in terms of his own time,
not ours. Yet his medical procedures cannot have been generally
very effective. Like his contemporaries, he was aware of neither
microbes nor viruses. Nor was he a proper anatomist. It is questionable if he seriously concerned himself with the most significant
medical idea of his time, the concept of the circulation of the
blood. For all his experimental bent, he persistently sought an all-
purpose nostrum, and in his "rubila powder" he came almost to be-

[169]

lieve he had found one. The fame of this preparation far transcended the limits of New England; it enjoyed the esteem of some of the most respected European practitioners. Of its ingredients we cannot be certain; two centuries later Dr. Oliver Wendell Holmes suggested that it consisted chiefly of diaphoretic antimony and niter in the proportion of 20:4; a little salt of tin may have been added, and there are hints of the presence of powdered "unicorn's" horn. One can imagine yet other horrors. But of its vigorous qualities we may be confident: Rubila was a purgative, one of the most powerful ever administered in the cause of healing. Winthrop himself warned that the normal initial dose of 8 to 10 grains should be greatly reduced in young children, and he advised particular caution in cases of vomiting or flux. A principal disadvantage of rubila was the difficulty experienced in keeping it down; its specific advantages even Winthrop failed to define very explicitly.[20]

But rubila could not contravene the confidence of his patients. This was, after all, the ultimate proof. Winthrop held no doctorate of medicine (nor did many of the physicians of his century); his reputation was of the nonprofessional kind which affords in the long run the best guarantee against deliberate quackery. His practice, conducted always upon terms of the most perfect informality, experienced a prodigious growth. On March 10, 1656/7, he commenced a regular recording of his prescriptions, a habit which he continued, with certain interruptions, until at least the summer of 1669. From it we discover that he treated, over the entire period, at least *700 different individuals,* an astonishing figure when the whole population of New England (which as late as 1675 did not exceed 120,000) is considered. Aside from his possibly unfortunate faith in the Paracelsian method, with its emphasis upon chemical commotion, his procedures reflect an essential good sense, and his correspondence has much to say of the virtues of rest and moderation. Like many another physician, he does not appear to have achieved notable success in healing himself. Nor was the salutary effect of his personality always enough. In the summer of 1653, just as his medical activities were getting seriously under way, he was condemned to watch helplessly at the deathbed of his daughter Mary. She was not yet nine years old; they buried her among the Nameaug ledges beneath two broad stones. "Children are but lent, as all other comforts are," wrote his brother Samuel from St. Christopher's.[21]

B U T H I S children, even when healthy, cannot always have been a satisfaction. Fitz-John was of the "strapping" sort; now in his middle teens, he already was exhibiting the vigorous nonintellectualism which was to mark him the rest of his life. Wait, aged about eleven, was of a more studious nature; beyond any of the others he appears to have inherited his father's peculiar interests.[22] But New London was hardly a place of scholarly inspiration for even the most academically inclined. Therefore—it was probably in 1652—Winthrop packed both of them off to Hartford to study in less distracting surroundings. There they seem to have attended the school kept by Samuel Fitch, but their general supervision was undertaken by Governor John Haynes himself, and it is likely that they boarded with the widow of George Willys. The importance of the change was doubtless a little lost upon the sons, but not upon the father, who for all his worldly tastes was by no means unaware of what paternal responsibilities required in a Puritan society.

Let me only exhort you [he wrote Fitz] to have the feare of God before your eyes continually . . . and remember how pretious tyme is wch passeth irrecoverably. . . . You have the society of such a friend [Haynes?], whose example may be . . . for your good and an incitement to studiousness and virtue. Reade the scriptures daily, and for your other studies they wilbe the easier and delightfuller the more your intentions are fixed upon the same. I desire the Lord to bless you therein, and rest

Your loving father
John Winthrop.[23]

It was a letter such as his own father might have written; it was like few of his own. But no exhortations, godly or mundane, could make a scholar of Fitz, who became, in 1654, one of the first young men to be denied admission to Harvard College on grounds of academic deficiency. Winthrop remained hopeful in the fashion of New England parents and placed the boy in charge of a consumptive Cambridge tutor, Thomas Dudley, Jr. Dudley, who also was Winthrop's nephew, tried to be encouraging; he admitted that Fitz was seriously "behind," but expressed confidence (thoroughly unjustified) in his pupil's industry. Wait's performance was more satisfactory; by September, 1658, he was enrolled at Harvard as fellow commoner and "head" of the class of 1662, and if, for reasons long forgotten, he failed to graduate, Winthrop could hardly in good conscience condemn him.²⁴

In any case, the seventeenth century did not regard a bachelor's degree as an indispensable badge of learning. Winthrop himself was credited with considerable *expertise* in educational matters: In 1654 for all the presumed advantages of Boston and Cambridge, Samuel Symonds placed his son, Harlakenden, in Winthrop's charge at *New London;* between 1657 and 1664, Winthrop assumed general responsibility for the training—this time *not* at New London—of two additional nephews, sons of Samuel Winthrop, the West India planter; and in March, 1657/8, he was approached, in quest of academic preferment, by a Reverend Doctor Thomas Brown (Oxon. and Cantab.), who warranted himself proficient in law, physic, Hebrew, Chaldic, Syriac, Arabic, Greek, Latin, Italian, and French. Nor did Winthrop ever become estranged from Harvard; in 1659, he presented the college library with "many choice books to the vallue of twenty pounds," a conspicuously handsome gift, and by no means his last. Overseas, his reputation as a savant continued undiminished. "Where you are, is too scanty a stage for you to remaine too long upon," wrote Sir Kenelm Digby in the winter of 1654/5—and suggested his early return to England. "*Res augusta domi,* my duty to a numerous family, will not permit it," responded Winthrop. (His American roots were growing.) [25]

E Q U A L L Y undiminished was his ability to attract invitations to settle in neighboring communities. Roger Williams again hoped to see him in Providence; there even was mention of an ironworks there. But as suppliants the town and colony of New Haven were most persistent and came closest to success. New Haven desired him for the usual reasons: prestige, personality, and medical reputation (John Davenport had sought his medical advice as early as 1653). But he was coveted most for his flair for enterprise. And New Haven had need of stimulation. Though founded by men of resource, the plantation had proved an economic disappointment, and the Roundhead triumphs of the forties were inspiring, in the fifties, a debilitating counter-migration to England. Those who remained talked of a fresh start on the banks of the Delaware.[26]

New Haven's solicitations commenced in July, 1654; they rained upon Winthrop with little interruption for more than two years. They offered, free of expense, a proper residence; they undertook to perform the irksome chores of moving; they even promised a "cleanly and saving maid servant." New Haven was of course aware of the competitive bidding of Hartford and moved to vigorous counteraction. "It is thought," wrote the Reverend Mr. Davenport in April, 1655, "that [Hartford's] aire is infected." [27]

Winthrop disliked to reject other men's appeals. Yet there were good reasons why he should remain where he was. New London, if not precisely flourishing, was growing: Its commerce was sufficient, by 1654, to justify the appointment of a Connecticut customs officer and, the following year, of a full-time innkeeper. Winthrop furthermore was at the moment deeply absorbed in a design for the extraction of salt from the tropical shallows of Barbados, a venture which he hoped would enjoy an assured market and at the same time afford steady employment to his nonscholarly eldest son. It was therefore understandable that he should soothe New Haven with genial half-promises and that the ultimate deciding factor should be an exceptional prospect for another ironworks.[28]

New Haven Colony possessed, if nothing else, bogs. The yield of an unrecognized glaciation, they were among the most extensive in southern New England. Such bogs indicated iron. Neither New London nor the Connecticut River towns quite afforded their equal, a fact which New Haven was not slow to emphasize. Early in March, 1654/5, Winthrop paid a medical call upon Mrs. John Higginson [29] of Guilford (the lady was a daughter of the Reverend Henry Whitfield, builder of the great stone house), and he typically improved the occasion with a critical survey of the neighborhood. The bogs which he encountered were enough to touch off another of his enthusiasms, and at New Haven, on the sixteenth, he nearly committed himself on the spot. In any case, the principal citizens, men like Theophilus Eaton and Stephen Goodyear, still London-perfect in the exaggeration of business opportunity, were careful not to let him depart without concluding certain informalities. Back at New London, Winthrop scratched off glowing memoranda, and in November the New Haven town meeting indicated its willingness to proceed to the necessary subsidies. "Many hands are daily at worke for the iron busines," wrote Davenport to Winthrop on the twenty-second, "Onely your presence is wanting, to sett al things in a right course." Winthrop nevertheless continued to hesitate, and an additional year of solicitation was required before he could be induced to quit a stunned New London in favor of New Haven.[30]

The change, when it came, seemed permanent. Winthrop declined the proffer of a free residence, and the town presently sold him one—in terms of goats, f.o.b., Fishers Island. It was a considerable property; it included not only a dwelling—one of the finest

Winthrop's America

Scale of Miles
0 10 20 30 40 50

in the community and immediately adjacent to the manse of the Reverend Mr. Davenport—but also 267¼ acres of land outside the village. In the beginning, the ironworks promised much: The inevitable company, of which Davenport, Theophilus Eaton, Stephen Goodyear, Jasper Crane, and Winthrop held the principal shares, was organized as early as February, 1655/6; by the spring of 1657, a primitive furnace already was undergoing trial runs, while encouraging inquiries after its product were being received from the Bay. New Haven itself was a place of some distinction; certain of its houses were, by American standards, pretentious; many of them (though not Winthrop's) faced upon a spacious green, in the center of which rose one of the most elaborate meeting houses in New England, 50 feet square, with a tower, a turret, and casement windows aglitter with leaded panes. Save for its rectilinear pattern and wooden construction, New Haven resembled an Old World village of pleasant maturity. Certainly it surpassed New London; both Winthrop and—especially—Elizabeth were openly impressed.[31]

Yet, when all was said and done, New Haven did not afford a suitable environment for John Winthrop, Jr. Of all the New England plantations, it was the most uncompromising in its everyday Calvinsim. Its Sabbath was a weekly ordeal; not only were there the usual restrictions upon labor and travel, prohibited also were cooking, bedmaking, shaving, and the kissing of one's own children. Forbidden at *any* time were cardplaying, the celebration of Christmas or saints' days, minced pies, dancing, or the playing of musical instruments, the drum, trumpet, and jew's harp (!) excepted. There was a profound and unhealthy concern with sexual matters, in particular the lapses of others, and any misconduct was investigated, and officially set down, in such detail that a number of the seventeenth-century records of New Haven have yet to see twentieth-century print.[32]

Winthrop must have been well aware of these things, and even after he had ensconced himself beside Mr. Davenport, he appears to have maintained his private reservations as to this particular community. There is no indication that he ever was made a "freeman" of New Haven, town or colony, nor is there anywhere to be found that most solemn proof of a change of residence, a transfer of Church membership. Throughout he continued comfortable in the knowledge of practicable alternatives. New London was piteous in its appeals for his return and generous with hints of the early completion of his stone house. He could recall the proposals of Roger Williams, of Director Stuyvesant, and of Hartford. Moreover, the prospects of the New Haven ironworks soon began to pale. No genuine output was achieved that year, nor would be before 1663. Goodyear journeyed to England, doubtless in quest of capital, but died shortly after his arrival there. Save for goats and real estate, Winthrop himself was as good as insolvent, and another vague and complicated West Indian speculation, from which he had hoped to derive an overseas balance, came to naught, thanks apparently to the depredations of privateers.[33]

No doubt New Haven imagined it possessed him for good when in the spring of 1657 he chose not to attend the Connecticut Court of Elections. Perhaps he himself considered his political relations there had come properly to an end. But neither he nor New Haven sufficiently reckoned with the Connecticut urge to keep him. On May 21 the Hartford court chose Winthrop governor of Connecticut Colony and directed its secretary, Captain John Cullick, "to write a letter to Mr. Winthrop, as speedily as may bee, to acquaint him to what place the country hath chosen him, & to desire his present assistance as much as may be." [34]

It was a political masterstroke. At whose suggestion it was undertaken, no one can say. But its results were quickly obvious. Winthrop was gained for Hartford, saved for New London, and secured in perpetuity for Connecticut. For New Haven, the town, it meant the loss of its most popular resident. For New Haven, the colony, it would one day mean no less than the loss of its separate existence.

CHAPTER 13

His Worship, the Governor

THE highest political office in the gift of a seventeenth-century New England colony was the governorship, and John Winthrop, Jr., was probably the most accomplished politician in all that half-defined little Puritan world. Yet he received the call from Hartford without enthusiasm. The Connecticut magistrates were obliged to extend their invitation again, and yet again; they suggested housing and transportation at public expense, and in August a select committee was appointed "to treat" with Winthrop in person. Despite all this, the court sessions, general and particular, of half the gubernatorial year were conducted by the deputy governor, Mr. Thomas Welles.[1]

It was nevertheless inevitable that he should accept. His political coquetries were seldom intended seriously; one may venture to speculate why he troubled to engage in them at all. Winthrop performed the duties of governor of Connecticut for the first time on Thursday, December 3, 1657, when he presided over a regular meeting of the Hartford "Quarter Court." Beside him in the dim little meetinghouse sat Deputy Governor Welles and four of the assistants—John Webster, John Cullick, young Samuel Willys (just four years out of Harvard), and the elder John Talcott, Hartford men all, save Welles, who was of Wethersfield. Before him a self-conscious jury disposed of a calendar of minor civil actions. The proceedings were as uninspiring and, let us hope, as brief as the December afternoon. It was hardly a brilliant beginning, yet it certified to his commitment; Winthrop absented himself from no further sessions during the remainder of his term.[2]

New Haven was disconsolate—and a little angry. No one, except for Mrs. Davenport, offered to help him wind up his affairs. When he sought to sell his share in the ironworks, no one would touch it, and Winthrop was driven to lease his portion to William Payne and Thomas Clarke, Boston entrepreneurs with an appetite for ironmongery. (New Haven learned of this arrangement with unconcealed dismay; the town dreaded—with excellent reason—the class of laborers the Bostonians might bring with them.) Winthrop found the disposal of his house equally awkward, and the place was eventually rented, with unfortunate consequences to its maintenance, to nonentities. This lack of market was doubtless contrived; the town in fact hoped to use the house as bait to bring the Winthrops back. It was known that Elizabeth Winthrop preferred New Haven to all her other New England abodes, and when, more than two years later, the house at last was sold, she openly lamented "that they could not accommodate matters so that they might live in New Haven." [3]

Though Hartford could congratulate itself, it soon became obvious that Winthrop came as a public person only. Part of the victory was New London's, of which he would always remain a legal resident, and through the long remainder of his official life he made no effort to fix his private seat at Hartford.[4] He accepted without protest, as proper to his office, the comparatively sumptuous housing the colony was able to provide. He appears in the beginning to have occupied the former dwelling of John Haynes, one of the handsomest in the village, facing upon two principal streets and convenient to the meetinghouse yard, yet open to a pleasant outlook across the river meadows. Immediately to the south, a little tributary slipped quietly toward the Connecticut; beyond it, a rise of land bore irregular rows of houses and a conspicuous white oak. The Haynes property moreover included nearly 200 outlying acres, of which the income was presumably the governor's. Winthrop seems to have enjoyed these considerable perquisites for more than two years. In the spring of 1660, the executive residence was transferred to the house of Elder William Goodwin, which must also have been of a superior sort; it stood close to the Haynes manse upon a site of equal dignity.[5]

Winthrop moved his wife and five daughters to Hartford late in the autumn of 1657. Wait remained at Harvard; the unscholarly Fitz recently had sailed, in a restless mood, for England. Hartford was in the grip of an epidemic of measles, with which the girls promptly came down; Betty, now twenty-one years of age, very nearly succumbed.[6] Of the first months of Winthrop's administration, comparatively little is known. Much of Connecticut's daily public business was simply not recorded, and Winthrop's personal disinclination to keep a diary continued pronounced. A surviving letter of March 2 to Petrus Stuyvesant is humdrum, and a Particular (that is, Quarter) Court of March 4 was devoted to such problems as the identification of a sow and the "inhumane cariage" of one John Brookes toward his wife. Yet Connecticut was distracted by major worries. Winthrop arrived in Hartford to find the local church riven by the sort of obscurantist dispute which only a Puritan community could take very seriously. It was a dismal affair, which even so dedicated a theologian as Cotton Mather later admitted was almost as indefinable as the sources of the Connecticut River.[7] It was calculated to irritate a man like Winthrop, yet religious questions were, in a Puritan colony, public questions also, and Winthrop was now Connecticut's principal public officer. Hence we discover him—on a day not precisely known, but probably in December, 1657—serving as moderator to an unofficial ecclesiastical "debate," the spirit of which grew "exceeding high and deeply engaged." The General Court of March 24, 1657/8, the first over which he presided as governor, desired him to make additional efforts at mediation, and the dispute came to public attention at least four times in the course of the succeeding political year (during which he was deputy governor). On June 15, 1659 (again as governor) he presided over a last attempt to discover a formula. But all that could be achieved was an appeal to external authority, in particular the clergy of Massachusetts Bay, and the the Hartford Church divided irretrievably before the end of 1659. Its dissident party departed self-righteously for Hadley, Massachusetts.[8]

A special incident of his initial governorship was a judicial process against the wife of Joshua Garlick of Easthampton, Long Island, on charges of witchcraft. It appears to have been the first occasion upon which Winthrop, as a responsible magistrate, had anything to do with a case of this kind. There also were political nuances: Easthampton had formally accepted the jurisdiction of Connecticut on May 3, 1658, while Mrs. Garlick's trial was held at Hartford only two days later. The indictment charged "familliarity with Sathan," the "losse of lives of sevrall persons (with sevrall other sorceries)," and declared that Mrs. Garlick deserved to die. On the bench sat the usual Hartford magistrates—Winthrop, Welles, Webster, Willys, and Talcott—and prominent upon the jury were Matthew Allyn and Nathaniel Warde. We do not know that the verdict was influenced by instructions from the bench, but Winthrop likely was relieved when the jurors found the prisoner not guilty. However, the woman's husband was required to post bond for her good behavior, which would indicate that she was, if not a witch, an unpleasant neighbor.[9]

It is difficult to evaluate Winthrop's personal attitude toward sorcery. His own son, Wait, by no means denied its existence upon a later and more famous occasion, while Winthrop's Connecticut was, in the middle of the seventeenth century, repeatedly bemused with it. He himself had been profoundly interested in the occult, especially as it related to alchemy. Yet, from all that is known of John Winthrop, Jr., it is not illogical to suggest that he did not subscribe to the reality of witchcraft in his heart. Moreover, when the peak of the hysteria came to Connecticut in 1662, he was involved in a far more significant service to the colony, 3,000 miles distant.[10]

By the terms of the Fundamental Orders of 1639, Winthrop could not succeed himself as governor. However, he had given such satisfaction that he was chosen deputy governor, without a recorded contest, on May 20, 1658. He seems not even to have moved from his gubernatorial quarters; this was in fact unnecessary, as his successor, Thomas Welles, dwelt close at hand at Wethersfield. It was also rather fortunate. A discouraging Connecticut spring, with "frequent rains and other seasons," refused that year to yield to the usual delights of June; all summer the skies continued leaden and the ground wet, wreaking havoc with the harvest and—it was believed—spreading disease, either the original measles or its complications. Both Winthrop and his wife fell ill, the latter rather desperately so; Winthrop's correspondence grew heavy with death notices; and Hartford ordered that Thursday, September 8, be observed as a day of "solemne humiliation." Yet normal living did not quite come to a halt. There was no question of a quarantine. Nor was there any suspension of public business; the Connecticut courts, Particular and General, continued to assemble, and it is indicative that Winthrop continued faithfully to attend.[11]

P ERHAPS this devotion to duty was not wholly disinterested. At least one current issue struck rather close to home. Subsequent to Winthrop's removal to New Haven, the entire Pequot region had experienced a violent falling out, chiefly political but with an accompanying religious quarrel which produced the resignation of

Mr. Blinman. Early in 1657, the residents of the easterly regions of New London had expressed, in town meeting, a desire to establish a separate corporation of their own. A party from the older and more westerly districts rose in opposition, and the dispute was carried before the Connecticut General Court. This was not at all to the taste of the secessionists, who at once sought a town charter from Massachusetts. The Bay responded with caution, but the old question of jurisdiction over the Pequot country had nevertheless been reopened. Meanwhile, pending a final disposition of the problem, the disaffected inhabitants organized themselves into a semiautonomous body called the "Asotiation of Poquatuck Peple." [12]

Direct correspondence between Hartford and Boston quite failed to produce an accommodation. At last, in a letter of August 8, 1658, the Connecticut magistrates invoked (with the assent of Massachusetts) the Articles of Confederation and appealed to the commissioners of the United Colonies. [13]

This brought the dispute still more intimately to Winthrop's attention. He had been elected, in May, not only deputy governor but also, with John Talcott, a United Colonies commissioner. Winthrop left Hartford, probably in Talcott's company, about August 26; the annual meeting of the United Colonies got under way in the handsome new town house at Boston on September 2. It was the first which Winthrop attended in an official capacity. For the Bay, and in opposition to the claims of Connecticut, sat his former colleagues of the Massachusetts council, John Endecott and Simon Bradstreet; neither, he knew, would be an ineffective advocate. For Plymouth and New Haven, and therefore in judgment, sat, respectively, Thomas Prince and Josiah Winslow, and Francis Newman and William Leete; men of political seasoning, save possibly the youthful Winslow, whose reputation was as yet chiefly military. Winthrop would one day come to know—and to respect —Leete the best. [14]

The commissioners of the United Colonies were of a distinctly deliberative habit, and the decision of the Plymouth and New Haven commissioners was not handed down until September 16: The "Pequot country" they defined as extending from "Nianticke to a place called Wecopaug"; it was of such a size, they felt, as might "conveniently accomodate two plantations." For this reason, and because they were "tender of any Inconvenency or Disturbance," they drew a line up the Mystic River "soe farr as the Pond by lawthorn [Lantern] hill and thence from the middle of the said pond to run away upon a North line." The territory to the east of this boundary would belong to Massachusetts, to the west, to Connecticut. Such a partition of the "melon" could hardly be rationalized into a victory for Connecticut; the pressures of the moment had clearly prevailed against the best that Winthrop could offer. Massachusetts at once incorporated the "Asotiation of Poquatuck Peple" into the town of Southertown. Understandably, Connecticut was in no mood to accept the decision as permanent. An attempt to raise the question again the following year came to nothing, but the final issue, in 1664, was to be Connecticut's and—in a special sense—Winthrop's own.[15]

Last, but not least, upon the commissioners' agenda of 1658 was the question which had been posed by the initial appearance in New England of the Society of Friends. The reception accorded these first "Quakers" had been various, but almost everywhere hostile. In the beginning, Massachusetts feared they might be witches and subjected them to a peculiarly inhumane confinement, followed by deportation. New Haven decreed banishment, branding, and (upon a fourth offense) a boring through of the tongue with a hot iron. Connecticut, less intense in such things, simply forbade their entry and fined those who gave them "unnecessary entertainment"; heavier penalties were left to local discretion. Even in Rhode Island, the Quakers were not universally popular.[16]

The difficulty with the pioneer Friends was their hunger for martyrdom. No one in New England was really disposed to do other than expel them, yet they stubbornly persisted in returning. By 1658, they were reckoned a regional menace and a fit subject for action by the United Colonies. The response of the commissioners was, within the context of the New England Way, eminently reasonable. On September 23, they adopted an "Act," recommending to the general courts of the member colonies the adoption of a standard procedure which first would banish, second would maim and banish, and, upon a third return, put the culprit to death. To this all the commissioners put their signatures without qualification—all except Winthrop. He signed indeed, but with the stipulation that he considered the document "a query and not an Act." [17]

In the whole record of John Winthrop, Jr., there is nothing more revealing than this. Nowhere is there a better example of his special kind of behavior in a sticky situation. He could see little merit in the imposition, upon religious grounds, of such disabilities, yet he understood that his point of view could not possibly prevail. Hence this faintest suggestion of disapproval, without rancor or offense to public sensibilities—and without prejudice to his own public future. Once again, there are those who might prefer that he had assumed an open, unequivocal, and utterly impractical, position. Such behavior is for proselyters, not politicians, and Winthrop, in matters of religion, was not the proselyting kind.

Though the Friends were aware of his delicate role, they never ceased, in their quiet but relentless way, to urge him to an avowal of religious toleration.[18] A particular gadfly was the eccentric William Coddington, who laid Winthrop under a periodic bombardment of Quaker literature. Winthrop endured it politely for more than a decade, but at last, in 1672, he could bear it no longer. An especially heavy salvo of tracts, enclosed in a letter which heaped abuse upon the religious practices of Connecticut, produced what nothing else had ever achieved, a statement, from Winthrop, of his private religious position. He stood, he wrote Coddington, "in the firme beliefe of those truths of the holy Scriptures, which are not of any private interpretation, as that knowne place, of the epistle of the Apostle Peter, mentioneth, but holy men spake, as they were indeed by the holy Ghost," and he commended a reference to Hebrews 1:1–2.[19] It was an adequate, though hardly eloquent, assertion of orthodoxy. But there was another, and better minted, side to the coin. If his personal religious commitment remained uninspiredly regular, if he could see no early future—officially, in Connecticut—for the kind of tolerance which came to him so easily, these did not mean he could not practice it in private. "[I should like to] . . . returne yu thancks for the many civillities I received from yu when I was in New England," wrote the Barbadan Quaker Constant Sylvester, in 1659. Roger Williams, who personally disliked the Friends, commended Winthrop for his "prudent and moderate" attitude toward them. We furthermore are assured that, in 1660, he entertained, "with a loving respect," an associate of the unfortunate Mary Dyer.[20] Finally, among his papers, in his own handwriting, we discover the following:

The Synods at Savoy determination about withdrawing

Although the magistrate is bound to encourage, promote & protect the professor & profession of the Gospell & to manage & order civill administration in due subservience to the interest of Christ in the World . . . ; yet in such differences about the doctrines of the Gospell, or Waies of the worship of God, as may befall men exercising a good concience, manifesting it in their conversation, & holding the foundation, not disturbing others in their way or worship that differ from them, there is no warrant for the magistrate under the Gospell to abridge them of their liberty.[21]

The Synod of Savoy (October, 1658) expressed the advanced viewpoint of the English "Independents" of the late interregnum. The date of Winthrop's transcription is unknown.

HIS PUBLIC visits to the Bay were seldom without their private aspects, and he attended the United Colonies sessions of 1658 with a head full of family problems. One of these was the welfare of Fitz, who seemed to be encountering too much success for his own good. He had stepped, in Britain, into the very midst of the right people. His stepgrandfather, Hugh Peter, occupied sumptuous apartments within Whitehall itself. His uncle Stephen Winthrop boasted an impressive military reputation (on the winning side) and had married "well"; though near death from a respiratory ailment, the skeins of his influence ran far. Moreover, Fitz's maternal uncle Colonel Thomas Reade was governor of Stirling Castle in Scotland, and family rumors indicated an early lieutenant's commission there.[22] Such prospects were encouraging, yet they inspired John Winthrop, Jr., to another of his rare exhortations to virtuous living. "Be careful to avoid all evill and vaine company," he wrote Fitz on September 9. "Be not drawne . . . into tavernes or alehouses or any houses of company of evill fame. I have often forwarned . . . you against wine and strong drinke, which if it were only for your health, you should carefully shun . . . ; It never agreeth with the constitution and lungs of any of our family." [23]

But Fitz was not the greatest of his worries. His eldest child, Elizabeth—still called "Betty" within the family—had for some time been courted by a young clergyman, the Reverend Antipas Newman, who had been called, under conditions of controversy and without formal ordination, to a pulpit at Wenham, Massachusetts. The initial reactions of the Winthrops were not entirely happy; they ranged from sympathetic (Mrs. Winthrop), through cautious (Betty herself), to violent antipathy (which was the feeling of Fitz and Wait). The grounds for opposition were clearly snobbish and financial, and they seem to have been dissipated, so far as Winthrop was concerned, when Newman acquired "a very convenient house." He talked Wait into acquiescence, wrote comfortable words to Fitz, and made arrangements to convey his land at "Salthouse Point," near Salem, as a dowry. Even so, Wait wrote

to his brother in September, 1659, that Newman was "far in-
ferioure" to their sister, and there is evidence that Fitz nursed sore
feelings as late as the summer of 1661.[24]

Affairs of this nature took up much time. The commissioners
concluded their sessions of 1658 on September 23, but Winthrop
did not reappear in Hartford—soaked by uninterrupted days of
rain—until the evening of November 1. It is unlikely that he or
his wife witnessed Betty's marriage to Mr. Newman, which took
place at Wenham ten days later; weddings were not yet, in that
Puritan world, occasions for the gathering of families. But everything issued, by contemporary standards, happily enough. Mr.
Newman acquired, in his pulpit, an unexceptionable reputation
and, by his wife, six children, of whom only one seems to have
died in infancy.[25]

JOHN WINTHROP, Jr., was now nearly fifty-three years of age.
His wonderful vigor had scarcely declined, yet time had distilled
out of him some of the old tendency to distraction, and he was steadily and, on the whole, easily coming to terms with his destiny. That
it was before all else political he himself must have realized. He of
course would never lose his magnificent curiosity; and his interest
in natural phenomena, if anything, increased. But his enthusiasm
for enterprise had become less pronounced. There would be no
further new plantations. He retained his connections with Tantiusque and the New Haven ironworks, but at a distance; already
William Payne had written to express "wonder you should soe
much necklect youer owne bisnes." [26]

Connecticut was still a colony of secondary consequence. As late
as 1660, only eight of its towns saw fit to furnish the data for their
taxable property, and the sum of the figures received totaled less
than £75,000—"country" currency. Nevertheless the administration of its government demanded talents of a superior order. Connecticut's affairs, if not yet authentically great, were growing stead-

ily more complicated. They were by no means confined to the maintenance of ordinary good order, though the General Court contrived, in the Puritan manner, to expend much time upon such matters. Most disruptive of the public peace, however, were the questions—technical, theological, and (one suspects) personal—which continued to shake the religious structure. In the background, there loomed by this time the awkward question of the Half-Way Covenant, that is, whether baptism should be permitted the children of those who, though baptized themselves, had not been received as Church members. There also were clusters of special difficulties: Injured sensibilities lingered on at Hartford, where John Cotton, Jr., "supplied" in 1659 and gave such offense that a private vision, followed by a public apology, was found advisable. The disposition to schism spread to Wethersfield, where the pastor, the Reverend John Russell, and a principal layman and politician, "Lieutenant" John Hollister, fell into a savage quarrel, which led presently to Hollister's excommunication and ultimately to the removal of a large part of the congregation to Hadley, Massachusetts. Such disorders were still deemed public questions and inevitably involved Winthrop. But, much as he stretched forth the arm of conciliation, it proved next to impossible to still this kind of troubled water. He did preserve his own equanimity, and the letters which he sent off to the discomfited friends of Mr. Cotton were models of tact.[27]

His theological perplexities were only the worst; the current concerns of state exhibited a marvelous multiformity. In the summer of 1659 appeared David, Connecticut's pioneer Jew, whose techniques of barter drew from the General Court a fine of 20 shillings. Sharper still was the behavior of Captain John Penny, an Anglo-Saxon of Barbados, who undertook in the autumn of 1659 to disrupt the Anglo-Dutch commerce of Long Island Sound; the mollification of his victims required weeks of correspondence between New Amsterdam, New Haven, and Hartford. Uncouth collisions between certain Indians upon the lower Connecticut spread to Pequot River and led to further "troublesome businesse" before the United Colonies. Yet Connecticut continued to develop; 1659 witnessed the beginnings, as Connecticut towns, of Norwich and, on Long Island, of Setauket (later called Brookhaven).[28]

That Winthrop did not renounce such intricacies in favor of another personal enterprise was a measure of his final maturity. (He did think nostalgically of England.)[29] He absented himself but little from Hartford, and his attention to public affairs continued commendably regular. When, at the elections court of May 19, 1659, he was raised again to the governorship, he seems not to have protested. Neither did he demur when chosen a United Colonies commissioner as well.[30]

Nor was this all. On January 14, 1659/60, there died at Wethersfield Mr. Thomas Welles, deputy governor and governor-apparent for 1660—"very suddainly, being very well at supper and dead before midnight," wrote Winthrop to his son at Cambridge. This of course broke the normal reciprocal sequence—and inspired Connecticut to extraordinary action. On April 11, 1660, the General Court, gathered under Winthrop's presidency, "thought meet to propound" whether the existing limitation (Article 4 of the Fundamental Orders) upon the gubernatorial succession ought not be lifted, and Secretary Daniel Clark was instructed to include the question in the regular warrants sent out in preparation for the next elections court, due to assemble on the nineteenth of May.[31]

The court met as planned. Both magistrates and deputies, without observable opposition, voiced approval of the change. Immediately thereafter—again without observable disapproval—they re-elected John Winthrop, Jr., governor of Connecticut. It is possible that they already intended that the office should be his, literally, for life. They referred to him as "worshipful" and voted him an additional annual salary of £80.[32]

Winthrop himself may not have witnessed this ultimate political tribute; he recently had been stricken with an alarming illness, from which he recovered very slowly.[33] But it would appear that he voiced no objections. From his sickroom he wrote to his brother Samuel on May 24 that though he preferred the seaside and his "accomodation & cattle about N. Lond:," nevertheless, "Providence & a call of God & the desire of the people have detained me heere [Hartford] some years and at present." [34]

The present was to occupy most of his future.

CHAPTER 14

Backgrounds for Crises

THUS Winthrop had found his vocation, which was high public service in a frontier community.

He doubtless was relieved to discover that his regimen did not demand too rigorous a self-discipline. He was not obliged to abandon his remarkable avocations. Courts, schisms, and Indian alarms seldom would deny him sufficient leisure for the speculations and experiments of which he was so fond, and he usually could continue that most fortunate of beings—a perceptive seventeenth-century man, able, without the obfuscation of overwhelming data—to marvel intelligently upon a fascinating world.

Winthrop, in fact, was never more prolific with "scientific" undertakings as in the years of his heaviest public responsibilities. A surviving correspondence with Samuel Hartlib, carried on between 1659 and 1661, reveals a remarkable virtuosity; included are not only the inevitable alchemy and, especially, medicine but also astronomy, physics, and a surprisingly imaginative approach to political economy. Of particular interest was his possession of an astronomical telescope, *10 feet* in focal length; though its performance seems to have left something to be desired, it was probably the first such instrument to be used in English North America.[1] Hartlib was a perfect foil for Winthrop; he was acquainted with practically every savant in Europe and made it his business to keep abreast of the latest "philosophical" developments. He apprised Winthrop of the activities of the renowned—men like Comenius, Glauber, Morian, Digby, and Johann Sibert Kuffler—and placed him in touch with interesting new personalities, including Dr. Benjamin Worsley and the youthful William Brereton.[2] He furthermore supplied, apparently gratis, large quantities of recent literature, both printed and in manuscript.

Winthrop was profoundly grateful. His replies were as prompt as conditions permitted, and he attempted to reward Hartlib with advice as to the treatment of a stubborn case of the stone. (Except for the "powder of sea-horse pissle," his recommendations—mineral waters and a careful diet—have a modern ring.) Of his other comments two deserve special notice, not so much for their scientific consequence as for what they reveal of Winthrop himself. "I wish," he wrote Hartlib in August of 1660, "you could prevaile with Dr. Keffler [*sic*] to bury that fireworke [a crude submarine mine] in oblivion. . . . There are meanes ynough knowne to the world of ruin and destruction to mankind both by sea and land." He deplored equally the experiments which Hartlib himself was conducting upon a perpetual motion machine—on the ground that such a device would be abused by the rich by depriving the poor of gainful employment. "Rich men commonly reape the benefits of invention to make them more rich, and the poore yet more miserable and uncomfortable," he observed. Though it would be too much to proclaim him North America's first Marxist, Winthrop had in fact acquired certain of the classic attitudes of an economic liberal in an underdeveloped environment. For one thing, he little doubted the virtue of cheap money. In a letter to Hartlib in the spring of 1661, he commented with approval upon a "book of a Banke," issued by William Potter, of which the central thesis was a currency based upon land. However, Winthrop felt this did not go far enough and suggested, with a startling instinct for the future, a monetary system which should operate without any standard at all. Nor did he confine this idea, or his interest in Potter, to a single letter.[3]

That Winthrop should adopt the favorite panacea of the insolvent is hardly surprising: He remained close to insolvency himself. By the spring of 1660, his New London interests had fallen into a deplorable state; a difficult winter was partly to blame, and so was his absence in Hartford, but the worst problem was the eternal deficiency in suitable manpower. Winthrop did possess an indentured servant or two and also (on terms unspecified) one "neger." But an incompetent young laborer had seriously damaged the equipment of his sawmill; on Fishers Island his horses roamed unbroken and unbranded; while his great stone house on Nameaug had shown little progress since 1654. Winthrop's overseer, John Tinker, was not inefficient, but was prone to discouragement and spoke guardedly of throwing up his position in favor of operating a tavern—which, the year following, he did. Elaborate speculations in sugar, conducted in association (at the Bay) with his brother Deane and (in the West Indies) with his brother Samuel, began badly, continued worse, and yielded, over a period of twelve years, little or nothing. It may have been simple financial pressure which led him to dispose, on March 13, 1660/1, of much of his residential land at New London. He talked also of the sale, at the Bay, of Ten Hills. There even were times when he seemed to lose his appetite for America. "We are heere as men dead to the world in this wildernesse," he wrote Hartlib in December of 1659.[4]

Yet Winthrop's naturally sanguine nature guaranteed a swift recovery from this sort of depression. The appearance at New London of an actual ocean-going vessel inspired him to issue a memoir upon its commercial advantages that would have done credit to a twentieth-century chamber of commerce.[5] If he was driven to dispose of real estate, it was at this very period that he became involved in the most momentous—for himself and Connecticut—of any of his land speculations.

T H E A N N A L S of the so-called Atherton Land Company [6] are of extraordinary length and complexity; they far transcend the years of John-Winthrop, Jr., and penetrate deep into the following century. Its beginnings were not unusual; it was a scheme of land engrossment, to be carried out at the only slightly concealed expense of other interests, both English and aboriginal. The exact circumstances of the company's birth are obscure, but it is clear that the principal father of the enterprise was Winthrop's Boston agent, the ubiquitous Amos Richardson, and that the original participants numbered seven: Richardson, Winthrop, Major Humphrey Atherton, Richard Smith, Sr., Richard Smith, Jr., Lt. William Hudson, and John Tinker. It was a curious group. Atherton, whose interest in the undertaking grew so deep that it came presently to bear his name, was a leading resident of Dorchester, Massachusetts, and major general of the Bay militia; though gifted in the arts of political and financial manipulation, he seems not to have been personally very likable, and his accidental death in 1661 was proclaimed "a judgment." The Smiths, senior and junior, operated, free of the effective control of any authority, a well-known trading house on the western shore of Narragansett Bay. Lt. William Hudson was of Boston and also of considerable military repute (he had seen much active service overseas in the parliamentary army). In an early listing of the partners, the name of John Winthrop, Jr., led all the rest, but it is obvious that he contemplated no active role. The flavor of Massachusetts Bay was of course apparent.[7]

It is necessary to consider the motives which impelled Winthrop, at a time of great personal stringency, to commit himself to such an enterprise. That Richardson (and, by implication, Atherton) had his eye upon the Narragansett country he must have known; Richardson's initial acquisitions, derived from a convenient Indian early in the summer of 1659, embraced much of the western littoral of Narragansett Bay, and Winthrop received a description of the tract before the end of July. He must also have been aware that the purchase was scarcely consistent with the sovereignty of Rhode Island, as per its charter of 1643/4, and that it violated a recent statute, of that colony, prohibiting the alienation of Indian land within its jurisdiction without the express authority of its General Court. But if he sought to use the company as a means to abet the eastward aspirations of Connecticut, there is no positive proof of it, and his later disposition to compromise the matter suggests that he did not subscribe to such a policy without reservations.[8]

Rhode Island's reaction was swift. From Portsmouth there came at the end of August an official protest, addressed to the commissioners of the United Colonies, whose annual meeting was expected at Hartford within a week. The Rhode Islanders received little satisfaction: The reply of the commissioners was meaningless, while Winthrop, as governor of Connecticut, appears to have offered no comment whatever.[9] Moreover, there gathered at Boston, on November 4, a significant conclave of the "Atherton" proprietors which Winthrop is known to have attended and which arranged for the subdivision of the lands already claimed. Provision also was made for the inclusion of additional partners, and Edward Hutchinson, at whose house the meeting was held, was formally admitted into the company.[10]

This was by no means the end of it. A "troublesome businesse" had sprung from the misbehavior of the Niantic Indians (a branch of the Narragansets whose sachem was Ninigret); they had engaged in an extralegitimate foray upon Uncas's Mohegans and had slain in the process a native servant of Jonathan Brewster— "at Mistris Brewster's feet, to her great affrightment." This perpetration was compounded in the spring of 1660 by another misdemeanor—the peppering, with eight or more bullets, of a house at the new English plantation of Mohegan, allegedly for the purpose of killing Major John Mason.[11] It was exactly the sort of conduct to which the English refused to become accustomed, and Connecticut did not hesitate to express its official indignation—first to the United Colonies meeting of 1659 (which effected little or nothing) and second to the several commissioners in a formal letter, dated June 11, 1660, which broadly hinted that Connecticut might not help the other United Colonies members with their Indian difficulties in the future unless something positive was done. Winthrop's approval of this latter communication may be assumed.[12]

There is nothing to indicate who first recognized the possibility of translating the punishment of the Narragansets into the aggrandizement of the Atherton Company, but the techniques employed are plain enough. The United Colonies meeting for 1660 was held at New Haven from September 6 through 17; Winthrop himself attended as commissioner from Connecticut, and this time the "troublesome businesse" produced more than talk. The commissioners agreed "to require and force the Narragansets to a just satisfaction" and appointed a special group of representatives to demand of Ninigret and other appropriate sachems either the delivery of the Indians responsible or 595 fathoms of wampum.[13] The representatives (Captain George Denison, Thomas Minor, and the trader-linguist Thomas Stanton) confronted the Indians before the month was out. As might have been expected, the natives could produce neither the culprits nor—at once—the wampum, and on September 29, *in the presence of Richard Smith, Sr.,* Ninigret and two associate sachems pledged "all our whole country" as a guarantee of payment of the fine within four months. (A copy of this mortgage, *in Winthrop's handwriting,* survives.) [14]

Thereafter the plot thickened rapidly. Acting not only for himself but in the name of eighteen additional associates, including

Winthrop, Humphrey Atherton concluded on October 13 an agreement with the Indians whereby his land company undertook to furnish the wampum at once—in return for the mortgage. Foreclosure could be ordered if the Narragansets failed to make good within six months. Moreover the cost of the "loan" was manipulated upward by the addition of a service fee of 140 fathoms—this to defray "the charges of divers messengers and others employed in reference to the same." On November 16, the whole 735 fathoms were received by Winthrop in behalf of the United Colonies from the hands of Captain Edward Hutchinson. Though questions of ultimate jurisdiction remained conspicuously unresolved, the entire southwesterly quarter of modern Rhode Island appeared effectively to have been bagged for the Atherton interests. It was a procedure such as would be repeated, with variations, across the continent. It long would disturb the peace, not only of the Narraganset Indians but of Massachusetts Bay, Rhode Island, Connecticut, the officers of the Crown, and John Winthrop, Jr.[15]

D o w n f r o m the Scottish border hills there marched in the winter of 1659/60 Fitz-John Winthrop, captain-lieutenant in Colonel Thomas Reade's regiment of foot, a principal unit of the forces of General George Monck. Fitz had served with some distinction; a few weeks before, there had been a promotion.[16] Now he was swinging southward into the political vacuum which had been left in England by the death of the great Protector and the fall of his incapable heir. It was a march of much consequence—for England, which it would leave a realm again, and for New England, whose ability to enjoy an undisturbed political privacy would never be thereafter quite the same.

Hints of the restoration of King Charles II already were reaching America. A letter to John Winthrop, Jr., from a "Capt. Peverel," dated November 8, 1659, spoke of administrative chaos and hinted that General Monck was at heart a Royalist.[17] In the course of the following summer, Winthrop received a long and remarkable communication from John Maidstone, Jr., a distant collateral relative and former intimate of Oliver Cromwell; it presented an intelligent critique, from the Roundhead viewpoint, of the Civil Wars and their aftermath, but ended upon a note of desperation: "I entreat your advice, by the next opportunity . . . what encouragement persons may have, if times press them, to transport their families into New England." [18] Other shreds of rumor followed, especially by way of New Haven, where the Reverend Mr. Davenport still clung to the hope that Old England might continue "godly." Winthrop, significantly, was most immediately concerned with the possibility of civil strife involving Fitz.[19]

The rumors had substance: As early as May 29, 1660, Charles II entered London amid unprecedented demonstrations of loyalty. That the return of the monarchy meant changes for more than merely Britain became quickly evident. Charles faced, with a marvelous graciousness, unnumbered sycophants; and among them seemed to be every living man (or woman) who ever had acquired a grievance against New England. Included were a leading merchant of Boston, Massachusetts, Captain Thomas Breeden, whose attitude appears to have been derived from simple royalism; Henry, Earl of Stirling, who fancied himself the rightful heir to Long Island; a number of English Quakers, who were distressed over the position of their "Freinds in New England"; the heirs of Robert Mason and Sir Ferdinando Gorges; the surviving stockholders of the Saugus ironworks; and John Gifford, also of the ironworks, whose preferred dissatisfaction was the alleged misappropriation, by the Reverend Hugh Peter, of funds for missionary work among the Indians.[20] But the most persistent complainer was a remarkable and mercurial former resident of Massachusetts named Samuel Maverick.

Maverick's quarrel with the New England Way dated from the

time of Dr. Child and his remonstrants, with whom he had been associated and fined. About 1650, he had removed to the less rigid atmosphere of New Netherlands, whence he now bombarded the new Lord Chancellor, Clarendon, with unsolicited advice. "[The New Englanders] . . . are a greate and Considerable people," he wrote early in 1661, "and the sooner reduced the better." He was quick to point out that neither Connecticut nor New Haven possessed a valid patent and furthermore recommended that a "generall Governor" be placed over all New England "with all convenient Speed." (He even predicted that such an official would be "joyefully and thankfully" received by three-quarters of the inhabitants.)[21] Yet Maverick was not merely captious. His objections were political; of the country itself he retained a favorable opinion. In a "Brief discription of New England," which he shortly prepared for the Council of Trade, he praised Winthrop's Pequot plantation and described Hartford as "a gallant Towne, and many rich men in it."[22]

Stuart theory was by no means averse to a centralized power, to which colonies could be subjected with administrative nicety. But Charles II also was blessed with a happy combination of sloth and political intuition, and his advisers were on the whole aware that every policy has its practical limits. A royal colonial bureaucracy there was—based upon precedent—yet it now was permitted to proliferate into a jungle of committees, subcommittees, and councils, until within a year and a quarter the situation was such as to render any genuine efficiency impossible.[23] This was by no means a universal misfortune; it speedily was discovered that any over-delicate business could be fed into the machinery and lost to view with a minimum of fuss. As early as May 17, 1661, a stiff dispatch, intended for "New England," was permitted quietly to expire upon the king's own council board, and from New Netherlands Samuel Maverick soon was protesting that "some have no desire that those persons in New England should be reduced."[24] Indeed, the helter-skelter royal administration eventually would provide an imperfect, yet viable, defense for New England's autonomy.

This the leaders of New England could hardly grasp at once. Definitive notice of the Restoration arrived at Boston on July 27, 1660, in the persons of the fleeing "regicides," Whalley and Goffe, and their comments and a disturbed Puritan imagination together raised it to the status of public calamity. The responsible leadership refused, however, to panic. There followed a useful interval in which to consider an effective response; at Hartford, Winthrop was aware of developments before the middle of August, yet he did not have to cope with anything royal and official until May of the following year. Connecticut buzzed with private discussion, but the minutes of the General Court of October 4, 1660, contained not a single reference to His Majesty. At Boston, Governor Endecott was able to delay matters until December, when new and disturbing advice from overseas produced a special meeting of the Massachusetts court and the dispatch of carefully worded addresses to the king and both Houses of Parliament.[25]

It was at this point that Winthrop and his colony were moved to action. In February, 1660/1, magistrates and deputies toiled across the wintry terrain to an extraordinary session of the General Court, wherein it was agreed, as a matter of policy, that Connecticut should address and petition the king "for his favour, & for the continuance & confirmation of such privileges & liberties as are necessary for the comfortable settlement of this Colony." This was ratified, once again as policy, by another meeting of the court a month later.[26]

It will be observed that neither Massachusetts nor Connecticut formally had moved to *proclaim* Charles II as king. There were no exhibitions of joy; the Connecticut action of March was taken in the midst of a calendar of quite ordinary business, and the session moreover was concluded with the appointment of "Wednes-

[201]

day three weeks" (April 3, 1661) as a day of "solemne humiliation." The die, however, really had been cast. It may have been a
soul-searing experience for a man like Governor Endecott, but
Winthrop, with his respect for reality, suffered small discomfort.
Even the news of the execution of his own father-in-law failed to
move him to unprofitable heroics, and when, early in June, a band
of purists at Oyster Bay on Long Island spoke of secession from
Connecticut and the Empire, he countered with a plain evaluation
of the facts. "My serious advise . . . is to desist from any such
actions as may tend to a ruin [?] of yourselves," he concluded.[27]

Long before the Hartford court took public notice of the
Restoration, Winthrop had sensed what course might be necessary.
In 1659, he had toyed with the idea of a voyage to England upon
private business, but when, in October of 1660, he considered the
matter anew, he spoke also of "the occasions of this colony," and
he went so far as to write his brother-in-law Colonel Thomas Reade
(Fitz's commanding officer) asking that Connecticut be brought to
the favorable notice of General Monck. By February, his intentions were widely known, even to his brother Samuel at St. Christopher in the Antilles. "And indeed," declared Samuel, "I thinke
the affaires of yor country may want the interposicion of some discrete person, & that timely." [28]

"Discrete" Winthrop indubitably was, and he now proved it
abundantly in connection with the celebrated episode of the fugitive regicides, Whalley and Goffe. This affair of the "judges" will
bear a partial retelling,[29] if only to demonstrate how effectively
Winthrop made use of it to establish, for himself and his colony, a
reputation for good sense and cooperative loyalty. Edward Whalley and William Goffe had directly participated in the condemna-
tion of the first Charles; since their arrival in America in July of
1660, they had been quietly residing at Cambridge, Massachusetts.
During the winter, however, word came of their exemption from

royal pardon, and it was thought advisable that they should move out of the Bay region to a place less convenient to officers of the Crown. This, at the end of February, they did, traveling overland, via Hartford, to New Haven, where they found sanctuary in the comfortable manse of John Davenport. Nothing further transpired until the beginning of May, 1661, when there arrived at Boston a royal order, two months' old, directing their seizure by any competent public official. Endecott swallowed his predilections and complied—acting in the king's name, but in such a fashion that the pursuit would itself convey a sufficient warning. Copies of the king's order were sent off to the governors of Plymouth, New Haven, and Connecticut; that to Winthrop was carried by Thomas Kirke and Thomas Kellond, youthful merchants of Stuart sympathies, both of whom were endowed with powers of arrest. Brisk riding brought them to Winthrop's door by the night of May 10, and a Connecticut governor stood face to face for the first time with the accredited representatives of the English Crown.

Winthrop found himself in a comfortable position; he knew perfectly well that the fugitives were not in his colony. One need not imagine his behavior—the gracious reception, the helpful attitude, the cordial understanding—for it still is preserved, among the public records of the Crown, in the official report of Kirke and Kellond themselves: "The honnble. Govnr. carried himself very nobly to us, & was diligent to supply us with all manner of conveniences . . . & promised all diligent search should be made after them [the regicides] in that Jurisdiction, wch. was afterwards performed." Nor was this all. Early the following morning, Winthrop ushered them from Hartford in person and at Wethersfield placed them in the hands of one Martyn, with instructions to speed them in dignity beyond the limits of Connecticut to the Guilford residence of Governor William Leete of New Haven Colony.

Winthrop could reasonably anticipate that New Haven, clinging still to its special godliness and moreover actually harboring the fugitives, would strengthen, by a kind of reversal process, the Connecticut image already established. Nor did he anticipate in vain. The same report preserves the essence: the chilly welcome, the scarcely concealed procrastination, the legal excuses, even a vignette of Governor Leete, wailing upon the stairs of a New Haven tavern that he "wished he had binn a plowman that never binn in office since he found it so weighty."

All this eventually reached Whitehall, where appropriate notice was taken. Winthrop, his public point made, may well have rejoiced in private that Whalley and Goffe were never apprehended.

THE ROYAL pursuit was safely out of sight, but the royal authority could not be put out of mind. Connecticut might be represented as unimpeachably loyal, but it possessed no political legitimacy, which was a thing the England of the later Stuarts rather rigidly insisted upon. For Connecticut, therefore, the great desideratum was a royal charter, similar to that of Massachusetts, but with geographical clauses in the manner of the Warwick Patent.

Such a document would naturally require some doing. As a beginning, two things were indispensable: a formal address to the king, expressing allegiance, and a suitable petition, praying that His Majesty would be pleased to provide the coveted patent. Both had already been approved in principle, and when the Court of Elections assembled at Hartford on May 16, Winthrop was ready with a provisional draft of the address. It was long and freighted with platitudes; there may have been those who thought it noisome. It likened the return of Charles II to a new and dazzling star, whose beams had "filled the worlds hemisphere and appeared also over the great deeps in this our Horizon"; it intimated that Connecticut had remained loyal at heart throughout the interregnum; and His Majesty was implored "to accept this Collony, your owne Collony, a little branch of your mighty Empire." "It is hard to see," a Connecticut historian has remarked, "how Winthrop could have read the document with a straight face." [30]

Doubtless to settle the queasier Puritan stomachs, Winthrop's draft was submitted for possible revision to a select committee of nine, which also was charged with drawing up a petition to the king, with composing letters to "noble personages" in England, and with the management of "al other matters respecting our . . . Patent." But the committee was dominated by Winthrop, and there is no evidence of a substantial modification of the address. Of greater significance was the "postscript" with which Secretary Daniel Clark concluded the minutes of the session:

> This Court doth desire and authorize our Worshipfull Governor (who speedily intends a voyage to England,) to agitate and transact the affairs of this Colony in reference to our Address & Petition to his Majestie, or respecting our Pattent, according as he shall receave further instructions from the Comittee appointed to compleat those matters, takeing in the advice and Counsell and consent of such Gentlemen and freinds as may be excited and procured to be active with him in and about the premises.

It was Winthrop's call to his greatest public endeavor.[31]

CHAPTER 15

The Charter Journey

MAJOR negotiations between political interests are seldom spontaneous; nearly always they require a meticulous preparation by at least one of the parties concerned. Such was the approach of Connecticut to King Charles II in 1661.

The May elections court had adjourned until the final Wednesday in August (the twenty-eighth), but Winthrop suddenly found it necessary to call an extraordinary session for June 7, a move which seems to have been precipitated by the arrival of a fresh packet of overseas news. Most of the magistrates managed to attend; even the select committee was ready with a complete order of business: the address (perhaps slightly amended), a petition, and an elaborate set of instructions under which Winthrop, as agent, was to operate. All received formal ratification before the day was out.[1]

Though properly respectful, the petition made Connecticut's position very clear. Geographically, the colony desired a royal equivalent to the Warwick Patent (lost, it was explained, "by fire . . . or some other accident"); politically, it sought a reproduction of the charter of Massachusetts Bay. In addition, it was suggested that the burdens of a wilderness environment might suitably be re-

lieved by a grant of immunity from customs duties.² The moon
and the planets were, perhaps as an afterthought, left out.

The instructions may have been prepared by Winthrop himself.
They were at once precise and flexible. The governor was directed:
to seek the advice and counsel of Lord Saye and Sele, the Earl of
Manchester, Lord Brooke, and others of the surviving Warwick
patentees; to discover, if possible, an authentic copy of the Warwick Patent; to improve upon it, if found, with appropriate inser-
tions from the Bay charter; and, if not found, to press for an
entirely new document to comprehend a strip of territory from the
bounds of *Plymouth Colony* "unto the Delliway River, or as far as
may be granted that way." An approved list of Connecticut
patentees and "associates" was also provided. However, lest Winthrop find himself lacking in room to maneuver, the court took
care to invest him with power to depart from the letter of his instructions whenever he should see fit. In addition, there were prepared, in the name of the court, two official communications, one to
Lord Saye and Sele, the other (very probably) to the Earl of
Manchester. (As Puritans turned Royalist, these particular peers
would afford the best kind of entree to the right circles.) ³

There remained the question of Winthrop's expenses. The
March meeting of the General Court had suggested an appropria-
tion of £500; this the session of June 7 confirmed, and the treasurer, John Talcott (the younger) was directed to provide the governor with a letter of credit. It was drawn up and executed nine
days later.⁴

OFFICIALLY and for the time being, Connecticut could do no
more. Yet Winthrop could not simply relax in anticipation of a convenient ship. The Restoration had set the political ants to scurrying
over all New England: Everyone was talking of charters. Massachusetts, of course, possessed one—of royal origin and still technically valid—but the colony's reputation overseas was such as to

recommend an early reaffirmation. Rhode Island also had a patent, but not of royal issue; an entirely new document was indicated. Plymouth enjoyed no political license whatever; and already Governor Prince had signed a petition to the king, praying (with a courageous disregard of the facts) for a "confirmation of the Religiouse and Civill liberties and privileges conferred by pattent from your Royall Grandfather . . . & since further inlarged by your most Illustrious Father." More precarious still was the case of New Haven, extralegal, ill-tempered, and suspected—correctly—of harboring regicides. With the possible exception of Plymouth, the interests of no sister jurisdiction wholly coincided with those of Connecticut.[5]

Winthrop was only too conscious of what for so long had gone unmentioned—that Connecticut's pretensions were inconsistent with the existence of New Haven as a separate entity. A fully successful suit, by Connecticut, would logically involve the termination of the latter's independence. Of this New Haven was entirely aware, and it was inevitable that the little colony should make a serious effort to secure a charter of its own. The details of the story are shrouded by the kind of nebulosity so often generated by "delicate" transactions. Yet some general observations may be ventured: (1) An influential party in New Haven, led by John Davenport, vigorously opposed any amalgamation with Connecticut, particularly on royal terms. (2) Connecticut, as a whole, regarded New Haven as fair game. (3) Winthrop thought absorption to be both desirable and inevitable, but preferred it should be carried out with the acquiescence of at least a respectable portion of the absorbed. (4) Governor Leete of New Haven was personally inclined toward a federal union under a common royal patent.[6]

Most redolent with controversy are the relations between Winthrop, Davenport, and Leete. It has been asserted not only by aggrieved contemporaries but by a competent modern scholar that Winthrop failed to maintain a modicum of good faith. This seems a little unfair. He took pains throughout to avoid promises. He must have known the nature of Leete's position, which the latter in fact made little effort to conceal, declaring before witnesses that "he did desire Mr. Winthrop to take them under the lines of his patten if he could, that is, to cast the skirt of his garment over us. Not but that wee would keep our goverment still." But Winthrop little relished an awkward episode between Leete and Davenport, with both of whom he was on terms of personal friendship, and he offered firm proposals to neither. Leete even traveled to Hartford to bargain; but he came away without an agreement, and for days thereafter Winthrop simply dispensed comfortable generalities from a distance. To be sure, in a letter of May 24, he mentioned the possibility of a voyage for England and assured Leete that "you may please to command me what your occasions require of any office of law." But when Davenport wrote on June 16 to urge that he delay his journey for at least a year, he seems not to have answered at all until he was irretrievably on his way.[7]

As to the untidy situation in the Narragansett lands, Winthrop for the time being did little.[8] He made no approach of any sort to the Rhode Islanders; toward Massachusetts and the Atherton interests he remained curiously silent. Indeed, save for his transactions with Leete and Davenport, he was careful to avoid any proceedings with the public authorities of another New England colony. That he sought to conduct his negotiations free of commitments is most clearly suggested by the arrangements for his transatlantic passage: He sailed in a *Dutch* vessel from Fort Amsterdam, which was not only unusual but also inconvenient; barring shipwreck, he would not be conveyed directly to England at all.

H I S   P L A N S were nevertheless deliberate. On June 21, 1661, he wrote from Hartford to Director Stuyvesant to inquire about available shipping. Stuyvesant replied that three ships would soon be ready to sail, of which he recommended the largest, named *Trouw*, as "most convenient for your honnor; soe in regard off the ship Master, which speackes good English." As the vessels were intending to proceed in company, Stuyvesant would hold all three.[9]

Winthrop tried not to keep the Dutch waiting. He had compounded his last medical prescription on June 10; his final "particular" court had been held on the fourteenth; and on the twentieth he had arranged a fresh lease (for nine years!) of his share in the New Haven ironworks. On July 3, he executed a power of attorney in favor of his wife. By July 5, the agonizing farewells had been said, and he had slipped quietly from Hartford.[10]

It was likely that he was accompanied by his son Wait and the Reverend Mr. Stone, though this cannot be fully substantiated. But his passage to Manhattan can be described absolutely, thanks to the lamentations of William Leete: Winthrop proceeded the entire distance by water, via Saybrook and Long Island Sound, leaving the governor of New Haven helpless on the shore, clutching a petition to the king, which he had been so naïve as to suppose might be carried by Winthrop in person. It was a little discourteous. But, once again, it was not dishonest.[11]

Petrus Stuyvesant was a thorough realist. He tendered the Connecticut governor an elaborate reception, of which the spirit was unmistakably military. When Winthrop appeared, on July 8, before the tip of Manhattan, saluting cannon consumed 27 pounds of gunpowder; during his stay in the town, he enjoyed the constant attendance of an armed body of burghers; and when, on the thirteenth, *Trouw* sailed with the others from Brooklyn, he was conducted aboard not only by the director himself but by a special detachment of soldiers. As his ship was warped into the bay, 53 additional pounds of powder burst into martial thunder.[12]

It was a miserable voyage, with much foul weather; *Trouw*, for all her suitability for distinguished passengers, fell far behind her

[210]

accompanying vessels, and Winthrop later confessed to "much sickness." He was now fifty-five years of age; his physical vigor, though still extraordinary, was on the decline. His relations with the bilingual captain are unreported, but he was moved to alleviate the boredom by keeping a journal, of which only the final portion has survived.

A discouraging progress through the Channel and the North Sea brought them at last to the Frisian Islands, where, on September 3, *Trouw* cast anchor in the face of awkward headwinds. Winthrop continued into the Zuider Zee aboard a vessel of less critical draft, but nearly two days additional were required to reach a haven beside the handsome brick lighthouse at Enkuizen. Thereafter his progress, by land, was more rapid; and by the morning of September 6 he was in Amsterdam.[13]

Winthrop tarried in the city for nearly a week. The reason is unclear. It is known that he had an "interview" with the directors of the Dutch West India Company, but this seems to have been no more than an exchange of amenities.[14] More likely he sought, after two months of shipboard and eighteen years of New England, to savor again a genuinely urbane atmosphere.

At The Hague, which he reached on September 12, he may have transacted more significant business, for the English ambassador then in residence was none other than his cousin George Downing. Downing had come, in a manner of speaking, very far. Reared amid the paraphernalia of the New England Way and intended by his parents for a Puritan pastorate, he long since had turned—in the ultimate sense—worldly. Brilliant, empirical, and of boundless personal selfishness, he had won favor, office, and a recent knighthood. He was hardly Winthrop's sort, but could offer useful advice.[15]

Whatever the confidences of Downing, Winthrop was in no mood to linger, and on the evening of the thirteenth he boarded, in the River Maas, a "great ship" for England. There followed a hectic contest with winds, tides, and channels; but the vessel made Harwich within forty-eight hours. Before him now were only the remembered highroads of his youth. He traversed them without incident, and on September 18, 1661, he entered London.[16]

I t   w a s the last year but five of the old medieval city. Odorous, confined, and crazy-angled, dominated still by Gothic St. Paul's, it throve hugely amid a sudden rededication to the material. Its upper-class streets were gay with ribbons, sashes, and golden buttons; pedestrians were jostled by unprecedented numbers of sedan chairs; and the evenings were uproarious with the singing of the semi-intoxicated. The newly resurrected theaters flourished. They offered, thanks to the employment of *actresses,* a distinctively suggestive fare, of which a current favorite was a revival of John Ford's *'Tis a Pity She's a Whore.*[17]

Winthrop eschewed the gayer side of the Restoration—less, one suspects, from disapproval than from a simple lack of interest. He secured comfortable lodgings in Coleman Street at the house of William Whiting, "next doore to the going in to Collman Streete Church yard, over against the Kings Armes." It was as sober a district as the City afforded. From its church the Reverend John Davenport himself had gone out to New England; Mr. Whiting was the son of a former treasurer of Connecticut; and the merchant-Puritan atmosphere continued thick. (The "Kings Armes" indicated not a tavern but an alley.) Though Winthrop may not have chosen such a neighborhood for its own sake, he found it well-suited to his purposes; Mrs. Whiting proved a gracious hostess and a certain "Sir John"—of unremembered surname—an agreeable fellow lodger.[18]

Precisely how Winthrop launched the business of the Connecticut charter is unknown. (His "Journal of my voyage" ended at Harwich.) Yet he must have understood from the beginning that his task would be neither simple nor straightforward. To discover the true Warwick Patent, if one existed, would have been helpful;

he also had with him the letters to the Earl of Manchester and to Viscount Saye and Sele, and he no doubt made use of both. But it is uncertain whether Manchester took early notice of him at all, while the aging Saye and Sele had quitted town altogether and was literally waiting for death at Broughton Castle, near Banbury. Indeed, Winthrop never saw Saye and Sele again, and his letter was conveyed by James Richards, a merchant of Massachusetts Bay, with whom the governor had been on close personal terms.[19]

The response of Saye and Sele was as much as could be expected of a feeble, gout-ridden old man. He wrote Manchester; he advised Winthrop to "attend" the earl in person; and he suggested that Winthrop seek out a certain Jessup, sometime clerk to the Lords and Gentlemen, who was said to be still in London. But Saye and Sele did not post off his replies until the middle of December, and neither he nor Manchester nor the shadowy Jessup nor a search of the papers of the late Mr. Edward Hopkins could yield anything more significant than a "copy of that copy" of the Warwick Patent which George Fenwick had supposedly exhibited to the Connecticut magistrates in 1644.[20]

This obviously would not do. Winthrop in fact had never put much faith in the Warwick Patent; as overseas governor for the Lords and Gentlemen he had long ago suspected its essential unreality. He therefore took care to develop alternative avenues, and it was one of these which led finally to the Connecticut Charter of 1662.

Upon his arrival in London, Winthrop had lost no time in calling upon his old friend Samuel Hartlib. His purpose was practical as well as intellectual: Hartlib was a man of wonderful versatility, competent in affairs of the intellect, but also in the world of "influence." Though he had been identified with the fallen Protectorate, the Crown did not care actively to persecute him, and the circle of his acquaintances—his "Inner College"—was such that he retained at his fingertips an exquisite knowledge of current goings on.

Winthrop could use this kind of help. He was all too aware that his colony could not hope to press its suit free of the interjections of exterior interests. Already the Atlantic was dotted with ships, bearing letters and petitions—some in the care of particular agents, others addressed to Winthrop himself in the hope that he would be willing to undertake his neighbors' business. Late in September, the Atherton associates, through their secretary, Edward Hutchinson, besought him "to interpose his wisdom in the present juncture that we may not be given up to Road Island for Government" and commended his attention to a system of boundaries which would virtually have eliminated Rhode Island from the map. A concurrent communication from William Leete must have been positively embarrassing: The New Haven governor suggested "that you & wee could procure one Pattent, to reach beyond the Delaware," but at the same time made it clear that he still preferred a federal union and hopefully included, for action by Winthrop [!], New Haven's separate petition and address. There came also a letter from Governor Thomas Prince of Plymouth, enclosing *his* colony's petition and urging that Winthrop should exert his influence in its behalf. (Prince indicated that Plymouth was "not a litell greved" that it had not learned of Winthrop's mission to England until after his departure.) [21]

Winthrop complied, albeit without enthusiasm, with Prince's request; Plymouth's petition reposes, still unacted upon, among the public records of the Crown. But he refrained from forwarding the New Haven matter through the customary channels. For the latter colony he had plans of his own.

Another colonial spokesman—of a sort—was Samuel Maverick, who had arrived in London to urge his recommendations in person. It was probably Maverick who was responsible for certain "Privat Agitations" which came to Hartlib's notice on the evening of October 9 and which the latter thought so important that he brought them to Winthrop's attention by special messenger. Hartlib need not have gotten the wind up; even he did not yet realize

[214]

that though the mills of the Restoration ground slowly, they did not grind particularly fine. His note, however, contained important advice. Winthrop was reminded that "no businesse can bee done here at Court without some interest" (a go-between), and he was urged to make, "with all convenient speed," the personal acquaintance of Benjamin Worsley. "Mr. Worsley," noted Hartlib, "hath much the eare of the Lord Chancellour, and I believe in reference to the Plantations Hee is Privy to most Transactions." This was if anything an understatement. We have the contemporary assurance of the Lord Chancellor's lady that Worsley was the principal author of the Navigation Act of 1660, and he thereafter served long, and at a handsome retainer, as an adviser in matters pertaining to overseas colonies. Nor was this Worsley's only faculty. He was widely recognized as a "natural philosopher" of advanced views, precisely the kind of man whom Winthrop could most effectively impress. Hartlib himself expressed it aptly: "I believe you will finde Mr. Worsley according to your own heart's desire relating to any Publique Good, Just Liberty of Conscience, and any sort of ingenious kinde of Improvements." [22]

The Connecticut governor must have proceeded to Worsley's lodgings [23] almost at once. Of what transpired there we have no direct evidence; it would have been the kind of conference which is seldom reduced to writing. That nothing immediately came of it should surprise no one; such transactions call for the nicest kind of mellowing—beneath the surface.

Winthrop was wise enough not to hasten matters. He was not a man who was easily bored, especially in a city like London, and his personal interests alone were sufficient to fill the remaining autumn weeks. A sound beginning had been made, and he could afford to be patient.

EVEN AT a distance of more than 3,000 miles, he was never for long beyond the concerns of his family. Hardly had he arrived in

England when he was cited, together with his cousin Benjamin Gostlin and the more distantly related Edward Rainsborough, to appear the following Easter term before the Court of King's Bench to answer an obscure suit brought by one Prudence Martyn. (The details and the final issue escape us.) From New England Elizabeth sent word of a new and serious romantic interest between their daughter Lucy and Edward Palmes, a rising young merchant of New London; she personally thought well of the match, but desired her husband's comments. She appended the inevitable shopping list: two "very good" beds—"one green, the other blew"—also plates, cups, and spoons. She also inquired, naïvely, if there were any prospect of her sharing in the estate of her late drawn-and-quartered stepfather.[24] A stream of communications arrived from John Payne of Boston, half-literate and burdened with the woes of the New Haven ironworks.[25] Winthrop's replies are mostly lost. We do have a letter to his younger daughters, stiff with the formality of an erudite parent who does not quite know how to approach children: "Be careful in your duty to your mother & in reading & learning out of God's Word, & your catechisme . . . learne to write." [26]

His major private concern, however, was his eldest son. Fitz-John was still something less than a comfort; for all his military reputation, he continued to exhibit the habits of a large breed of puppy. His regiment had been disbanded; he was out of employment; he fancied himself in love; and he needed money. He was not slow to approach his father for funds, and when Winthrop responded with a dissertation upon the virtues of thrift, Fitz suggested, with youthful logic, a winter holiday in France! It was perhaps just as well that the young man was temporarily forbidden to enter the cities of London and Westminster, a technical disability consequent upon his service under the Protector—and one which his father took significant pains to remind him.[27]

I N T H E midst of everything—rumors of state, private interruptions, and the irrational behavior of youth—Winthrop continued to find time for the company of those who, like himself, delighted to speculate upon the natural world and to dabble with "ingenious improvements." Here again Hartlib provided a peerless entree, and it was not long before the Connecticut governor had made the acquaintance of as remarkable muster of savants as the seventeenth century could afford. Of a number of these friendships we can be positive: William Brereton, Sir Robert Moray, Henry Oldenburg, Robert Boyle, Elias Ashmole, and Dr. John Wilkins; there is evidence, possibly valid, of additional celebrities, including Isaac Newton, John Milton, and Christopher Wren.[28]

With William Brereton, Winthrop soon contracted an important alliance. Thanks to Hartlib, they had been transatlantic correspondents for some time, and, shortly after the beginning of October, the young aristocrat wrote from Cheshire to welcome Winthrop to England and arrange a personal meeting. Brereton was, according to Pepys the diarist, "a very sober and serious able man," yet of an easy graciousness, exactly the kind of person which Winthrop found most congenial.[29] Their friendship led to the happiest consequences. Brereton had become associated with an informal group, or "college," of forward-looking intellectuals, which for years had been wont to gather in learned conference, most often in the spacious chambers of Gresham College in Bishopsgate Street. This association was now in the process of formal organization; the king himself had expressed his interest, and, though there was as yet no charter, the members already spoke of themselves as "The Royal Society." It was no ordinary fellowship. It was not identical with Hartlib's "college," but numbers of Hartlib's group were included, notably Robert Boyle and Mr. Hartlib himself.[30]

It appears to have been Brereton who first conducted Winthrop into the lordly Gresham precincts to present him to the assembled Fellows, "seated civilly on the rising benches that faced the famous green cloth table." [31] It was a gathering of distinction: Boyle, with homely fox face, but quietly intelligent eyes; Dr. John Wilkins, whose finely chiseled features radiated, above a clergyman's neckpiece, an irrepressible, worldly enthusiasm; Henry Oldenburg, vast and Germanic, yet a master of exquisite English; and Scottish Sir Robert Moray, veteran martyr in the Stuarts' cause, but devoted above all to chemistry.[32]

Winthrop was understandably enthralled, and it is obvious that the Fellows recognized in him a kindred spirit. On the evening of December 18, 1661, Brereton proposed him for membership, and, at a meeting held on January 1, he was admitted. There is no record of opposition; aside from a simple statement of Winthrop's election, the society's journal indicates only that Oldenburg presented a paper "concerning a new manner of cutting the stone out of the bladder," that Dr. Wilkins demonstrated "his Engine for Hearing," and that a court favorite, Sir Robert Paston, submitted his name.[33]

It was an authentic honor. Winthrop was not only the first resident of North America to be made a member of this famous body, he was received at a time when the society stood on the threshold of perhaps its most splendid period. Winthrop furthermore enjoyed the distinction of "Original Fellow," for his name appears as such on the first formal list compiled by the society in 1663, following its incorporation by the Crown.[34] Nor was he to take this newest dignity lightly. It could not have been better tailored to his private tastes; moreover, he cannot have been unaware of the peculiar relation between the green-cloth table at Gresham College and the antechambers of Whitehall.

CHAPTER 16

The Connecticut Charter

LATE on Christmas Eve of 1661, Winthrop returned to his Coleman Street lodgings, following a long day at Westminster. Though weary, he took time to scratch off a half-legible note to Fitz, who still was marooned in Hertfordshire by the king's proclamation. He refrained, in the New England fashion, from comments upon the holiday season, and he did not disclose the nature of the day's business. Yet it may have been of capital importance, perhaps even a conference with the principal secretary of state, Sir Edward Nicholas, in his comfortable apartments beside the Thames.[1]

For at last there was a noticeable activity among the dispensers of favor, productive of slight, but electric, responses through the intricate hierarchy of influence. By the sixth of January, they appear to have brought Winthrop into delicate discourse with an unlikely quartet: a former rear admiral, a Barbados merchant, a transoceanic scamp, and his own seafaring cousin, Benjamin Gostlin. Admiral Nehemiah Bourne was an authentic salt, with a long background of merchant shipping at Massachusetts Bay and of sea battles with the Dutch under the Commonwealth. "Colonel" Thomas Middleton was an aging London merchant of kaleidoscopic interests, all fitted to his personal advantage: landed interests in North America, commercial interests in Barbados, and a "place" at court as an adviser upon overseas colonies. (He later became, in the Navy, an associate of Samuel Pepys, who thought him very competent.) The third individual, "Capt. Scott," was almost certainly the mysterious and complicated John Scott, then a resident of Long Island, but currently in London. He was a young man of twenty-nine, with a past full of questionable curiosities; he was well known in Massachusetts and had become a member of the Atherton Company. He seems to have come to England to fish, on grounds of a boyhood enthusiasm for Charles I, for royal gratitude. He was one of the few men for whom Winthrop ever developed a cordial dislike, and there is no question that he was the most controversial figure with whom the Connecticut governor ever had to deal.[2]

All that is known of Winthrop's business with this curious group is derived from a single note, dispatched by Bourne to Winthrop on the morning of Monday, January 6, 1661/2, wherein Bourne dropped a number of unusual remarks. He said he would "accomodate Capt. Scott" with 50 more than he (Bourne) had promised —provided Captain Gostlin paid off a previous debt. He had no doubt that Winthrop would influence Scott "so farr in so just a case (which I entreate yow to do for me)." He referred to a previous conversation concerning Middleton and announced he was ready "to pay him [Middleton] money." He was unwilling to force Middleton to perform anything greatly against his will, but if Middleton would "do it" following a payment, Bourne would "pay it in" for him—always provided Gostlin was willing to extinguish his debt. Bourne concluded by requesting Winthrop to extend his kindest regards to both Gostlin and Middleton.[3]

It is of course possible that these obscure comments reflected but an ordinary adjustment of private credits. Nevertheless, in view of what was about to happen, one may suspect the presence of something more. Furthermore Scott would appear again—in a strictly political context and with reference to the Connecticut Charter.

IN WHAT manner Winthrop saw to the presentation of Connecticut's petition, no one can say. But it is known that it was not submitted in its original form. Preliminary negotiations might be unconventional to the point of irregularity, but any *documents* were expected to conform to a rigid prescription of phrase and syntax. The language of the Hartford court, though respectful enough, did not meet the requirements, and upon the advice of someone competent in such matters, Winthrop recast the entire petition. Even this was found to be unsuitable, in part because Winthrop personally signed it.[4] Only a third draft, incorporating a further modification of text and without a signature, bears the endorsement of Secretary Nicholas—indisputable evidence that it was at last in proper form.[5]

Though patent solicitation at the court of Charles II involved much private greasing of wheels and, one suspects, of palms, centuries of usage had reduced the official procedures to a precise standard. The initial hurdle was the Privy Council—"His Majesty in Council"—which in that period often included the king in person; it was to this body that the proposed charter, with petition attached, must first be submitted. Winthrop was ready for this highly critical transaction by February of 1661/2.[6]

A favorable issue was by no means assured. He not only must cope with the whimsical instabilities of the highly placed; he faced competition from without. Rhode Island had appointed, as its agent at court, Dr. John Clarke, a well-known physician and religious liberal, whose circle of associates rivaled Winthrop's. Clarke already had placed an "address" in the hands of the Council for Foreign Plantations and was busy with the composition of supplementary appeals. Likewise haunting the antechambers was Colonel

Thomas Temple, a principal resident of Boston, Massachusetts, who sought confirmation of a semimythical fief in Acadia; he in no way impinged upon Winthrop's aspirations, but threatened to occupy too much of the Privy Council's time. Even the Bay might provoke embarrassment; it by now had forwarded more than one address, and two of its representatives, Simon Bradstreet and the Reverend John Norton, were even then on the high seas.[7]

But it was Winthrop who first submitted a petition in authentic form directly to the king in council. The date was likely February 12, 1661/2. The details are undocumented. The episode has indeed given birth to a pleasant story,[8] to the effect that Winthrop presented his sovereign with "an extraordinary ring," a gift to his grandfather Adam "by King Charles I," a gesture which so pleased the second Charles that His Majesty reciprocated with a miniature of himself. This anecdote is certainly apocryphal; for one thing, Adam Winthrop had been dead for nearly two years when Charles I ascended the throne; for another, there exists no primary evidence of its authenticity. Yet the tale can scarcely be out of harmony with the spirit of the proceedings. One can imagine the scene: the sumptuous council chamber, the glittering council, perhaps the king in person, easy and affable for all his overadornment, and before them the governor of Connecticut, quietly but suitably garbed, respectful but never for an instant a sycophant, his homely face aglow, his presentation couched in precisely the right phrases. It was the supreme test of his extraordinary personality, and it did not fail him: Petition and charter draft were graciously received.

The Privy Council ordinarily referred such business to the Council for Plantations for further study. Yet Winthrop's petition was endorsed, over the signature of Secretary Nicholas, directly to the attention of the attorney general, Sir Geoffrey Palmer, with instructions "to advise & certifie what Powers, Previledges, Estate and Interests hee thinkes fit for his Majesty to grant unto the

Peticioners." This was significant; it meant the elimination of a full step in the normal procedure. Nor was the attorney general wanting in dispatch; the papers were back before the Privy Council within days. Sir Geoffrey's opinion was almost wholly favorable. He indicated that the powers desired by Connecticut might properly be granted, "saving only as to the freedome from Customes, the consideration whereof I humbly conceave to be proper for the Lord [Treasurer], or others to whom the care of your Majesties revenues belongs." [9]

The council continued auspicious. On February 26, it ordered that all persons with New England interests should attend the council board on Thursday, March 6, at three in the afternoon and that Winthrop and Colonel Temple "bee Summoned and required" to appear. What this portended is unclear, but it is plain that Winthrop did not face serious additional scrutiny. Precisely two days later, on February 28, came the decisive transaction, the "Warrant to Prepare a Bill," wherein both the attorney general and the solicitor general were directed to draw up a "King's Bill," or provisional charter, for Connecticut. The inspiration for such speed is not known, though it may be guessed at. But once the warrant was issued, Winthrop could reasonably assume that the worst of his uncertainties were at an end. Save for the exemption from customs, the warrant contained virtually all that he had sought.[10]

Winthrop's relief was understandable; he even thought of returning to New England by a regular late-spring sailing. However, his charter still faced a long and intricate procedure: the preparation of the king's bill (in triplicate), the affixing of the royal signature (on the third copy), the medieval progress through the Office of Privy Signet (where the third copy remained), the Office of Privy Seal (where the first copy was left behind and the second expanded into a "Writ of Privy Seal"), and Chancery, where the Lord Chancellor's signature (upon the second copy) provided authority for the engrossing of the patent itself. This last function was performed by the clerk of patents, whereupon the document was ready for final validation under the Great Seal, which was attached by the Chancery officer known as "Lord Keeper of the Great Seal." Though there was small danger that this elaborate regimen would be disrupted by external influences, it was necessary from time to time to urge the process along, and for weeks Winthrop continued to haunt the passages of Whitehall. He found this "very confining," but continued to hope for an early conclusion.[11]

Amid this esoteric machinery there must have been those who thought well of the Connecticut governor; for example, the lord privy seal, Baron Robartes, had been connected by marriage with the second Earl of Warwick and was of a character similar to Winthrop's own.[12] The writ of privy seal was indeed secured as early as April 23 (which thereby became the formal "date" of the charter). Yet the engrossment, and the passage of the Great Seal, were not completed until the afternoon of May 10. This represented a considerable delay. The preparation of two original copies of the patent, suitably executed upon parchment, required time, but hardly seventeen days. It is most likely that the final sealing was held up pending the liquidation of certain expenses, both regular and, it must be assumed, irregular. The formal fees, payable to the clerks of the Hanaper, came to no more than £14/09/04, thanks, said Winthrop, to the favorable attitude of the Lord Chancellor. The whole of Winthrop's "costs" must, of course, have been enormously heavier, but by how much will probably never be known. Estimates have run as high as £6,000 (Roger Williams); a respected modern historian has suggested £600. The latter is doubtless closer to the truth.[13]

Whatever the figure, it is evident that Winthrop had serious difficulty in meeting it. For months his Connecticut letter of credit had raised eyebrows rather than the £500 it stipulated, and it yielded not a penny until May 3. Even then it was taken up by a syndicate of merchants and at a discount. How Winthrop had paid his expenses in the meantime no one knows; and to get his £500 he now undertook, in the name of Connecticut, but under his own endorsement, to lay down at New London, prior to November 30, 2,000 bushels of wheat at 3.5 shillings per bushel and 1,200 bushels of pease at 2.5 shillings. This represented a book value of £650, a not excessive markup in view of subsequent developments. The Connecticut court was prompt to levy an extraordinary tax in kind, and the wheat and pease were in hand at New London by December. But Connecticut was not England, and as late as the summer of 1664 the associated merchants had received nothing.[14]

Winthrop had won his charter. The task had required rather more time than he had anticipated, and he had missed a hoped-for sailing with his old friend Captain Peirse. Yet he was content. "[The charter] . . . is so full & large in the grants & privileges therein that I hope none will thinke much of the cost," he wrote Samuel Willys. He indeed had secured an extraordinary document. Connecticut now was spread on royal parchment from the Massachusetts line on the north to the "sea" on the south (sound or ocean unspecified), and from "Norrogancett River, comonly called Norrogancett Bay" [!] to the Pacific. Its existing government was given royal certification: Public acts were of course to be performed in the king's name, but in practical terms Connecticut would enjoy something very like independence. What had been established extralegally was now legally fixed by reference to the ancient tenure "as of our Mannor of East Greenewich, in Free and Comon Soccage." (For Englishmen, and even for Anglo-Americans, it has ever proved useful to drape new facts with old precedents.) [15]

Winthrop now hoped that he might be back in Hartford before

the end of November.[16] He reckoned without an aroused competitor. Unknown to him, his happy position would be undermined within forty-eight hours.

"Dr." John Clarke, agent for Rhode Island and Providence Plantations, had not seemed a serious threat. His commission had been drawn up by the Rhode Island General Court as early as October of 1660, but he had made no obvious move until January, 1661/2—when he had presented an improperly worded address to an inappropriate authority. His additional suits were in similarly bad form, and by February Dr. Clarke had slipped once more into a state of quiescence. The general character of Winthrop's business was of course no secret, and it was rumored as early as March 27 to be "allmost finished." Yet Clarke lifted not a finger to intervene. This and the fact that he had not resided in America since 1651 appear to have led Winthrop to suppose that he was hardly a genuine representative.[17]

But Clarke was neither spurious nor wholly lackadaisical. His lack of vigor may have been derived in part from a simple lack of funds,[18] and when the details of the Connecticut charter became, after May 10, more widely known, he was literally driven to action. Once in motion, he revealed himself a stubborn adversary.

Clarke continued slow to master the arts of petitioning. The first of two new communications, dated May 14, bore a thoroughly unconventional salutation, "My Lord o King," and apparently was entrusted for delivery to a London alderman. The second, in May 16, was of similarly unprofessional quality. Yet Clarke did make his case plain. He asked for a review of Winthrop's charter, "for as much as therby he hath injuriously swallowed up half of our Colonie"; he requested a patent for Rhode Island, "as good and ample . . . as yor majesty have given & confirmed unto our neighbors"; and he suggested a firm frontier between the two jurisdictions, either by agreement between the parties or by royal decision. In some fashion unknown, these unlikely documents came presently to the attention of Lord Chancellor Clarendon. They furthermore made an impression, thanks, perhaps, to an existing acquaintance between Clarendon and Clarke.[19]

Though the two originals of the Connecticut charter were fully authentic, they were not yet in Winthrop's possession, but in the hands of the clerks of the Hanaper and the master of the Rolls for purposes of "enrollment." [20] Pending physical delivery, Winthrop had left town upon a visit to his widowed aunt, Lucy Downing, at her residence at Hatley, near Cambridge. Clarke likewise experienced delay; the entire court was for the time being distracted by the official landing, at Portsmouth, of the king's intended bride, Catherine of Braganza, and the consequent pomp and circumstance quite eclipsed the concerns of New England. Even after his return from Hatley, Winthrop still had no inkling of an attack upon his charter. Then, at the end of May, the bolt fell. The full details do not survive, but it is certain that Clarke confronted Winthrop on Friday the thirtieth and made his position known. It also would appear that Clarendon ordered the return of the originals. Winthrop was appalled; months later, he still felt he had been subjected to "a great wrong." To Clarendon he wrote, on June 7, that the whole situation had come as a surprise and that he could hardly yet believe that Clarke's commission was genuine. He was especially piqued that the issue had not been raised earlier, and his disappointment over the postponement of his sailing plans was bitter.[21]

It cannot have eased Winthrop's discomfort to realize that he once again faced financial embarrassment. This time he possessed not even a dubious letter of credit, yet the defense of his charter would require unspecified sums. In despair, he turned to Robert Boyle and Thomas Temple, and it was doubtless Boyle who took him to Henry Ashurst.

Ashurst proved a handy port in a storm. He was enormously

wealthy; he was by nature philanthropic; and he was an intimate friend of Boyle. He furthermore was deeply interested in missionary work among the North American Indians and was associated with Boyle in the newly (and royally) reorganized "Corporation for Propogating the Gospel in New England." [22] Ashurst was not disposed to quibble; he offered Winthrop the money he needed— upon reasonable, but well-defined, personal terms. Winthrop accepted, undoubtedly with relief.[23]

The Connecticut governor did have a supplementary card with which to play, an imprecise grant of land, allegedly made in the reign of the first Charles by one of the dukes of Lenox to the father of Samuel Willys. Samuel's cousin Thomas dwelt in nearby Ratcliff, and there is evidence that he and Winthrop actually discussed the matter—a conversation which led to an unhappy misunderstanding and charges that Winthrop's behavior had been "farr from upright." [24] But insofar as Winthrop fought at all for his charter upon grounds of precedent, he continued to emphasize the Warwick Patent with its Narragansett "River."

Boyle and Temple remained helpful. At Winthrop's request, they drafted an "expedient," of which the identity is problematical, but which seems to have proposed an arbitrary boundary 12 miles to the west of the western shore of Narragansett Bay. In the presence of Winthrop, John Scott, Samuel Maverick, and Winthrop's son Wait, they urged Dr. Clarke to accept it. Clarke refused.[25]

Fortunately, Winthrop had retained the services of William Thirsby, a well-known barrister of the Middle Temple, and of a junior colleague, a Mr. Laurence. Thirsby's initial recommendation was to get at least one of the originals of the charter to Connecticut as quickly as possible. This was easier proposed than performed. The last of the regular sailings already had dropped down the Thames, and both copies of the charter were still in the hands of Clarendon. "I could doe no other than to desire my lord

Chancellor his favour that I might have it to send away," reported Winthrop—and one would give much to know what thereupon transpired in his lordship's chambers. For the favor was granted almost at once; *both* copies were released to Winthrop, though on condition that he forward one of them to Connecticut "by the first opertunity"—which was precisely what he sought to do! One of the "charters" was hastily placed in the care of the merchant James Richards, "to be packed up with his best things"; somewhere in the lower river or in the Downs, it was carried aboard ship. The vessel entered Boston harbor in September, coincident with the annual meeting of the United Colonies, and there Richards delivered the document into the hands of the Connecticut commissioners, Samuel Willys and John Talcott.[26]

Meanwhile, in London, the impasse intensified. Clarendon was favorably disposed to both Clarke and Winthrop and, upon a midsummer date it would be convenient to remember, ordered the two into his presence in an effort to discover a mutually acceptable ground for discussion. It was a public audience, likely held amid the stately surroundings of Worcester House; present was the ubiquitous Captain Scott and probably also Boyle. It proved a rather dramatic episode. Clarke was, with all his talents, a natural gadfly, and he now turned such a torrent of abuse upon the Connecticut governor that Clarendon was moved to inquire before the whole assemblage if he were not ashamed of himself. It was, his lordship added, a wonder that Winthrop "could have the patience to bare itt." Yet Winthrop retained his poise—and quietly terminated the discussion by referring Clarke to his lawyers.[27]

Winthrop's conduct continued flawless. He confined his laments to his personal circle. He withdrew from town—upon "family business," he said. He instructed Thirsby to offer no concessions beyond the "expedient" previously proposed—unless Rhode Island should sue out a genuine charter of its own. But if a reduction of the Connecticut grant should become unavoidable, he wondered if the "contentment" of his people might not be best assured by the issue of an entirely *new* Connecticut patent. The fault would then be the Crown's, not his, and any ill-feeling against Rhode Island would be minimized. "Sir," he wrote Thirsby, "I hint these things, but I leave it to your judgment [*sic*] what to advise." [28]

Meanwhile Clarke had discovered that Winthrop had got one of his charter originals out of England. He was understandably furious and rushed to Thirsby with additional charges. Through Thirsby, Winthrop replied that the document was not his "to dispose of otherwise then to send it to the colonye . . . except I had express command to the contrary"—which technically was true. At the same time, he arranged for the "second original" to be delivered to Thirsby for safe keeping, pending its dispatch to America; in addition, he provided an informal copy for the lawyer's personal reference. The second original was presently on its way, in whose charge or in what vessel we cannot be sure. It was probably in Connecticut before the end of November.[29]

There unquestionably were moments when Winthrop permitted himself to hope that Clarke would abandon the contest and disappear from the scene. He had been absent from home for more than a year and was quite naturally eager to bring his task to a conclusion. But he was too much a realist to count upon so happy an issue. Clarke, moreover, was of the sort which thrives upon opposition. He by no means was through with Winthrop, and he now arranged to have the Rhode Island petition redrawn in accordance with protocol and presented to the Privy Council, by which on September 22, it was certified as acceptable, and forwarded for comment to the Council for Foreign Plantations.[30]

Clarke also had taken care to lubricate the machinery. The Council (or Committee) for Plantations stood primed to act; as early as September 15, its secretary, Colonel Frowd, had been directed to bring "all orders and papers relating to New England and Barbadoes" to a meeting posted for the twenty-fifth. New

England was thereupon "seriously debated and discoursed," and a charter for Rhode Island was approved in principle. But the inconsistency between the Rhode Island and Connecticut positions must have been too apparent, for at this point the council sought refuge in delay and announced that a settlement of intercolonial squabbles must await the dispatch, to *America,* of a royal commission. It was a typical administrative evasion, for all that the council comprehended such dignitaries as the Duke of York, and Lords Clarendon and Albemarle.[31]

That Winthrop was responsible for this stay in Rhode Island's progress cannot be proved, though he is known to have been in town on the previous evening.[32] It was, of course, a fortunate development from his point of view. Yet the whole business was once more at a standstill. What, and when, would be the end of it, no one could say.

CHAPTER 17

Avocation, Evasion, & Arbitration

NOW that Dr. Clarke's proposals had been launched into authorized channels, Winthrop became for all intents and purposes a prisoner of the metropolis. Week upon week he attended the appointed meetings of the Plantations Council, but the issue of Connecticut and Rhode Island was as repeatedly postponed. He himself could obtain no formal hearing.[1] As the autumn days darkened into another December, it became evident that Clarke enjoyed an influence almost, if not quite, equal to Winthrop's own and that he was using it so to wear his rival down that Winthrop would throw up the argument and return to New England.

Clarke seems not to have apprehended the true quality of John Winthrop the Younger. With all his pleasant instinct for accommodation, the Connecticut governor was capable, whenever the situation warranted, of a monumental stubbornness; he now proposed to outlast even Dr. Clarke. Perhaps the latter had not reckoned with the unaccustomed range of his interests—and of his consequent immunity from tedium. The Royal Society, in particular, afforded an unsurpassed alternative to despondency.

Never for a moment had Winthrop treated his membership in the society as mere ritual. As early as July 9, 1662, he stood beside the green-cloth table to read his first formal paper, "The Manner

of Making Tarr and Pitch in New England, etc." Almost simultaneously he prepared for Robert Boyle an elaborate dissertation
upon Indian corn and its uses, which so impressed his friend that it
was rearranged for delivery before the whole society on December
31. On September 24, he presented still another paper, "Concerning the Building of Shipps in New England," wherein he cited his
region as deserving the interest of the Royal Navy, not only in
terms of raw materials but on grounds of economy; it must have
fitted in appropriately with an accompanying parcel of "Thoughts"
by Dr. Jonathan Goddard upon the growing of timber in England. In January, 1662/3, the society asked him to examine and
report upon a New England–built vessel in the Thames, and in
March, when once again he could hope for an early return to
America, he was requested to undertake, with leads, balls, and a
valve-fitted cylinder, a study of the open Atlantic. Furthermore,
upon his departure in April, he left with Henry Oldenburg the
rough draft of an essay upon paper money and its use in trade and
commerce.[2]

Nor was this quite the sum of it. It was probably early in
1663—and thanks to the assistance of Dr. Benjamin Worsley—
that Winthrop acquired a well-constructed astronomical telescope,
only 3½ feet in focal length, but a far more satisfactory instrument
than the 10-foot apparatus with which he had been experimenting.
"I seldom looke upon the Constellations of the heavens, or the
planetts . . . with my telescope," he wrote Worsley seven years
later, ". . . but the most grateful memory of yourselfe is fresh to
my thoughts & soule." The glass would presently confront him
with an interesting possibility—and it is likely that it came
ultimately into the possession of Harvard College.[3]

Less in tune with his special nature, but quite inevitable in the
circumstances, was his association with the Corporation (or Society) for the Propagation of the Gospel in New England. The
president of this famous organization was Robert Boyle; Henry

Ashurst was its long-time treasurer; while Winthrop, as the principal executive of a New England colony, held essential responsibility for a section of its work overseas. He was consequently much in
evidence at the society's rooms in Cooper's Hall in Basinghall
Street. Winthrop observed that a fundamental difficulty was
finance and suggested, with a sound paper logic, that the Indians
should not only be instructed but put profitably to work. They
might, he told Boyle, produce hemp, flax, tar, and wheat and, as
an extra benefit, serve as a market for English manufactured
goods. The idea was not, of course, original; it was as old as the
American dominions of the Castilian Crown. Winthrop moreover
chose to disregard what he knew of the aboriginal nature; in the
careless spirit of his younger days he estimated a capital of no more
than £5,000, which he declared should be recovered by the end of
five years "at the farthest." (It is of some significance that he suggested the Narragansett Country as the most suitable place in
which to begin.) [4]

Strangely enough, there is small evidence that Winthrop devoted himself much to medical matters, either during that autumn
or at any time during his stay in England. He did become familiar
with a certain Dr. Constable and may have revealed to him the
formula of his rubila powder. But the record is otherwise blank. It
is more remarkable still that he apparently failed to seek out his
former protégé, George Stirk, who is known to have been in London and who, under the name of Starkey, had achieved considerable fame in both medical and alchemical circles. Stirk had emphasized the chemical medicine of Paracelsus and, especially, of
Helmont, and it is a matter for wonder that Winthrop was not
frequently in his company. Possibly they had quarreled, but of this
there is no direct evidence.[5]

O n t h e evening of February 17, 1661/2, Winthrop sat in his
Coleman Street lodgings, writing to the Reverend Mr. Daven-

port, 3,000 miles away in New Haven. Outside, an unprecedented windstorm littered the streets with bricks and tiles, but Winthrop scratched off only comfortable words: New Haven need not worry over the fugitive regicides; there was "no more speech" concerning them in England. Upon his own affairs (which even then were in the hands of the attorney general), he offered almost no comment, hinting only that he might transmit additonal "thoughts" early in the spring.[6]

It was so characteristic! That he seriously intended the annexation of New Haven there can be no doubt. But there must be no warning—especially of the kind which alarms—there in particular must be no bluster. To this day, John Winthrop, Jr., stands tallest in the midst of the nearly universal good will of his opponents.

His next parcel of "thoughts" went off to Davenport on May 13, three days after his charter had passed the seals; again they were as pleasant as they were imprecise. Apparently the first specific word New Haven received of Winthrop's doings was the Connecticut patent itself, which Willys and Talcott triumphantly exhibited to the United Colonies commissioners near the close of their September sessions. The Massachusetts and Plymouth members examined the document with "favor," but Leete and Fenn of New Haven were taken openly aback and noted on the margin of the day's minutes that they could not "as yett say that the procurement of this Pattent wilbe acceptable to us or our Collonie." [7]

The charter was conveyed to Hartford by Lieutenant Thomas Bull, a militia officer who accompanied Willys homeward. (Talcott was delayed in Boston by illness.) It was received by the magistrates with delight; indeed, they cast discretion to the Indian summer sunshine and announced to the inhabitants of New Haven Colony and of eastern and central Long Island that they now were so fortunate as to live under Connecticut's jurisdiction. New Haven was cordially invited to send representatives to the Hartford General Court on October 9, at which time the ceremonies of formal union would be celebrated. At Southold, Captain John Young was urged to forward the annexation of *all* Long Island, the Dutch extremity included.[8]

This was unfortunate. The prospect of Connecticut rule was not unpopular with the Anglo-Long Islanders, and certain New Haven towns of the mainland began openly to waver. But at the core, at Milford, New Haven and Branford, there was sturdy opposition, of which the Reverend Mr. Davenport was at once the leader and the image. So thunderous were his objections that the freemen of New Haven Colony, in special meeting on November 4, voted to reject any sort of union until the United Colonies, the Crown, and Winthrop had been consulted.[9]

Moreover, the situation was further exacerbated by the unexpected intervention of Captain John Scott, who came briefly to America late in the autumn to observe, and doubtless to exploit, the local political waters. He announced that neither New Haven nor Long Island need regard itself as under the Connecticut patent, and the Hartford assistants presently learned that New Haven—and the Shelter Island Sylvesters—had retained his services as an overseas agent. There were further discussions, of a private and inconclusive sort, and Daniel Clark wrote Winthrop in November that "we hope there wilbe a Loving concurrence and Accomodation twixt ourselves and N: Haven." But three weeks later John Allyn dispatched a second letter to elaborate upon the doings of Scott and to warn he might return to England at any time.[10]

In London, Winthrop knew by February how awkward the New Haven question had become. Nor was the situation improved by the prompt reappearance of Scott. Whether Winthrop now moved to bring matters to a head or whether his hand was forced by others is not certain. But sometime before the end of the month, there was a conference, at which certain New Haven representatives complained of unauthorized "acts of sovereignty" within their territory, and they were not really satisfied when Winthrop pointed out that the "businesse" was yet in the discussion stage and that his colony had "appointed a committee" to negotiate. Thereafter the proceedings are documented in detail.[11] On the morning of Monday, March 2, Winthrop made his way to the secret lodgings of the Reverend William Hooke, once Davenport's colleague at New Haven, later Cromwell's personal chaplain, and now living in bitter, fugitive, self-righteous retirement. With him went three spokesmen for the New Haven establishment: Nathaniel Whitfield, Major Robert Thompson (an intimate friend of the late Edward Hopkins who in 1659 had purchased the famous Guilford manse of the Reverend Henry Whitfield), and the by now slightly sinister Scott.[12] Mr. Hooke at first "desired to be spared" their company, but he presently agreed to moderate a formal discussion between Winthrop and the others. It was a curious episode: a debate wherein the Connecticut governor was outnumbered three to one and faced an umpire whose obvious sympathies were with his opponents, but which nevertheless afforded the best kind of opportunity for his talents. He was superb. He spoke to New Haven's *"former* Liberties in Church and Commonwealth" and hinted—for Hooke's particular consumption—that these stood nowadays in imminent peril of destruction. He protested "that it was not his Intention that . . . [New Haven] should have beene thus dealt with" by his colleagues at home nor that any of New Haven's liberties should be in the least infringed. But he took parenthetical note of Leete's concept of a federation, and he declared, facing his opposition squarely, that it was his most profound desire that they might enjoy those liberties "as much to the full, as ever you did." It was a very snowstorm of reassurance, yet it contained not a single concession or a definable promise.

The New Haven emissaries (with the unconcealed support of Mr. Hooke) at once desired that Winthrop should write his associates in America, restating his position and requesting that they should "not crosse" anything which he as their agent chose to undertake. This he was quite willing to do. (For the sake of good feelings, he would agree to almost anything that was gracious—and imprecise.) So cordial, indeed, became the atmosphere that the members of the New Haven party soon found themselves admitting to a personal belief in a union of the colonies and to a private "wonder" that so many New Haven residents failed to agree. The Winthrop personality had never achieved anything so extraordinary.[13]

The text of his letter was discussed and agreed to on the following day. Addressed to Deputy Governor Mason, it asked that Connecticut forbear from further political activity—without New Haven's consent—within New Haven's limits; it suggested that further pressure would represent a violation of Winthrop's trust, and it indicated that the New Haven representatives in England had "thereupon forborn to give you or me any further trouble." Then came, as at a scorpion's tail, the essence of the thing:

> [The New Haven agents] do not doubt but upon further consideration there may be such a right understanding between both governments that a union & friendly joining may be established to the satisfaction of all, which at my arrival I shall endeavor (God willing) to promote. . . .[14]

A true copy of this letter was provided for the information—and we may suppose the consternation—of New Haven Colony. The original, signed by Winthrop, was dated March 3. But though it signified much, a covering letter which he addressed privately to John Mason and the Connecticut General Court revealed even more. Following a careful review of his transactions with the New Haven men, he earnestly recommended a suspension of further attempts to extend Connecticut's sovereignty over areas "wherein controversy or trouble" might develop. As specially sensitive, he cited New Haven, Long Island, Westchester, and "Mr. Sylvesters" [Shelter Island], but not, be it noted, the Narragansett country. And he concluded on a curious note: "Let me begg this further favour that you will please at your next election to leave me out. I spare to trouble you with the reasons at present." [15]

The reasons can only be guessed. He may have been suffering from simple weariness. Yet one is tempted to discover a more subtile purpose, a process whereby his colony could enjoy an unrestricted ability to maneuver, while Winthrop, his public connections severed, undertook to receive, as a good-humored private martyr, the barbs and arrows of those whom he had outwitted.

A F U S I O N with New Haven could now be assumed; it was but a matter of time. Not so the Narragansett question; here Winthrop faced a far more difficult antagonism. His New Haven opponents were divided. The Rhode Islanders were not; indeed, a fundamental disparity of outlook would presently disrupt the harmony of his own side. Winthrop, as always, remained mindful of the possible, but his associates, both of Connecticut and of the Atherton Company, were so infatuated with their antipathy toward Rhode Island as to lose all sense of proportion. Nor did 3,000 miles of intervening ocean help clarify matters.

Major embarrassments were prompt to appear. During the autumn of 1662, the Atherton partners posted off a succession of commentaries upon the Connecticut charter; they naturally were gratified; some were so fond as to suppose it might presage Rhode Island's extinction. But their pleasure was clouded by a fear that Winthrop would fail to maintain a consistently rigid position—a consequence, perhaps, of Winthrop's own letters and, certainly, of the remarks of John Scott, who arrived in Boston at the beginning of November. "We are bold," wrote Edward Hutchinson on the ninth, "to crave of you to consider what you yield to before you yield, and whatever you do to reserve our particular interest," and on the eighteenth he dispatched, by way of proof that Rhode Island had no right to exist, a copy of an obscure "patent" of December, 1643, which had passed no one's seals, but which had granted the Narragansett region to Massachusetts.[16]

The anxiety of the Atherton Company was understandable. The Indians had long since failed to make good upon their commitment of 1660, and in the spring of 1662, Ninigret had performed, with Hutchinson and other company representatives, the traditional (English) ceremony of land transfer by "turf and twig." [17] They were in no mood to allow such a cup to be dashed from their lips, and it was doubtless to insure Winthrop's consistency that they now employed the artful Scott as an additional agent. Scott was back in England before the end of winter.

Thus Winthrop's difficulties with Dr. Clarke were compounded by the dissatisfactions of his own colleagues. He nevertheless continued to hew to the line of patience. He remained in touch with Clarke through "private friends": A written proposal, apparently his, carries the date of December 19, and on February 16, 1662/3, he and Clarke made use of a public ship-launching to meet directly and informally. But no cracks yet appeared in Clarke's obstinacy; by the beginning of March he was talking of a "new publique hearing" before the Privy Council; he recited the distresses not only of Rhode Island but of New Haven; and he threatened action more obstructive still. "I feare," wrote Winthrop to Connecticut, "he waites as formerly to give me trouble when the ships are just ready to goe out." [18]

Winthrop had reason for discouragement. Once again he found himself in severe financial embarrassment, and early in February he was obliged to seek an advance of £1,500 from John Harwood, a City merchant of long experience in the New England trade. Harwood was amenable, but only upon iron terms: There would be no pledging of Connecticut's faith and credit, only of the personal property of Winthrop and his heirs—the black lead mine at

Tantiusque, the whole of Fishers Island, plus other tracts in Connecticut and Massachusetts, 50,000 acres in all, together with 100 head of cattle, 400 sheep, and 400 goats. The loan would become due and payable on August 6, 1669, at "the Insurance Office scitutate on the West side of the Royall Exchange, London." It would plague Winthrop to the end of his days.[19]

Yet a solution was nearer than he supposed. Clark was not to stand indefinitely pat. Within weeks his bluster softened to an open willingness to compromise. The reason is unknown. But Winthrop was quick to hasten the thaw. On March 17 he abruptly transferred his entire share in the Narragansett lands to Fitz, Wait, and three of his daughters, a maneuver which not only reduced his direct interest in the controversy but likely disrupted the plans of John Scott. He and Clarke presently agreed to a panel of arbitrators: William Brereton, Dr. Benjamin Worsley, Major Robert Thompson, Captain Richard Deane, and Captain John Brookhaven. Brereton and Worsley were of course friendly to Winthrop; Thompson's sympathies are uncertain, though perhaps leaning to Rhode Island; Deane was a close associate of Dr. Clarke; while Brookhaven's identity is unclear (he may have been an aging sea captain of Puritan past). But whatever the balance of feelings, the group was accepted by both Winthrop and Clarke as competent to pass judgment upon their differences.[20]

The arguments were formal and vigorously pressed. The Rhode Islanders charged that Winthrop had taken out his Connecticut charter "otherwise than according to the limitts and bounds expressed in a former Patent." Yet Winthrop continued to invoke the Warwick precedent; he declared he had made a special effort to avoid "Ambiguity of Phrase"; he claimed he had proceeded under specific Connecticut directives and in conformity with the terms of the Atherton purchase; and he emphasized that he acted only as an agent—there was, he maintained, "no privat aime that might Byasse him." He produced geographic data: the fact that no Rhode Islanders actually resided within the "Narragansett" region and that an insular Rhode Island would contain more people per square mile than would Connecticut. He made much of his "duty," both to his colony and to the Atherton Company, but he intimated the possibility of concessions—if approved by higher authority.[21]

The arbitrators announced their decision early in April. (Two official copies, regularly inscribed upon parchment and endorsed by Winthrop and Clarke, each to the other, were dated April 7.) It was a peculiar settlement—nor was it to afford a permanent solution. The boundary between the two jurisdictions was established at the *Pawcatuck* River, and any consequent revision of the Connecticut charter was avoided by the inspired device of transferring the name "Narrogancet River" to the Pawcatuck. Fishers Island and the Quinibaug Lands above New London would remain in Connecticut. The rights of private property were not to be interfered with by either colony. But the arbitrators further declared "that the proprietors and inhabitants of that land claimed or purchased by [the Atherton Company] . . . shall have free liberty to choose to which of those colonies they will belong." In view of the known attitude of the Atherton investors, this was quite inconsistent with the Pawcatuck frontier. Winthrop, ever empirical, cannot have objected, but why Dr. Clarke failed to take formal exception to it is a mystery.[22]

Yet if the award could settle nothing in America, it did end, for the time being, the London contest of Clarke and Winthrop. Clarke's terrier instincts subsided, while Winthrop appears at once to have lent his special talents to the promotion of Rhode Island's own patent. Again his procedures were not of a sort that could be confided to a public record. But a rapidly rising administrative star, Sir Henry Bennet, later indicated that the Rhode Island charter of

July 8, 1663, owed more to "the good opinions and confidence we had in . . . Mr. Winthrop" than to any other factor, while a standard historian suggests that he might have been the vital influence behind the inclusion of the unprecedented "freedom of religion" clause.[23]

That Captain John Scott had deliberately been excluded from the arbitration is obvious. It no doubt was Winthrop's doing; he by now desired to have as little business with him as possible. But Scott was a man of persistence, nor could Winthrop wholly ignore him. Scott still could claim to represent the Atherton Company and when he learned the details of the settlement with Dr. Clarke went straightway to Winthrop to demand that the entire issue be reopened. The Connecticut governor found it hard to be cordial; he declared himself "very averse" to Scott's whole position and made it plain that he would tolerate no further rocking of the boat.[24] Scott for the moment withdrew. But it soon would become clear that he did not regard the question as closed.

W I T H   T H E conclusion, favorable or no, of his argument with Dr. Clarke, Winthrop was understandably loath to permit anything to delay his departure. Yet there was much which might have detained him: the meetings of the Royal Society, the incomplete status of Rhode Island, a dabbling in a poorly defined new enterprise for salt and potash. Moreover, there was held at Whitehall on April 12 an unusual session of the Privy Council, attended by the king in person, at which New England matters occupied the entire agenda and during which His Majesty declared his intention "to send some commissioners thither . . . to reconcile the differences at present amongst them." That Winthrop attended is almost certain (it indeed may have been his sole direct encounter with his sovereign), and it was probably on this occasion that he extended his most effective aid to the Rhode Islanders. There is evidence that he delighted everyone, in particular the king and Clarendon, and that he acknowledged, respectfully but rather carelessly, that the dispatch of the Royal Commissioners might require a revision of his own charter.[25]

This was a thundering admission. Perhaps, in the face of such grandeur, he could do nothing else. On the other hand, he may have felt that the benefits of humble acquiescence could be enjoyed without serious risk. He must by now have been aware of Stuart misapprehensions in transatlantic matters; the king himself failed to grasp the distinction between Massachusetts and New England, and there is proof, in the hand of another rising undersecretary, of official confusion between Winthrop of Connecticut and Winslow of Plymouth. Even before the end of 1663, the same undersecretary was noting the date of the Rhode Island patent as 1661 or 1662![26]

Winthrop did miss one desirable sailing. But this would be his last frustration; another vessel stood ready to leave, and he embarked with such haste that he failed to say a proper farewell even to William Brereton. Somehow he contrived to round up Fitz and Wait and three indentured servants and get them onto the ship before she dropped down the river.[27]

It was his final view of London, and the last of his ocean crossings. The name of the vessel cannot be stated, nor the day of her departure. But the voyage must have been singularly happy. Seldom have winds carried a sailing craft so steadily westward through middle latitudes; they appear to have been out of sight of land for no more than a month. To be sure, the Royal Society's apparatus for oceanic soundings failed of a "perfect triall": "The motion of the waves unhookes the lead, &c.," reported Winthrop. But it did serve to occupy his time. He furthermore undertook a careful study of the difficulties involved in the determination of longitude, the results of which he incorporated into an extremely perceptive commentary, wherein he concluded that the deficiencies of available instruments, especially timekeepers, reduced the most meticulous efforts to "meere guessing." [28]

He kept no ordinary diary. There was nothing catastrophic of which to take note; and the drab Massachusetts coast lay before him by the earliest days of June.[29]

CHAPTER 18

Studies in Aggression

ON June 17, 1663, perhaps earlier, Winthrop reached Connecticut. The nature of his welcome can be imagined. He had been absent for more than twenty-three months. But now he was home for good—bound forever to the stark little villages and their uncomfortable God.[1]

He still was governor; his third reelection *in absentia*, on May 14, had been routine; moreover, he found himself as well a commissioner to the United Colonies. His personal concerns were in such disarray that he could ask to be excused for the time being from attendance at public functions.[2] But this relief cannot have lasted long. The churches of the colony were rocking with the question of the "Half-Way Covenant," a pious tumult which persisted for months and eventually required the governor's personal intervention. So too did the eternally nasty controversy over the Wethersfield pastorate. Worst of all in the official opinion was an effort to introduce the Anglican style of worship, a problem which Winthrop and the General Court were well advised, in the face of the Royal Commission, to treat with caution. (They even managed a convincing display of reason and understanding.) But Winthrop did not press for genuine toleration; the Lord's Supper was significantly denoted an "ordinance"; and the issue, as soon as practicable, was forgotten.[3]

An early and constant responsibility was the reorganized Society for the Propagation of the Gospel. This was a task for which it is most charitable to say that Winthrop had no flair. He had hoped to place his Indian work program in the hands of his brother-in-law, Colonel Thomas Reade, a man of pronounced military instincts, but the colonel had lately died, while a renewed acquaintance with the natives quickly soured Winthrop's faith in their capacity for sustained labor. Within a year, he had quite abandoned his notions and was recommending a reappraisal of the society's whole effort.[4]

But his paramount responsibility remained the Connecticut charter and the question of whom it was to comprehend. He had found awaiting him in Hartford a letter from Petrus Stuyvesant, in which the Dutch director bade him welcome, spoke heartily of permanent frontiers, and otherwise whistled at the margin of New Netherlands' grave. A week later, John Davenport wrote from New Haven to express his confidence that Connecticut would never undertake to destroy Christ's Kingdom. There was no recent word from Rhode Island, but Winthrop had quickly been given to understand that the boundary at the Pawcatuck was unacceptable to his own colleagues.[5]

I N A S E N S E, Mr. Davenport did misplace his trust: New Haven was not to be destroyed; it was being absorbed. The process was already well under way. Whether or not Winthrop intended it, Connecticut had taken little note of his pleas for delay. (Connecticut—and Winthrop himself—later implied that his letter of March, 1662/3, to John Mason had never been received.) In any case, the Hartford government had continued to act on the premise that its charter meant immediate annexation. On March 20, 1662/3, a Connecticut committee of three had waited upon the

New Haven magistrates with detailed and (it must be admitted) reasonable conditions of union, but the New Haven men demurred, on grounds of consulting their General Court. Moreover, the latter proved, when it met, far from acquiescent; on May 6, it issued a crashing remonstrance, of which the indignation was exceeded only by the verbosity.[6]

A fair estimate of Winthrop's tactics demands constant reference to three factors: (1) Connecticut was committed to union; there is no surviving evidence of opposition to it within Winthrop's colony. (2) Public opinion in New Haven was divided into two principal factions: the stalwarts of the Davenport tradition and those who, like Governor Leete, were disposed to accept some kind of accommodation. (3) The Connecticut governor sought to encourage the amalgamation with a minimum of injured feelings. It was a situation which called not only for the nicest kind of management but likewise for a quantity of ordinary luck. Winthrop contributed the former as could no other in New England; his touch was so light that to this day it is difficult to account for all of his actions. The luck would appear in due course—as so often it does in favor of the astute.

Winthrop's most useful ally was probably the governor of New Haven. William Leete resembled Winthrop in his ability to turn a pleasant, but meaningless, phrase and to insert substance between innocuous lines. But he occupied an awkward position, exposed constantly to the pious pressures of the Davenport party. Leete learned of Winthrop's arrival almost as soon as the latter was in Hartford, but he lay temporarily in agony from a toothache and did not get off a letter until June 25. Leete made his position abundantly clear. He was sorry that Winthrop's charter had not provided for *two* colonies (this was, for Leete, the official New Haven position), but he confided that he had rejected the latest Connecticut proposals merely as a "respite of all actings" until Winthrop's return, which Leete hoped would prove "the medium to bring a comfortable issue to our perturbing exercises." He acknowledged there might be "violent fomentations," and he warned that Winthrop's letter to Major Mason was being variously misrepresented. Nevertheless, he was sure that all would "come to a fair reconcilement in due time." [7]

But even Winthrop's presence failed to reduce the tension. John Davenport wrote that the concept of two colonies under a common charter was Leete's "private doing," quite without official sanction, a position which he presently underscored with a personal appearance at Hartford. Winthrop behaved with a maddening evasiveness; he even found himself unable to find a copy of the Mason letter. The wrath of Jehovah thereupon descended on Leete; his next letter (July 20) to Winthrop might have been dictated from Davenport's own pulpit: "You would please to send us a plaine, positive & particular answer in writing to this question, viz., whither the contents of that your letter [to Mason] shalbe performed to us or no, according to the genuine sense [!] thereof." (A copy of the Mason letter was carefully enclosed.) [8]

In the face of such opposition, Winthrop felt it wise to avoid a decisive encounter until time and the natural fermentation of events should produce a more comfortable atmosphere. A session of the General Court (now styled, in the language of the charter, the "General Assembly") had been called for August 19, but Winthrop did not propose to attend and be pressed into something rash by overzealous colleagues. He therefore pleaded personal business at Boston, which may possibly have been authentic, and the forthcoming meeting of the United Colonies—also at Boston, but not expected to get under way before September. To Mason and the assistants he recommended the creation of a "small committee," with which to pay a "loving visit" to New Haven whenever opportunity offered. To John Davenport he sounded the changes, for what they were worth, upon the merits of union: "Reverend & very honored Sir the more I looke upon the weakened condition of your plantation, in this wild wast, the more need there appears to be," and so on.[9]

Yet Winthrop's absence in Boston represented more than simple evasion. Connecticut's designs required not only the capitulation of New Haven but the approval of the United Colonies, whose Articles of Confederation guaranteed the integrity of each member.[10] Naturally Connecticut would expect to face, at this particular meeting, some solemn and very embarrassing questions.

The 1663 session of the United Colonies of New England got under way on Thursday, September 3, at which time all the commissioners exhibited their credentials: Simon Bradstreet and Thomas Danforth for Massachusetts, Thomas Prince and Josiah Winslow for Plymouth, William Leete and Benjamin Fenn for New Haven, and John Winthrop and John Talcott for Connecticut. (Bradstreet, as senior commissioner for the host colony, was asked to preside.) Thanks to extensive and significant discussions concerning New Netherlands, New Haven's complaint against Connecticut was not presented until the seventeenth. Signed by Leete and Fenn, it specified a number of impolitic interventions within their colony's limits and requested an explanation.[11]

Connecticut's response, though hardly more than a paragraph in length, required two days to compose. It was, under the circumstances, a masterpiece. The Winthrop touches were obvious: the protests of friendly intent, the citation of "amicable propositions," the smoothly contrived phrases, the absence of enforceable promises, everything which might render it both gracious and meaningless. It could hardly be acceptable to Leete and Fenn, though the former hinted his true attitude when he declared that "it is not knowne how farr those propositions mencioned wilbee satisfactory to our people nor what Issue will be attained." The matter was thus, under the rules of the commissioners, deposited in the neutral laps of Bradstreet, Danforth, Prince, and Winslow.[12]

It has been said that Massachusetts and Plymouth thereupon

sprang, with ringing words, to the assistance of the underdog. The neutrals indeed thought it "meet to declare" that New Haven was a separate and distinct jurisdiction, not to be infringed upon by any other United Colonies member without a breach of the Articles of Confederation. But the airing of further particulars was postponed until the next meeting (to be held a year later at Hartford!), "unlesse in the mean time ther bee an amicable uniteing for the establishment of theire peace, the which wee are perswaded wilbee very acceptable to the Naighboring Collonies." It would be difficult to discover here anything else than a veiled invitation to union. Both Leete and Winthrop must, in their special ways, have made their positions clear.[13]

Winthrop returned to Connecticut at the beginning of October, in ample time for the autumn assembly. Hardly was he home, however, when he fell ill, of what disease he did not say, but there is suspicion that he used his complaint as another convenient means to dissociate himself from certain embarrassing proceedings. The assistants and deputies were indeed in an expansive mood, little disposed to moderation in matters affecting their manifest destiny. They authorized the local magistrates at Southampton and Easthampton (Connecticut municipalities on Long Island) to exercise jurisdiction at Southold (a New Haven dependency) and published, by joint resolution, their "dissatisfaction" with those New Haven towns which continued to assert their independence. "Wee also do expect their submission to or Goverment," they declared, "according to or Charter and his Majestyes pleasure therein exprest."[14]

We cannot say that Winthrop opposed this kind of behavior. It is perhaps not too much to suggest that he was following a delicate, two-sided policy wherein he permitted his colleagues to provide the unpleasantness, while he stood conspicuously aside, the very image of good will, prepared, when the time came, with soothing reconciliation. His illness, genuine or no, removed him from the assembly chamber at precisely those moments when the business was at its bluntest, and near the end of the session, "having been againe ill in the night," he advised the assembly, by messenger, of his "dissent from any actions . . . otherwise than by amicable treaties." To this, the assembly paid no more heed than to his now-celebrated letter to John Mason, which was a strange response to the governor whom they would annually re-elect for seventeen unbroken years.[15]

Once more it is possible to charge Winthrop with dissimulation —and once again one must consider whether this would be altogether fair. His goals, proved through three centuries, were in no way reprehensible. His techniques, though perchance refined beyond the purview of a pedestrian morality, worked in ways which were always humane. And there are few who would not pause in admiration before so exquisite a display of the political arts.

Conservative New Haven still could hope for royal protection, but the Crown was bemused and far away. Closer at hand was New Netherlands, and a number of the ultrapure considered removing there, but New Netherlands, though still hospitable to English immigration, was not an English jurisdiction. New Haven —already hooked—twisted and turned. Its General Court decided for another appeal to the king, appropriated £300 toward the expenses, and voted a special tax to provide the money; but the levy raised only disaffection, which openly was encouraged by Connecticut partisans. Davenport and Nicholas Street issued a crabbedly eloquent plea, "New Haven's Case Stated," but it reconstructed few of the rebels.[16]

Winthrop, patient angler, simply permitted his fish to tire. Though resumed negotiations led to nothing immediate, he bided his time, detached, but constantly available, on the periphery of events. In February, 1663/4, he accompanied another "committee" to New Haven, but did not endorse its written—and once more rejected—proposals, and when, in April, a man was arrested at Guilford (New Haven Colony) and put on trial at Saybrook (Connecticut!), he kept carefully out of the affair. His most positive move was private: When Leete, who still could not bring himself to confront Davenport with the truth, gave tacit support to a confiscation of the property of Connecticut sympathizers, Winthrop turned very sharp, reminding the New Haven governor that such behavior was inconsistent with his "freedom of spirit" and that it would "directly tend to further difference and discord." Winthrop went further; he quietly gathered, within New Haven's territory, sworn testimony to indicate that Leete was in essential sympathy with Connecticut rule.[17]

Then, early in the summer of 1664, came the decisive development, for which the most accomplished of negotiators must sometimes wait. Rumors, which lost little in the spreading, told of an abrupt turn in the Stuart program for North America, whereby New Netherlands and a distressingly unspecified portion of New England would, by virtue of force and *another* charter, be converted to a proprietorship under the king's brother, the Duke of York. Subsequent information reduced the enormity of it only slightly. Moreover, everyone knew that the duke was no flexible Puritan but a dedicated Papist. The New Haven struggle was over: A John Winthrop would be infinitely preferable to a James Stuart. To be sure, the requirements of dignity at first produced not amalgamation but a program for the defense of New Haven by Connecticut under the terms of the Connecticut charter. But the problem, for Winthrop, was essentially resolved. The rest of the proceedings were routine: the typically indecisive consent, in September, of the United Colonies and the provisional adjustment of its voting rules; the Connecticut plan, in October, for adding New Haven members to its assembly and council; the decision for union (reluctant still) of the New Haven General Court in December; and the formal act of submission on January 5, 1664/5. Two days later, the final embers of resistance were extinguished when the *Town* of New Haven bowed to the inevitable.[18]

"I suppose," observed John Mason, "it might have been more comfortable for them and our selves . . . [if conclusions could have been reached sooner], but better late than never." Winthrop expressed no such minor resentment. Upon Leete and Davenport he bestowed respectively praise and comfort. It was as if there had been no difficulty at all.[19]

WHEN Winthrop sailed from England in the spring of 1663, he had left behind, dissatisfied but undismayed, the redoubtable "Captain" John Scott. Of this curious young man it at least can be said that he was almost totally immune to the Winthrop personality. This may appear strange, as the two possessed much in common. Each had a nose for enterprise; each was a born politician; both were masters of negotiation. Yet a subtile difference set them apart—and often at loggerheads. For the plain truth is that Scott was an adventurer, while Winthrop was a builder. The disparity is everywhere evident, but nowhere more strikingly than in the testimony of those whom each had outmaneuvered. Winthrop's victories were acceptable. Scott's, somehow, were not.

It will be recalled that Scott had taken vigorous exception to the outcome of the Winthrop-Clarke arbitration. "I cannot deem those termes . . . any way to answer your desires," he wrote Edward Hutchinson on April 29; [20] indeed, Winthrop's ship had hardly faded from view before he was resorting to every intriguing art in an effort to undo the settlement. Scott was a serious antagonist. He possessed important friends—"connections" would be perhaps the better word. He enjoyed especially close ties with Sir Joseph Williamson, an officer-courtier of numerous talents, including scholarship, but marked most of all by an instinct for the main chance. Williamson currently served as confidential secretary to the Principal Secretary of State Sir Henry Bennet. Another significant acquaintance was Thomas Chiffinch, an aging bureaucrat with a marvelous collection of offices, including Comptroller of the Excise and New Imports, Page of the Backstairs, and Keeper of His Majesty's Closet and Pictures. The offices, and a notorious brother named William, have endowed him with a reputation for unscrupulous behavior that seems not to have been fully deserved.[21] However, it was through Thomas Chiffinch, not William, that Scott conducted the greater part of his business. From Scott himself we learn that he took "a potent Gentleman" into the Atherton Company; the royal archives disclose, atop a list of the Atherton associates, the name of Thomas Chiffinch; while Scott further indicates that he expended £60 upon a "parcel of curiosities" wherewith to "gratify persons that are powerful." There are hints of yet other disbursements.[22]

Nor were Scott's efforts entirely in vain. "Wee have been given to understand," declared King Charles on June 21, "that our good Subjects . . . [of the Atherton Company] are . . . dayly disturbed and unjustly molested . . . by certain unreasonable and turbulent Spirits of Providence Colony. . . . Wee have therefore thought fit hereby effectually to recommend the said Proprietors to [the] neighborly Kindness and Protection . . . [of Massachusetts Bay, Plymouth, New Haven, and Connecticut]." It was as unimpeachable a license to aggression as the most prejudiced Puritan could have desired. It was likewise an earnest of official confusion: The charter of Rhode Island emerged from the seals within less than a month, complete with the Pawcatuck boundary and with appropriate reference to the late arbitration, but without clear specification of the Atherton rights.[23]

Moreover, the transactions at Westminster were by no means synchronous with developments in New England. The Connecticut assembly had made it clear, as early as October of 1662, that it regarded the Narragansett country as its own. To this Rhode Island had reacted with horror and suggested, in the manner of

[255]

New Haven, that any disruptive action be postponed until after Winthrop's return. A kind of lull indeed set in and continued until the third of the following July. It was then that the Atherton proprietors, unaware alike of the king's letter and the imminence of the Rhode Island patent, gathered at the trading house of the Messrs. Richard Smith to signify, as per the arbitration, their political loyalty. There could be no question of the result; Connecticut was chosen by acclamation. Twenty associates subscribed their names (and four their marks) to a formal petition, addressed to the Hartford magistrates, begging for immediate annexation. Among the signatories were Fitz and Wait Winthrop, but not, it should be noted, their father.[24]

Connecticut responded, on July 10, with a meeting of the governor's council. Whether Winthrop personally presided is unknown, but it is reasonable to assume that he did. Neither he nor the assistants were loath to proceed to the formalities. They pronounced the inhabitants of Narragansett a "plantation," of which Captain Edward Hutchinson, Lieutenant Joshua Hewes, and the elder Richard Smith were constituted selectmen, and the younger Richard Smith the constable. Rather significantly, the newborn jurisdiction was christened Wickford—after the native place of Winthrop's lady. Its limits were suggestively unspecified.[25]

Nothing in these proceedings could be held to violate the Winthrop-Clarke agreement. But it was asking too much to expect the Rhode Islanders to accept them, especially after the receipt that autumn of their own patent. There occurred, inevitably, public confrontations and private fisticuffs, nor was the situation clarified by the persistence, on both sides of the Pawcatuck, of a certain preference for *Massachusetts*. As early as December, Winthrop was sufficiently disturbed to send off a semiofficial complaint to his semiofficial friend, Dr. Benjamin Worsley, in which he cited "violent disposessions," contrary to guarantee, at the hands of Rhode Island. Winthrop had yet to see the formal text of the Rhode Island charter, but someone had told him that the entire April agreement had been omitted therefrom. He also reported that Connecticut had thus far received no offer to discuss any differences.[26]

Rhode Island was finally heard from during the following March, a formal protest, signed by Governor Benedict Arnold and his deputy, that listed "mayhem and torts" allegedly perpetrated by Connecticut agents east of the Pawcatuck. Rhode Island suggested negotiations. Winthrop responded typically: He procrastinated (on the ground that the Connecticut assembly would not meet again until May); he counterprotested (citing the destruction of hay west of the Pawcatuck); and he adopted an air of friendly moderation. "I am very unwilling," he declared, "to fill your eares with complaints, being rather studiously desirous there should be all righteous waies promoted of loving & amicable correspondence." He further suggested that both colonies create a permanent body of commissioners with which to resolve not only current but all future differences. The idea had merit, and doubtless he meant it when he subscribed himself as "your reall freind." [27]

But Winthrop was not so naïve as to suppose that friendship demanded automatic capitulation to an opponent's point of view. At a council meeting on April 2, 1664—over which he is known to have presided—the organization of Wickford was further perfected. Hutchinson, William Hudson, and the elder Smith (all Atherton associates) were named "commissioners" for "the Town and the places adjoyning within the Colony of Connecticott[!]"; appeals from their decisions were directed to the county court at New London; a militia was prescribed (six exercises per year); and a "suitable orthodox minister" was recommended (Mr. Edward Brewster). Hutchinson and Hudson, being present, took their oaths on the spot.[28]

Rhode Island was infuriated. Late in May, Roger Williams, though named an assistant under its new patent, was hard pressed to prevent the forcible expulsion of the Smiths by a neighborhood mob. In a lengthy letter to Winthrop, he deplored the selfishness of man and, in particular, of Englishmen, but he applied some judicious pressure of his own with the information that Massachusetts was about to compose its differences with his colony. Williams concluded with the hope that Winthrop, Mason, and "some of the grave elders" might be moved to a similar purpose. However, it was not until July 20 that Connecticut made formal reply to the Rhode Island letter of March 10, and then it merely suggested that representatives be selected by each side to run the boundary. This the United Colonies commissioners, meeting in September, endorsed for what it was worth.[29]

Affairs therefore continued dangerously imprecise. Moreover, they were soon to be further unsettled by the interposition of the Crown itself.

O F A L L the regions brought into controversy by the Connecticut charter, Long Island presented the greatest complexity. The conflicting positions of Connecticut and New Haven already have been noted. Furthermore, west of the boundary of 1650, yet within the Connecticut patent as broadly interpreted, the Dutch West India Company continued to give the law to a growing and increasingly English population. Under the circumstances, the Hollanders were loath to disturb the *status quo,* while Connecticut was eager to revise it. Into this distracted environment a third influence now thrust itself in the person of the unfathomable John Scott.

Scott had returned to America in the late autumn of 1663, bringing with him a quantity of backstairs information which he was careful for the time being not to divulge. He was not long in sniffing out Connecticut's true intentions and within a month appeared at Hartford, all charming and personable, in quest of advantage. Winthrop, for once, was taken in. He was of course aware of Scott's entrees at court, and when the young man drew up a letter, full of "dropped" names and addressed to Joseph Williamson, which seemed to give unqualified endorsement to all of Connecticut's aspirations, he turned suddenly cordial. Scott was named magistrate at Ashford (Setauket) and Connecticut commissioner for all of Long Island. He soon was holding court in his own house at Setauket, assisted by John Talcott, John Young, and Richard Woodhull.[30]

Among the closets of Whitehall, Scott had gotten wind of the plans of the Duke of York for the reduction of New Netherlands. He apparently had revealed nothing of them at Hartford, but now, on Long Island, he began to hint what was in prospect, suggesting that the Connecticut claims would be superseded and even implying that he had come as the duke's agent. Long Island was by this time in a condition so fluid that Scott could contrive what he would. Dutch authority in the western towns already was being flouted by a band of irregulars, and before the end of December Scott himself led a company of 150 men, horse and foot, over the frontier. Trailing a cloud of partly armed onlookers, he progressed from village to village, issuing ambiguous proclamations. But at Hempstead, he openly endorsed the Duke of York, and at Breuckelen (Brooklyn) and other ethnically Dutch communities he boldly flew St. George's Cross.[31]

In the face of even so flagrant a challenge, the realistic Stuyvesant preferred speech to combat. Early in January, he sent representatives to Scott, who disclosed nothing concrete, yet conveyed the impression that he still was acting for Connecticut. When Scott's activities threatened to destroy even the pretense of Dutch authority, the director went in person and late in February, at Hempstead, agreed to permit the "English" to govern the English-speaking towns for twelve months or until a proper boundary could be determined.[32]

Under normal circumstances, Winthrop might have condemned

such a performance in public, but commended it in private; Scott's filibusterings had already half destroyed the Dutch will to resist. However, it was apparent by now that Scott was not serving Connecticut's advantage. His pronouncements either had been vague or had made no mention of Connecticut at all. Moreover, he began to suggest that a further pressing of the Connecticut claims would constitute, in the face of York's plans, little less than treason. Before a public meeting at Easthampton (far without the Dutch limits) he declared Connecticut's behavior to be virtual rebellion, that he would so inform the king, and that thereafter the Connecticut people "should not be able to govern themselves fore months." [33]

For Winthrop and the assistants, this was enough. They did not, as one has asserted, call the assembly into special session, but they did set forth the whole matter at the next scheduled opportunity, which was in March. The assembly's response was vivid, if not notably sound from a legal point of view. It drew up an elaborate bill of particulars, noting such diverse malfeasances as defaming the king, tumultuous carriages, receiving bribes, profaning the Lord's Day, and "Acting treacherously to the Colony of Connecticutt"; and it ordered Scott's arrest by appropriate officers in New Haven, Milford, Branford, Stratford, and Fairfield. (Since only Stratford and Fairfield as yet appertained unquestionably to Connecticut, the challenge to the identity of New Haven Colony was obvious.) [34]

On March 21, the Connecticut marshal, Jonathan Gilbert, presented himself before the magistrates' court at New Haven with charges and specifications. He received little satisfaction. New Haven still clung to its posture of independence; the court was indeed willing to try the case, but not in the name of Connecticut. As luck would have it, Scott himself was present; to the magistrates he declared his willingness to face prosecution in any except a Connecticut court; to the discomfited Gilbert he handed a semiofficial letter wherein he pronounced the Connecticut authorities "guilty of heinous crimes." He thereupon departed across the Sound to Setauket, escorted by a dozen New Haven men of the separatist persuasion.[35]

Connecticut wasted no more time with New Haven. Setauket was in any case a Connecticut town, and on the twenty-seventh a posse of sixteen sailed over from Fairfield and overpowered Scott at his own residence. He in due course was committed to the Hartford jail, laden, according to one witness, "with a long Iron Chaine." It was an unpleasant business, and Winthrop was besieged with protests. Not all were disinterested: "You now see," wrote John Davenport, "that we have abundant cause to refuse union with that Colonie, which multiplies injuries against us, without ceasing." [36]

Winthrop kept his own counsel. Indeed, there is evidence that he once again tried to dissociate himself from the less genteel proceedings. While Scott was being hustled into irons, the governor was reported "forth of the Towne, busy with Some Gentlemen from the bay," and he tarried through much of April at New London. It was not, on the face of it, very straightforward; the wife of the prisoner, distracted by worry and in an advanced state of pregnancy, invited his attention to Pontius Pilate. Yet the principal evidence of kindness in the record of Scott's incarceration survives in Winthrop's handwriting.[37]

Winthrop even managed to avoid presiding at Scott's trial, held late in May before the Particular Court at Hartford. It was just as well; the proceedings hardly represented English justice at its best. Essentially the same colorful charges were preferred, supplemented by a new one relating to "a certaine Indian Queene," known as "the Sunk Squaw," from whom Scott was alleged to have embezzled a large tract of land. The process required several days; the verdict was guilty—on all counts. The sentence was a fine (£250), loss of political and judicial rights, imprisonment at the pleasure of the court, and ultimate banishment from the colony. Scott was at once packed away in a "Garrit," three stories above the ground.[38]

Yet his treatment turned suddenly more lenient. We are assured of visits by his father-in-law and even by his wife. These were followed, in July, by the prisoner's escape, down all three stories, "by the help of some Rop. . . ." He returned directly to his home in Setauket. There was no hint of a hue and cry. For it suddenly had become desirable that Scott should no longer in any way resemble a martyr.[39]

CHAPTER 19

Benevolent Conquest

PETRUS Stuyvesant, director general of the Dutch West India Company in New Netherlands, was a person in whom a substantial common sense contended unceasingly with a violent emotion. It was much to his credit that the former ordinarily prevailed; only on infrequent occasions did his passions burst forth unchecked. The popular legend of his ungovernable temper is as inaccurate as it is unfair.

Precisely how, or when, Stuyvesant was apprised of Winthrop's charter is uncertain, but he must have recognized at once that his New Netherlands lay squarely within Connecticut's zone of westward expansion. Nor was Connecticut loath to confirm the impression. Weeks before Winthrop's return from England, the Hartford assembly had presented the Dutch with a clear statement of its intentions. Stuyvesant may have hoped that Winthrop's return would quiet the situation. But the latter afforded little comfort. He expressed his "great thanks for those favours when I was beginning my late pilgrimage from your citty," but remained otherwise noncommittal.[1]

Connecticut, moreover, increased its pressure. On July 10, 1663, the Hartford council dispatched John Talcott to the English-speaking, but Dutch-governed, plantation of Westchester, with thinly disguised instructions to arrange its annexation. (Winthrop's involvement is not certain, but he cannot have been unaware of what was going on.) Stuyvesant sensed the danger before Talcott was well out of Hartford; on the same day he wrote bluntly to Winthrop, demanding a categorical statement as to whether Connecticut would honor the treaty of 1650, and three days later, in an obviously inspired letter from "Monades" (Manhattan), the Plymouth merchant Thomas Willet urged a public reassertion of the existing frontier.[2]

Winthrop continued indefinite. To Willet he endorsed the virtues of "the settling and continuance of peace," but forbore any specific pledge until his assembly should meet; furthermore, he said, his "occasions" required a return to Boston. "I came now up," he explained, "rather upon a visit to my family and friends, then [*sic*] with any intent of officiating." To Stuyvesant he wrote, politely but plainly, that negotiations by letter would be of little use. He would prefer, he said, a face-to-face discussion, preferably at Hartford and after the September meeting of the United Colonies. Indeed, if Stuyvesant could wait until after the October session of the Connecticut assembly, so much the better.[3]

Stuyvesant refused to fall into any such trap. On September 9 he abruptly appeared, flanked by a deputation, before the United Colonies commissioners at Boston and demanded assurance that the Hartford articles of 1650 would continue intact. Winthrop and Talcott, sitting for Connecticut, were visibly embarrassed; they cited the absence of notice and "humbly craved" that the whole matter be postponed until the next meeting—docketed for the following year at Hartford. The other commissioners were equally uncomfortable and endeavored to resolve the dilemma by pronouncing the 1650 articles binding—saving always the rights of the Crown and of Connecticut, "by theire Charter and late graunt from his Majesty." [4]

This inspired verbiage satisfied neither party. Its transparency was patent to the Dutch, while Winthrop and Talcott charged the United Colonies with venturing beyond their proper jurisdiction. Statements and arguments were bandied about for five additional days. No conclusions were reached. Stuyvesant came near to losing his famous temper, charging (with some justification) that Talcott and Winthrop made "frivolous Reply." [5]

T I M E   W A S not on the side of the Hollanders, and the director knew it. Frustrated at Boston, he now determined to force a direct confrontation. It was a gallant, if hopeless, effort. Stuyvesant chose not to participate in person; likely he feared for his own self-control. But he sent representatives of stature: Cornelis Van Ruyven, secretary and receiver general of New Netherlands; Oloff Stevenszen Van Cortlandt, burgomaster of New Amsterdam; and John Laurence, a merchant of English origin, the last to serve as an interpreter. They departed Fort Amsterdam at sunrise on October 5 aboard "Dirck Smith's sloop." They reached Hartford, on horseback, about four o'clock on the afternoon of the eighth, which was the first day of the Connecticut autumn assembly. [6]

From the beginning, it was obvious that the Dutch could hope for very little. They were permitted to leave a written communication at the Hartford meetinghouse, but were barred from direct speech with the assembly and were quartered with the marshal, Jonathan Gilbert, on the extremity of the village. [7] They moreover discovered the presence of "deputies" from a number of their own towns, including Westchester and Rustdorp (Jamaica). Early the following morning, they waited privately upon Winthrop, who received them with characteristic courtesy, but treated their questions with a frustrating equivocation. When the Hollanders inquired as to the assembly's reaction to their note, the governor replied he had no "correct information on this subject, as he left the meeting a little while after, being very much indisposed." Later in the day, the Dutch were faced with a select committee, consisting of Matthew Allyn, John Allyn, and John Talcott, but not Winthrop, which proved less genial and more to the point. They were told, "in a long harangue," that the English towns on Long Island must be placed henceforth under Connecticut and that the articles of 1650 had been superseded by the patent of 1662.

Winthrop once again took care to withdraw himself from the less pleasant passages. On Saturday, October 10, the committee belabored the Dutch all morning; Winthrop and the committee tendered them a noonday dinner. On Sunday morning, October 11, Winthrop escorted the visitors to church; in the evening he entertained them at supper at his own residence; and when the meal —and the sabbath—were at an end, he gave them easy assurance that his colony laid no claim to New Netherlands, only to the territory stipulated in its patent. But he waved aside a request to put this into writing and pretended honest confusion when reminded that New Netherlands and the charter lands were to a great extent identical.

On Monday, the twelfth, the Dutch were simply kept waiting. On the thirteenth, they again were confronted by the assembly's committee, which advised that the deputies from Long Island and Westchester refused to continue longer under Dutch rule. The vis-itors, clutching at straws, cited Winthrop's assurances. "The Gov-ernor," retorted the committee, "is but one man." They had, they added, no legal knowledge of New Netherlands and could have none until the Crown of England should recognize its existence. They did tender another noonday dinner, this time at the "Town Hall," but the amenities were disrupted by further argument, wherein the English appear to have cast off all pretense of de-corum. (There typically is no evidence that the governor was present.)

Late that afternoon, the visitors were told that a final communi-cation would be placed in their hands on the following day. As a last gesture, possibly of despair, they paid their parting respects to Winthrop, whom they found gracious as ever. He assured them he wished the negotiations had gone better, but that the *assembly* had moved otherwise (!).

Stuyvesant's agents had their note and were ahorse by half-past eight in the morning. The farewells were minimal, while the note they carried was addressed to the director general "at the Manados," not New Netherlands. Yet Winthrop maintained the pose of peacemaker for a little longer. Confined near the close of the October assembly by another of his illnesses, he urged, by letter, the avoidance of force. "I conceive it might be necessary," he added, "that some fitt persons might be sent to know the true state and condition of those plantations towards the dutch . . . and to have power to treat with the duch Generall concerning them." [8] (Diplomats have ever been a special breed of spies.)

Stuyvesant was appalled. In a forlorn letter to Amsterdam, he foresaw only "bloodshed and, with bloodshed, which they seem only to wish, loss of all we possess" unless adequate reinforcements were forthcoming. Yet Winthrop desired neither slaughter nor, in its ordinary sense, plunder. He sought hegemony—as much as would be feasible without recourse to arms. He may have been "but one man," yet he contrived to restrain the more belligerent Connecticut spirits. The Hartford assembly did receive the town of Westchester "as a member of this Corporation" and declared that "all the land between the sayd West Chester and Stanford [*sic*] also doth belong to the Colony of Connecticut." But it also announced that it would refrain, for the time being, from asserting its authority over western Long Island, *provided* that Stuyvesant did the same. [9]

The pressure upon the Dutch was not, of course, withdrawn. John Scott was, for a time, a part of it, and after Scott the assembly openly commissioned Samuel Willys and Matthew Allyn to visit Long Island "to settle the Govermt. on the West end" according to Scott's Hempstead agreement. Thenceforth the engulfment developed apace: On March 19, 1663/4, Connecticut announced that the English-speaking towns would be absorbed on grounds not of language and nationality but of charter right. Later in the spring, the standing council ordered the residents of the same towns to "yield obediance" only to officials chosen "according to the advice of the Collony of Connecticut; and all pretended officers are to stand by." At the May elections meeting, the assembly accepted representatives from Hempstead, Jamaica, Newtown, and Flushing, and once again declared Long Island to be "one of those adjoining Islands expressed in the charter." By May 21, John Talcott was preparing to collect Connecticut taxes there.[10]

N o r d i d Winthrop himself remain much longer in isolation. He presided in person over the assemblies of March and May and at the latter permitted himself to be put at the head of yet another Long Island committee. He undoubtedly felt by this time that things had proceeded so far—toward chaos—that his personal intervention was in order. He was in western Long Island by mid-June. Vanished now was any suggestion of dissimulation. Accompanied by Matthew Allyn, Samuel Willys, and John Young, he made the rounds of the English towns—Hempstead, Flushing, Jamaica, Middleburg, and Gravesend—removing as he went the greater number of Scott's appointees and replacing them, always carefully in the king's name, with men of Connecticut sympathies. Poor Stuyvesant went, with part of his bureaucracy, to protest—and encountered a Winthrop smooth as ever, but like flint. Before a knot of obviously English bystanders, he was read the plain facts of political life: This was the king's land, allotted to Connecticut by royal patent, and all who therein dwelt were His Majesty's subjects and liege men. In vain did the director expostulate; Winthrop remained polite but inflexible. The Dutch position was, he asserted, plainly invalid, the Connecticut claim perfect. The Dutch must therefore give way. One may marvel that Stuyvesant could restrain himself.[11]

It was the political high tide of John Winthrop, Jr. Before him and his Connecticut colony, New Netherlands lay already in an advanced state of disintegration. He may be pardoned if he permitted himself the dreams of a much younger man, and the dreams would have been more exalted still had he known what really lay along Connecticut's deeded ribbon to the South Sea. He may be pardoned if he thought again of enterprise, of real estate, engrossed in his own behalf, and when a certain Indian, by name Tobaccus, "freely" conveyed to him the southern half of Long Island from modern Islip to and including Patchogue, no one was astonished.[12]

But political tides are seldom slow to subside. Winthrop's continued at flood for less than a week. On June 18, at Huntington, he was handed a hurried note, covered with the untutored, half-Dutch scrawl of John Underhill. It listed rumors from Boston: A squadron of English frigates was approaching New England to "settle government and reduce the Dutch." Five hundred soldiers were aboard and a thousand small arms. "My respecktse," concluded Underhill, "to my frense atending you." [13]

Connecticut was not to be heir to North America after all.

T H E D U K E of York's expedition of 1664 was not quite a bolt from the blue; John Scott already had hinted it. Yet a full and accurate concept of what was afoot developed only slowly. Massachusetts received its first dependable advice in mid-June; Stuyvesant at Fort Amsterdam waited until nearly July. Winthrop's knowledge grew piecemeal in the course of his return from Long Island to Hartford, but only by July 4 were Underhill's rumors essentially confirmed.[14]

In England, the decision had been dilatory, the preparations precipitate. The ancient and persistent "Stirling" claim to Long Island had been quieted—with promises of the Stuart sort—as early as 1662, but the famous duke's charter of March 12, 1663/4 was not submitted to the royal secretariat until February 29. The speed with which it was perfected bore witness to the eminence of its recipient; its inconsistency with previous patents disclosed either a grand confusion or a lordly unconcern with existing commitments. To be sure, the free and common soccage of the manor of East Greenwich was once again invoked, but this time the grant was to an individual, not a corporation. Far more disturbing were the territories described: the present State of Maine between the St. Croix and the Kennebec (with an extension northward to the St. Lawrence); *all* the islands from Nantucket westward to Manhattan and Staten; and the whole of the mainland *from the Connecticut* to the Delaware. It must have startled Winthrop almost as much as it did Stuyvesant.[15]

Even before the patent, seals dangling, was formally in hand, the Crown was working to give it reality. As early as February 25, a royal warrant directed the officers of the ordinance to prepare an estimate of arms and ammunition necessary for "New England," and on the twenty-ninth the Clerk of Signet was ordered to prepare a bill authorizing an initial expenditure of £4,000. There followed a spate of almost frenzied activity. Subsequent "stores of war" exceeded £2,000 additional. Someone suggested that the liquidation of New Netherlands might be combined with the regulation of New England, and it was thereupon decided that the expedition against the Dutch should be carried out by the same Royal Commissioners which the Privy Council had authorized the previous year. Their final commission, with appertaining instructions, was ready by April 25.[16]

To entrust a military venture to a group of this kind would seem the height of folly, and nothing so fatuous was in fact attempted. Command of the military effort was placed in the hands of one of the commissioners, and the individual selected for this responsibility was of admittedly superior qualifications. (The Duke of York, though gravely deficient in political acumen, had an occasional knack for choosing effective subordinates.) Colonel Richard Nicolls had just turned forty. The younger son of a Bedfordshire barrister, his Royalist roots ran deep; while yet a youth, he had captained a troop of horse, and during the whole exile of the interregnum he had clung loyally to York's entourage. Nicolls enjoyed unquestioned access to the Restoration great—in 1660 he had been made groom of the duke's bedchamber—yet one can discover in him nothing of the traditional placeman. He was, in a word, Winthrop's sort, a man of curiosity, intelligence and pronounced moderation. This was most fortunate not only for Winthrop and Connecticut but for Stuyvesant and New Netherlands as well.[17]

The other selections were less happy. Colonel George Cartwright was an officer of little competence; aside from his services in America, we know merely that he was of Ossington in Nottinghamshire. The abilities of Samuel Maverick were more obvious—but so were his prejudices. Least suitable of all was Sir Robert Carr, an obscure knight of Ithall in Northumberland, whose record as commissioner and the possession, as his *heir*, of a natural son, would indicate a character not of the firmest. The Maverick appointment, though questionable from the New England point of view, was at least understandable. No one knows who discovered Cartwright and Carr, but Sir Joseph Williamson, who was, with all his faults, a man of perception, approved of neither. He described Cartwright as "a for all fopp"; Carr he dismissed as "weake." [18]

Thanks to the reports of "several persons"—one thinks immediately of Maverick and Scott—Whitehall possessed a not inaccurate notion of the capabilities of New Netherlands. This and the limited Stuart resources insured an expedition of only moderate strength. There were four vessels, of which two were listed as fourth rate and one as fifth, while the last was a chartered mer-chantman. *Guinea*, the flagship, carried between 26 and 30 guns; *Elias*, a captive from the Dutch in 1653, may have had as many as 36. *Martin*, the fifth rate, mounted 14; the merchantman, *William and Nicholas*, may have had 10. The quantities of personnel and equipment are still less certain. There may have been 450 men of the sort called "troops"; Stuyvesant referred to four effective companies, but expanded their numbers to about 1,000. Among the initial estimates for the operation we find 500 firelocks, 200 pikes, "carabins," 2 mortar pieces, 24 halberds, and 2 "brasse sakers with field carriages." Also recommended were 300 spades and shovels—in case of a prolonged siege.[19]

Such, very generally, was the force that Nicolls took out of Portsmouth Roads in mid-May to change the history of North America. His voyage across the Atlantic was not conspicuously prosperous. He had hoped to sail in company to Long Island Sound, where refreshment and reinforcements would be available at a reasonable distance from his objective. But he met with head-winds, and later, in the fogs of the fishing banks, his ships lost touch. *Martin* and *William and Nicholas* put into the Piscataqua settlements on the afternoon of July 20; Nicolls, in *Guinea* and with *Elias* in company, anchored off Nantasket, in the approaches to Massachusetts Bay, on the twenty-second. It was some days be-fore the two groups could rediscover each other and recombine.[20]

Nicolls was prompt to proclaim his mission. Letters went off at once to Hartford; the Massachusetts council he approached di-rectly. At Boston, his reception was far from gracious. The Bay openly dragged its feet; Nicolls was told that his propositions would necessitate a special session of the General Court, and he still was at Boston, seeking pilots and logistical aid, on August 10.[21]

At Hartford it was otherwise. To be sure, the Reverend John

Whiting had hurried in from Massachusetts with all the undigested rumours, including a dreadful hint of direct royal taxation. But Winthrop retained his poise; there was no panicky summoning of his assembly. He moreover had reason to believe that Nicolls at least was no martinet; among the dispatches from the king's ships was a letter, from Sir Robert Moray of the Royal Society, urging his cooperation and commending Nicolls to his attention in the most cordial terms. Moray clearly knew when to promote a friendship, for the two were positively made for each other. "I am not a litle proud I had some litle hand in your acquaintance," Moray wrote in 1665, "which I do not doubt but is cultivate by both to your mutuall satisfaction." [22]

At Fort Amsterdam, Stuyvesant now knew of the English intentions, but not of the arrival of the duke's "frigates." Rather pitiably he endeavored to distract the New Englanders by implying, through the embarrassed Thomas Willet, that the Mohawk Indians harbored "evill intentions" toward them, and he thereupon passed up the Hudson to Fort Orange, in part to convert the suggestion into reality. But neither Winthrop nor even the Boston magistrates were diverted for an instant from the principal issue; the former pointed out that the Mohawks were so distant as hardly to constitute a threat, save possibly to the settlements above Springfield, and spoke comfortably of reports from up river as to the friendly disposition of such Mohawks as actually were in the region. The plans of the English were, if anything, hastened. By the beginning of August, a Dutch coaster arrived at Manhattan to report being chased by an English man-of-war, and when, on August 15, Stuyvesant at last returned from Fort Orange, he found his little capital in a state of confused alert, with men poking at its fortifications and an eight-day ban upon the brewing of high-percent beer.[23]

Winthrop was prepared, for reasons both public and personal, to cooperate fully with Nicolls. On July 29, the latter wrote to an-

nounce that all his ships had at last assembled at Boston and to ask
the Connecticut governor to meet him at the west end of Long
Island. Shortly after August 7 (he compounded a final medical
prescription on that date), Winthrop proceeded to New Haven,
where he would be in a more favorable position to learn of and
respond to any movements of the English squadron. There, on the
sixteenth, he received word that Nicolls was temporarily in Long
Island Sound and had requested the able-bodied English of Long
Island to meet him at Gravesend on Monday, the twenty-second.
(It is evident that Nicolls preferred to avoid the tricky currents of
Hell Gate in favor of the circuitous, but far safer, approach of the
Narrows.) [24]

Winthrop moved at once. With Fitz-John and Samuel Willys,
he crossed to Long Island by shallop, and he already was in
Gravesend when *Guinea* first showed her topsails in Lower Bay on
the sixteenth. Two days later, the other vessels were up; all four
made anchor in the shelter of Coney Island.[25]

Gravesend was normally a village of 300, but now it became a
throng. To the local able bodied were added contingents (some
serving again under the remarkable John Scott) from the other
English towns, while the king's ships presently debouched several
hundred more. Amid the bustle, Nicolls and Winthrop met for the
first time—whether on quarter deck or village green is of no consequence. It is enough to say that the happy expectations of each
were borne out; Winthrop, in fact, soon found himself one of the
English commander's more intimate advisers.[26]

Having come ashore, Colonel Nicolls proclaimed the duke's
patent in the presence of "a great number" of regional worthies—
and of Winthrop—and invited their cooperation. The worthies
were nothing loath, nor was Winthrop for all that his vision of a
trans-American Connecticut had gone aglimmering. Patriotic
tongue in loyal cheek, he "openly declared" that none of the New
England colonies had ever possessed a legal claim to Long Island

and that his own government had "intervened there to serve the King's interests as the nearest English jurisdiction"! (There still survives, in his own handwriting, a draft of "A narrative of the proceedings of the General Assembly & Councel of Connecticut Colony in reference to the English plantations upon the west end of Long Island toward the Manhatoes Iland inhabited by the Dutch," which smoothly justified, in terms of the new dispensation, all that had previously transpired; it was a paper of considerable acumen, and may well have been handed Nicolls at this particular juncture.) [27]

Nicolls's good sense was fortified by a comfortable impression of superior strength. He improved his position steadily, yet without unseemly haste, with the clear intention that the thing should be carried off without bloodshed. To Stuyvesant's initial inquiries, he responded with a brief, almost informal, recommendation of surrender—on liberal terms. He took steps to stop the flow of provisions from Long Island to New Amsterdam. Already he had firm assurance that the neighborhood English would refuse any Dutch call to arms.[28]

It was precisely Winthrop's kind of operation—an inexorable application of pressure, seasoned with good will—and Winthrop indeed had much to do with its development. In conference with Nicolls, he urged additional and unprecedented liberality, including, it would seem, freedom of navigation by Dutch residents in Dutch vessels for the time being and for the future! This was scarcely in the spirit of the colonel's instructions, yet Winthrop was not categorically rebuffed. "Mr. Winthrop," wrote Nicolls on the twenty-second, "I do assure you that if the Manhadoes be delivered up to his Majesty, I shall not hinder, but any people from the Netherlands may freely come and plant there . . . and such vessels of their owne country may freely come thither, and any of them may as freely return home in vessels of their own country . . . , and thus much you may, by what means you please, assure the Governor." Winthrop at once drafted a personal letter to Stuyvesant, incorporating the nicest balance of bellicosity and generosity; he was very specific as to the possibility of free trade, yet Nicolls, Carr, and Cartwright promptly endorsed it over their own signatures.[29]

The business was now at a decisive stage. On the twenty-second, Nicolls sent off a second and more elaborate proposal—in charge of a delegation of four, led by Cartwright. Three days later, Winthrop carried his own letter to Manhattan by rowboat, under a white flag and in the company of a committee of New Englanders, including his son Fitz and Samuel Willys. Stuyvesant received them in a wharfside tavern; he was understandably stiff, but Winthrop appears to have applied all the charm he could muster. He appealed to the director's reason, referred to past amenities, and, finally, upon his departure, handed over the letter. This appears to have provided the inspiration for Stuyvesant's best-remembered tantrum, for it was Winthrop's note which the Hollander tore to fragments—lest its extraordinary suggestions should become public knowledge. Even so, the director appreciated the hopelessness of his position. His reply to Nicolls conveyed official defiance, laced with legal and historical citations, but this and his anger were chiefly for posterity and for honor's sake. Already he had privately noted to the attention of his company directors that Long Island was gone, that his own people were disaffected, and that the loss of New Netherlands was certain.[30]

Serene in the knowledge of decisive superiority and with Winthrop constantly at his elbow, Nicolls continued his pressure. All his land forces were by this time ashore on Long Island, and now he marched them to the ferry landing opposite New Amsterdam, while two of his frigates, gunports agape, were posted directly before the town. It is said that Stuyvesant, in a frenzy of despair, had to be restrained from firing upon them. But his fundamental good sense quickly reasserted itself; he was thoroughly out-

manned and outgunned, and his whole supply of powder and lead
did not exceed 3,000 pounds. Nicolls himself was careful to refrain
from unnecessary provocation, and when, on August 25, Stuyvesant suggested a further parley, he ordered the captain of his
flagship in no circumstance to initiate a bombardment.[31]

The terms of capitulation were hammered out on the twenty-
seventh at the director's own "bouwerie" beside the East River.
Protocol still required that neither Nicolls nor Stuyvesant should
meet, but the negotiators selected by each side were nevertheless
persons of consequence. For the Dutch, there acted one of Stuyvesant's council, John de Decker, also Captain Nicholas Varleth,
"Commissary of Wares and Merchandises" and the governor's
own brother-in-law, the Reverend Dr. Samuel Megapolensis (who
is said to have prevented the director from opening hostilities),
Burgomaster Cornelis Steenwyck, former Burgomaster Oloff
Stevenszen Van Cortlandt, and Schepen (Alderman) Jacques
Cousseau. For the English, Nicolls named two of the Royal Commissioners (Carr and Cartwright), and—very significantly—four
New Englanders: John Pynchon of Springfield, Thomas Clarke of
Boston, Samuel Willys, and John Winthrop, Jr. There appears to
have been little hard bargaining. The Arcadian surroundings made
for easy discourse and so did the sight of the English frigates, riding quietly in the late summer haze, up river and down. The most
awkward problem was the question of who was to pay for the
homeward passage of the West India Company's garrison.
(Steenwyck, Cousseau, and Varleth agreed privately to underwrite
this particular expense, to prevent, it is said, any possibility that
the negotiations might break down.) The twenty-three articles of
capitulation were perhaps not quite so expansive as Winthrop had
hinted, but they were undoubtedly liberal. Generally speaking, no
private interest, either of person or property, was to be molested,
while those public and corporate assets that were movable might
be disposed of freely for a period of six months. The Dutch would

enjoy liberty of conscience and (for the time being at least) of trade with the Netherlands. The sole political disability was an oath of allegiance to the English sovereign. It was a remarkable settlement—and much in the Winthrop manner.[32]

The ceremonies came on August 29. The exhibit of commissions and orders and the exchange of ratifications were completed at eight o'clock in the morning beneath the old windmill, close by the west bastion of the fort. There followed a series of martial exercises: The Dutch soldiers marched from their works, bearing banners, arms and drums; two companies of English moved self-importantly in; and detachments from a third company occupied the town gates and the town hall. Etiquette insured that Winthrop should witness everything at close range, but the New England rank and file were kept—at the specific request of the Dutch—on the far shore of East River.[33]

New Amsterdam had become New York, and Fort Amsterdam Fort James. Seldom has an aggression of equal consequence been so humane.

CHAPTER 20

Connecticut, Winthrop,
& the Royal Commission

WINTHROP did not choose to savor the aftermath of victory in conquered New York; it was necessary, he said, that he should appear at the meeting of the United Colonies, which had been scheduled for Hartford on September 1. But one may question that this was his real reason. Although he was "taken" at New Haven with a fever and did not reach Hartford until about the tenth, he seems not to have participated in the remaining sessions, which continued through three days more.[1]

The plain fact was that the occupation of New Netherlands had not been Connecticut's triumph. It had done little to remove the uncertainties posed by the Royal Commissioners and the policies they purported to represent. An accommodation, he knew, must come—and upon more than one issue. He naturally was careful to retain his outward composure: "I saw the towne upon the Manatos Iland reduced to the obedience of our Soveraigne," he wrote Lord Clarendon on September 25, "and we hope also it wilbe a meanes of the future peace, & good of these his Majesties adioyning Colonies." [2] But fond speculations could not of themselves resolve the question of how far, east or west, Connecticut now really extended.

The westward problem was the more urgent, and indeed Winthrop appears already to have taken steps toward its settlement. In the midst of the uncertainties and formalities of the "reduction," he had managed at least one private conversation with Nicolls on the boundary matter, in which it would seem were developed the outlines of a reasonable compromise.[3] The details are vague, but we may suppose, in view of subsequent developments, that Winthrop offered the Hudson Valley and the islands in return for the rest of the mainland west of the Connecticut River. We may assume also that his principal task was now to ease this realistic medicine down the throats of his own constituents.

If so, his procedures were typically subtle. The United Colonies spoke of *collective* bargaining with the Royal Commissioners; but from this he kept carefully aloof. In October, the Connecticut assembly established a permanent committee on boundaries, of which the governor was not to be a member, and which was specifically charged not to "give away any parte of the bownds of our Charter." Yet the same session created a particular committee to negotiate with the Royal Commissioners, of which Winthrop was made chairman and which the assembly invested with power to "issue the bounds" between Connecticut and the duke's patent "so as in theire judgments may be to the satisfaction of the [Connecticut] Court."[4]

At no time did Winthrop suggest that negotiations had already been conducted. Nicolls still stood, officially, upon the duke's charter, and it likely was to convey the impression, at Hartford, of a little necessary bribery that Winthrop arranged for a number of gratuities to go forward to Fort James. In September, he diverted thereto a quantity of foodstuffs (allegedly the whole of Connecticut's current surplus) with instructions that it should be kept out of the reach of speculators and sold to Nicolls alone on Nicolls's terms. In October, the assembly voted a straight gift of 500 bushels of just-harvested grain, while in November the governor dispatched, from his personal herd on Fishers Island, a number of saddle horses. If fiction this was, it was universally regarded as genuine. As soon, in fact, as the October assembly was out of the way, Winthrop felt it safe to proceed to open conclusions. He did encounter delays: Early in November, he was diverted by the religious bickerings of Wethersfield. A little later, he got away toward New York only to be stopped, at Fairfield, by another illness. Nicolls, moreover, was plagued by distractions of his own.[5]

Winthrop did not get all the way to Fort James until the final days of November. (Even then, he evinced little disposition to hurry; en route he took time to examine minutely a "great tall oake," from which lightning had stripped the bark in curiously perfect spirals.) With him went Matthew Allyn, Nathan Gould (or Gold, a leading resident of Fairfield), James Richards (who first had carried the Connecticut charter to America), and Fitz-John Winthrop; at New York they were joined by two representatives from eastern Long Island, John Howell of Southampton and John Young of Southold. For the duke appeared Nicolls, Cartwright, and Maverick. A pioneer historian avers that the discussions were "too long here to be recorded," but it may be questioned that this actually was the case. An agreement was reached by the thirtieth of November, yet Winthrop in the meantime had found it possible to pass many pleasant hours in the company of an erudite Dr. Sackville and other ornaments of the Nicolls entourage. One gets the impression, indeed, of a formality, arranged in advance; only the Long Islanders (who sought to continue under Connecticut rule) appear to have given any trouble.[6]

This is not to say that the boundary of November 30, 1664, was conspicuously satisfactory in all of its parts. The exclusion of Connecticut from the offshore islands was plain enough, but the mainland frontier was so imprecisely drawn as to suggest a last-minute Puritan deception. From the Sound the line was to follow "the Creek or river called Momoronock [Mamaroneck], which is reputed to be about twelve miles to the east of West Chester"; above the head of tide it would run arbitrarily north-northwest "to the line of the Massachusetts." This boundary was presumably not to intersect the Hudson River at any point, yet it actually did so, when extended, at the Highlands. Nicolls had second thoughts in the matter as early as February, and the entire frontier was re-negotiated in 1683 to approximately the location of the present state line.[7]

Like all compromises, the agreement satisfied no one absolutely. Howell and Young refused to sign it, and they continued to badger Nicolls—though, curiously, not Winthrop—through the remainder of the winter. Thomas Pell, long the principal land speculator of Westchester, charged bitterly that Connecticut had sold him out in violation of its own charter and hinted an appeal to the United Colonies. Nicolls himself had technical reason to dread the reaction overseas; though his private instructions had designated Long Island as a special objective, he took care to explain his mainland concessions at length, citing in particular Connecticut's prior occupation and its precedent patent. There would be, he concluded, no profit in insisting upon the whole of the duke's stated bounds unless all New England could be reduced to his rule.[8]

Winthrop, who respected reality before all else, gave way to no lamentations, nor did, officially, his colony. If he feared for his rights to Fishers Island, he did not dramatize the question, and three years later it was quietly reconveyed to him as an "Intire Enfranchised Township, Manor & Place of itself," for a quitrent of "one lamb upon the first day of May if the same be demanded." Nicolls was equally unworried; he had the measure of the Stuart court, nor could he bring himself really to resent the complaints of Howell and Young. "I am too well Naturd," he told the Connecticut governor, "to deale harshly though with the worst of men." [9]

VITAL THOUGH it had been to describe a boundary with the Duke of York, it was not the most complicated of Winthrop's difficulties. Nor was it necessarily the most dangerous. The Royal Commissioners not only had been charged with securing the duke's American territories, they also were expected to reduce the New England colonies to some measure of discipline. Precisely what the Crown had in mind was, as usual, rather vague. But there seems not at this point to have been any serious intention of imposing a centralized police state: Surviving memoranda in the hand of Sir Henry Bennet emphasize such matters as the use of the king's name in public acts and the display of the king's arms at official functions; customs and the regulation of trade are mentioned also. (Least in accord with the Puritan position is a suggestion of liberty of conscience.) The formal instructions carried by the commissioners did not depart significantly from the memoranda; those for the "visitation" of Connecticut indicated some concern over the colony's "most rigid Presbiterian [*sic*] government" and directed an investigation of the territorial uncertainties with Rhode Island, but they cited Winthrop as a man "of whom Wee have a good opinion." Moreover, private addenda urged special caution in dealing with religious questions.[10]

Winthrop was not uninstructed in the nuances of Whitehall; he possessed, in Robert Boyle, an unofficial observer with access to very particular circles. Boyle was ideal for the purpose: He was personally sympathetic; he was a member of the Council for Foreign Plantations; and his special position in the Society for the Propagation of the Gospel justified a steady correspondence, wherein it was convenient to insert comments of a political nature. In July of 1664, just as the greater part of New England was contemplating the arrival of the Royal Commissioners with self-righteous apprehension, Winthrop received private assurance from Boyle that the king intended "not any Injury to your Charter, or the Dissolution of your sivil Gouerment, or the infringement of your Liberty of Conscience and that the doeing of these things is none of the business of the Commissioners." This was perhaps a little optimistic, but Boyle showed himself a perceptive adviser when he suggested some harmless expressions of loyalty and affection as being "most acceptable." The principal danger in dealing with the commissioners would be, he concluded, a "want of right understanding betwixt them & the planters." [11]

No one in New England was so accomplished in the expression of loyalty and affection as the governor of Connecticut. "Your Lordships Commands for the reception of the Honorable Commissioners," he wrote Clarendon in September, "shalbe attended with all imaginable indeavors according to the capacity of this our wildernesse condition, and with all dutifull observance." "Good Mr. Governor," responded the Lord Chancellor, "I . . . do find by the Comrs. that they have beene very civilly treated by you, with wch. his Majtie. is well pleased." At Fort James, Nicolls continued favorably impressed. The laws he prescribed for the English of the duke's province reflected Connecticut practices, and he so embraced the Winthrop point of view as to eject John Scott, forever as it proved, from North America. Nor was the happy atmosphere permitted to be compromised, from Connecticut, by any Puritan outbursts. [12]

As things turned out, the commissioners, as a body, never came to Hartford at all; to an astonishing degree, they accepted Connecticut on faith. They did initiate a formal inquiry at New London on March 25, 1665, but were careful not to press for anything unreasonable. They submitted four "propositions": (1) All householders should take an oath of allegiance, and the administration of justice should be in the king's name. (2) The sole requirements for the franchise should be a "competent estate" and "civil conversation," with no religious clauses. (3) Freedom to worship was suggested—if consistent with good order. (4) Former laws and "expressions in laws" derogatory to the king's majesty should be repealed and expunged. [13]

Formal reply came from the assembly in special session on April 20; it might have been phrased by Winthrop himself—and likely was. Allegiance and the king's name posed no problem; lip service was already in established policy. The suffrage matter was adequately side-stepped with the declaration that "our order for admission of freemen is consonant wth. that proposition." The recommendation of freedom of worship carried its own solution: "We know not," declared the assembly, "of anyone that hath bin troubled by us by attending his conscience, prouided he hath not disturbed the publique." (Religious disconformity remained, in Connecticut, a rather certain apple of public discord.) As to the statutes derogatory to His Majesty, the assembly protested its ignorance of anything of the sort.[14]

Connecticut, under Winthrop, was learning a lesson of infinite merit: It mattered not so much what a colony did, provided it was done graciously!

YET RELATIONS with the Royal Commissioners were by no means confined to a doffing of hats. The problem of the Rhode Island boundary remained conspicuously unresolved. Hardly were the commissioners settled in conquered New York when Governor Benedict Arnold sought to present the issue; he was for the time being rebuffed; New York lacked, explained Nicolls, suitable "entertainment." But in a letter to Winthrop in October, 1664, the colonel referred to the Narragansett country in a fashion hardly conformable to the Connecticut point of view. In his reply, Winthrop "humbly suggested" that no decision be made in the premises until Nicolls again could visit Boston (the headquarters of the Atherton Company!) "where your honr. will have more leisure to heare & consider of those cases."[15]

It was a difficult season in which to undertake any visit. Winthrop likened Hartford, in January, to a "near frozen desert," ice floes encumbered the Connecticut River, and when the Rhode Islanders again pressed for action, he could request an indefinite delay without appearing unreasonable. Nicolls failed to reach Boston at all; Carr, Cartwright, and Maverick arrived only in February. They at once were beset by a bevy of Atherton shareholders, so voluble with denunciations of Rhode Island that Carr wrote in alarm to Hartford, suggesting an immediate conference in the Narragansett country itself. Winthrop did not respond for many days and, when he did, cited God, the weather, and the ice as grounds for further postponement. He no doubt was playing for time—either until the situation could be clarified or even (vain hope!) until Carr, Cartwright, and Maverick would abandon the business and disappear. But the commissioners proved of sturdier temper than he expected, and, following an uncomfortable journey by way of Plymouth, they appeared at the Rhode Island settlements on the afternoon of March 4.[16]

Word of their arrival must somehow have reached Hartford, for Winthrop abruptly ceased his procrastinating. Well before the middle of March, he was on his way to the Narragansett country in the company of Fitz-John and Samuel Willys; the floes miraculously disappeared, and his progress was so rapid that he had arrived at the Pawcatuck by the evening of the thirteenth. Here he received a note from the commissioners requesting a meeting for Thursday, the sixteenth, at the house of Mr. John Porter at Petaquamscut. Winthrop at once pushed forward to Wickford (a village of Connecticut and Atherton loyalties) and blandly suggested that the conference might better be held there, at the residence of Captain William Hudson (an active Atherton associate).[17]

The commissioners were not deceived; they insisted upon Petaquamscut. The details of the proceedings are hazy. Winthrop must have cited the usual documents; the Atherton proprietors offered a symbolic quitrent and suggested six beaver skins annually for ten years. The commissioners, however, had acquired a remarkably favorable impression of the Rhode Islanders. Their decision, rendered on March 20, destroyed for the time being any hope that an Atherton-Connecticut claim might be made good to the east of the Pawcatuck. The disputed territory was not, it is true, ceded outright to Rhode Island; it was to be organized, pending a final disposition, as a "king's province" and administered by royal appointees. But the Pawcatuck boundary of Winthrop and Clarke was again delineated, and the appointees were all Rhode Islanders, including governor, deputy governor, and assistants. Worse yet, the foreclosure upon the Indian mortgage might be voided whenever the natives should contrive to raise their 735 fathoms of wampum, any grants made in the region by Massachusetts, or "that usurped authority called the United Colonies," were pronounced invalid, and any settlers dwelling thereon were to vacate their lands by September 29. Warming to their task, Carr, Cartwright, and Maverick reasserted their award at Warwick on April 4 in still more precise terms.[18]

The Atherton associates were naturally stunned. Yet there is no evidence that Winthrop experienced special distress. He could hardly object to the Pawcatuck line. He furthermore could not help but notice that the commissioners had taken no steps to void any Connecticut act in the area. Moreover, the eviction of bona fide settlers was too arbitrary to last; the commissioners themselves had second thoughts in the matter, and on August 2 Carr and Maverick issued an amendment from Boston, suspending this particular clause until the king's pleasure was known. Nicolls, too, would have none of it, and on September 15 he softened the whole Warwick proclamation with a personal order.[19]

The problem of the Narragansett country had not, in fact, been quieted at all; there remained ample opportunity for maneuver.

But it may fairly be asserted that Winthrop was not, on this occasion, to blame.

THE REMAINING questions between Connecticut and the commissioners were more easily settled or, better still, evaded; indeed, they had been effectively reduced before the New London conference had ended.[20]

One of them, if pressed by a legalist, might have been awkward. In 1635, the moribund Council for New England had invested one of its stockholders, the second Marquis of Hamilton, with 3,600 square miles of territory east of the Connecticut River (which was spelled, conveniently as it transpired, "Converticu"). Now, in 1665, the third Duke and Duchess of Hamilton were attempting confirmation of the grant. Did Connecticut, asked the commissioners, care to comment? [21]

No one knew better than Winthrop that the most effective way in which to dispose of a rival land patent was to postpone serious action upon it. He promised the commissioners that his assembly would study the question, and indeed the special session of April 20 directed Samuel Willys and James Richards to draw up a suitable reply. When, or in what circumstances, this was rendered is not known, but it was, as finally embellished, a typically Winthropian piece of goods. It protested the assembly's ignorance of any "Converticu" River; it chanted the doctrines of the Warwick Patent; and it cited thirty years of possession and the charter of 1662. It expressed the hope that "his majesty would be graciously pleased to silence the claim of Duke Hamilton," and it improved the occasion by suggesting that the king might designate New London(!) "a place of free trade for seven, ten, or twelve years, as his royal heart shall incline to confer as a boon upon his poor, yet loyal, subjects." [22]

This legerdemain was sufficient to render the Hamiltons innocuous for years to come. They never again would be a concern to

Winthrop; a final appeal of the widowed duchess was denied by the Council of Trade in 1697.[23]

Of greater potential embarrassment was a private petition of William Morton of New London, presented to the Privy Council the previous autumn, requesting action against the "treasonable Words spoken by several Persons" in the village. This had been referred across the Atlantic to the commissioners and subsequently was fortified with a letter from Lord Clarendon direct to Winthrop, wherein the latter was urged to consider the case in private. The governor proceeded not only privily but at leisure. In March, he put off the commissioners with gestures; we hear, in due course, of a "committee" and ultimately are assured that every exacerbation has been soothed. Winthrop was palpably aided by the death of John Tinker, who had been Morton's particular bête noire, but he was most particularly relieved that Clarendon had suggested a local, Connecticut solution.[24]

A T T H E beginning of April, 1665, the commissioners quitted New London in excellent humor, obviously assured of Connecticut's loyalty. They had not been so impressed by its physical amenities: "This Colony," they reported, "hath many good Rivers & Harbours . . . [and] many scattering towns, not worthy of their Names." It was an apt description, though they had not in fact seen much of the region. A full year later, Nicolls acknowledged that Connecticut had yet to be fully visited; he did not anticipate, however, "two dayes worke for us, & not the least appearance of a refractory disposition." [25]

The desired impression had been conveyed. Valid or no, the commissioners had swallowed it without reservation. Their regard for Winthrop continued unconcealed; as early as May, Nicolls was endeavoring to persuade him to settle in New York, offering "one of the best houses" free of expense and intimating that "some matters considerable may be putt into practice by yr. assistance and

[289]

knowledge." The happy reaction was a little slow to reach England. Cartwright sailed for home in midsummer, but was intercepted on the high seas by a Dutch privateer and compelled to jettison his papers. Carr arrived at Bristol, mortally ill, in May of 1667. But their reports and those of Nicolls and Maverick, forwarded according to custom in numerous copies upon several vessels, began presently to arrive at Whitehall.[26]

Images, once fixed, are difficult to dispel. That of a bumptious and uncooperative Massachusetts Bay persisted, through numerous countercurrents, to the green at Lexington. That of a loyal and reasonable Connecticut helped guarantee a practical independence so broad that the colony's early and hearty participation in the American rebellion of 1775 is a matter for wonder. The influence of geography may be admitted; whole generations of imperial administrators failed to notice Connecticut. Yet it is not inappropriate to suggest, as a factor in its happy condition, the habits established during the fifteen unbroken years of the ablest of its colonial governors.

CHAPTER 2 1

The Art of Gentle Politics

O N E of the pleasantest episodes in the history of colonial America was the cordial relationship between Richard Nicolls and
John Winthrop, Jr. During the four years in which the colonel
held court at Fort James, they never once experienced a personal
falling out.

This was the more remarkable in view of the striking dissimilar-
ity of their respective communities. New York was compact, built
of brick, and accessible;[1] Hartford unkempt, of clapboards, and
remote. New York already conversed in many tongues; Hartford
was monolingual. New York worshiped variously; Hartford, for
all its pretended tolerance, still sought a single way to God. There
was a topographic variation also. Hartford's river, though of
majestic proportions, was of moderate influence; it did not dominate even New England. The Hudson, by contrast, was the key to
North America, and anyone charged with its administration was
obliged to think in continental terms. Nicolls reflected this clearly;
from the beginning, he was concerned with fundamental forces—
English and French, Protestant and Catholic, European and
aboriginal. Winthrop, growing old beside the Connecticut, his
avenue to the west now severed forever, experienced no such
pressures, and, for all his extraordinary sophistication, he aban-

doned, within months, the pursuit of empire in favor of a judicious, if not very splendid, isolation.

That the policies of Connecticut and New York were not necessarily compatible became evident as early as the winter of 1664/5. Nicolls, at the foot of the Hudson corridor, sought the firmest possible arrangement with the Iroquois Five Nations, then (and for a full century to come) the dominant native influence in that part of America. The Five Nations were not, however, on the best of terms with the ill-assorted "Northerne Indians" of the upper Connecticut, and Nicolls naturally wondered if Winthrop might not lend his good offices to promote an intertribal agreement. Winthrop's reply was cordial; he went even so far as to arrange an exchange of Indian "prisoners." But he had experienced too much of native prejudices to anticipate a genuine accord and was manifestly unwilling to expend much effort to get one.[2]

The disparity of viewpoint became still more pronounced when Nicolls proposed a program for intercolonial defense. Rumors of an Anglo-Dutch war were running through New York as early as March of 1665, and in April the colonel approached Connecticut with a formal "motion," suggesting joint action in case of invasion. This Winthrop referred "with all earnestness" to the special assembly of April 20, but it was for the record only. The deputies balked at once, claiming that such an undertaking would expose their own plantations. Subsequent discussions at the May elections meeting elicited similar excuses.[3]

Formal hostilities with the Dutch had indeed been declared; definitive word reached America in June, embellished with horrid rumors of the intentions of the Dutch Admiral de Ruyter. Nicolls took advantage of the excitement to renew his overtures for an alliance; he reminded Winthrop that the safety of New York was of "the greatest Consequence" to Connecticut, a proposition which he underscored with a personal appearance, on the evening of June 28, at Winthrop's own threshold. Winthrop's response was as

gracious—and as unsubstantial—as he could make it; he already
had called his assembly into another special session for July 6, and
he assured Nicolls that his proposal would, in due course, be reex-
amined. But the assembly once again did nothing. Citing Ruyter
and the Indians, it concentrated its efforts upon neighborhood defense.[4]

Winthrop tried not to appear too blunt. He spiced the fiction of
cooperation by posting Fitz to Fort Albany in the role of liaison
officer, and he implied that the United Colonies might present
something interesting in September. But his true attitude became
clear when, Dutch admiral or no, he took his family upon an
August outing to Fishers Island. The United Colonies brought
forth nothing at all; Winthrop went to Boston in person, but Governor Prince of Plymouth was ill and unable to attend, the
atmosphere was thoroughly distracting, and no formal meetings
were held. It was not, as Winthrop took pains to point out, a suitable time for decision. Nicolls appears thereafter to have abandoned
his efforts for the season. His private relations with Winthrop continued excellent. But he complained to Sir Henry Bennet (now
Lord Arlington) that he had suffered "much Tryall . . . of our
neighbors of Conecticott."[5]

The winter of 1665/6 was exceptionally severe for all; Nicolls
wrote from New York that the town had been "bound up . . .
with a longer frost than was ever knowne in these parts"; at Hartford, Winthrop's wood bill came to £7/15/00. Yet the spring of
1666 failed to soften Connecticut's aversion to military adventures.
In April Nicolls transmitted suggestive reports of the movements
of the *French* and Indians, but in May the Hartford assembly
again devoted itself to local concerns, nor is there evidence that
Winthrop, who presided, attempted to influence it otherwise.[6]

Nicolls's rumors had substance; late in June came royal letters
(dated the twenty-second of the preceding February) proclaiming
war with Louis XIV. These, and French probings into the Iro-

quois country, inspired yet another and more earnest plea from Nicolls, who now asked that a Connecticut contingent be sent to Fort Albany to strengthen the frontier.[7]

Nicolls unfortunately emasculated his own argument by concluding a military agreement with the Mohawks (the nearest of the Five Nations). This placed the New Englanders in a situation of genuine embarrassment: *Their* Indians, of Algonkian speech, were pledged over generations to hatred of the Iroquois. Thus, when Winthrop placed Nicolls's proposal before his assistants, their dismay was patent. Their reply, dated July 11, was signed by Samuel Willys, but undoubtedly was drafted by the governor himself. Its tone was not, strictly speaking, negative, but its plain purpose was to keep Connecticut, with a minimum of fuss, out of such a war. It recommended that the French and the Mohawks be permitted to "trie it out awhile" by themselves and that the English effort be confined to a naval blockade of the St. Lawrence; this, it was claimed, would put the French into "so bad a condition that they may be far easier dealt withall." On paper, it was not unlike the strategy which ultimately ejected France from North America, but under the circumstances of 1666 it was wholly inapplicable; English sea power was in no condition to undertake anything of the sort, and Winthrop himself would soon suffer grievous personal losses because of its inability to protect the most ordinary shipping routes.[8]

Winthrop understood perfectly well that even so refined a beating about the bush would hardly satisfy a man like Nicolls. He therefore transmitted the colonel's suggestion to Massachusetts Bay, and his assembly, met once more in special session at the end of July, took positive steps to improve its communications with Fort Albany. Winthrop also made an honest effort to resolve the Indian dilemma; with neighboring sachems he held private talks (which appear to have prevented their going openly over to the French), and he joined personally with the Bay authorities in sponsoring an intertribal conference at Springfield. Always he kept Nicolls informed of developments.[9]

These gestures kept the colonel mildly confused. When the powwow at Springfield ended in nothing, Nicolls was disposed to censure, not Connecticut but Massachusetts. "The orders of the [Boston] Generall Court are so misterious," he wrote Winthrop, "that I cannot build any coniectures of good neighborhood or assistance upon any occasion whatsoever from them." He even ventured—hopefully—to predict the early dissolution of the United Colonies and suggested—openly—the secession of Connecticut.[10]

One cannot blame Winthrop for continuing the pantomime. Late in August, he proceeded again to Boston, where (officially) he passed the greater part of two months in military conclave with Sir Thomas Temple (the "governor" of Nova Scotia) and the Bay magistrates. But we may wonder how seriously it was intended. The conferees agreed, in sound New England fashion, to endorse an expedition by sea—but there were no ships. The overland route to the enemy was rejected "by reason of the many lakes and rivers, dismall thickets and Rocky mountaines." (It is of interest that *Winthrop* was commissioned to "explain" the New England position, by letter, to the Privy Council; a concurrent message to Nicolls strongly emphasized England's naval inferiority—which was indeed not inconsistent with the facts.) [11]

The play was continued through the winter and into the following spring. The destruction wreaked, late in the summer of 1666, by De Tracy's expedition into the Iroquois country had so disturbed Colonel Nicolls that he wrote Winthrop in November to suggest, in plain disregard of the American climate, an immediate campaign of retaliation. Winthrop was careful not to explode. Nicolls's suggestion was accorded an exhaustive study by a committee of his assistants, and the Connecticut response was posted solemnly back on December 24. It politely declined the proposal:

Affairs of such importance must await action by the full assembly; it now was winter (Hartford was alleged to have been smitten by eight snowstorms already); furthermore, the governor had developed a "paine," which would keep him close to home. In January came authentic snows of such severity that communications with the shore were lost until the beginning of March.[12]

Meanwhile the Royal Navy, ill-managed and outgunned, came close to losing control of the English Narrow Seas; Dutch privateers roamed the Atlantic, and French raiders wreaked havoc among the Caribbean sugar islands. Thereupon the Crown, with the self-assurance of despair, thought of New England and on August 28, 1666, drew up additional royal letters, urging a joint colonial effort in the West Indies. Thanks to the London fire and the total disorganization of shipping, the royal wishes did not become known in America until the following March. There was of course no chance that New England would undertake such a thing, but once more Winthrop took pains to establish a loyal impression. "Honorable Sir," he wrote the Massachusetts governor, Bellingham, "Having received his Maties. letter . . . we desire that you wilbe pleased to convene the councell of . . . the Massachusett, that we may have the opertunity therby to consider with your selfe & them about these his maties. commands." And wearily, for he was now sixty-one, he set out again across the soggy wilderness toward the Bay. At Boston the formalities were duly transacted, with results which everyone knew in advance. The New Englanders proclaimed themselves "very sencible" of the sufferings of their "deare countrimen of those Caribee Islands," but, alas, they could do nothing. There were 3,000 Frenchmen "upon the lakes behind us" who moreover possessed seven seagoing men-of-war. The Iroquois-Algonquin difficulty—which was genuine enough—was set forth at length. Food was short and so, still, was shipping. (Once more it was Winthrop who was detailed to break the bad news to Whitehall.) [13]

The remainder of the spring was rendered dismal by almost constant rains. Winthrop struggled back to Connecticut by way of Springfield, too late for the greater part of the May assembly and admittedly close to exhaustion. The ritual of his reelection cannot, in the circumstances, have been of much comfort. He rode into Hartford on the night of May 10, and when, on the following morning, he found a committee of notification already on his door-step, he responded with his written resignation. This the assembly declined flatly to accept. Back came another committee, packed with members of consequence—the elder Willys, Gold of Fairfield, Bishop of New Haven, Wadsworth of Hartford. Winthrop endeavored to explain: He pointed to his private affairs, long neglected; he cited his war losses. The committee declared that it understood, but the resignation remained rejected. Winthrop thought of making himself a figurehead: "I accept the place," he told the assembly, "only so there may be no trouble nor interruption in the course of & of the proceedings in the court & government, upon this condition that I may have liberty at any time to be absent." At this the deputies raised his basic salary from £80 to £112 and freed his property from taxation for a year. He was not of the figurehead sort, nor did the colony want him that way.[14]

Thanks to rumors of an Anglo-Dutch armistice and a lengthy interchange upon the native dilemma, Winthrop managed to hold off the importunities from Fort James. Peace was indeed concluded before the end of July, but communications continued so chaotic that the colonies received no definite word for months. As late as September, Winthrop still thought it prudent to side-step—gracefully—a suggested conference with Nicolls. This time his excuse was the devastation wrought by a coastal storm of tropical origin.[15]

He had kept Connecticut out of war—war of the risky kind that is waged between the evenly matched. It was a characteristic response. There was no question of doctrinaire pacificism; no one appreciated better than he the virtues of force. But always he in-

[297]

sisted that it should be overwhelming—and therefore humane. And he must have suspected that Quebec was no Fort Amsterdam.

As WINTHROP thus developed, with so light a touch, his intricate diplomacy, his personal affairs were falling into a deplorable state. A complicated effort to reduce his debt to Henry Ashurst came to nothing. The New Haven Ironworks—though the General Assembly had authorized "some meet person" to dispense alcoholic drinks on the premises—yielded no profits. His Pequot holdings had a way of attracting a multiplicity of troubles. The control of his latest salt venture was transferred, under dubious circumstances, to Sir George and Philip Carteret, court favorites with an eye upon the region soon to be known as New Jersey—"a place," said Winthrop, "which I know not nor have ever heard where it is." He was hard put to meet his most ordinary expenses; a bill for shoes and shoe repair was paid in the winter of 1665/6 by the treasurer of Connecticut, John Talcott, with a draft on his salary.[16]

Once more, in August of 1668, but in vain, he endeavored to relieve himself of his public responsibilities with a letter of resignation.[17] Connecticut again would not permit it—which was fortunate. The little colony still was subject to the intensities—not always religious—which so often accompanied English Puritanism and to which Winthrop afforded the best kind of counterpoise. The quarrel with Rhode Island had by no means been quieted. Hardly had the Royal Commissioners concluded their mission when Connecticut moved to resume its claim to the Narragansett country. Winthrop neither encouraged nor attempted to stifle the aggression; he accompanied it. He was prepared, no doubt, to take advantage of any promising opportunity. But he endeavored to divert his associates from extreme positions, and when this particular phase of the contest was over, no one had been irreparably injured.

The affair had been reopened in the autumn of 1666 with the arrest, under Connecticut authority, of certain Narraganset Indians, within their own country, on charges of pilferage. From Newport, Governor Brenton protested directly to Winthrop, but his letter was delayed by unprecedented snows, or so Winthrop claimed, and no reply was returned until the end of the succeeding April. Winthrop was by this time at Boston for the conference on the French war and thus comfortably removed from the pressures of his constituents. His reaction was suggestive: His initial draft made open reference to Connecticut's charter rights, but his actual letter contained no word of anyone's patent; it merely suggested that Indians discovered with stolen goods should be made examples of and advised that the victim of this particular larceny would personally acquaint Governor Brenton with the details.[18]

At Hartford, his colleagues were not so moderate. In October, 1667, the assembly threatened jail to any Rhode Islander who should attempt to engross any land west of the Pawcatuck. The following spring, it bluntly asserted its "liberty of claime" to the Narragansett country and dispatched a committee (which did not include the governor) to order Rhode Island out. It declared the Winthrop-Clarke agreement of 1663 invalid, on the ground that Winthrop's commission had been terminated the moment the patent of 1662 had passed the seals, and it denied the legality of the "King's Province" of 1665 because Nicolls had had no hand in it. There followed two years of battledore and shuttlecock, too tedious for elaboration. Certain of the Atherton associates urged a decisive showdown, even at the risk of violence. Yet in Rhode Island, Governor Brenton played his cards in the Winthrop fashion; confronted by the Connecticut committee, he protested that he could not assemble his council "on a suddaine, by reason of the distance of places." Winthrop, himself grave and remote above his impatient deputies, took little direct part. But his influence was not unfelt; as early as October, 1668, a particularly inflammatory petition from Captain Edward Hutchinson was simply "left upon file," and the assembly moved not only to "take the advice" of Richard Nicolls but to suggest a meeting of commissioners from each colony. Neither device yielded anything immediate; Nicolls was on the point of departing for England, while Rhode Island asserted there was nothing to negotiate. But open conflict had at least been postponed.[19]

Yet Winthrop continued perfectly willing to work for the reannexation of the Narragansett country. In a farewell letter to Nicolls, he requested his friend to acquaint the king with the unsettled situation, "hoping your honor will represent the case so clearly to his Matie. that he may be pleased to give his Royall order for the confirmation of it, to that originall condition as to Civill administrations, & their properties, it was setled in before & since confirmed by his gratious letters pattents." Yet he strove always to avoid unilateral boorishness. Nowhere was this better indicated than in an extraordinary communication he presented in May, 1670, to his own General Assembly. Most of Connecticut was by this time in a mood to force Rhode Island into some kind of conference, and the assembly now took action, not only to appoint a negotiating committee (of five), a date (the second Tuesday in June), and a place (New London) but also to proclaim that the committee would, in case of refusal to treat, take matters into its own hands and proceed thereafter as duly constituted public officers in the Narragansett lands. Winthrop, presiding, appears to have done nothing to halt these transactions, and they were quickly incorporated into an official letter to the governor and council of Rhode Island. But five days later, on May 17, he wrote privately to the assembly, reminding them of his agreement with Dr. Clarke and expressing his vigorous "dissent from exerting power of Jurisdiction of the people [east of the Pawcatuck] until his Maties. pleasure be further knowne or the matter issued by a treaty betweene some impowered from this Colony and Road Iland." [20]

This did not torpedo the conference, nor was it intended to do so. But Winthrop sniffed heavy weather; as in the New Haven crisis, it was time to dissociate himself from the proceedings, and hold himself apart, unidentified with any unpleasantness, prepared, when the occasion permitted, with his healing arts. The assembly's pressure indeed produced results, and the conference actually was held. But the governor kept carefully away from New London, and when three of the Connecticut representatives (James Richards, Deputy Governor Leete, and Winthrop's own son-in-law, Edward Palmes) went, prior to the meeting, on a snooping expedition into the disputed area, he pretended ignorance of their "transactions." The conference, held under conditions of strict punctilio, failed utterly; both sides agreed that the "Narragansett River" should be their boundary, but Rhode Island equated it with the Pawcatuck and Connecticut with the Blackstone, and on June 16 the delegates parted in restrained dudgeon. [21]

Three of the Connecticut commissioners (John Allyn, James Richards, and, this time, Fitz Winthrop!) thereupon crossed the Pawcatuck and proceeded to acts of sovereignty over the whole of the Narragansett bush. They promptly were confronted by Rhode Island officials, who declared them under arrest; they responded by arresting the Rhode Islanders. They returned, without physical molestation, by another way, still proclaiming Connecticut; their final pronouncement was issued at Stonington on June 23. [22]

It had been no more than a demonstration. But a scuffle, with mild bloodletting, did break out, on July 11, at Wickford, and Winthrop thereupon intervened. He assumed an unexpected position, chiding Allyn and Richards (though not Fitz!) for failure to establish an effective judicial apparatus. "I dare confidently to assure you," he wrote, "that the only last hope of . . . [Rhode Island] is grounded upon the wonted slowness and moderation of your motions." This hardly squared with his own behavior. Winthrop was not always a master of simple English; possibly he meant on this occasion to convey that if serious risks were taken, they should not be taken half-prepared.[23]

He continued, to the end, empirical. But he was distracted, too, and weary. In July, en route to Boston on personal occasions, he sent his resignation once again to the assembly.[24]

THE RHODE Island dilemma would continue indefinitely: "The story of the long-drawn-out negotiations between the two colonies would easily fill a volume," remarks one of the ablest of American colonial historians.[25] But the contestants remained, in general, on speaking terms. This was not always the case when a Connecticut village fell to quarreling over religious matters.

Religion and public policy were still inextricably associated in New England, and any question of doctrine or ecclesiastical administration continued, per se, to be a political problem.[26] One of the most disrupting issues was that of the "Half-Way Covenant"—the notion that baptism might be afforded the children of persons who had not been received as church members. Religious conservatives tended to deny its validity, the less meticulous (who, significantly, embraced most of the younger leadership) tended to accept it.

Such differences of doctrine and procedure bore a curious relationship to the annexation of New Haven. Of all New England communities, New Haven Colony had been the most Mosaic in spirit, and its disinclination to union with Connecticut had derived to a large extent from a desire to preserve its pharisaical purity. No one grieved more for the old New Haven than the Reverend John Davenport. Though he continued on excellent personal terms with the Connecticut governor, the smoothest of Winthrop's unctions never quite relieved his discontent. Winthrop had been so

tactful as to ask Davenport to deliver the Connecticut election sermon for 1666 (the first before the fully unified assembly), but the
old Puritan declined, pleading "weighty reasons . . . which may
more conveniently be given by word of mouth." Davenport presently was calling loudly for a synod of the Connecticut clergy.[27]

Nor was this the worst embarrassment. Religious altercations
were shaking the individual churches—in Windsor and Hartford
especially. So unsettled was the situation that the assembly, in October, issued a call of its own for a synod, to meet upon the third
Wednesday in May, 1667. Winthrop was not present (he was at
Boston discovering reasons why New England could not lend a
hand against the Dutch), but he became involved enough upon his
return. Davenport continued to play the gadfly. He dispatched,
uninvited, a delegation of the overgodly to inquire into the difficulties of the Hartford Church; and he declared the assembly's
synod to be out of order. Winthrop did his best to quiet him (the
name of the gathering was changed from "synod" to "assembly"),
but Davenport nonetheless came up from New Haven to use it as
a sounding board. His observations must have been vigorous;
some of them were carried, fourth-hand, to Colonel Nicolls, who
at once envisaged an assault upon the Church of England. Winthrop reassured him: "I am of *your* opinion that surely Mr. Davenport is a wiser man than to use any unfitt expressions," he wrote.
The "assembly," in any case, came to nothing; three divines of
special eminence, expected from the Bay, were unable to come, the
weather turned unseasonably warm, and many of those present,
being elderly, "could not well beare it . . . & began to be ill, & so
adiorned." [28]

The governor must have suspected that such doctrinal rows
could be settled neither neatly nor permanently. Indeed, they required the attention of the General Assembly on at least four occasions over the next two years. He was doubtless relieved when an
imperfect *modus vivendi* at last was reached in May of 1669,

whereby feuding congregations might separate (with the approval of the assembly) and at the same time divide the town monies allocated to church support. "All persons," observed the assembly, "being allso approved according to lawe as orthodox and sownd in the fundamentalls of christian religion may have allowance of their perswasion and profession in church wayes or assemblies without disturbance." This must have been yet more to Winthrop's liking.[29]

The churches at Windsor and Hartford presently did separate, the latter for good. It was not fully in accord with perfectionist conceptions. But the device at least had the virtue of workability. "It is good newes," wrote Deputy Governor Leete in April of 1671, "to hear of the two churches at Hartford thriving in their distinct state." [30] Winthrop cannot have disagreed.

H E o F course did not confine himself to crises. One of the merits of his administration was the improvement of the public efficiency to a point not unrelated to the public convenience. During 1665 and 1666, a system of county courts was introduced at Hartford, New London, New Haven, and Fairfield, and the old "Particular Court" of governor, deputy governor, and assistants became a court of appeals, under the style of "Court of Assistants," which now was to meet twice a year, on the Tuesdays preceding the regular semiannual assemblies. Taxation being largely in kind, a complex of storage facilities was provided for the colony "revenues." Each county was required to erect its own jail, and a basic statute was passed to deal with the eternal problem of squatters. By the spring of 1669, Connecticut living had become sufficiently complicated to inspire the colony's pioneer speed law; directed against those who "are apt to be injurious to their neighbors by their disorderly riding in the townes, whereby the lives of themselves and others are hazarded and endangered," it restricted them, within settled areas, to "an ordinary and easy hand gallop." Violators faced a fine of five shillings.³¹

However, Connecticut politics continued as unsophisticated as those of an English shire; there was much factiousness, but nothing resembling organized parties. There unquestionably did exist an informal "establishment" of officeholders; the same names appear, year upon year, upon the lists of magistrates and deputies. On the other hand, the franchise seems to have been exceptionally broad. As of March, 1670, the population of Hartford was about 721, of whom 117 were freemen; Windsor contained 754 persons, with 112 freemen; Wethersfield 349, with 58 freemen.³² English conceptions, applied to an environment with abundant land, already were yielding (without the aid of theoreticians) a representative democracy.

Less effective was the instinct to confederate. Nicolls's expectations had not been entirely misplaced, and the United Colonies were distinctly less potent in the late sixties than before. It was partly Connecticut's—and Winthrop's—doing; the engulfment of New Haven and the pressure against Rhode Island had stirred the apprehensions of Plymouth Colony, which likewise was small, and which felt easier behind a buffer. Winthrop and Talcott served as commissioners at Boston in September of 1669; and when they sponsored a resolution, based upon the Connecticut charter, that Rhode Island's "intrusion" into the Narragansett region was "very unjust and unreasonable" they were not supported by Plymouth. All present agreed, however, that the confederation seemed "to be Greatly weakened and at present uselesse"—unless the articles were so revised as further to weaken it.³³ It would require a major disaster to restore the organization, though only temporarily, to its initial vigor.

Winthrop was seldom so lacking in perception as this, and his marvelous sense of proportion seems to have been fully restored when, the following spring, Katherine Harrison of Wethersfield was brought before the Connecticut Court of Assistants on charges of witchcraft. She was tried by a jury which reflected contemporary attitudes and found her guilty. But the matter did not end there, nor on the scaffold. How the business was managed we do not know, but the May General Assembly (over which the governor presided) referred the case to a special session of the Court of Assistants (without a jury). And the court (Winthrop presiding) declared on May 20 that it could not concur with the jury's verdict "so as to sentence her to death, or to a longer continuance in restraynt," and the prisoner was released on condition that she pay her "just fees" and seriously consider leaving Wethersfield—for her own safety and "the contentment of the people who are her neighbors." [34]

John Winthrop, Jr., was, before all else, humane.

CHAPTER 22

Scientific Observer

IN his several efforts to escape the burdens of public life, Winthrop repeatedly pointed to the demands of his private affairs. No doubt he had reference chiefly to his financial and business problems, but these were by no means all. He had departed from London in 1663 with an informal commission as the Royal Society's correspondent for North America, and it was not long before letters began to arrive from the society's secretary, Henry Oldenburg, with suggestions as to suitable areas of investigation. His eagerness to comply may be assumed.

The savants of Gresham College seem to have been to some degree affected by standard Old World, wishful thinking concerning the New; from the beginning, they indicated a special interest in mineral deposits. Winthrop was unable to supply much early information. His public concerns with New Haven, Long Island, and New Amsterdam precluded extensive field trips. He had received, he said, an interesting specimen of marcasite from an Indian of the interior, but the "warres among the heathen" rendered any thorough investigation out of the question. He did transmit some information upon the Indians themselves. To Robert Boyle, whose purview embraced both the Royal Society and the Propagation of the Gospel, he forwarded two papers in Latin, warranted the work of two young aboriginals who had been Hebraically re-designated Joel and Caleb and enrolled at Harvard. Winthrop had been so impressed (as he seldom was by Indians) that he wondered if the Royal Society might not be interested also.[1]

H I S M O S T notable early data were, however, astronomical. These derived from his new 3½-foot telescope and the occurrence of certain fortuitous phenomena.

On the evening of August 6, 1664, shortly before leaving Hartford to join the Nicolls expedition before New Amsterdam, Winthrop undertook an examination of the planet Jupiter, which was then in a favorable position for observation, not far from opposition in the constellation Sagittarius. It was a clear and pleasant night, but marred with "poor seeing"; Winthrop himself noticed that the "bright activity" of the planet's light interfered with the images of the fixed stars in its immediate neighborhood. Nevertheless, several intervals of careful observation led him to suspect that the little disc in his telescope was accompanied by *five* satellites instead of the usual four. Winthrop was called away from Hartford almost at once, perhaps on the following day, and he never thereafter was able to confirm his suspicion. He was amply aware of the pitfalls—the deficiencies of his instrument, the mysterious habits of optical illusion, the presence, in the background, of the most opulent portion of the Milky Way. Indeed, he broached the matter to no one until the end of the following January, when he revealed it in a letter to Sir Robert Moray of the Royal Society. "I have been in much doubt whether I should mention this," he wrote, "which would possibly be taken from a single affirmation of a mistaken novelty, but I thought I would rather beare such sensure than omitt the notice of it." The letter never—because of the Dutch—reached its destination, and when no comment came from England, Winthrop must have equated silence with "sensure." He did not write of the matter again until the autumn of 1670, and then not to Moray.[2]

Winthrop's extra satellite was, of course, no dependency of Jupiter. The authentic fifth moon demands, for visual observation, a modern achromatic telescope of at least six inches aperture, far larger and more refined than Winthrop's, and indeed it continued unrecognized until 1892. But there remains the question of what Winthrop did see. He reported that his mysterious object did not twinkle, and it furthermore happens that Uranus and Neptune, both of them easy, though not obvious, "telescopic" objects, were at the time of his observation in the same region of the sky as Jupiter. But they were not really close enough, nor were they located on the plane of Jupiter's principal satellites. Moreover, none of the brighter asteroids seems to have been in the neighborhood. It is therefore safe to assert that Winthrop observed a *star*—in an area notably rich therein. (The most careful student of the problem suggests H.R. 7128, listed in *Schlesinger's Catalogue of Bright Stars*.) [3]

Much less controversial was the appearance, in 1664, 1667/8, and 1671/2, of three naked-eye comets, and here it is possible that Winthrop's reports, coming from the New World, possessed real value. The comet of 1664 was first recorded in November and proved one of the most spectacular objects of the century, being visible to the naked eye for seventeen weeks. It is a commentary on the rising habits of Winthrop and his usual associates that he failed even to hear of this early morning phenomenon until the beginning of December. A period of cloudy weather intervened, but thereafter he made a number of careful observations. The comet was by then passing the Earth, very erratically, on its outward track from the sun: "It was a little before day neere the meridian," he wrote Oldenburg, "and the come or blaze of it streamed westward. It had a strange erratick motion to the westward besides the swift declination to the southward." Six more days of gloomy skies followed, but "the next clere night after there appeared a blazing starr at the beginning of the night in the meridian in a very high northerly declination and the coma of it streamed to the eastwards." Winthrop wondered if there were not *two* "blazing starres" rather than one, and inevitably he heard, though never confirmed, that others had witnessed two such objects in the sky simultaneously.[4]

The second comet, that of 1667/8, was little noted in Europe, being chiefly visible in the Southern Hemisphere. New England, ten degrees to the south of Old, must have enjoyed a rather better view, for Winthrop was aware of the object within ten days of its discovery and referred to it in a letter of March 5 to Richard Nicolls. He included therein some intelligent comments, but there is no mention of this particular body among his surviving reports to the Royal Society.[5]

On February 28, 1671/2, Wait Winthrop reported from Boston that still another "blaseing starr" had appeared in the northeastern sky at four o'clock in the morning two days before. But Wait's letter was not delivered for nearly two weeks, and Winthrop was never able to find the object. (No one appears to have told him that it had almost no tail.) Yet he forwarded his reports, for what they were worth, to Oldenburg.[6]

Winthrop's astronomical accomplishments were, in fact, of comparatively small consequence, because of his lack of suitable instruments (his telescopes seem not to have been equipped for measurements) and most of all to the multiplicity of his distractions. There was once an element of bad luck: Word from the Royal Society of a predicted transit of Mercury—October 25, 1664—arrived too late to be of use. His interest in the improvement of telescope optics was genuine, and he still was working in 1668 to perfect an instrument of eight or ten feet. But he was in no sense a dedicated observer. It was very likely his own 3½-foot glass which he presented to Harvard College in the winter of 1671/2, a gift considered so handsome that President Chauncy conveyed his personal thanks from his deathbed. The telescope was accompanied by "a modell of a supporter" (base, or mount), two "drawers" (pullout tubes), one eye piece, and a "large and learned" letter explaining its use. Winthrop requested early confirmation of its performance; unfortunately he did not live to hear that it might, thanks to observations of the Great Comet of 1680 (Halley's), have contributed to Newton's *Principia*.[7]

Winthrop remained much in the minds of the Harvard Fellows not only as an intellectual ornament but as a head of government. Harvard, an infant institution in a difficult environment, already had become the first land-grant college in English-speaking America, and certain of its endowments were not only within Connecticut but under dispute. Here Winthrop's position was rendered specially embarrassing by the counterclaims of an institution—not yet in being—which Connecticut might call her own. He likely found it more congenial to lend his advice, which earnestly was solicited, as to President Chauncy's successor.[8]

I T I S curious to record that Winthrop's interest in minerals somewhat declined in his later years. He may have been simply discouraged. As late as 1671, he reacted with enthusiasm to a rumor that Prince Rupert had perfected a method for the manufacture of *cheap* steel, yet his letters to England contained comparatively little about iron or ironmaking in America. He had, indeed, come reluctantly to the conclusion that New England held slight immediate promise for a metallurgical industry. An occasional Indian might bring in a nugget (usually of copper), but always the source was unspecified, and year after year he put off serious wilderness prospecting, pleading the interminable tribal wars. (One may wonder if the real reason were not his own advancing age.) He furthermore had learned that New England was deficient in a

number of essential materials, such as chalk, flints, and lime. In
1668, he rationalized his wartime shipping losses with the suggestion that they had saved him worse involvements: "I might have
buried more in an antimonie Mine . . . had not such accidents
prevented," he declared.[9]

However, he had in no way lost his magnificent curiosity, and
his friends of the Royal Society made certain it was kept well
honed. It still was an age wherein the intelligently inquisitive
could make real contributions to knowledge. Wrote Henry Oldenburg in 1667,

> Sir, you will please to remember that we have taken to taske the whole
> Universe. . . . It will therefore be requisite that we . . . entertain a
> a commerce in all parts of the world with the most philosophicall and
> curious persons. . . . We know yr. ingenuity, experience, and veracity,
> the best qualities of a man and a Philosopher; and we doubt not but you
> will let us share in the happy fruits thereoff. . . . Give us at last a visit
> by a Philosophicall letter.[10]

Oldenburg and others forwarded the latest "philosophicall" literature, ranging from the printed *Transactions* of the society to
discourses attacking the Roman position upon the Eucharist. Most
significant of all were the reports upon "Mr. Boyles Continuation
of the [Experiments] concerning the Spring and weight of the
Aire." "I hope," ventured Oldenburg, "the new English in America will not be displeased with what they find the Old English
do . . . as to the matter of improving useful knowledge." In
1668, a considerable lot of material was brought from Europe by
no other than Petrus Stuyvesant, who seems to have harbored no
permanent resentment against either Winthrop or English New
York.[11]

To Winthrop, such things were a delight. Inevitably, there were
times when he wearied of his drab little colony, "so greatly separated," as he once expressed it, "from happy Europe." He therefore was doubly appreciative of those friends who had given him

"part of that content with which Christendom is so constantly & abundantly satiated, which yet makes my condition seeme the more unhappy that I am at such a distance from that fountaine whence so many rivelets of excellent things do streame forth for the good of the world." [12]

In 1670, perhaps earlier, Winthrop was asked by the society to compile "a fresh, a faithfull and ample Naturall History of New England." This he declined to undertake, arguing—with a poorly sharpened quill—that the English had been too short a time in America. The interior, he pointed out, was not at all known, while the reports of natives were "many tymes uncertaine and need good examination & further inquiry." He did provide the society with most un-Linnaean arrays of data and specimens—mineral, vegetable, and animal—and there arrived at intervals in London a perfect hodgepodge of acorns, horseshoe crabs, hummingbirds' nests, milkweed fibers, and common beach sand, together with remarks upon tides, comets, wheat rust, caterpillars, and the manufacture of tar. Winthrop took obvious pleasure in submitting and commenting upon his specimens. Sometimes he exhibited a wry humor: He regarded certain stunted, yet mature, American White Oaks as a distinct species; growing inland upon deficient soil, they bore numerous acorns, although no more than waist high. "It would seeme a strange hyperbole," he observed, "to report of a country where the swine are so tall that they eat acornes upon the tops of standing growing oakes, but it will appear not to be a riddle to those that shall see acornes . . . upon these little oakes." The hogs of the neighborhood were, he added, extremely fond of them.[18]

The Royal Society was happy to receive almost anything from the New World; Winthrop even inquired if he should furnish examples of poison ivy! He did ship, in a carefully nailed box, an example of "Hony combe stone" (barnacles) from Fishers Island. But the greatest astonishment was elicited by the hummingbird's nest (and eggs), the horseshoe crab, the milkweed fibers, and (rather oddly in view of its world-wide distribution) the starfish. The nest was accompanied by an uncommonly perceptive description of the bird itself and the "humming noise it maketh whilst it flieth from flower to flower sucking hony like a Bee." Neither hummingbirds nor horseshoe crabs being native to the Old World, both produced an understandable flurry. Several of the society even wondered if the sharp tail of the "horsefoot" might not be the animal's forepart. They pronounced the starfish extraordinary. The entire lot was carried in March of 1670 to Whitehall, where the king examined everything "with no uncommon satisfaction." [14]

GRESHAM College as yet had achieved little consistent discipline of mind; brilliance often was confounded by naïveté and even, on occasion, by superstition. The remarkable Theodore Haak never ceased, through all his rational speculations, to acknowledge the capricious interventions of the Deity. Winthrop himself was never loath to ascribe the inexplicable to the supernatural. When, late in 1665, he received a letter from one Thomas Mall of Youghal, County Cork, describing the "touch" healing of a certain Gratrick, he covered it with solemn annotations. He esteemed the "Virginia snakeweed" a serious specific for rattlesnake bite and dispatched a sample to London. And when the fish population of a large pond near Watertown, Massachusetts, expired en masse, he wrote *Robert Boyle* to inquire "whether any natural cause can be knowne or whether . . . [it is] only to be looked upon as supernaturall." [15]

Sometimes he found it difficult to separate the significant from the insignificant. In the spring of 1673, an earless hog was observed on Noddles Island in Boston Harbor, and Winthrop went to enormous pains to forward the animal to England. Nor was he always careful to verify the tales which came to him secondhand. He seriously believed that certain of the waterspouts of tropical latitudes (which he never had visited) were "blown up by some sea monster." He also gave full credence to stories of a "miraculous overturning hill" beside the Kennebec River in Maine; he thought the phenomenon "very certain," but this time the Royal Society failed to agree. "Concerning the overturned hill," advised Secretary Oldenburg, "it is wished that a more certain and punctuall relation might be procured of all the Circumstances of that Accident." [16]

H E W A S, of course, more than a dilettante. Much of his philosophical correspondence dealt with highly practical matters, and the Royal Society itself was deeply interested in the application of knowledge to man's convenience. Then, as now, New England agriculture was subject to a variety of blights, molds, and insects, and Winthrop's were among the first intelligent commentaries thereon. He repeatedly referred to the "wheat blast" and its spread, by 1670, from Massachusetts Bay to Connecticut and eastern Long Island; he noted the immunity of peas, barley, rye, and Indian corn, but failed to grasp the role of the bayberry; indeed, he admitted he knew not whether the difficulty derived from natural causes or from "blasting from heaven." His allusions to insects were understandably more precise; he described the "tent caterpillar" and its fondness for deciduous foliage, but he was most concerned by the ravages of "a kind of black caterpillar"—derived, he said, from a mothlike fly—which devoured the leaves and blossoms of apple trees.[17]

Not all his data were so dismal. He reported that the colonists now grew two varieties of wheat; one, planted in the *spring*, he called "summer wheat" and furnished samples. He spoke of efforts to extend the range and increase the yield of Indian corn, and he hoped a late-ripening strain would succeed in England. He discussed methods for producing charcoal from any sort of wood. A fire at Farmington, Connecticut, in December of 1666 (seven fatal casualties) inspired him to a discussion of building practices in New England: Most dwellings, he wrote, were of white oak and commonly "shingled" (roofed) with the same material, although white cedar was preferred when available. He cited "four good stone houses" (one of which must have been his own manse in New London) and four with slate roofs. But a great many New England buildings still were thatched, chiefly with salt-water creek grass, a material which Winthrop did not consider more inflammable than shingles, provided it was well compressed. He had proved this to his satisfaction at his farmhouse at Ten Hills by holding a lighted candle against the thatch from beneath! Creek grass also had been found effective as fertilizer.[18]

In 1670 the Royal Society undertook an inquiry into a new "Hypothesis of the Fluxe and refluxe of the Sea" and wrote for confirmation of the rumored tides of the Bay of Fundy. Winthrop had seen no more of these than he had of West Indian waterspouts, but on this occasion he transmitted his secondhand information with caution and supplemented it with a description of the tidal currents at Hell Gate, near Manhattan, with which he actually was familiar. He still hankered to elaborate upon his "designe for the advance of trade," which he had left with Brereton in 1663, but seems to have felt it too controversial to press, and in 1670 abandoned it gracefully on grounds of lack of time.[19]

The Royal Society drew no positive distinction between the natural and the political; it was as eager to develop the king's dominions as to discover celestial mechanics. "How happy it would be," wrote Oldenburg in the spring of 1669, "if there were an Union of all our English Colonies for free communications with mutuall assistances: taking in the Bermudas and other isles, wch. the English inhabite, they cannot be lesse than a million of people." He asked for maps—and evidently needed them, for he believed that the New England and Virginia plantations lay only 100 miles apart. Dr. Benjamin Worsley, still very much *en rapport* with the

Council of Trade, wrote copiously the following year upon current official thinking, to which Winthrop responded pleasantly but with caution: "I am glad that such matters are under the consideration of so many honorable, worthy and judicious persons, I hope God will guide your consultations for a generall advantage to the English, as well in their swarmes, as in the hives." [20] He could accept natural laws more readily than imperial.

Winthrop experienced much difficulty in maintaining steady communications with his English colleagues. Many of his letters (and specimens) were dispatched from Boston, which long since had become the premier seaport of New England, even of the Connecticut Valley. But even Boston's communications were by no means certain. In 1666, an elaborate parcel of reports and specimens was confided to a vessel which fell in with Dutch privateers; everything aboard was flung into the sea. Another ship was lost through natural causes. One packet from London came to Winthrop via Virginia and New York, another, as we have seen, in the baggage of Petrus Stuyvesant. A particularly heavy assortment of material arrived, in 1670, with John Pell, Jr., son of the renowned Cambridge mathematician and heir of Thomas Pell of Fairfield, to whom Winthrop extended appropriate amenities. His most expeditious consignment went to England in charge of his nephew Adam Winthrop, but a number of his successful shipments were simply directed in care of Daniel Colwell, Chief Searcher of the London Customs House.[21]

Those who delight in minutiae may yet compare with profit the reports which he drew up wtih those which actually were delivered.[22]

It is noteworthy that Winthrop's correspondence with the Royal Society had comparatively little to say of chemistry or medicine. In the summer of 1668, he referred to his occasional use, internally, of mercury dulcis—and advised caution in the ingestion of such preparations. But that was about all. To assume a declining personal interest would be manifestly false, yet, as age began at last to dilute his wonderful vigor, his medical activities slowly lessened. No continuous record of prescriptions survives for the years after 1669. He did endeavor, with fair success, to train up Wait as a practical physician, and his sickroom references never wholly ceased. He remained confident of the merits of rubila: It was, he wrote Wait in March, 1670/1, "the surest thing I know to take away the wormes & the cause of them," and he even ventured, the following year, to declare it effective against smallpox, provided it was given at the onset of the disease. In the summer of 1671, he prescribed, by post, for a victim of West Indian dysentery (sal tartari prepared as a cordial powder, aloe pills, and, of course, rubila), and, in the autumn of 1674, also at a distance, for two children in Rhode Island. But he grew short of medicaments and lamented his inablility to attend in person.[23]

That Connecticut needed a proper successor became steadily more obvious. During one of his absences at the Bay, his own wife was stricken with what rather clearly was appendicitis; the housewives of Hartford applied herbs to her side and she was purged, with difficulty, with rubila.[24] (She survived for reasons beyond calculation.) Winthrop himself often resorted to similar procedures, but he long had suspected that rubila was risky in cases of lower abdominal pain.

Nevertheless, no younger practitioner appeared who could fully take his place, though Winthrop thought he had found one when, in 1674, John Lederer appeared briefly in the colony. So remarkable was this young man that it seemed as if Connecticut had acquired a second, albeit Teutonic, Winthrop. Lederer had migrated, a half decade before and while still in his early twenties, from his native Hamburg to Virginia. He had been a student of medicine, but he was most of all a natural scholar and observer; his expeditions into the Southern Appalachians in 1670 are still remembered with respect. Why he left Virginia, and then Maryland, to come to Connecticut no one knows precisely. That he should nevertheless appeal to Winthrop was a foregone conclusion, and in November of 1674 we find him practicing medicine among the settlements of Fairfield County, very likely under the governor's personal patronage. For a few weeks all went magnificently; his patients esteemed him highly (though at least one of them expired), and the young physician's letters were full of the kind of discourse in which Winthrop delighted most.[25]

But Lederer appears to have labored under a youthful inability to remain in one place (another similarity, be it noted, to Winthrop!) and hardly was he established on the coast of Fairfield when he announced his early departure for Europe, via the West Indies. He protested he would return, but a letter to the governor, describing the alchemical experiments of the Chief Justice of Common Pleas at Barbados, is the last evidence history affords of this wonderful young man.[26]

For Connecticut, it was unfortunate. Winthrop was by this time sixty-nine years of age.

Uncomfortable Old Age

EARLY in March, 1667/8, there arrived at New York, by way of Maryland, Colonel Francis Lovelace, successor to Nicolls as governor of the duke's province. Commissioned almost a year previously, Lovelace was happily another example of York's penchant for adequate appointments. Of ancient and cavalier lineage, he was related on his mother's side to Sir Edwin Sandys of the Virginia Company and to the poet George Sandys, and as a very young man had campaigned through Wales for the first Charles. Though hardly of Nicolls's stature, he brought to his post certain respectable qualities, of which the most conspicuous was an initiative tempered with caution. (His major failing was love of official minutiae.) [1]

It must not be supposed that Nicolls departed under a cloud; he remained in New York beside his replacement, on terms of the most perfect cordiality, until mid-August. Significantly, it was his first consideration to present Lovelace to Winthrop, a pleasant encounter which took place amid the Spartan facilities of Stamford, Connecticut, before the end of March. (Winthrop later expressed his gratitude that the visitors "could excuse the unsutable accomodations of such a village.") [2]

The Connecticut governor was favorably taken with Lovelace,

but he could not conceal his distress at Nicolls's departure. The two had developed an extraordinary *rapport;* it is revealing that Winthrop, in the months immediately following Lovelace's arrival, provided Nicolls with certain semiofficial "tattle" in language so figurative as to be meaningless to Lovelace—and in fact to posterity. Nicolls was equally cooperative. "Pray send mee," he wrote on June 16, "the whole process against Capt. Scott at Hartford that I may evidence what a knave he is." Such courtesies were more than formal; each friend took care that the virtues of the other were suitably proclaimed among the highly placed.[3]

The Lovelace appointment presaged much for the future; his penchant for administrative tidiness reflected the tastes of the Duke of York and his increasing influence at Whitehall. But the changing atmosphere was as yet little felt in America, where Lovelace grew essentially into another Nicolls. The retiring governor had left behind, as provincial secretary, Matthias Nicolls, who was not only steeped in the attitudes of his former superior but committed to their continuation. Matthias—no relation to Richard— was a lawyer of superior abilities. Though he owed his appointment to Samuel Maverick, he was not a placeman; from the beginning he took the New World seriously. When he came, he brought his family. He had been chiefly responsible for the "Duke's Laws" of 1665 and would live to serve the city of New York as mayor and the province as judge and speaker of the assembly. It is not too much to say that his influence with Lovelace was decisive. Most of all, he was a man of affable nature and grew steadily more intimate with Winthrop and, in particular, with Fitz.[4]

Lovelace, like his predecessor, tried repeatedly to promote a treaty of the formal, Old World kind between the Iroquois Confederacy and the Indians of Northern New England, and once again Winthrop chose not to lend much help. He submitted the standard reasons: personal distractions, the lateness of the season, an illness, at Boston, of his wife. He also pointed out that aboriginal agreements were inherently unstable and declared that the New England natives actually dreaded a peace more than war for fear that some advantage might be taken of them. Lovelace, like Nicolls, persisted; he announced he would visit Connecticut and early in December, 1670, appeared with a small official party at Milford, on the Connecticut shore of Long Island Sound, whence he dispatched an express to Hartford, urging that Winthrop come down in person for a discussion of "all affaires." Lovelace and his companions lingered at Milford for five full days, but Winthrop failed to appear. Once more the Connecticut governor deplored the unpropitious season—though the weather had been unusually mild—and pleaded his responsibility to a "dear sick friend" (his wife, who was in fact again ill). He also protested that Lovelace had been expected at Hartford and that the substitution of Milford might be construed as a "meanes to diverte" the New Yorkers! To Alexander Bryan, to whom, as Milford's first citizen, fell the unenviable task of soothing the visitors, Winthrop wrote that "nothing was intended but for great respect & honour, it being impossible that there should be any other from myselfe to a person so much honored in my heart," but he also commended Bryan for refusing to commit himself to a "motion" proposed by one of Lovelace's subordinates.[5]

Winthrop did take care to remain in touch with Fort James. He transmitted European intelligence as a matter of course. He in particular kept Lovelace informed of his *absences*, which were frequent enough, usually at Boston, but also, in September, 1671, at Plymouth, to which he went for a conference upon the insolent behavior of a Wampanoag sachem called Philip. His colony seems to have cooperated adequately in the establishment, during the winter of 1672/3, of a regular monthly post between New York and Boston, via Hartford, and if the service failed to match expectations, the deficiencies appear to have developed at the Boston end.[6]

Early in April of 1672, rumors reached Hartford of an outbreak of hostilities between France and the Netherlands. They little disturbed the springtime quiet, yet they in fact presaged the second of the Restoration's unprofitable Dutch conflicts, and it was not long before Winthrop again found himself technically at war—and in exactly the same position with Lovelace as with Nicolls eight years before. There was the usual royal letter, urging offensive action, Winthrop's call for a special assembly (it met on June 26), the hurried measures for local defense, and the inevitable notice to Fort James that no sizable contributions need be expected from Connecticut. The principal difference was the entry of Winthrop's family into the military hierarchy: His son-in-law, Edward Palmes, was given general command of the 2,000 man militia—in place of John Mason, deceased—while Fitz was put in charge of the forces of New London County.[7]

There was also, early in September, an appropriate meeting of the United Colonies, once more at Plymouth; Winthrop attended in person, traveling the roundabout inland route via Springfield, but his concern with the emergency was not so profound as to prevent his writing home for various pharmaceuticals or to improve the occasion with personal business at Boston, Salem, Wenham, and Ipswich. Moreover, the Plymouth sessions dealt chiefly with the final amending of the Articles of Confederation and scarcely at all with the war.[8]

THE TRADITION of escapism runs strong in America, and it began in New England in the seventeenth century. The dominance of domestic concerns in the midst of external crises was already remarkable; Connecticut in particular had turned inward, developing slowly into a minor, but authentic, entity, returning, year after year, the same magistrates, consuming its own food, exporting a little more, shipping (chiefly through Boston) small quantities of lumber and livestock. Its 20 merchants (as of 1679) were reck-

[323]

oned also small, and so were its 24 registered vessels. Annual imports did not come to £9,000. Between 1671 and 1672, the value of its taxable property rose only from £141,195 to £147,368.[9]

The colony was not, however, stagnant; its growth, if unspectacular, was healthy. Winthrop's final years witnessed a steady refinement of its political structure: In May of 1670, it was enacted that freemen should no longer be obliged to attend the elections meetings in order to vote for the principal magistrates, and in October it was ordered that lists of nominees for assistant should be drawn up by the autumn assemblies. (These changes produced no significant rotation of personnel, nor was it thought fitting to suggest any alternatives to Winthrop or to Deputy Governor Leete.) During the following year came steps toward a revision and republication of the Connecticut legal code; Winthrop served for months on a select committee, and the new code was ready for the press by October of 1672. The printer was Samuel Green of Cambridge, producer of the Indian Bible, and though the assembly required that every family in the colony should purchase a copy, Green's services remained unpaid as late as July of 1674. Connecticut was more prompt to assure the Privy Council overseas that it was not its "purpose to repugn the Statute laws of England." [10]

The administrative routine was spiced from time to time with teapot tempests, not always religious. In August of 1671, certain residents of Lyme and New London (Winthrop's son-in-law, Palmes, among them) exchanged fisticuffs over a tract of tidal meadow near Black Point. Happily there were no injuries, and the participants—pending referral to the courts—concluded hostilities by "drinking a dram together." But such was the importance of salt hay that the case attracted wide notice; Winthrop was himself called to testify before the Hartford County Court and submitted an elaborate deposition which remains to this day not only a major commentary upon early New London, but also the sole primary evidence of the famous incident of Bride's Brook. (In the winter of 1646, Winthrop had, in his capacity as Pequot magistrate, married a youthful couple from Saybrook; he stood within his own territory on the eastern margin of a small stream, which he took to be the westerly limit of his plantation, while the bride and groom faced him from the opposite side, regarded as Saybrook's. Bride's Brook is still so called.) The meadow question was carried ultimately to the assembly, where the governor temporarily left the chair in order to plead New London's case; the affair was not concluded—essentially by halving the melon—until October, 1673. Meanwhile the assembly, under Winthrop's presidency, urged amicable boundary pacts upon eight additional towns.[11]

In May of 1672, there was brought up from New London County the first case of incest in the experience of the colony; the situation was rendered doubly difficult by the absence of any statute in the premises. Winthrop clearly was disinclined to have anything to do with the matter; the assembly returned the case to the county court for a more precise finding of probability, and when it appeared again before him and the Court of Assistants in June, he tried once more to avoid unpleasantness by inquiring of the local clergy whether scripture required those guilty of such a crime to be put to death. He no doubt was relieved when a journey to Boston precluded his presiding at the final trial, held in October; even then Deputy Governor Leete requested, and received, a final ratification from the assembly, where Thomas Rood was sentenced to death and his daughter Sarah to be so whipped "that others may heare an feare." [12]

Winthrop was aging. He was less disposed than formerly to grapple with uncertainties, and he shied from unconformity. He may have been responsible for the gracious treatment extended Assur Levy, a leading merchant of New York, who came to Hartford that year to plead the case of a fellow Jew, one Jacob Lucena. But when a Rhode Island Quaker, Henry Bull, requested his intervention in the religious policy of Massachusetts, his refusal was

blunt: "I know no cause to doubt but that godly persons in authority are well instructed already & grounded in these necessary rules,
wch. the lord hath beene pleased to dictate unto them in the Scriptures." His clothing, though carefully tailored from the best obtainable fabrics, was now almost invariably of black or a "sadd"
color.[13]

YET UNCERTAINTIES had a way of thrusting themselves upon
him. Of the Narrangansett territorial question, there was neither issue nor end. Connecticut's land lust continued unabated: "This is one
of the gods of New England," observed Roger Williams in 1670.
There was little modification in the Hartford strategy, which was
to render lip service to a negotiated settlement—and to threaten,
in case of failure, unilateral action. Rhode Island was more flexible; in addition to defensive countermoves, Newport resorted to
appeals to the Crown and even sought the sympathy of not-quite-
Puritan Plymouth. Though stubborn as to their rights of jurisdiction, the Rhode Islanders were otherwise not unreasonable, and a
respectable amount of Connecticut steam must have been dissipated when, in November of 1672, they suddenly validated all
previous transactions of the Atherton Company. However Connecticut took effective advantage of a venerable row between
Roger Williams and one William Harris, which had slowly developed into an unseemly tussle between Baptists and Quakers, less,
one suspects, over matters of religion than of land surveys. Harris
was, according to Williams, a mere adventurer, but at least he suggested a fresh approach to the whole imbroglio and petitioned the
king to constitute *all* the New England governors a special court to
settle *all* issues. In August, 1675, the Privy Council issued parchment commissions for the purpose, but by that time a far more serious crisis had precluded early action.[14]

Winthrop continued to find the Narragansett business at once
disrupting and embarrassing. He did not have to be reminded of

his agreement with John Clarke or of its repudiation by his own assembly. He was not unwilling to see the region become part of his colony, but he continued to distrust the strong-arm methods favored by many of his colleagues. If force there must be, it were better that it be used without stint, yet the longer he considered the events of 1670—the denial of his public undertakings, the failure at New London, and the brawl at Wickford—the more certain he became that he wanted no part of them. From Boston, whither he had gone with his wife, he penned, on October 7, the most convincing of his resignations and let it privately be known that he thought himself poorly used. The assembly, of course, would have none of it: "For many waighty considerations, we doe declare that we cannot give way to any such thing." To make certain the governor would give way instead, an intimate pressure was conveyed through female channels. "Truly," wrote Elizabeth Stone to Elizabeth Winthrop, "I looke at ourselves as an undone people if the Gouernour should wholy desert us." The assembly also took care to express its feelings with more than words, and in the following spring Winthrop's public salary was raised again—to £150 per annum.[15]

One may be pardoned for tracing, without absolute documentation, the Winthrop influence upon what followed. It was, thanks to his extraordinary position, equivocal. When, in April, 1671, Rhode Island commissioned one John Crandall the Conservator of the Peace in a district claimed by Stonington, Connecticut, Hartford made much ado over "sedition" and "rebellion," yet in October the assembly, under Winthrop's presidency, put off all prosecutions until the following spring. When, in June of 1672, Newport hinted, in the face of possible foreign invasion, that it might now be considered for membership in the United Colonies, Winthrop proved friendly to the idea. But Connecticut could react with rapier thrusts: "We must needs say . . . we cannot but see you [Rhode Island] never intended any composure or compliance in the thing in controversy" is a fair example (January 29, 1671/2), and Winthrop was unable to prevent further alarms and excursions within the disputed lands. (One of these, in June, 1674, produced "tumultuous interruption" at the hands of the Rhode Islanders.) [16]

None of it can have been to the taste of a man who, at the age of threescore years and eight, desired nothing so much as retirement.

S E V E N T E E N T H - C E N T U R Y New England displayed a persistent interest in matters of communications and health. A typical Winthrop letter, written to his younger son, Wait, on November 27, 1671, described in detail "a very convenient journey" from Boston to Hartford, the streams being low and free from ice; moreover, upon his arrival on the night of Wednesday, November 22, he had "found your mother and sister [probably Martha] in good health." That this happy condition continued throughout the winter we are assured in a second letter, to Fitz, dated April 7, 1672. [17]

It was seldom that a Connecticut family enjoyed so favorable a winter—and for the Winthrops it was the last. Trouble appeared in the early summer of 1672; the colony was stricken with an epidemic, of what nature an undisciplined medical terminology does not make clear, but we learn of "ague," and Winthrop observed that those receiving early doses of his rubila recovered quickly. Yet two deaths occurred on August 22, and at the same time Mrs. Winthrop was prostrated by profuse nosebleeds. [18]

One gains the impression of a deteriorating situation not only in Connecticut but everywhere in New England. Margaret Lake, Elizabeth Winthrop's eldest and best loved sister, died in September, and in October died—tragically, at the height of his considerable powers—the Reverend Antipas Newman, the husband of Elizabeth's eldest child. Moreover, the governor, early in November, was suddenly and desperately stricken. Elizabeth did what she could to save him and succeeded, but distracted in mind and probably close to exhaustion, she was unable herself to escape the disease. Nor was she able to contest it for long, and between seven and eight o'clock of the evening of Sunday, December 1, Elizabeth Reade Winthrop died. Her age was fifty-eight years, and she had been, without brilliance but prudent and effective, the wife of the younger John Winthrop for more than thirty-seven. They buried her in the yard of Hartford's First Church, "just by the south side of Mr. Stones monument, within thre or fower feet." [19]

Winthrop was crushed. The depth of his grief may be measured by the fact that he turned for weeks from the Royal Society view of the world to seek solace among the religious precepts of his East Anglian childhood. "Thus God is pleased to deprive us of our best earthly injoyments," he wrote his widowed daughter, "that we might seriously seeke for our cheife comfort in him & be weaned more from this world & these fading things below." "My losse is irreparable," he told a sister-in-law nearly two years later, "& my sorrows continued and no other way to be alienated but in the consideration of the sovereign will of the Lord to wch. we must submitt." These were extraordinary words from John Winthrop, Jr., nor could there have been, for his wife, a more authentic tribute. [20]

His own condition remained precarious for a long period; indeed, the very core of his vigor had been broken. It was a dismal winter, and the governor watched the dimming of its afternoons from his bed in an upper chamber. His unmarried daughters, Martha and Anne, tended him faithfully, but as late as mid-February he could arise only for brief periods by the fire. Even in mid-April he could not yet "beare the aire, only to step out into the garden a few minutes, & in againe." He participated in the May assembly (and was duly reelected), but on its final day (Saturday the seventeenth), he suffered an "aguish distemper." In a letter of June 20, he boasted of returning health, but others recommended a rest at the shore, and he still confessed himself unable to "ride any journey." [21]

Most significant of all was his conveyance to his daughter Lucy and her husband, Edward Palmes, of his farm at Niantic and the stone dwelling-house at New London.[22] He called these a dowry, but inasmuch as the young couple had been wed for more than a decade, it more clearly resembled a bequest.

I N T H E midst of the torrid summer of 1673, Colonel Francis Lovelace came at last to Hartford, accompanied by Matthias Nicolls and three personal servants. The entire party was entertained for four nights and three days at Winthrop's own house—"I believe to good content," reported the Connecticut secretary, John Allyn. The discussions which took place must be imagined; no proper record survives. Connecticut, of course, offered no military alliance. However, Secretary Allyn thought Matthias Nicolls a "sweet natured gentn." [23]

Lovelace departed, in a steady rain, but escorted by a full complement of outriders, on the morning of Tuesday, July 29. He was in New Haven by nightfall, and there, on the following morning, he was stunned to learn that a large Dutch fleet had appeared before New York. A day later came rumors that Fort James was under assault and that the enemy had "breakfasted" upon his personal livestock on Staten Island.[24]

The facts were worse. The enemy had come in overwhelming strength, 21 vessels of assorted tonnage, with a landing force of 800. New York was thoroughly surprised and absolutely helpless. Resistance was token, bloodshed minimal. Captain John Manning surrendered Fort James on the thirtieth, and immediately the Dutch commanders Jacob Binckes and Cornelius Evertsen renamed the place "New Orange" and proclaimed a subordinate, Captain Anthony Colve, governor. The towns on western Long Island were directed to capitulate within forty-eight hours; those to the east within five days. Poor Lovelace, in a frenzy of despair, rushed into the vortex of the disaster and fell shortly himself into enemy hands.[25]

The Dutch were prompt to send probing expeditions into Long Island Sound, and the rumors of their intentions were more disturbing still. The danger to Connecticut was obvious, yet the situation was not wholly bleak. Winthrop could not afford to lose control of the Sound, but control of the Sound required possession of the greater part of Long Island, and possession of Long Island might conceivably lead to its ultimate reannexation. The English inhabitants would hardly object: Many months prior to the appearance of the Dutch, three of their towns had petitioned the Crown to be returned to the "Government and Patent of Mr. Winthrop." And in these latest circumstances they were not slow to call upon Connecticut for aid.[26]

Winthrop's initial moves were routine. He forwarded the news to Governors Leverett at Boston and Coddington at Newport, and he called the Connecticut assembly into emergency session. Magistrates and deputies gathered in Hartford as early as August 7, with at least 18 of 24 towns represented. They were plainly frightened. For the first time in their history, they established a "Grand Committee" with extraordinary powers, including the impressment of men, animals, vessels, and equipment of all sorts. (To the committee were named Winthrop, Leete, the assistants, and five leaders of the militia.) A special flying column of 500 dragoons was authorized—at least on paper.[27]

Toward the enemy, the colony turned an official face of brass. A note was drawn up to the Dutch commander, "rideing in Hudson's River at New Yorke," declaring that Connecticut *and the United Colonies* would defend their interests—in particular Long Island east of Oyster Bay. This was carried to New York by Hartford Assistant James Richards, who first had brought the Connecticut charter to New England, and by William Roswell of New

Haven, who could speak Dutch, but neither was authorized to undertake any negotiations other than to suggest the establishment of a local neutrality. At New York, they refused to confer with certain emissaries from Southampton, nor would they linger for discussions with the recently paroled Lovelace. As soon as the Dutch reply was in their hands, they departed for Hartford. That so abrupt an interchange was wholly wise may be questioned; the Southampton representatives were naturally discouraged, while the uncrowned Prince of Shelter Island, Nathaniel Sylvester, at once assumed that his bread was buttered on its Dutch side and began openly to recommend submission.[28]

The Dutch themselves were little disposed to compromise; though their reply said nothing of the mainland, it made very clear their intention to occupy the whole of Long Island. Yet Winthrop had reason to hope that his reference to the United Colonies would not prove without foundation. Toward the end of an unprecedentedly wet August, the United Colonies commissioners gathered in emergency conference at Hartford; still half an invalid, Winthrop permitted Leete to preside, but the danger was such that an outward unity was quickly achieved, and on the twenty-seventh the meeting issued a unanimous declaration that an injury to one member would be regarded as an injury to all.[29]

Winthrop may wishfully have supposed that this alone might give the Dutch pause. The final day of the United Colonies sessions found him in buoyant spirits; he even turned jocund over the rain. "There be," he wrote Governor Leverett, "too many generall evils of these tymes that may crye to heaven against us, but for what speciall cause the clouds so often weepe it were good we could find out. The Lord be pleased to cause the pleasant dew of Herman to descend upon Zion." But his easy confidence was only hours long. Hardly had the commissioners quitted Hartford when letters arrived from eastern Long Island full of additional rumors and a disposition to surrender. Winthrop instantly dispatched a postrider to call the commissioners back, but they demurred, citing, in tones reminiscent of his own evasions, the possibility of another meeting at Boston, the "sicknesse" of Hinckley of Plymouth, and the public alarm which their return to Hartford might occasion.[30]

Winthrop, in fact, discovered himself in the former shoes of Richard Nicolls. There was no early reassembly of the commissioners. The Massachusetts court did go into special session in mid-September, but following three days of consideration it declared that any joint operation was "not expedient at present" and took steps, Connecticut fashion, to arm *itself*. For the time being without allies, Winthrop reacted to the threat across his narrow sea like a Tudor before a Hapsburg. He understood that the ultimate element must be force. "It were good," he wrote privately, "to equippe a stronger fleete of Frigats then they have and to spend twenty thousand pounds more in a very sufficient land army of land forces to dislodge them . . . rather then to suffer such an enimy to settle [on Long Island]." Yet he cautioned against any undertaking not in overwhelming strength, and he still hoped, a little wistfully, that a settlement in Europe might render local hostilities unnecessary.[31]

The Dutch themselves were hesitant to carry matters too far. A considerable segment of their fleet departed at the close of the summer, and if the New Englanders had thus far failed to move, their capabilities remained considerable. At the end of September, Governor Colve ordered two of his subalterns to Southold to administer an oath of allegiance, but the island English took instant note of their lack of armament, and the greater part of them refused; only Oyster Bay, Huntington, and Setauket had, by the middle of October, made token compliance.[32]

The crisis naturally dominated the Connecticut October assembly. Even so, it was treated with a curious deliberation; Secretary John Allyn, still young and of a hair-trigger disposition, later remarked that he could "blush to relate it." More appeals, desperate on the wings of rumor, came from the Long Islanders, yet Hartford still indicated its preference for an intercolonial intervention. Samuel Willys and Fitz-John Winthrop were indeed dispatched across the Sound as Connecticut agents, but without adequate support and in an ordinary coaster; they carried impressive commissions, but their private instructions discouraged any resort to violence. However, the Dutch were sent a second note, dated October 21 and signed by Secretary Allyn, of which the tone was blistering: Colve was told to cease interfering with eastern Long Island on pain of direct assault upon his "headquarters"; there was intimation also that Connecticut would meet any Dutch barbarities with retaliation upon his "boores and open dorpes." So stern indeed was the note that Colve placed the bearer of it, John Banks, in unceremonious confinement.[33]

These tactics were Winthrop's. They were designed to avoid bloodshed and keep the Dutch talking, until such time as New England might collect a decisively superior force, and for this we have the governor's own testimony. They proved for the moment successful. Colve spoke defiance, but continued to shadowbox; another delegation of oath-taking commissioners, ordered eastward at the end of October, were insufficiently armed for anything crucial, and when they fell in with Fitz and Willys, there occurred nothing more dramatic than a stiff-necked exhibit of credentials and a simultaneous appeal to the citizens of Southold. The latter promptly declared for Connecticut, by salutes of musketry and otherwise, and the Dutch forthwith abandoned their mission, "as we clearly perceived that we should be unable to effect anything." [34]

The Long Islanders breathed more easily. They liked the military look of Fitz and requested his permanent services. The Hartford Grand Committee responded by making him "Sarjt. Major over the Military forces of his Maties. subjects" on the island, and there even was talk of making him the core of a provisional government. At Manhattan, Colve was furious; on November 14 he released John Banks from durance to convey a note, in peremptory Dutch, to "Mr. John Winthrope commanding at Hartford," wherein he threatened to oblige those responsible for such "unright-measured proceedings to change their evil undertakings." Winthrop was not seriously disturbed. Banks reported that Colve was "a man of resolute spirit and passionate," but not conspicuously popular with his own people. The season was late. Moreover Winthrop now could hope for early action from the Bay; the Hollanders were disrupting Massachusetts shipping, and Wait wrote from Boston that the threat to Long Island was "well resented here by all." [35]

Yet the governor understood that the Dutch had received no decisive check and with Fitz's "Sarjt. Major's" commission went private instructions to treat Long Island as a primary concern, even at the expense of New London. Fitz crossed the Sound again late in November, but he returned to the mainland for the winter and was actually visiting in Hartford when, early in February, the next emergency arose. A Dutch captain in a captured Boston ketch had put in at Shelter Island, demanding provisions; Nathaniel Sylvester parted with "twelve barrells," how willingly no one can say, but the adjacent English towns once more called for assistance. Nor was Winthrop now disposed to look the other way: To his council he recommended the immediate dispatch of "a sufficient number of men" to Long Island and sent off appeals of his own to Boston.[36]

Fitz returned to Southold, amid additional rumors, on Saturday, February 22. He brought with him less than a militia company, which hardly was "sufficient," for on the following Monday morning the Dutch appeared before Southold in "handsome order" with *four* vessels—one ketch, one "snow," and two sloops. Guns were trained on the village, and there debarked the extraordinary Mr. Sylvester, in the role of broker, with a demand for surrender. To this Fitz replied, in effect and in the king's name, no, and the Hollanders cleared for action. Fitz feared himself out-numbered, and he must in fact have been outgunned. Yet he had an eye for terrain; he posted his fifty men expertly among the neighboring hillocks, and though hostilities were opened with much smoke and commotion, there seem to have been no casualties whatsoever. Moreover the enemy sustained a psychological sur-prise. They had not expected anything so brisk, and they presently broke off the action and sailed ponderously away.[37]

No military engagement could have been more to the gov-ernor's taste, and Fitz was suitably commended—though parodox-ically his father undertook simultaneously to lecture him upon the merits of hasty fortifications. It also marked the war's climax in North America. Fitz continued on Long Island in a state of alert, while Massachusetts promised naval aid, this time with specifica-tions as to tonnage, armament, and personnel. But no serious en-counters occurred thereafter. (At Southold, Fitz's little expedi-tionary force quickly developed a characteristically American distaste for "overseas" service and clamored to go home.) [38]

Hostilities had in fact been terminated in Europe on February 9 with a mutual restoration of captured places; New England had the definitive news early in May. But for some time thereafter the issues of New York and Long Island continued unsettled. Repre-sentatives from Southampton, Easthampton, and Southold peti-tioned the Hartford assembly "for their continuence" under Connecticut; moreover, the response was openly sympathetic, though the Winthrop caution was evident in a qualifying clause, "as farr as shalbe in our lawfull power from his Maties. gracious grant in his Charter," nor was any Long Islander received as a deputy. At Manhattan, also, Anthony Colve continued to hope that the peace terms did not apply to him; he tried at first to sup-press them and was obviously loath to abandon his raids upon English shipping.[39]

Not only did the restoration of ducal New York require time; it threatened Winthrop and his colony with serious embarrassment. It was too logical to assume that their intervention on Long Island had not sprung entirely from selfless patriotism, and the governor himself went to suspiciously elaborate pains to rectify such an impression. The situation at New York remained uncertain for months: The new English governor, Edmund Andros, arrived in October, but without the vessel containing the greater portion of his garrison and armament, while Colve still pretended he had received no competent orders to evacuate. Andros and his staff were permitted ashore, but the atmosphere continued tense, and there were incidents. It was against this background that Winthrop wrote Fitz, on the night of October 30, suggesting a private talk at Hartford, to be followed by an equally confidential approach to the Long Islanders, "that you might advise them and dispose them to some handsome and fitt way for attaining their owne satisfaction." [40]

The purpose of this was clear. Nothing, of course, came of it. Winthrop continued above all to honor reality, and when word arrived, in November, of the actual recession of New York, his son was promptly diverted to Manhattan in the role of welcomer, accompanied by the ever-useful Willys and fortified with appropriate documents, both public and confidential, in his father's own hand. Fitz did not relish his errand, but his reception was unexceptionably cordial, thanks to the tone of his documents and to the obvious fact that Connecticut had abandoned all hope for Long Island. Indeed, no one troubled to question the past; even the collaborating Nathaniel Sylvester was quietly forgiven.[41]

Thus was concluded Winthrop's second foreign war as governor of Connecticut. There had been no victory and no annexation. But his colony had suffered neither bloodshed nor disapproval officially expressed.

His final military occasions would be less happy.

CHAPTER 24

Conclusion in Crisis

DURING the winter of 1674/5, Winthrop turned sixty-nine, still governor of Connecticut, but hopefully free at last of extraordinary public crises.

His physical condition remained precarious; as late as the preceding August he had decided not to risk a journey to the Bay and had confined himself to brief rides in the immediate neighborhood of Hartford.[1] His private affairs continued chaotic. Many of his debts—especially those to the merchant, John Harwood, and to his sister-in-law, Priscilla Reade—remained unpaid, and his overseas letters were heavy with the pleas and reassurances of a frontier entrepreneur: wheat blast (which now afflicted Connecticut and "you know very well that corne is the mony of these parts"), cargo losses, anticipated (but usually unfulfilled) sales of land, and the intricacies of commodity exchange. Other distresses included the prospect of Fitz's marriage to a certain widow (the father advised caution), Fitz's dissatisfaction at having to share the Pequot lands with his sister Lucy, the mortgage—and the lack of fencing—upon Fishers Island, a boundary controversy with William Parks, and a vexing shortage of salt (which meant driving his Connecticut livestock to the Boston market). His medical activities were probably less discouraging; the outcome of his treatment of a severe accidental gunshot wound is unknown, but somehow there had come to his attention the virtues, as a tonic, of cod liver oil.[2]

On Thursday, May 13, 1675, the assembly reelected him governor as a matter of course. Winthrop protested orally—though he permitted himself to be sworn—and precisely a week later submitted a written request that he be allowed to step down, citing the "troubles & paines of some infirmities" and a desire to visit England. That his intentions were genuine is obvious from the tone of his letter, which verged on the pathetic. Somehow the magistrates and deputies induced him to stay on, if only temporarily. But on June 24 he addressed another letter of resignation, with seal affixed, to Leete and the assistants, and on July 28, he executed a power of attorney in preparation for an early departure.[3]

Nonetheless, he found himself postponing his plans, both for repose and for England, before the middle of August. Less than a year remained to him, yet now he faced, simultaneously and still as governor, two of his colony's most profound emergencies.

THE FIRST derived from Whitehall, which had fallen into another of its efforts to perfect the organization of its overseas empire. There had been a typical rearrangement of structure, the Council for Trade and Foreign Plantations being replaced by a select committee of the Privy Council itself, and there were special hearings wherein it was charged that the New England colonies had taken improper advantage of the recent war. A "census" of New England—with emphasis upon Massachusetts—was compiled, and a small regional library (25 titles) was recatalogued. One receives the impression of an administrative reform, a redefinition in the interests of precision, with little reference to political wisdom, the kind of process of which the Duke of York was becoming the symbol.[4]

The duke in fact was prepared with a special contribution: a reorganization of his New York proprietorship exactly in accordance with his patent of 1664, the modifications of Winthrop, Nicolls, and the Royal Commissioners to the contrary notwithstanding. This meant, among other things, the absorption of the mainland as far east as the Connecticut River, including the towns of Hartford, Saybrook, and New Haven. To dispel any uncertainty, the duke was invested, on June 29, 1674, with a new charter, "reciting and confirming" all the benefits of the old.[5]

To govern this improved domain, York sent out that summer Edmund Andros, a man whom an unfortunate juxtaposition of events has endowed with an unsavory reputation, but who must nevertheless be regarded as another of the duke's adequate appointments. Andros (1637–1714) was of good family, of impeccable Cavalier background, and, under most circumstances, of conspicuous ability. He was more administrator than politician and characteristically was devoted to the carrying out of orders, yet in certain situations he displayed a common sense far in advance of his master. His association with John Winthrop, Jr., was too brief, and under conditions too difficult, to lead to a notable friendship, but it is significant that Fitz-John always held Andros personally in high esteem.[6]

Though Connecticut's wartime doings on Long Island had attracted the half-suspicious notice of Whitehall, Andros preferred not to make much issue of it. He may not have been greatly taken in by a "handsome, true & full narrative" which Winthrop had prepared against his coming nor by a supplementary tract, celebrating the necessity of going to the aid of "those few people . . . standing out wth. undaunted courage agt. the dangerous assaults . . . [of a more powerful enemy] to the vindication of the honour of the English of this wildernesse." Andros, however, was openly concerned with the boundary at the Connecticut River. There was no question of his duty here; his commission required it, and in additional instructions, dated April 6, 1675, the duke reemphasized the need "to preserve the utmost limitts for me that my Patent gives me title to." The reemphasis was scarcely required. Andros made York's position abundantly clear in a formal letter to Connecticut on May 1; he even enclosed copies of the 1674 patent and his own commission. "You'l see," he declared, that the Connecticut River marked the proper boundary, and he did "not doubt" that Connecticut would cede the appropriate territory forthwith.[7]

These papers reached Hartford on Wednesday, May 12, the day preceding the opening of the elections assembly. Winthrop drafted the Connecticut reply in person; it was approved by the assembly on the seventeenth and at once returned over Secretary Allyn's signature. Andros was told in effect that Connecticut would honor the compromise of 1664, but otherwise must stand upon its own patent. Indeed, the "loyalty of his Majties. poore people in this wildernesse" demanded it; Connecticut could not properly "dispose" of the king's lands or subjects, "and therefore according to or. obliged duty, we are firmly resolved (as hitherto) by the gracious assistance of Allmighty God, to continue (in obedience to his Matie.) in the management of what we are betrusted with." [8]

It is probable that, up to this point, neither Winthrop nor the assembly took Andros at face value; though a "day of publique humiliation" was prescribed for June 2, it was inspired not by Andros but by unfavorable weather. Moreover, Winthrop, in a simultaneous and private letter, disregarded the whole boundary question amid bland comments upon European news; he even advised Andros of his own imminent retirement. But Andros intended no pantomime. He responded at length and with sharpness; he accused Connecticut of unfairness (toward the duke) and of open tyranny (in New Haven), and he taunted its principal officers with "disobedience & refractionesse." Moreover, he confided these comments to no casual bearer but to a pair of commissioners, officially designated and under orders to demand an answer within a week.[9]

They were at Winthrop's door by June 8. The governor at once perceived that Andros was not to be shrugged off, and he penned a personal reply the following day. Typically, he sought delay. He advised that the deputy governor and most of the assistants "of this his Maties. Colony" were scattered about "upon his Maties. Service" and could not be assembled within a week, but he promised that Andros's letter would be considered as soon as possible and an answer returned. He again hinted his early departure, but was "not doubtfull" that a personal meeting could in the meantime be arranged.[10]

Winthrop got Leete and the greater part of his assistants into special conclave at Hartford on June 16, and an official response was composed. We may suppose that Winthrop provided the text: Its tone was restrained, and a willingness for discussion was reexpressed, but it conveyed no hint that Connecticut would go further than a recertification of the boundary of 1664. This, to Andros, was unacceptable, and, following a council meeting of his own, he sent back, on June 28, his final declaration. Toward individuals he proposed to be generous: Existing officeholders would be reconfirmed and the privileges of the Church—and liberty of conscience!—protected. But there would be no further discussion of the duke's right to the lands west of the Connecticut, and he announced his arrival within a few days to take possession. Moreover, any further opposition would oblige him to pronounce the whole colony in a state of rebellion.[11]

All this was echoing through Hartford's lanes by July 5. Yet it did not signal a major emergency, for Connecticut in the meantime had been confronted with another and distinctly more dreadful prospect.

Except for the agonies which accompanied the initial European occupation, New England has experienced no crisis more severe than the Indian war which bears the name of the Wampanoag sachem Philip. Merely to cite it as a final proving between Stone Age and Renaissance men is not enough. A fully satisfactory understanding requires an examination of the attitudes, situations, and capabilities of both whites and aborigines.

The first planting, in New England, of more than a dozen or so English had been that of the Pilgrim Fathers late in 1620. Their distresses were authentic enough, but at least they experienced no serious difficulties with the natives. There were, in fact, few natives to reckon with, because of European diseases lately introduced. So complete had been their ravages that the sole important collision of Indian and European so far experienced in southern New England had been the war with the Pequots in 1637.

The Englishman of the seventeenth century harbored few notions as to the "equality" of the North American native. Nor was he loath, especially when the Indian appeared in small numbers, to shoulder him aside in a fashion calculated to inspire resentment. For these things the Englishman should not perhaps be blamed. But two fundamentals he failed essentially to grasp: the possibility that the native population might restore itself and the fact that the use of improved weapons is, of all the techniques of a superior civilization, the easiest to master.

Any estimate of the Indian potential is necessarily founded upon inadequate data. They were semiagricultural and spoke dialects of a basic speech (Algonkian), but their organization was so primitive that neither the colonials who faced them nor the historians who have examined them since have been able satisfactorily to define their multifarious fragments. There were indeed groups in the vicinity of the Bay towns—hopefully half-Anglicized—which still bore the Massachusetts name. To the east of Narragansett Bay were the Wampanoags, heavily pressed between Rhode Island and Plymouth, of which a principal sachem was "King" Philip. Between Narragansett Bay and the Pawcatuck River were the Narragansets, more numerous—and even more inchoate. Through eastern Connecticut and northwestward into the interior regions of Massachusetts, the forests were strewn with aboriginal flotsam and jetsam, of which only the southerly fragments had been reduced, by Uncas, to a degree of discipline. The total native numbers are impossible to state; it has been supposed that about 3,500 took arms, during 1675 and 1676, against the English. The precise figure is of little consequence. Far more significant was the Indian's ability to convert European weapons to forest campaigning; indeed, King Philip's War must be regarded as an early and notable example of the kind of well-armed, yet primitive, guerrilla operation which has since proved so effective against white men in alien environments. There existed but one flaw in the native technique: the inability to organize under a genuinely central direction.[12]

To evaluate the English is simpler, yet not without uncertainty. The census of New England, compiled in 1675 for the Committee of Trade of the Privy Council, reported the region contained "about 120 thousand Souls, 13 thousand Famylyes, [and] 16 thousand that can bear Armes." But even assuming these data to be exaggerated, it is obvious that the European potential greatly exceeded the native. That the colonists were themselves unable to achieve a perfect unity is notorious, yet they proved in this respect infinitely superior to the Indians. Their real deficiencies were two: an initial, and very Anglo-Saxon, disposition to underestimate the opposition and an inability—characteristic of more than one North American frontier—to distinguish between friendly and hostile natives.[13]

The outbreak of the struggle is easier to document: It came, fol-

lowing a brief period of tension, along the Wampanoag strip between Plymouth and Rhode Island; hostilities were well under
way by the final week of June, 1675. The immediate causes were
typical: English presumption, mutual misunderstanding, and an
Indian sense of grievance. Not so certain is the extent to which it
was planned in advance, by Philip or any other, but it clearly was
more than spontaneous. There just as plainly were efforts toward
an intertribal cooperation, but these were not uniformly effective,
and one gets the impression that Philip, as an organizer, proceeded
empirically and with little regard for the long term.[14]

The first musketry had hardly thudded across the Swansea clearings before Plymouth and Massachusetts were deeply committed; Rhode Island, on the other hand, would never be, for reasons
easy to discover but difficult to elaborate. The Connecticut towns
received word variously and by installments, but of particular importance was a letter dispatched on June 13, well in advance of
hostilities, to Winthrop by Roger Williams, advising that the *Narragansets* were exhibiting unmistakable signs of disaffection. This
development on the colony's very frontier guaranteed a vigorous
reaction when, on the thirtieth, word reached Hartford of the outbreak of fighting.[15]

Thus, by July of 1675, Connecticut found itself supremely
threatened from opposite directions. Winthrop could still hope for
the best, but he already was condemned to die in harness.

T H A T   S U M M E R proved one of the most hectic in the governor's
experience. The first advices, from New London, were edged with
panic: All the Indians were about to rise; even the Mohegans
could no longer be trusted.[16] Things had not in fact reached so
desperate a pass; the majority of the Narragansets still hesitated
to commit themselves, while an effective Narraganset-Mohegan
rapprochement was all but unthinkable. The situation was, how-

ever, awkward. Edward Palmes, who should have commanded the militia, was in England, while Fitz-John lay helpless at New London with temporary, but severe, illness.

At Hartford, Winthrop acted with conspicuous speed. He gathered the nearest magistrates (Allyn, Talcott, Willys, and Richards), ordered emergency reinforcements (30 "dragoones" and 10 "troopers") toward New London, and sent off suitable warnings, including a special express to Andros at New York. He called the assembly into special session for July 9. Wait Winthrop, who chanced to be in Hartford, was named to the command of the New London County militia in place of his brother—suggestive indication of how far Connecticut had become a family affair. All this was completed on the first of July. Yet Winthrop was in no dedicated mood; on the same day he handed the magistrates present the last of his formal resignations.[17]

He meant it seriously. Through the rest of the month he seems to have appeared at no public function, save for two meetings of the magistrates on the seventh and eighth.[18] But his influence was by no means unfelt; it could hardly be otherwise in a time of such troubles.

Edmund Andros, 120 miles distant at Fort James, was awakened by Winthrop's express at three o'clock in the morning of July 4. His own council was assembled within hours, and before evening he himself had embarked down the Sound in two sloops "about the Indian Troubles." This was subterfuge: Andros was not greatly worried by King Philip; his real purpose was to take advantage of Connecticut's distraction to establish the duke's frontier. This, indeed, he made little effort to conceal; in a note to Winthrop he expressed appropriate concern—and indicated his early arrival at the Connecticut River, "his Royall Highnesse bounds there." [19]

Andros anticipated that things should go peaceably, and he brought no considerable force. That he was frustrated was due to the alertness of Connecticut and a piece of ordinary luck. The luck came first: A minor native powwow at "Podunck" [20] had been promoted by the current excitement into a major conspiracy against the towns of Saybrook, Lyme, and Killingworth; the matter came, on July 7, to the attention of the Connecticut council (it was one of the sessions attended by Winthrop); and a special force, under Captain Thomas Bull, was sent down river to help organize a defense. Bull's orders deserve notice: "You are desired to be very carefull of keeping such watches and wardes as you shall find necessary for the discoverie of an enemie." The foe was not, however, clearly defined, and Bull reached Saybrook with unprecedented dispatch. Moreover, it is known that Winthrop and the assistants already were aware of the approach of Andros.[21]

Thus, when the New Yorker appeared off Saybrook the following morning, he found the place already under arms. The result, for Andros, was a prolonged embarrassment. He at once sent ashore the popular Matthias Nicolls, who spoke awkwardly of assistance against the Indians—and took in no one. A number of militiamen, en route eastward toward the Narragansett country, were held at Saybrook fort, and a dispatch, superscribed "Haste, haste, post haste—upon his Majestyes speciall service," was conveyed to Hartford within hours. Connecticut's reaction was uncompromising: A letter, issued the same evening in the name of the governor and council, directed instant resistance to any armed landing. The New Yorkers were to be advised to proceed to the eastern shore of Narragansett Bay, "for there is the seat of warr." "And you may," it concluded, "represent to Major Andros how inconvenient it is to make a discomposure amongst his Maties. subjects at such time as this is." [22]

That Winthrop had a direct hand in this is fully documented.[23] It is not so certain that he played an intimate role during the remainder of the episode, which the day following fell to the official charge of the special assembly. The die, in any case, had been cast; he had authorized a fight, if it should be necessary. Fortunately Andros had no stomach for such a conclusion. He lingered off Saybrook fort for days, swinging forlornly upon his cables, trying to save face. On the twelfth, he even came ashore in considerable pomp, but without weapons, to read a bootless proclamation. Bull responded with a stern counterpronouncement, sent down by the assembly, while his militia stood close to their arms. Andros was profoundly humiliated, but attempted nothing rash; the following day he departed. It is pleasant to recall that his good sense received, the following winter, the endorsement, "for the present," of the duke.[24]

The Andros threat, though neutralized, left aftereffects, not all of them unsatisfactory from Winthrop's point of view. No one could be sure that New York had really been quieted, and on July 12 the assembly named Winthrop and James Richards—both "intending a voyage to England upon their own occasions"—as special representatives of the colony at Westminster. Winthrop was, of course, a logical choice: "Yu," wrote Alexander Bryan from Milford, "would doe more then a hundred of us." The idea fitted the governor's inclinations perfectly. If his resignations were not to be entertained, his essential wishes could now be met; an agent could, as in 1661, be a governor *in absentia*.[25]

The Saybrook confrontation also could not help but affect the response to the Indian danger. Wait Winthrop had marched eastward from Stonington early on July 8 at the head of 120 men, 60 English of New London County and 60 Indian allies. Though his military experience was minimal, he had acquired, by association, a certain feeling for leadership, and he now pressed forward with vigor. He felt, indeed, that a confident display would discourage sympathy for Philip among the Narragansets, and before the day was over had drawn from the aged, but still voluble, Ninegret a promise to turn over any Wampanoag refugees to the English.

No word of the Andros affair reached him until, on the ninth, he had made junction with the forces of Massachusetts and Plymouth, encamped—120 strong—before Smith's trading house at Wickford. Yet the crisis with New York at once inspired Hartford to caution. On the twelfth, the assembly posted orders to Wait, directing his return to Stonington, and a letter to Massachusetts, explaining that it had become necessary to "stand upon our guard in other parts." [26]

With these also the governor was in cordial agreement, though not entirely because of Andros. He still regarded the Narragansets as a potentially valuable buffer between Connecticut and the hostile Wampanoags and was furthermore convinced that militia demonstrations, the taking of hostages, and similar tactics were a poor prescription for their continued good will. He assumed, during July, no public position in the matter; he still hoped for an early departure and remained through days of stifling humidity at his residence, leaving all official activity to Leete. He did not, on the other hand, fully isolate himself. He was consulted informally and probably often, and he let his ideas be known in an extensive private correspondence. He grew concerned over the strong-arm inclinations of Wait: "To have an open breach wth. Naragancet," he wrote his son, "may be of worse consequence then they [Massachusetts and Plymouth] are aware. Its best to keepe & promote peace wth. them, though wth. bearing some of their ill manners and conniving at some irregularities." He enclosed an additional letter to the attention of the other commanders, wherein he warned against deliberate violence toward what was after all the strongest Indian complex in the region. "I believe there is difficulty ynough wth. that one enemy," he declared, "& why to stir up an other before an issue wth. the first." He was privately encouraged when he learned that Wait and the other commanders had signed a "treaty" with certain available sachems and were withdrawing from the Narragansett country.[27]

NEVERTHELESS, he failed to get away for England. The assembly on July 9 had created a "standing" council, competent to act in "all" situations, provided the governor or deputy governor was present, and when, at the beginning of August, Leete's occasions required his withdrawal from Hartford, Winthrop once more found himself committed to public duty. It was not inappropriate. The Indian war swept suddenly, like flame along a trail of powder, into the northern interior; an English scouting expedition was nearly cut to pieces on August 2 near Brookfield, Massachusetts, and the village itself went up in smoke the following day. The news put Winthrop and five of his council into emergency session at one o'clock in the morning of the fifth, and thereafter there were almost daily meetings as the inland Nipmucs, without significant direction, yet perfectly attuned to forest tactics, carried arson and butchery into the upper Connecticut Valley.[28]

Winthrop and his colleagues faced the danger with candor—and considerable initial wisdom. Not only were militia units hurried upriver; much emphasis was laid upon the use of native Mohegan auxiliaries, a policy which Massachusetts could hardly bring itself to approve. Their most unfortunate move was to advise against the disarming of those valley Indians who had committed no hostile acts, for a number of these subsequently took the field against the English.[29]

The situation worsened steadily. New England's miseries were not eased by the onslaught, that same August, of a tropical hurricane, while the tidings from the north turned so ominous that the Connecticut council on the eighteenth discharged Secretary Allyn from his responsibilities as United Colonies commissioner and transferred them to the governor in person. Leete was recalled to Hartford, and on Thursday, the nineteenth, Winthrop presided over his final council meeting. The commissioners were due to assemble at Boston on September 9; Winthrop left Hartford about August 28. It was his last view of the clustered roofs beside the gentle curve of river and the long skyline ridges.[30]

H E T R A V E L E D the whole distance by water, over the circuitous beat about Nantucket Shoals. It was not for immediate fear of the Narragansett route (horses for his use at Boston were conveyed over-land without incident); he simply could no longer bear such a journey; furthermore, he had thought it wise to take Anne and Martha with him. The voyage proceeded without extraordinary delay, and on Thursday, the ninth, he was present with the other commissioners for the most crucial of all the gatherings of the United Colonies.[31]

Winthrop's Connecticut colleague was James Richards; Plymouth also sent its governor, Josiah Winslow, plus the experienced Thomas Hinckley; Massachusetts, though host colony, was represented not by Governor Leverett but by Thomas Danforth (who presided) and William Stoughton. (Both were, however, men of public stature.) [32] The initial proceedings went briskly enough. The Plymouth men presented a formal memorandum of the events leading to the current hostilities, and all the commissioners did thereupon "agree and conclude" that a state of war existed, that it must be prosecuted jointly, and that an additional 1,000 men should be put into the field, of which 500 were to be "Dragoones or troopers with longe Armes." [33] Formal sessions were suspended at this point until November 2, but nearly all the commissioners, including Winthrop, remained at Boston in an advisory capacity. Nor was their activity merely supplementary; the situation of inland Massachusetts deteriorated to catastrophe, and reports of continued ill-humor among the Narragansets promised even worse. The commissioners even resorted, on September 28, to an extraordinary "day of Humiliation," during which five of the Bay's most eminent divines preached and prayed, and it is recorded that "the Lord did Help." Yet danger provokes recrimination: As early as September 21, Leete wrote from Hartford, complaining of the insufficiency of the Massachusetts effort. On the twenty-fourth, the commissioners voted to assume direction of operations on the upper Connecticut, but the Hartford council announced, on October 7, the withdrawal of their forces unless the campaign were adjusted to their own specifications, and "most" of them, including the Mohegan scouts, were actually recalled before the end of the month. Winthrop's colleague, Richards, quitted Boston, October 4, on his personal concerns, and when his Hartford barn and warehouse were accidentally destroyed by fire, refused to return. The displeasure of Plymouth and the Bay was manifest, and as soon as the formal meetings resumed in November, their commissioners resolved "that the withdrawing of their brethren of Connecticott in a time of so great extremity is . . . a very awfull & tremendous providence of the Lord . . . [and] an absolute violaccōn of the maine ends of the Articles of Confederation." [34]

Winthrop on the whole kept his head. Following the valley disasters of early October, he wrote frankly to the Connecticut council that this must be regarded as a widespread rising and that he feared the Narragansets might indeed be involved. Later, when "very pregnant" reports indicated actual Narraganset participation, he composed a paper to suggest how they might, by sharp increases in the numbers of the ready militia, be induced to desist. Yet he still worked strenuously to discourage any retaliatory action against them. "I haue heard," wrote Roger Williams approvingly, "that you have bene in late consultations *semper idem, semper pacificus,* & I hope therein *beatus.*" Winthrop must have been heartened when, on October 18, there was staged at Boston a little ceremony to certify the Anglo-Narraganset agreement of July 15, but the ratification paper was marked by three sachems only, and when the official November sessions began, it was clear that his fellow commissioners preferred something more decisive. He nevertheless struggled to the end. Richards had neither returned nor been replaced, and Winthrop suggested that, in the absence of a Connecticut colleague, he himself was incompetent to act. The others were not impressed; they merely declared themselves a quorum and behind closed doors took the initial steps toward a military expedition against the Narragansets.[35]

It was characteristic of Winthrop that, once the decision had gone against him, he should work without equivocation to insure that the campaign should succeed. He signed, without evidence of dissent, the formal instructions sent by the commissioners to Connecticut on November 12, and he even argued in private letters their necessity. He did try, successfully, to spare Ninigret. But upon Connecticut's Major Robert Treat, he urged, on December 18, an unlimited cooperation with Connecticut's allies.[36] It was the day next before the Great Swamp Fight.

This famous encounter, the greatest Indian battle, and the bloodiest, in the annals of New England, requires no elaboration. How many Narragansets—men, women, and children—perished in the snowy tangle no one knows, but scores of the English died also, including many from Connecticut. It was doubtless instrumental, in the long run, in the defeat of the Indians, but at first it hardly seemed so, for the wrath of the surviving natives was swiftly turned upon any English within convenient reach, the Rhode Island settlements in particular. Winthrop wrote presently to Samuel Willys that the whole affair had been unnecessary.[37]

It was his last winter, and quite without serenity. (He even failed to take note, on December 21, of an eclipse of the moon.) Amid its alarms and calamities, he could never repress his yearning for England, but his health again turned uncertain, and he dared not risk an early crossing.[38] He took part, when he was able, in the business of the commissioners, but there were occasions when he could not bring himself to face the bleak walk to the Town House, and papers had to be brought to him for approval. In January and February, there was a disposition, largely self-derived among the commissioners, to hopefulness, and even Winthrop ventured, in a typically Anglo-Saxon rationalization, that the "common people" of the enemy had no doubt "beene unwillingly envolved." But most transactions were dismal, and for Winthrop particularly so when Connecticut, like a classic "ally," once more announced itself overburdened and underappreciated.[39]

Yet he remained loyal to his special instincts, and the last of his official papers are pleas for moderation—toward captive Indians, facing slavery in the Antilles, and Indians still at large, but disposed to capitulation. At stake, he declared, was no less than "the issue of this desolating war"; there furthermore was the very practical question of the enemy retaining a "sympatheticall" attitude toward "those poore English in their hands." [40]

Not even his personal concerns could be quieted. As usual he had hoped to acquit himself of his ancient liabilities to the London merchant Harwood by selling real estate, but there could be no serious market for land exposed to scalping parties. Somehow he achieved credit for £140 with Richard Smith of the Wickford trading house, but Smith became so involved in the war himself that he could not make an intended voyage for England until spring. Even then, the application of such credit to a particular debt was by no means assured. "Deare Cousin," wrote Winthrop to Samuel Reade on March 14, "I desire you . . . to deliver him [Smith] of the bond & to cancell it & to give him your full discharge." It was the last of his private letters to survive.[41]

W I N T H R O P's final illness developed before March had ended. Its nature is unspecified, but we may assume the kind of respiratory ailment which afflicts late-winter New England to this day and which, until the coming of antibiotics, was so perfectly calculated to carry off the feeble. On Thursday the thirtieth he already lay prostrate, but was visited in his chamber by the Reverend Increase Mather, accompanied by his elders. For a time he appears to have held his own, which must be accounted remarkable, for disease that season struck down many who were far younger and more vigorous than he. But by the Tuesday following it was manifest that the end could not be far off, and his world shrank inward, to center upon Puritan shadows, kindly enough, but untrained in reassurance and a little too concerned that he should indicate approval of a final will and testament. By the next dawn even the shadows were gone. It was the morning of Wednesday, April 5, 1676. He had lived seventy years and—lacking eight days—two months.[42]

T H E S O R T of man he had been can be to an extent measured by the response to his passing. "Know yee not that a great man is fallen this day in this or. Israel," declared the surviving commissioners, "a gentlman every-way lovely & full of love." The public observances were as large and dignified as Boston, still half-mature and desperately beset, could make them. Governor Leverett tendered his own house for the receipt of the corpse; the Bay assembly pronounced him "a publique ornament, honour & blessing." The New England Way afforded no last rites of a religious character, yet his final journey through the rutted lanes to the Old Burying Ground was long remembered. There, on a chilly April afternoon, the remains of the younger John Winthrop were interred beside those of his father.[43]

It was the contemporary custom to mark the passing of the distinguished with poetic lamentations, but those for Winthrop were extraordinary. "Upon the Death, and much lamented loss, of that excellentlie well accomplisht Gentleman, John Winthrop Esquire" (64 lines) was the contribution of one "amiculus E.C." Stephen Chester (1639–1705) of Wethersfield, Connecticut, submitted a "Funeral Elegy" of 60 lines, from which

> Oh may this dismal loss ne'r be forgot
> Per Plimouth Boston, and Connecticot

is sufficient quotation. And Benjamin Tompson (1642–1712, a Massachusetts schoolmaster and physician) published, in his *New*

Englands Tears For Her Present Miseries (London, 1676), an elegy "Upon the setting of that Occidental Star John Winthrop Esq; Governor of Connecticott Colony" (72 lines), also a supplementary effort in broadside, entitled "A Funeral Tribute to the Honourable Dust of that most Charitable Christian, Unbiassed Politician, And unimibable [*sic*] Pyrotechnist John Winthrop, esq: A Member of the Royal Society, & Governor of Connecticut Colony" (88 lines).[44]

There was doubtless much sincerity, if little artistic merit, in these efforts. In any case, the younger John Winthrop has almost invariably impressed those who have come after him. "A blessed land was New England," wrote Cotton Mather, "when there was over part of it a governor who was not only a Christian and a gentlemen, but also an eminent philosopher. . . . Wherever he came, still the Diseased flocked about him, as if the Healing Angel of Bethesda had appeared in the place." Palfrey, nineteenth-century apologist for New England Orthodoxy, was less sanguine, but Winthrop clearly has appealed to the scholars of the twentieth. "Eager, outgoing, genial, responsive, modern," is the summation of Samuel Eliot Morison, ". . . the finest flower of [New England's] aristocracy." His death, declares T.G. Wright, "broke one of the chief links that kept the best of the new world in touch with the best of the old." [45]

Yet the most impressive of his accolades—and the most suitable —was extended while he still lived, and it is pleasant to know that he must have been aware of it. "You are," wrote Henry Oldenburg in a letter of March 10, 1671/2, "a person most curious and able, and of a nature prone to pardon." [46]

A finer compliment could hardly be bestowed upon any man.

$\mathcal{N}otes$

CHAPTER I

The Backgrounds & the Beginning

1. This was in the mansion house at Great Stambridge, Essex. For a partial description thereof, see letter of Thomas Hawes to John Winthrop, Sr. (hereafter referred to as JWS), May 22, 1628, *Collections,* Mass. Hist. Soc., Series 5, I, 182–87.

2. The well-balanced, housewifely character of Mary Forth Winthrop is made very clear in the "experiencia," or religious diary, of JWS. See *Winthrop Papers,* I, 162–63, 163*n*, 165.

3. Hawes to JWS, May 22, 1628, *Collections,* Mass. Hist. Soc., Series 5, I, 182–87.

4. R.C. Winthrop, *Life and Letters,* I, 10–11.

5. For this first successful Winthrop, see *ibid.,* I, 11–19; "Winthrop Pedigree," *Winthrop Papers,* I, 1; and Morgan, p. 3. Groton Manor included appurtenances in the parishes of Groton, Boxford, and Edwardstone. Its annual value was quoted at £21/01/08, plus the patronage of Groton church. Following its transfer to Adam, it was to be held in capite of the Crown by "the service of the twentieth part of a knight's fee and the payment of 42s., 2d. as tithe into the Court of Augmentations on Michaelmas each year . . ." (Latin) Patent Roll, 35 Henry VIII, part 14, m. 5, quoted in *Winthrop Papers,* I, xiii, 7–11. Certain outlying lands were in effect under lease to the lord of Groton. For a listing of these, see *ibid.,* I, 107–8.

Groton, Suffolk, is today often pronounced "Growton," and it almost certainly was so expressed in the sixteenth and seventeenth centuries. See spelling in "Acquittance" of Sir Henry Appleton, Bart., December 24, 1613, *Winthrop Papers*, I, 174.

6. As the father of the first successful Winthrop was also named Adam, it has been the practice of Winthrop genealogists to refer to Adam I, Adam II, and Adam III—Adam (1498–1562) being the second. One reason for the preferential treatment enjoyed by Adam III appears to have been the extramarital alarms and excursions of an elder brother. See *ibid.*, I, xv, 12–13, 38–39 and Morgan, p. 4.

7. His first marriage was to Alice Still, who died, with her infant, upon her initial childbed, but who brought him influential connections, especially her brother, who later became a bishop. His second was to Anne Browne, the daughter of a wealthy clothier of neighboring Edwardstone, who successfully mothered his children, including John Winthrop of Massachusetts. R.C. Winthrop. *Life and Letters*, I, 47–51; "Winthrop Pedigree," *Winthrop Papers*, I, 1.

8. He matriculated fellow-commoner at Magdalene College, Cambridge, in 1567, but took no degree. *Ibid.*, I, 46n.

9. *Ibid.*, 134n.

10. Morgan, pp. 4–5; *Winthrop Papers*, I, 111.

11. R.C. Winthrop, *Life and Letters*, I, 27–42.

12. *Winthrop Papers*, I, 34–36.

13. Ms. diary of Adam Winthrop, Additional Mss. 37419, British Museum.

14. *New England Historical and Genealogical Register*, XVIII (1864), 184; R.C. Winthrop, *Life and Letters*, I, 60, 63n; Muskett, ed., p.43; "The Will of John Forth of Much Stambridge in the Countie of Essex Gent . . . ," *Winthrop Papers*, I, 173 and n; Ms. diary of Adam Winthrop, Additional Mss. 37419, British Museum; see also *Winthrop Papers*, I, 87–88.

15. *Ibid.*, I, 6, 60n, 176n.

16. R.C. Winthrop, *Life and Letters*, I, 60; *New England Historical and Genealogical Register*, XVIII (1864), 184; *Winthrop Papers*, I, 65 and n; Shaw, II, 133.

17. Ms. diary of Adam Winthrop, Additional Mss. 37419, British Museum.

18. *Ibid.*

19. *Ibid.; Collections,* Mass. Hist. Soc., Series 3, VIII, 296; R.C. Winthrop, *Life and Letters,* I, 62; *Winthrop Papers,* I, 6, 151 and *n;* Statement by the Rev. Archibald Brian Bird, rector of Groton and vicar of Edwardstone, to the author, November 1, 1959.

20. See Adam Winthrop diary, Additional Mss., 37419, British Museum; also Mss. Parish Registars, Groton and Great Stambridge, and *Collections,* Mass. Hist. Soc., Series 3, VIII, 296–98. There is some confusion in the data as to Forth Winthrop; Adam Winthrop's diary records his birth as December 19, 1609, but the Great Stambridge Parish Register indicates his baptismal date as January 10, 1610/11. In his "Visitation of Suffolk" in 1612, the Richmond Herald, John Raven, noted Forth Winthrop as being one year of age. *Winthrop Papers,* I, 171 and *n.*

21. For a good deal of information as to the comings and goings of JWS, see Adam Winthrop's diary.

22. To be "lewdly disposed" did not, in the seventeenth century, indicate an extraordinary interest in sexual matters; it meant the simple enjoyment of earthly things. See R.C. Winthrop, *Life and Letters,* I, 59–60.

23. JWS "Experiencia," *Winthrop Papers,* I, 163 and *n.*

24. *Ibid.,* I, 88*n;* letter, the Reverend Frank Hughes, rector of Stambridge, to the author, April 3, 1960.

25. R.C. Winthrop, *Life and Letters,* I, 69–74; *Winthrop Papers,* I, 154–69.

26. JWS, "Experiencia," *ibid.,* I, 168.

27. *Ibid.;* see also Adam Winthrop's diary.

28. There is naturally little direct certification of young Winthrop's attitudes in early childhood, but, given the peculiar and abundantly documented characteristics of his later years, it appears legitimate to assume them.

29. *Winthrop Papers,* I, 176; Muskett, ed., p. 113.

30. John Forth's will specified that he should be buried "within the parishe Church of Stambridge." See *Winthrop Papers,* I, 176. But "there is nothing to mark John Forth's grave, either in church or churchyard." Letter, the Rev. Frank Hughes to the author, April 3, 1960. For John Winthrop's comments, see *Winthrop Papers,* I, 168.

31. *Ibid.,* I, 173 and *n.*

32. *Ibid.,* I, 162, 169.

33. They had removed to Groton certainly before winter. See "Acquittance" of Sir Henry Appleton, Bart., to JWS, December 24, 1613, *ibid.*, I, 174; also *Collections*, Mass. Hist. Soc., Series 4, VI, 574.

34. R.C. Winthrop, *Life and Letters*, I, 243.

35. Information from parish register, St. Bartholomew's Church, Groton, in James Savage, "Gleanings for New England History," *Collections*, Mass. Hist. Soc., Series 3, VIII, 296–98.

The Rev. Thomas Nicholson had been rector of Groton since 1583 and was getting on in years. Information as to Groton rectors is recorded upon a plaque in St. Bartholomew's Church, Groton, and is based on the parish register.

36. R.C. Winthrop, *Life and Letters*, Vol. I, chap. 5; *Winthrop Papers*, I, 51*n*, 183*n*.

37. *Ibid.*, I, 30*nn*, 51*n*, 100; Adam Winthrop Diary, Additional Mss. 37419, British Museum.

38. JWS "Experiencia," R.C. Winthrop, *Life and Letters*, Vol. I, chap. 5; see also *Winthrop Papers*, I, 182–90.

39. These varied events were noted by Adam Winthrop in his copy of Bretnor's *Almanack* for 1617. *Winthrop Papers*, I, 215–18.

40. Notestein, pp. 117–18.

41. *Winthrop Papers*, I, 145–46; A.F. Leach and E.P. Steele Hutton, "Schools," in Page, ed., II, 344.

The imperfect records of seventeenth-century English grammar schools are a minor frustration of many twentieth-century English headmasters. Conversation of author with R.W. Elliot, M.A., headmaster of King Edward VI School; Bury St. Edmunds, November 2, 1959.

42. R.C. Winthrop, *Life and Letters*, I, 436; *Winthrop Papers*, I, 217.

43. R.C. Winthrop, *Life and Letters*, II, 123–26, 370–71; *Winthrop Papers*, I, 179 and *n*, 180, 218; JWJ to Samuel Winthrop, May 24, 1660, *Collections*, Mass. Hist. Soc., Series 5, VIII, 61.

44. M.R. Pirani, *A Short History of the Cathedral of St. James the Greater, Bury St. Edmunds, Suffolk* (place of publication not cited, 1959), pp. 3 f.

45. Page, ed., II, 306, 318; *Winthrop Papers*, I, 276–77, 284, 285–86, 314; oral information supplied the author by R.W. Elliot, M.A., headmaster of King Edward VI School, November 2, 1959.

46. Page, ed., II, 317; *Winthrop Papers*, I, 276–77, 279–80, 284,

285–86, 314; letter R.W. Elliott to author, December 11, 1959. The school *itself* possesses no record that JWJ ever attended. See S.H.A. Hervey's *Biographical List of Boys Educated at King Edward VI Free Grammar School, Bury St. Edmunds, from 1500–1900.*

CHAPTER 2

Maturity Deferred

1. The best studies of English Puritanism as it affected colonial activity in North America are to be found in the several works of Perry Miller. They are profoundly scholarly and should be avoided by those who shrink from hard and abstract thinking. But there are no alternative works of equal excellence, and if Professor Miller is rich in complexity, it is because of his subject. He furthermore has performed a sterling service in scotching the notion that the religious motivation in the settlement of New England was merely incidental.

2. For an admirable exposition of this attribute, see Morison, *Intellectual Life.*

3. Adam Winthrop's policy was gradually to transfer his holdings, and the economic and judicial responsibilities that went with them, to his eldest son. The process had begun as early as September, 1606. See Adam Winthrop Diary, as quoted in R.C. Winthrop, *Life and Letters,* I, 425. By May 10, 1620, JWS was competent to draw up a will wherein the lands were assigned to his children, chiefly JWJ. See *ibid.,* I, 151–53, and *Winthrop Papers,* I, 250.

4. *Ibid.,* I, 180 and *n,* 181, 243–47, 257–60, 270–71.

5. Notestein, pp. 261–62; Morgan, pp. 21–22.

6. Maxwell, p. 24.

7. *Winthrop Papers,* I, 341*n.*

8. JWS to Margaret Tyndal W., April 9, 1622, *ibid.,* I, 368.

9. Maxwell, pp. 13–14; see also John Speed's Map of Dublin (1610, enlarged and edited copy in Dublin Civic Museum).

10. *Ibid.,* pp. 11–13, 40, 44–45, 51.

11. *Ibid.,* pp. 28–29. *Dictionary of National Biography* (*DNB*), LVI, 40–42. The vice-chancellor of Trinity, Dublin, was the well-known James Ussher, who devoted his life to the union of altar and

throne. But Ussher was in England while JWJ was at Trinity, Dublin. Maxwell, p. 55; W.B.S. Taylor, *History of the University of Dublin*, p. 219.

12. Maxwell, *History of Trinity College*, pp. 29, 44, 46–48. JWS to JWJ, August 6, 1622, R.C. Winthrop, *Life and Letters*, I, 172.

13. In the winter of 1622/3, JWS felt it necessary to extract from his son a written promise to apply himself to religious speculation. In March, 1623/4, he warned him against reading a certain book upon classical monuments with other than a "sober mind and sanctified heart." *Winthrop Papers*, I, 280–81.

14. Maxwell, pp. 17–18; *Winthrop Papers*, I, 274.

15. Notestein, p. 139.

16. He was no doubt in Holy Orders; JWS in a letter to JWJ, October 3, 1623, refers to "your reverend tutor." *Winthrop Papers*, I, 288–89. See also Maxwell, pp. 59–60.

17. *Winthrop Papers*, I, 271–77, 282–83; R.C. Winthrop, *Life and Letters*, I, 172–76, 179–80.

18. *Winthrop Papers*, I, 288–89, 313–14.

19. *Ibid.*, I, 182–83, 272, 280–81, 283–84, 311, 312 and *n*, 313. The Downings' infant son was the famous Sir George Downing of Downing Street.

20. *Collections*, Mass. Hist. Soc., Series 3, VIII, 296–98; *Winthrop Papers*, I, 319–22.

21. *Ibid.*, I, 320–22; Inner Temple Register, quoted in R.C. Winthrop, *Life and Letters*, I, 203. *Students Admitted to the Inner Temple, 1547–1660* (London, 1877), cited in *Winthrop Papers*, I, 241, 318*n*, gives the date as November, 1624. The private correspondence already cited is sufficient indication that this date is in error.

22. Bellot, chaps. 2 and 3, also p. 264; London County Council, pp. 7, 9; Notestein, pp. 86–88.

23. Bellot, chap. 6.

24. Notestein, p. 87; *Winthrop Papers*, I, 320–21. Not all students, however, could be thus accommodated.

25. Robert was the second son of Brampton Gurdon of Assington, Suffolk, a rather lavish country seat on the margin of the Stour Valley. *Ibid.*, I, 318*n*. Robert's elder brother John later won renown as a parliamentary stalwart and regicide, but never faced the block. *DNB*, XXIII, 353.

26. *Winthrop Papers*, I, 335–36. Peterborough Court nowadays serves as a loading area for the *Daily Telegraph*. See also Wheatley, III, 77.

27. Anne (Winthrop) Fones had died in May, 1619. *Winthrop Papers*, I, 238–39.

28. R.C. Winthrop, *Life and Letters*, II, 240n.

29. Elizabeth's passionate nature is evident in her subsequent career, certain details of which will be touched upon later. She has more recently achieved considerable renown as the heroine of Anya Seton's *The Winthrop Woman*. But there exists no positive evidence that there was, as in the novel, a frustrated love affair between Elizabeth Fones and John Winthrop, Jr.

The sign is mentioned in a number of letters, for example, JWS (Groton) to JWJ (London), *Winthrop Papers*, I, 333.

30. This is sufficient proof that these particular Waldegraves were not the celebrated Roman Catholic clan. Indeed, the Waldegraves were connected by marriage to the Suffolk Cloptons. See R.C. Winthrop, *Life and Letters*, I, 209–10.

31. *Winthrop Papers*, I, 334–35 and illustration facing p. 334.

32. *Ibid.*, I, 333–34, 335–36, 338–40.

33. *Ibid.*, I, 331–32, 335–37 and nn. Both Barnardiston and Barrington flatly refused to sit on county commissions for administering the loans. Barrington (1570–1628) was by marriage an uncle of Oliver Cromwell.

34. *Proceedings*, Mass. Hist. Soc., XVI, 144; *Winthrop Papers*, I, 340–41; R.C. Winthrop, *Life and Letters*, I, 214–18; Morgan, pp. 22–26. The Court of Wards and Liveries was not a very highly respected institution. It supervised the real estate of "King's Wards," that is, those who held land directly of the Crown and were not yet of age. It was prolific in graft, though there is nothing to indicate any dishonesty on the part of John Winthrop or of his fellow attorney, Emmanuel Downing.

35. Notestein, p. 88; *DNB*, XXVIII, 119; *Winthrop Papers*, I, 374n.

36. *Ibid.*, I, 329–33, 337–38; 347–48; R.C. Winthrop, *Life and Letters*, I, 236–37. The location of JWS's "chambers" is evident in a letter from Brampton Gurdon October 20, 1627, *Winthrop Papers*, I, 363.

CHAPTER 3

Two Voyages to Manhood

1. Muskett, p. 99; *Winthrop Papers*, I, 347*n*–48; R.C. Winthrop, *Life and Letters*, I, 236–37.

2. The situation is discussed, nowhere with special clarity, in many works. See Gardiner, Vol. VI, chap. 60; also Acton *et al.*, eds., IV, 131 ff.

3. For the correspondence that led to Winthrop's appointment, see *Winthrop Papers*, I, 347–48, 350–51; also R.C. Winthrop, *Life and Letters*, I, 236–40.

4. *Winthrop Papers*, I, 352–53. For Hervey (d. 1642), see *DNB*, XXVI, 292. But Clowes, II, 65, says *Due Repulse* carried Vice Admiral Lord Lindsay, not Hervey. A sketch of Thomas Best (1570?–1638) is in *DNB*, IV, 418–20; see also *Winthrop Papers*, I, 344 and *n*.

5. Oppenheim, pp. 121, 124, 202, 212, 251; article on Phineas Pett (1570–1647), *DNB*, XLV, 104–6; *Winthrop Papers*, I, 344.

6. *Ibid.*, I, 351–52, 355–56 and *n*; Gardiner, Vol. VI, chap. 60, *passim*.

7. *Winthrop Papers*, I, 352–53.

8. Williamson, p. 207.

9. For a general description of the Île de Ré operations, see Gardiner, Vol. VI, chap. 60; see also *Cambridge Modern History*, IV, 132.

10. *Winthrop Papers*, I, 359–60; see also Gardiner's *History of England*.

11. Trevelyan, p. 138.

12. *Due Repulse* appears to have been so well disciplined that there was little sickness in her company. *Winthrop Papers*, I, 359–60.

13. Williamson, p. 207; R.C. Winthrop, *Life and Letters*, I, 248–49.

14. *Ibid.*, I, 404.

15. *Winthrop Papers*, I, 374–76, 378, 379; II, 3. JWS was also rather heavily in debt. This was partly incident to an enterprise involving his second son, Henry, who had departed with a colonizing

group for Barbados, probably in December, 1626. *Ibid.*, I, 338*n*, 356–57.

16. Ms. Indenture, Close Roll, 4 Charles I, pt. 6, no. 15, Public Record Office, London. This is also printed in *Winthrop Papers*, II, 59–61. The indenture indicates an extent of less than 100 acres. But a series of unspecified parcels, known as "Brettes Crofts," undoubtedly amounted to a good deal more.

17. R.C. Winthrop, *Life and Letters*, I, 250–51.

18. *Winthrop Papers*, I, 386–87, 390–91.

19. *Ibid.*, I, 267–68, 402 and *n*, 403, 406, 408–9; II, 72–73; R.C. Winthrop, *Life and Letters*, I, 263–65; ms. Winthrop Papers, Vol. V, fol. 91, Mass. Hist. Soc.

20. *Ibid.*, I, 417*n*, 417–18; II, 80*n*; R.C. Winthrop, *Life and Letters*, I, 268; for Wyche see also *DNB*, LXIII, 193–94.

21. R.C. Winthrop, *Life and Letters*, I, 268, 270–71.

22. *Winthrop Papers*, II, 73–74.

23. *Ibid.*, II, 72 and *n*, 74.

24. *Ibid.*, II, 72 and *n*, 73. For Sir Isaac Wake (1580?–1632), see *DNB*, LVIII, 441–42.

25. *Winthrop Papers*, IV, 155–56. For Golius (1596–1667), see *ibid.*, 155*n*; also Hugh James Rose, VIII, 58–59.

26. *Winthrop Papers*, I, 410–11; II, 68–69, 75, 76 and *n*, 77.

27. *Ibid.*, II, 103–4.

28. *Ibid.*, II, 103–5, 154, 202–3.

CHAPTER 4

The Governor & Company
of the Massachusetts Bay in New England

1. Lucy Downing had written Winthrop on August 8 at Flushing, but he can hardly have received this letter prior to his sailing therefrom on August 10. *Winthrop Papers*, II, 104–5.

2. *Ibid.*, I, 78–79, 104–5, 338*n*, 356–57, 405–6; II, 66–69. This affair is featured, with suitable embellishments, in Anya Seton, *The Winthrop Woman.*

3. R.C. Winthrop, *Life and Letters*, I, 289.

4. *Winthrop Papers*, II, 94–95, 99–100.

5. JWJ (London) to JWS (Groton), August 21, 1629, *ibid.*, II, 150–51. For a perceptive comment, see Dunn, pp. 61–62.

6. The literature of the Massachusetts Bay Company is vast. Frances Rose-Troup's *The Massachusetts Bay Company and its Predecessors* is recommended to those who seek a sensible presentation of the technicalities.

7. Morgan, pp. 38–42.

8. Its full text is most conveniently to be consulted in Jensen, ed., pp. 72–84.

9. Frances Rose-Troup, pp. 88–102; Bailyn, p. 19.

10. Morgan, pp. 45–56; *Winthrop Papers*, II, 102–3.

11. Morgan, p. 49; *Winthrop Papers*, II, 159–61.

12. *Ibid.*, II, 202–3. JWS and JWJ doubtless met at Groton. The latter was home no later than October 5, 1629, and probably rather earlier. The former was not present at any Bay Company meeting in London before October 15. Osgood, p. 146.

13. Banks, p. 14; *Winthrop Papers*, II, 91–92.

14. *Ibid.*, II, 160–61, 171–72, 178 and *nn*, 193–94, 200–2; III, 33, 129; R.C. Winthrop, *Life and Letters*, I, 373.

15. *Winthrop Papers*, I, 32–33, 332–33; II, 155–58, 193–95.

16. *Ibid.*, II, 210–11 and *nn*.

17. Harry Andrew Wright, "Those Human Puritans," *Proceedings*, American Antiquarian Society, new series, L (1940), 80–84.

18. *Winthrop Papers*, II, 211–12.

19. *Ibid.*, II, 202–3.

20. R.C. Winthrop, *Life and Letters*, I, 382–93; II, 5–7; Banks, p. 65; Morgan, pp. 53, 84.

21. *Winthrop Papers*, II, 304–7; Morgan, pp. 57–65.

22. The nature of his activities is indicated very clearly in the appropriate correspondence published in *The Winthrop Papers*. The news doctoring involved chiefly the deletion of unfavorable developments.

23. They may even have joined in gentle adventures. In a letter to JWJ nearly thirty years later, Williams referred happily to "that Westerne Metheglyn [a spiced alcoholic drink], which you and I have drunck at Bristow togeather, &c." *Collections*, Mass. Hist. Soc., Series 3, X, 27. See also *Winthrop Papers*, II, 316–18 and *nn*.

24. Frances Rose-Troup, "John Humfrey," *Collections*, Essex Institute, LXV, 293–308; *Winthrop Papers*, II, 229–31, 304–7; III, 27–28, 31–33, 49–50, 51–54, 129–30; R.C. Winthrop, *Life and Letters*, II, 69–71, 73–75; Banks, pp. 62, 64, 85–86, 92–93; Muskett, p. 99. Downing's name appears frequently in the "company" correspondence printed in *Winthrop Papers*.

25. *Winthrop Papers*, II, 35, 300–1; III, 7–8.

26. Visit of the author, July 8, 1960; see also Pevsner, pp. 141, 245–46. For Sir Henry Mildmay (d. 1637), see *Winthrop Papers*, I, 1 (illus. facing), 295*n*, 442; II, 69; Muskett, pp. 7*n*, 45–47; Metcalfe, ed., *Visitations*, I, 250; Willson, pp. 163, 350; Mss. State Papers, Domestic (Charles II), Vol. LXII, fol. 47, Public Record Office, London.

27. *Winthrop Papers*, III, 1*n*, 1–6, 20–22.

28. R.C. Winthrop, *Life and Letters*, II, 34–35, 82–83, 170–71; *New England Historical and Genealogical Register*, XVIII (1864). 183.

29. *Winthrop Papers*, II, 71–73, 180 and *n*, 181, 186–91; III, 7–8.

30. *Ibid.*, II, 74, 78, 299–301, 300*n*, 325–27; III, 7–8, 27–28. For Dr. Wright, see *DNB*, LXIII, 118. Professor Andrews says the Winthrops secured £4,600 from Warren; see *Colonial Period of American History*, I, 387*n*. Warren did not prove a good landlord. In 1647, the manor house was already "much ruinous and falne to decay," and its current occupant was seeking a license to pull down half of it to repair the rest. *Winthrop Papers*, V, 154. The Groton seat of the Winthrops has, indeed, crumbled away long since. Only a vague depression, close to an ancient and derelict mulberry tree, is possible evidence of its location. That the tree grew in the kitchen garden before 1630 is a tradition which can be neither proved nor denied.

31. Groton Parish Register, quoted in *Collections*, Mass. Hist. Soc., Series 3, VIII, 297; conversation of author with the Rev. A.B. Bird (vicar of Edwardstone and rector of Groton), November 1, 1959. It is almost certain that Martha and JWJ were married by the curate, Mr. Leigh. Thomas Nicholson, the rector, was already feeble and nearly blind in 1626. *Winthrop Papers*, I, 334.

32. *Ibid.*, III, 16–17, 23–24.

33. *Ibid.*, III, 26, 28–29; II, 37.

34. *Ibid.*, I, 274, 330–31; II, 35, 299–300; III, 20–22, 33, 129.

35. Martha was born January 21, 1609/10. *Ibid.*, I, 104 and *n*.

36. *Ibid.*, I, 37. Dunn, p. 63, declares that JWJ was fined by the London Court of Aldermen.

CHAPTER 5

Massachusetts Bay in New England

1. *Winthrop Papers*, III, 1*n*, 1–6, 20–22, 31–33, 35–36, 41–49.
2. *Ibid.*, III, 58, 226–27. For Jacie (1601–63), see *ibid.*, II, 87*n*; III, 484–85; *Collections*, Mass. Hist. Soc., Series 4, VI, 452*n*.
3. Banks, p. 95; *Winthrop Papers*, III, 50–51. Deane Winthrop, who was nine years of age, was left in England to advance his schooling —in whose charge is not known.
4. *Ibid.*, III, 49–60.
5. It has been estimated that *Lion* sailed from London on August 23. Banks, pp. 94–95.
6. *Ibid.* The heaviest passenger list reported for *Lion* is 123. The 200-ton *Mayflower* carried 100 in 1620 and was crowded.
7. For the shipboard conditions faced by early voyagers to New England, see *ibid.*, pp. 3–10, 25, 27–28, 40–41.
8. Winthrop, *Journal*, I, 70.
9. *Ibid.*, I, 70.
10. *Ibid.*
11. *Ibid.*, I, 70–71.
12. Weeden, I, 81.
13. *Winthrop Papers*, III, 75, 81, 94; R.C. Winthrop, *Life and Letters*, II, 30.
14. Bailyn, pp. 26–27, 206*n*.
15. *Winthrop Papers*, I, 394, 472, 477, 480, 487, 496, 497–506; III, 57, 76–77, 81–85, 94–100, 104, 110–14, 116–18, 124–25; T.G. Wright, *Literary Culture*, pp. 32–34 and *nn*.
16. *Winthrop Papers*, III, 55–56, 57–61, 77–83, 90–91, 94–98, 110–14, 127. The eclipse was partial in New England, but a very small percentage of the sun's disk was covered. It did occur on October 3, 1632 (o.s.), but the band of totality extended from a sunrise point south of the eastern peninsula of Siberia, across the Pacific to Mexico, Central and South America, and ended at sunset at a point 200 miles east of the Orinoco delta. Oppolzer, pp. 270–71, plate 135.

17. *Winthrop Papers*, III, 142; Hutchinson, I, 24–25; Andrews, I, 433, 435; Morgan, pp. 90–91.

18. Shurtleff, ed., *The Records of the Governor and Company of the Massachusetts Bay in New England* (hereafter referred to as *Recs.* Mass. Bay), I, 95.

19. *Ibid.*, I, 79, 93.

20. *Ibid.*, I, 95–96; Morgan, pp. 110–11.

21. For the several forms of the Massachusetts assistants' oath, see Shurtleff, ed., *Recs.* Mass. Bay, I, 350, 352–53. The first oath did not include the king's name, which was added after the company moved to New England.

22. For Dudley (c. 1575–1653), see *DAB*, V, 484; R.C. Winthrop, *Life and Letters*, II, 91–93, 101*n*; Morgan, pp. 87, 103. For Ludlow, see J.M. Taylor, *Roger Ludlow*; *DAB*, XI, 493–94. For Pynchon, see Bailyn, p. 31; *Collections*, Mass. Hist. Soc., Series 4, VI, 369*n*; *DAB*, XV, 292–93. For Simon Bradstreet (1603–97), see *DAB*, II, 579–80. (He served as assistant in Massachusetts for the remarkable period of forty-nine years and twice, in a vigorous old age, as governor. His famous first wife was, of course, the Puritan poetess Anne Bradstreet.) Increase Nowell (1590–1655) is briefly sketched in *DNB*, XLI, 250. John Endecott (c. 1589–1665) is in *DAB*, VI, 155–56. For William Coddington (1601–78), see *Collections*, Mass. Hist. Soc., Series 4, VI, 312*n*.

23. Shurtleff, ed., *Recs.* Mass. Bay, I, 96–103.

24. This affair is presented in some detail, though with a Winthrop slant, in R.C. Winthrop, *Life and Letters*, II, 94–100.

25. *Winthrop Papers*, III, 100–1, 110–14, 124–25, 126–28; W.L. Grant, *et al.*, eds., *Acts of the Privy Council of England, Colonial Series* (hereafter referred to as *Acts, P.C. (Colonial)*), I, 183, 187.

26. Winthrop, *Journal*, I, 103, 104–5.

CHAPTER 6

Enterprise at Agawam

1. Shurtleff, ed., *Recs.* Mass. Bay, I, 103.

2. Winthrop, *Journal*, I, 97–98. See also William Hubbard, "A General History of New England," *Collections*, Mass. Hist. Soc., Series 2, V, 160–61.

3. Winthrop, *Journal*, I, 98. Its scattered hills are, however, glacial drumlins.

4. Edward Johnson, "Wonder Working Providence of Zion's Savior in New England" (chap. XXX), *Collections*, Mass. Hist. Soc., Series 2, III, 141–42.

5. Winthrop, *Journal*, I, 98; Waters, *Sketch*, p. 4; Thomas Prince, "Annals of New England," *Collections*, Mass. Hist. Soc., Series 2, VII, 36. See also *Essex Antiquarian*, I, 141; Frederick John Kingsbury, "John Winthrop, Junior," *Proceedings*, American Antiquarian Society, new series, XII, 301.

6. Shurtleff, ed., *Recs.* Mass. Bay, I, 104–8.

7. Ms. inventory at Whipple House, Ipswich, Mass.; *Proceedings*, Mass. Hist. Soc., Series 2, XI, 4–6; Waters, *Ipswich*, pp. 33–35; *Winthrop Papers*, III, 140.

8. Morgan, p. 169; Shurtleff, ed., *Recs.* Mass. Bay, I, 101–2; *Winthrop Papers*, III, 140–41.

9. *Ibid.*, III, 141, 142–43; Ms. inventory at Whipple House, Ipswich (see also *Proceedings*, Mass. Hist. Soc., Series 2, XI, 4–6).

10. Waters, *Ipswich*, pp. 33–35, 386. The earliest surviving reference to JWJ's house tract dates, however, no further back than 1654. It appears to have been 6 acres in extent and to have been on the south slope of Ipswich's Town Hill, near the lower end of present Wainwright Street.

11. R.C. Winthrop, *Life and Letters*, II, 418; *Winthrop Papers*, III, 146.

12. *Ibid.*, III, 131, 133–35, 137, 157–59.

13. *Ibid.*, III, 119n, 120–21. This letter cannot, as has been supposed, be dated c. May 1, 1633; it thanks JWJ and *Martha* for their recent hospitality, and Martha did not arrive in Agawam until the late autumn of 1633.

14. Yet it did become, within less than twenty years, the principal beef packing town in New England. See Johnson, "Wonder Working Providence," chap. XXX, *Collections*, Mass. Hist. Soc., Series 2, III, 141–42.

15. *Winthrop Papers*, III, 150–52, 162–63, 170.

16. Waters, *Sketch*, p. 11, citing Essex Deeds 2:260, 12; Waters, *Ipswich*, p. 464, citing Ipswich Town Records; *Records and Files of the Quarterly Courts of Essex County, Massachusetts* (hereafter cited as *Records and Files*, Essex Quarter Courts), II, 170n.

17. Shurtleff, ed., *Recs.* Mass. Bay, I, 114.

18. *Winthrop Papers*, II, 227 and *n*; *Collections*, Mass. Hist. Soc., Series 4, VI, 354*n*; Shurtleff, ed., *Recs.* Mass. Bay, I, 114–16.

19. For discussions of this famous session, see Frances Rose-Troup, pp. 117–21; R.C. Winthrop, *Life and Letters*, II, 113; Morgan, pp. 112–14. For the position of Ludlow, see Taylor, *Roger Ludlow*, p. 45.

20. Shurtleff, ed., *Recs.* Mass. Bay, I, 122–23; Waters, *Sketch*, pp. 8–9.

21. *Ibid.* It is curious that Waters, who (though without formal historical training) was ordinarily very meticulous, failed to indicate the source of this information.

22. The romantically speculative can consider the following: Winthrop's letters to his second wife are rather straightforward—at times practically business documents. But at *her* death, he wrote copiously of his sense of loss.

23. Ward (1578?–1652) is in *DAB*, XIX, 433–34; for Parker (1595–1677), see *ibid.*, XIV, 241–42. The name change to Ipswich was approved by the Court of Assistants at Newtown on August 5, 1634. Shurtleff, ed., *Recs.* Mass. Bay, I, 122–23.

24. *Ibid.*, I, 123–33.

CHAPTER 7

The First Return to Britain

1. Andrews, I, 408–14; W.L. Grant, *et al.*, eds., *Acts, P.C.* (*Colonial*), I, 199–202.

2. *Ibid.*, I, 199, 200–1.

3. Winthrop, *Journal*, I, 129; Osgood, III, 64; Shurtleff, ed., *Recs.* Mass. Bay, I, 123–25.

4. John Wilson is adequately sketched in *DAB*, XX, 336–337.

5. R.C. Winthrop, *Life and Letters*, II, 123, 126; Shurtleff, ed., *Recs.* Mass. Bay, I, 132–73 *passim*; Waters, *Sketch*, pp. 9–10; ms. inventory at Whipple House, Ipswich, Mass.; *Proceedings*, Mass. Hist. Soc., Series 2, XI, 4–6.

6. Winthrop, *Journal*, I, 164; William Hubbard, "General History of New England," *Collections*, Mass. Hist. Soc., Series 2, V, 180. JWS

states that JWJ and Wilson parted company at Galway, but a letter of December 26, 1634, from Joshua Hoyle to JWJ strongly implies that the two were together as far as Dublin. *Winthrop Papers*, III, 179–80.

7. *DNB*, XII, 156; G.E. Cokayne, *Complete Peerage*, IX, 358–60; ms. Winthrop Papers, 5.198, Mass. Hist. Soc. Winthrop almost certainly encountered Coote on this occasion; on his next journey to Britain he did not visit Ireland at all, and Coote and his son of the same name were at the same time occupied with the Irish Rebellion.

8. An Irish kern of the seventeenth century was a footsoldier of uncertain loyalty and no visible restraint.

9. *Winthrop Papers*, III, 179–80.

10. That Wilson remained with Winthrop as far as Dublin is further indicated in William Wilson to JWJ, March 6, 1634/5, *ibid.*, III, 193. But there is no evidence that the two traveled together thereafter.

11. Clotworthy is in *DNB*, XI, 126–27; see also *Winthrop Papers*, III, 187, 190–93, 195–96; IV, 230.

12. Leder, pp. 3–6, 158–159. William Hubbard indicates that Livingstone may already have been in correspondence with Massachusetts Bay. *Collections*, Mass. Hist. Soc., Series 2, V, 154.

13. *Winthrop Papers*, III, 187–88, 195–96; Winthrop, *Journal*, I, 164.

14. *Winthrop Papers*, II, 87n; III, 484–85; *Collections*, Mass. Hist. Soc., Series 4, VI, 452n; VII, 162n; Boynton, x, xii, xvi–xvii.

15. *Winthrop Papers*, III, 188–89, 226–27, 247, 248, 366, 388–89. But neither Boynton nor Jacie ever reached America.

16. *Ibid.*, III, 188–89.

17. *Ibid.*, III, 66, 175–78, 189–90.

18. *Ibid.*, III, 176.

19. The bibliography of Hugh Peter is large. A recent study is Raymond Phineas Stearns, *The Strenuous Puritan, Hugh Peter, 1598–1660* (Urbana, Ill., 1954). Biographical sketches are to be found in *DNB*, XLV, 69–77, and *DAB*, XIV, 496–98.

20. *Winthrop Papers*, III, 194.

21. Elizabeth Reade was baptized November 27, 1614. Ms. Parish Record, St. Katherine's Parish Church, Wickford, Essex.

22. *Winthrop Papers*, III, 195; Bannerman, p. 53; *DNB*, VIII, 5–7; Miller, pp. 266–67, 370; Jenkinson, pp. 189–90; Dale, I, 136; Goodwin and Britton, Vol. II, no pagination; Kent, pp. 120–21; visit of author to site, July 6, 1960.

23. Samuel Reade to JWJ, March 5, 1635/6, mentions Elizabeth Reade Winthrop as "my little sister," but this may refer to the fact that she was the youngest in her family. *Winthrop Papers*, III, 233–34.

24. "Last Will and Testament of Edmund Reade," *Proceedings*, Mass. Hist. Soc. V, 255–58; Muskett, p. 164; information posted on west wall of nave, St. Katherine's Parish Church, Wickford, Essex; visit of author, November, 1959. Elizabeth's letters are very few. Practically all are in the handwriting of amanuenses or of relatives. A legal document of July 5, 1661, which she personally signed, reveals an obviously painful effort. Ms. Winthrop Papers, 5.16, 20, 30, Mass. Hist. Soc.

25. *Ibid.*, 5.16. Appreciative references to "good Mrs. Winthrop" are more than ordinarily frequent in letters addressed to JWJ.

26. *Winthrop Papers*, III, 175, 176–78, 194–95.

27. Egerton Mss. 2395, fols. 27, 29, British Museum; Osgood, III, 69–71; Andrews, I, 420–23; *Winthrop Papers*, III, 194–95; IV, 340–41.

28. A ms. "Copy of a copy" of this "Warwick Patent" is in the Connecticut State Library, Hartford; it is printed in B.B. Trumbull, *A Complete History of Connecticut*, I, 423–24.

29. For discussions of the validity, or even the reality, of the Warwick patent, see Bates, pp. 8–10, and Andrews, II, 128*n*.

30. *Ibid.* Saye and Sele (1583–1662) is in *DNB*, XVIII, 433–36; for Brooke (1608–43) see *DNB*, XXIII, 163–64.

31. *Winthrop Papers*, III, 198–99.

32. *Ibid.* Lord Brooke did not sign Winthrop's commission, for reasons unknown.

33. *Ibid.*, III, 206; IV, 122 and *n*, 202–3; *Collections*, Mass. Hist. Soc., Series 5, I, 382–83; Albert Matthews, "Comenius and Harvard College," *Publications*, Colonial Society of Massachusetts (hereafter referred to as Col. Soc. Mass.), XXI, 175*n*; Basil Valentine, *Von den Naturlich und Obernaturlich Dingen* (Leipzig, 1624), Title No. 254 in Winthrop Library, New York Society Library.

Winthrop appears to have acquired already a reading knowledge of German. His membership in the Rosicrucian Order is an interesting but unproved possibility. J.W. Hamilton-Jones to author, January 11, 1965; Ronald S. Wilkinson to author, February 2, 1965.

34. For Hopkins (c. 1600–57), see *DAB*, IX, 207–8. That Nye (c. 1596–1672) did not return from exile until 1640 is implied in *DNB*,

XII, 279–82. But his presence in England and his connection with the "Lords and Gentlemen," in 1635, are attested by his correspondence with JWJ. For specific preparations, see *Winthrop Papers*, III, 191–92, 204–5, 208–10, 211, 213.

35. Banks, pp. 161–70; *Winthrop Papers*, III, 206–7.

36. Banks's data would indicate that Wilson and Peter voyaged remarkably to America in both vessels at once. But the senior Winthrop (*Journal*, I, 160) asserts that they arrived in America aboard the *Defence*. Other data are in *Winthrop Papers*, III, 201, 206–7. Vane (1613–62) is sketched in *DAB*, XIX, 191–93; see also Hosmer's *The Life of Young Sir Henry Vane*. Vane is said to have been issued a royal license to remain in Massachusetts for three years. Winthrop, *Journal*, I, 162.

37. *Ibid.*, I, 161; *Winthrop Papers*, III, 201, 206–7.

38. Winthrop, *Journal*, I, 161.

CHAPTER 8

The Fitful Years

1. Andrews, II, 69, 72–73; *New England Genealogical and Historical Register*, XXIX, 237–39; Bradford, p. 301.

2. Winthrop, *Journal*, I, 161–62, 165; Winthrop *Papers*, III, 209–10; Lion Gardiner, "Pequot Warres," *Collections*, Mass. Hist. Soc., Series 3, III, 137.

3. Andrews, II, 73–74; *Winthrop Papers*, III, 217–19, 228–29; Winthrop, *Journal*, I, 161–62, 169–72, 180; Shurtleff, ed., *Recs.* Mass. Bay, I, 164, 174, 371.

4. Andrews, I, 77–79; Shurtleff, ed., *Recs.* Mass. Bay, I, 170–71, 320–21, 371. It is interesting to note that Winthrop, though still an assistant, chose not to attend any sessions of the Massachusetts magistrates during the entire period. *Ibid.*, I, 145–71.

5. *Winthrop Papers*, III, 201–6, 209–10, 211, 213, 215–17, 232–33; Banks, pp. 153–54.

6. Gardiner's solid good sense is evident in his own history of the Pequot Wars. *Collections*, Mass. Hist. Soc., Series 3, Vol. III. He is sketched in *DAB*, VII, 138–39.

7. Winthrop apparently received, in Boston, a letter dated March 20, 1635/6. *Winthrop Papers*, III, 239. Gardiner's son, David, born April 29, 1636, is said to have been the first white child born within the present limits of the State of Connecticut. *Collections*, Mass. Hist. Soc., Series 4, VII, 52*n*.

8. *Winthrop Papers*, III, 246–47; Weeden, I, 123 ff.; Rose-Troup, p. 28.

9. Saybrook is supposed to have been named by George Fenwick. *Collections*, Mass. Hist. Soc., Series 4, VI, 364*n*.

10. *Winthrop Papers*, III, 255–56, 268–70, 273–75, 388–89. A great amount of surviving correspondence, much of it contained in *Winthrop Papers*, Vol. III, deals with the transshipments. Though medium-sized ships could, with luck and high water, ascend the Connecticut to Windsor, it ordinarily was quicker and safer to make use of local river smacks. A partially settled bill, submitted to William Pynchon, survives. Photostat in Conn. State Library.

11. *Ibid.*, III, 281–82. The complaint was referred to Winthrop, who simply endorsed it "Servants at Saybrooke their pro[test]."

12. The county town of Hertfordshire had been the native place of one of its ministers, the Reverend Samuel Stone. For the naming of Hartford, Connecticut, see J.H. Trumbull, *et al.*, eds., *The Public Records of the Colony of Connecticut* (hereafter referred to as *Col. Recs. Conn.*), I, 7–8.

13. *Winthrop Papers*, III, 274. For a discussion of Connecticut developments that spring, see Andrews, II, 79–81.

14. The bibliography of the Pequots is extensive. For a good brief discussion, see Van Dusen, pp. 33–35; see also Lion Gardiner's "Pequot Warres," *Collections*, Mass. Hist. Soc., Series 3, Vol. III.

15. This incident is described in Bradford, pp. 332–33.

16. Shurtleff, ed., *Recs. Mass. Bay*, I, 174; *Winthrop Papers*, III, 284–85.

17. Gardiner, "Pequot Warres," *Collections*, Mass. Hist. Soc., Series 3, III, 137–39; *Winthrop Papers*, III, 282–83. Stanton (c. 1615–78) became the best known Indian trader and interpreter in Southern New England; see Savage, IV, 167. It is significant that JWJ made use of him on this occasion to secure (in his own behalf) a land cession from the Niantic Indians. Deposition of Thomas Stanton, July, 1647, "Acts" of the Commissioners of the United Colonies of New England, David

Pulsifer, ed., *Records of the Colony of New Plymouth* (hereafter referred to as *Recs.* Plymouth Colony), IX, 103.

18. Gardiner, "Pequot Warres," *Collections*, Mass. Hist. Soc., Series 3, III, 137–39; Boston Record Commissioners, *Report* for 1630–99, p. 4; *Winthrop Papers*, III, 261–62, 283, 287–88.

19. *Ibid.*, III, 513; IV, 20–21.

20. *Ibid.*, III, 319–21, 366; IV, 21–22; Shurtleff, ed., *Recs.* Mass. Bay, I, 176–77.

21. The Mass. General Court, in an effort to improve the military efficiency of the colony, organized the militia into three regiments. JWJ was commissioned, December 13, 1636, lieutenant colonel of the Third Regiment, made up from Saugus, Salem, *Ipswich*, and Newbury. Shurtleff, ed., *Recs.* Mass. Bay, I, 185–87. See also *Winthrop Papers*, III, 385.

22. *Ibid.*, III, 369–85, 432–33; IV, 4–5, 11–13, 42, 104–5, 108, 140, 141, 155–56; Waters, *Sketch*, pp. 23, 39, 40*n*2, 41*n*1; Weeden, I, 169; *Records and Files*, Essex Quarter Courts, I, 9–12.

23. Waters, *Sketch*, pp. 24–25, declares that Fitz-John Winthrop was born in Boston (JWJ was at the time attending a meeting of the General Court at Newtown). However, there is no record of the infant's baptism there. Muskett, p. 27 and a death notice of December 1, 1707 (*Publications*, Col. Soc. Mass., XVII, 44*n*) indicate that he was born in Ipswich.

24. *Report*, Boston Record Commissioners (1630–99), pp. 8, 9; Lucy Downing to JWJ, January 28, 1640/1, implies an advanced pregnancy. *Winthrop Papers*, IV, 311. But there is no evidence of a surviving child.

25. *Ibid.*, IV, 3–4, 63, 64, 68–69; R.C. Winthrop, *Life and Letters*, II, 264–66.

26. *Winthrop Papers*, IV, 10–11, 13*n*.

27. Andrews, I, 489; George L. Kittredge, "Dr. Robert Child the Remonstrant," *Publications*, Col. Soc. Mass., XXI, 1–146; George H. Turnbull, "Robert Child," *ibid.*, XXXVIII, 21–53; Morgan, pp. 199–200. There is no indication of JWJ's interest in medicine prior to the 1640s.

28. Child to JWJ, c. May, 1641, *Winthrop Papers*, IV, 333–38.

29. S.E. Morison, *Intellectual Life*, p. 34; for John Dee (1527–1608), see *DNB*, XIV, 217. JWJ, by the terms of his father's will,

October 29, 1639, was to share his father's library with his stepmother. But the latter died before JWS, whose death occurred in 1649. R.C. Winthrop, *Life and Letters*, II, 251–52. Nearly all of the known remains of JWJ's library are in the New York Society Library, New York City.

30. Andrews, I, 452–54; Morgan, pp. 160–61; R.C. Winthrop, *Life and Letters*, II, 142–43; Shurtleff, ed., *Recs. Mass. Bay*, I, 177–84.

31. *Collections*, Mass. Hist. Soc., Series 4, VII, 52–56; Series 5, I, 233–34; Shurtleff, ed., *Recs. Mass. Bay*, I, 185–87, 191–95; *Winthrop Papers*, III, 381–82; John Mason, "A Brief History of the Pequot War," *Collections*, Mass. Hist. Soc., Series 2, VIII, 120–53.

32. Andrews, I, 478–79; Morgan, pp. 138–39. Battis's *Saints and Sectaries* is a more complete modern study.

33. Shurtleff, ed., *Recs. Mass. Bay*, I, 184–91, 194–95; Hosmer, p. 70.

34. Winthrop, *Journal*, I, 232–35.

35. Shurtleff, ed., *Recs. Mass. Bay*, I, 205–18; Andrews, I, 484–87.

36. Shurtleff, ed., *Recs. Mass. Bay*, I, 205–35 *passim*.

37. R.C. Winthrop, Life and Letters, II, 217–18, 418; Waters, *Sketch*, pp. 23, 24; *Winthrop Papers*, III, 500, 517 and *n*, 518; IV, 3–4, 10–14, 42.

38. Sketches of Saltonstall (1610–94) and of Stoughton (d. 1645) are in Hutchinson, I, 55*n*. Harlakenden (c. 1608–November, 1638) is treated in Winthrop *Journal*, I, 281 and *n*.

39. Shurtleff, ed., *Recs. Mass. Bay*, I, 227, 255, 287, 318; Winthrop, *Journal*, II, 48–49; *Collections*, Mass. Hist. Soc., Series 3, VIII, 191.

40. W.L. Grant, *et al.*, *Acts, P.C. (Colonial)*, I, 217; Calder, p. 45; *Winthrop Papers*, III, 484–88.

41. Winthrop, *Journal*, I, 274–275, 307; R.C. Winthrop, *Life and Letters*, II, 223–29.

42. *Ibid.*

43. Morgan, p. 161; W.L. Grant, *et al.*, *Acts, P.C. (Colonial)*, I, 227–30. A hostile critic of New England at this time was Lord Saye and Sele. *Winthrop Papers*, IV, 263–67.

44. Bailyn, pp. 46–47; Shurtleff, ed., *Recs. Mass. Bay*, I, 301–9,

318–34; M.B. Jones, "An Early Silver Mining Promotion in Massachusetts Bay," *Proceedings*, Mass. Hist. Soc., XXXV, 372; E.N. Hartley, *Ironworks*, p. 53.

CHAPTER 9

Adventure in Iron—with Diversions

1. *Winthrop Papers*, IV, 314–16; Winthrop *Journal*, II, 25, 31–32; R.C. Winthrop, *Life and Letters*, II, 240n; Shurtleff, ed., *Recs.*, Mass. Bay, I, 250; E.N. Hartley, *Ironworks*, p. 55. Thomas Weld (1595–1662), sometimes referred to as Welde or Welles, is treated in *DAB*, XIX, 627–28, and *DNB*, LX, 160–61.

2. Winthrop, *Journal*, II, 31. See also Raymond Phineas Stearns, "The Weld-Peter Mission to England," *Publications*, Col. Soc. Mass., XXXII, 188–246.

3. Wait-Still Winthrop (d. 1717) was born, probably at Ten Hills or Boston, February 27, 1641/2 and was baptized at First Church, Boston, March 6, 1641/2. Muskett, p. 27; *Report*, Boston Record Commissioners (1630–99), pp. 11, 13.

4. Winthrop, *Journal*, II, 32; Bailyn, p. 62; *Winthrop Papers*, IV, 343–44.

5. Winthrop, *Journal*, II, 32; JWJ to Elizabeth R.W., October 8, 1641, *Winthrop Papers*, IV, 341–42.

6. O'Callaghan *et al.*, eds., *Documents Relative to the Colonial History of New York* (hereafter referred to as *N.Y. Col. Docs.*), II, 150–51; *Winthrop Papers*, IV, 357.

7. *Ibid.*, V, 122–23; Shurtleff, ed., *Recs.*, Mass. Bay, II, 33. For the Forbes expedition, see Prendergast, pp. 74–75; Wedgwood, pp. 110–11; *DAB*, XIV, 497–98; XIX, 627–28; *DNB*, LX, 160–61. Lord Forbes is in Pierce, p. 12, and Paul, IV, 62; also in Cokayne, *Complete Peerage*, V, 547. It is curious to learn that Winthrop met the great liberal Protestant divine, the Reverend John Dury, at Forbes's lodgings. *Proceedings* Mass. Hist. Soc., LXXII, 58–62.

8. *Winthrop Papers*, IV, 368–69. For Comenius (1592–1671) and his English visit, see *Encyclopedia Britannica* (1895 ed.), VI, 182, and Albert Matthews, "Comenius and Harvard College," *Publications*, Col. Soc. Mass. XXI, 146–90.

9. For Tanckmarus (fl. 1632–52), see *Winthrop Papers*, IV, 361*n*, citing Kaspar Heinrich Starck, *Lübeckischer Kirken-Historie* (Hamburg, 1764), p. 796, and Heinrich Schneider, *Joachim Morsius und sein Kreis* (Lübeck, 1929), pp. 48–57. See also *Winthrop Papers*, IV, 361–62, 372.

10. *Ibid.*, IV, 356, 368–69; *Proceedings*, Mass. Hist. Soc. LXXII, 36–40.

11. *Winthrop Papers*, IV, 362–63. Sir William Boswell (d. 1649) is discussed in *DNB*, V, 440.

12. *Winthrop Papers*, IV, 368–69; *Proceedings*, Mass. Hist. Soc. LXXII, 36–40; E.N. Hartley, *Ironworks*, p. 56. Sir Henry de Vic (1599–1671) is in Cokayne, *Complete Baronetage*, III, 11. His wife was a relative, probably a sister, of Philip Carteret (1639–82), first governor of New Jersey.

13. Comenius (1592–1671), born Komensky, is sketched in *Encyclopedia Britannica* (1895 ed.), VI, 182. His acquaintance with JWJ and the alleged invitation to the presidency are asserted in Mather, II, 14. Though Mather is hardly renowned as a dependable source, Albert Matthews, "Comenius and Harvard College," *Publications*, Col. Soc. Mass. XXI, 146–90, presents exhaustive and, on the whole, impressive arguments for the validity of Mather's statement.

14. *Winthrop Papers*, IV, 368–69, 374–75; Wedgwood, p. 187.

15. E.N. Hartley, *Ironworks*, pp. 81–82.

16. *Ibid.*, pp. 61–62, 68–83; *Winthrop Papers*, IV, 371–72, 375. Holland (1599–post 1660) is sketched in *DNB*, XXVII, 199; Foley is in *DNB*, XIX, 355.

17. *Winthrop Papers*, IV, 379–80, 395–96, 415–16.

18. Hartlib (c. 1600–70?) is discussed in *DNB*, XXV, 72–73. Letters received by JWJ prior to 1661 indicate that he had become personally acquainted with Hartlib between 1641 and 1643. Digby's extraordinary career is sketched in *DNB*, XV, 60–66 and treated at length in Petersson's *Sir Kenelm Digby, The Ornament of England, 1603–1665;* in a letter to JWJ, January 31, 1654/5 (*Collections*, Mass. Hist. Soc., Series 3, X, 5–6), he deplored the wasting of so promising a philosopher upon the American wilderness.

19. *Winthrop Papers*, V, 122–23; Shurtleff, ed., *Recs.*, Mass. Bay, II, 34; III, 256; Morgan, p. 196; Weeden, I, 141; Andrews, II, 24.

20. *Winthrop Papers*, IV, 354–55, 357–59, 370–71, 377; V, 20–21, 28–29, 373.

21. JWJ was so angered by the whole proceeding that he drew up a petition to Parliament, citing details and soliciting compensation for subsequent losses. *Ibid.*, IV, 424–25.

22. *Ibid.*, IV, 424–25. JWJ took his assistant's oath at the meeting of the Mass. General Court, September 7, 1643. Shurtleff, ed., *Recs.*, Mass. Bay, II, 47.

23. JWJ "Discourse about the fittest place to begin the Iron workes," *Winthrop Papers*, IV, 425–27; see also *Proceedings*, Mass. Hist. Soc., Series 2, VIII, 13–14.

24. *Ibid.*

25. Morgan, pp. 176–84; *Winthrop Papers*, IV, 498–99, 500.

26. Though absent in England, he was reelected assistant both in 1642 and 1643. Shurtleff, ed., *Recs.*, Mass. Bay, II, 2, 33.

27. *Winthrop Papers*, IV, 422–23, 450–51; Shurtleff, ed., *Recs.*, Mass. Bay, II, 61, 81–82, 104–5, 125–28; E.N. Hartley, *Ironworks*, pp. 85–90.

28. The undertakers in London were openly objecting to the New England restrictions as early as the spring of 1645; Massachusetts stood, for the time being, pat. Bailyn, pp. 66–67; Shurtleff, ed., *Recs.*, Mass. Bay, II, 185–186; E.N. Hartley, *Ironworks*, pp. 92 ff.

29. Almost certainly Edward Hutchinson (1613?–75), son of the famous Anne, see Hutchinson, I, 169 and *n.* For additional data on lands, see Battis, p. 75; see also *Winthrop Papers*, IV, 359.

30. Ibid., IV, 498–99. For Osborne, see *ibid.*, also Savage, III, 319. E.N. Hartley, *Ironworks*, pp. 101–2 and *n.* The remains of Winthrop's furnace lie within the modern limits of Hall Cemetery, West Quincy, Mass.

31. *Winthrop Papers*, V, 5–8, 10–14, 21–22, 27.

32. Downing to JWJ, February 25, 1644/5, *ibid.*, V, 5–8, 51, 209, 261–62; R.C. Winthrop, *Life and Letters*, II, 382–83; *Proceedings*, Mass. Hist. Soc., Series 2, III, 190–91. The ultimately disastrous, and always complicated, fortunes of the Ironworks Undertakers—especially after they had removed their center of operations to the Saugus River—are recorded in great and scholarly detail by Professor Hartley in his excellent *Ironworks on the Saugus*. But I support Professor Richard Dunn's comment that Hartley should have given greater emphasis to the "transatlantic cross purposes" of Massachusetts and the undertakers in England. See Dunn, p. 88*n.*

CHAPTER 10

Journey Home—with Deviations

1. *Winthrop Papers*, IV, 465–66; Shurtleff, ed., *Recs.*, Mass. Bay, II, 71. "Pequot" was, however, about to become a major interest for JWJ.

2. *Winthrop Papers*, IV, 395–96, 495*n*, 495–97; V, 4–5; *Proceedings*, American Antiquarian Society, new series, XIII, 366; XIV, 475*n*. The names of King and Smith will appear again, the latter as a well-known purveyor to the Indians of the Narragansett region. Day (c. 1594–1668), though by profession a locksmith and not perfectly literate, is nevertheless famed as the (allegedly) first printer in English America. *DAB*, V, 163. Smith (d. 1664) is briefly sketched in Ellis and Morris, p. 70*n*; King is treated in George H. Haynes, "The Tale of Tantiusques," *Proceedings*, American Antiquarian Society, new series, XIV, 475. The Tantiusque region is southwest of modern Sturbridge and close to the Connecticut state line.

3. Shurtleff, ed., *Recs.*, Mass. Bay, II, 78–96 *passim; Winthrop Papers*, IV, 497–98.

4. *Ibid.*, V, 10–12, 21, 28–29.

5. *Proceedings*, American Antiquarian Society, new series, XIII, 113, 366; XIV, 472–95; *Collections*, Mass. Hist. Soc., Series 4, VII, 404–5; 5, VII, 404–10; VIII, 49–59. See also JWJ to Henry Oldenburg (secretary of the Royal Society), November 12, 1668, ms. in Letter Book W3, No. 21, Royal Society Library, London. (JWJ's copy of this letter, which is incomplete, is printed in *Collections*, Mass. Hist. Soc., Series 5, VIII, 129–37; also in *Proceedings*, Mass. Hist. Soc., XVI, 234–339. A copy of another, and supplementary, letter, of about the same date and possibly addressed also to Oldenburg, is in ms. Winthrop Papers 5.87, Mass. Hist. Soc.) It is interesting to discover that Dr. Child, for all his realism, had himself a difficult time forgetting JWJ's "black lead" mine. *Winthrop Papers*, V, 248; *Collections*, Mass. Hist. Soc., Series 5, I, 161–64.

6. The La Tour episode is discussed in many places, including the works of Francis Parkman. Brief treatments are available in R.C. Winthrop, *Life and Letters*, II, 311–18, and Morgan, pp. 191–93.

7. Those interested in the details may turn to R.C. Winthrop, *Life and Letters*, II, 280 ff., and Andrews, I, 450–52.

8. Shurtleff, ed., *Recs.*, Mass. Bay, II, 65; *Proceedings*, Mass. Hist. Soc., XVI, 111; *Winthrop Papers*, IV, 501; Pierce, p. 12; Paul, IV, 62.

9. Shurtleff, ed., *Recs.*, Mass. Bay, II, 54 ff. That Winthrop was comparatively unimpressed by what had taken place is suggested by his failure to introduce a similar arrangement into Connecticut. That colony did not acquire an assembly of two houses until some time after his death.

10. The standard work upon colonial and separate New Haven is Calder's *The New Haven Colony*. The Saybrook Plantation, as will shortly become evident, was on the verge of absorption into Connecticut.

11. The "Articles of Confederation" of the United Colonies are to be found in Pulsifer, ed., *Recs.* Plymouth Colony, IX, 3–8. (The printed "Acts of the Commissioners of the United Colonies in New England," Vols. I and II, comprise Vols. IX and X of the above.) For general discussions, see Constance McLaughlin Green, "New England Confederation," in Hart, ed., I, 230 ff.; Calder, pp. 111–15; Andrews, II, 98 ff.

12. *Winthrop Papers*, V, 115–16, 140–41, 221–23.

13. The position of Child is discussed with clarity and essential sympathy in Andrews, I, 487 ff., and in Morgan, pp. 198–99, 201. The classic defense of the official Congregationalism is in Palfrey, II, 165–85.

14. Morgan, pp. 201–2.

15. Andrews, II, 489–93; Morgan, pp. 181–83; Miller, pp. 269, 283.

16. Shurtleff, ed., *Recs.*, Mass. Bay, II, 62–74, 78–104; Winthrop, *Journal*, II, 289; *Records and Papers*, New London County Hist. Soc., III, 180–83; *Winthrop Papers*, V, 114, 118–20.

17. Evidence of the continued good relations between Child and JWJ is to be found in *ibid.*, V, 115–16, 140–41, 160, 181, 221–23.

18. *Ibid.*, IV, 46, 174–76; Morgan, pp. 175–76; R.C. Winthrop, *Life and Letters*, II, 251–52; *Proceedings*, Mass. Hist. Soc., Series 2, XI, 185–86.

19. Mayo, p. 56.

20. *Winthrop Papers*, IV, 366–67. This letter may have been written late in 1643, shortly after JWJ's return from England.

21. F.E. Hine, "Fishers Island, Its History and Development," *Records and Papers*, New London County Hist. Soc., III, 178–79;

Shurtleff, ed., *Recs.*, Mass. Bay, II, 71; J.H. Trumbull, *et al.*, *Col. Recs. Conn.*, I, 64–65; *Winthrop Papers*, IV, 338–39.

22. *Ibid.*, IV, 465–66; V, 1. Latham (d. 1685) is in Savage, III, 58. Thomas Peter is sketched in Caulkins, pp. 43, 46–47; and in *Collections*, Mass. Hist. Soc., Series 4, VII, 428n. That JWJ was probably at "Pequot" in June, 1645, is indicated by a letter from Roger Williams. *Winthrop Papers*, V, 30.

23. Uncas is sketched in *DAB*, XIX, 108–9; and in Ellis and Morris, pp. 26n, 27–28, 35. Pequot River is, of course, the Thames.

24. Miantonomo is in *DAB*, XII, 589–90. The episode is also treated by Constance McLaughlin, "New England Confederation," in Hart, ed., I, 231–33; in Ellis and Morris, pp. 331–33 and n; and in Calder, pp. 177 ff.

25. Shurtleff, ed., *Recs.*, Mass. Bay, III, 39 ff.; *Acts*, U.C. Commissioners, in Pulsifer, ed., *Recs.* Plymouth Colony, IX, 31–60; J.H. Trumbull, *et al.*, *Col. Recs. Conn.*, I, 130n.

26. This interesting wilderness travel diary has been printed several times. An English translation, with copious notes, is available in William R. Carleton, "Overland to Connecticut in 1645," *New England Quarterly*, XIII, 495–510. The entertaining original Latin may be found in *Proceedings*, Mass. Hist. Soc., Series 2, VIII, 7–12. See also *Winthrop Papers*, V, 100–1.

27. Fenwick is treated in *DAB*, VI, 329–30. He had been in a mood to throw up the whole Saybrook business as early as the autumn of 1642. Fenwick to Sir Thomas Barrington, *et al.*, October 10, 1642, Egerton Mss., 2646, fols. 181–83, British Museum. See also *Collections*, Conn. Hist. Soc., XXIV, 4–5. The deceased "Lady" Fenwick had been the widow of Sir John Boteler.

28. Possibly Jonathan Rudd, who appears frequently in the New London records.

29. See JWJ to Samuel Foster, no date, *Winthrop Papers*, V, 10. Foster (d. 1652) had many talents, but he was especially an instrument maker and mathematician; see *DNB*, XX, 62–63. The Long Island property originally belonged to Edward Cope, one of whose heirs transmitted it to JWJ (through the agency of E. Downing) on October 23, 1645. *Winthrop Papers*, V, 46–47.

30. *Ibid.*, V, 59–60, 68–69, 100–1, 114, 118, 119–20, 185–87; *Collections*, Mass. Hist. Soc., Series 5, VIII, 161; *Proceedings*, Mass.

Hist. Soc., LXXII, 58–62; Waters, *Sketch*, p. 34; Shurtleff, ed., *Recs.*, Mass. Bay, III, 78; J.H. Trumbull, *et al.*, *Col. Recs. Conn.*, I, 571. Margaret Lake (d. 1672) had been a resident of Saybrook, but had passed the winter of 1645–46 with John and Elizabeth Winthrop in Massachusetts. Mrs. Lake's husband, John, was separated from her, for reasons unknown, for many years. Caulkins, pp. 44–45, 47; Felt, p. 160; *Collections*, Mass. Hist. Soc., Series 4, VI, 129–30; 5, VIII, 163–64.

31. *Winthrop Papers*, V, 118. Coddington (1601–78) had found it prudent to withdraw from Massachusetts in 1638 because of his open sympathy with the cause of Anne Hutchinson. He did not necessarily find Mrs. Hutchinson a comfortable neighbor, however, and when she settled beside him at Adquidneck (Rhode Island) he moved to the other end of the island, where he founded Newport. *DAB*, IV, 258–59.

CHAPTER II

New London, Connecticut

1. The Fundamental Orders are discussed in many places; see Andrews, II, 102–11. Their full text is in J.H. Trumbull, *et al.*, *Col. Recs., Conn.*, I, 20–25.

2. Bailyn, pp. 53–55; Andrews, pp. 124, 125 and *n*; Mathews, pp. 23*n* and 24*n*; J.H. Trumbull, *et al.*, *Col. Recs. Conn.*, I, 566–68; II, 86, 138, 200.

3. Theophilus Eaton (c. 1590–1657/8) is discussed in *DAB*, V, 612–13, and in Calder, pp. 28–29. For John Davenport (1597–1669/70), see *DAB*, V, 85–87; also Andrews, II, 145–50. Early New Haven's development may be followed in Andrews, II, 150–55, 157–67 and Calder, esp. pp. 62–66, 147, 170–71.

4. The political, economic, and social development of Rhode Island and its conformity to the New England pattern may be followed in any standard work on colonial New England; see particularly Richman's *Rhode Island, Its Making and Its Meaning*.

5. See Chapter X.

6. E.E. Hine, "Fishers Island, Its History and Development," *Records and Papers*, New London County Historical Society, III, 178–79; R.C. Winthrop, *Life and Letters*, II, 360–61; true copy, deed of con-

veyance, JWJ to Edward Palmes and Lucy Winthrop Palmes, May 25, 1674, ms. Win. Paps. 5.134, Mass. Hist. Soc.; also, copies of deed, JWJ to James Rogers, March 13, 1660/1, *ibid.*, 5.26, 27.

7. The best discussion of early Pequot is still to be found in Caulkins's *History of New London*, which for all its lack of citation is usually sound with respect to *local* matters. See pp. 56–58, 62, 65–66, 73, 77, 81. Jonathan Brewster (d. 1659) was the eldest son of the famous William Brewster of New Plymouth. He moved to Pequot about 1649 with a background of Indian trading and established himself there in the same business. Caulkins, pp. 65–66; Savage, I, 244–45; J.H. Trumbull, *et al.*, *Col. Recs. Conn.*, I, 209. Robert Parke (d. February, 1664/5) came from Lincolnshire and was early interested in Massachusetts. He was a leading resident of Wethersfield, Conn., in the early 1640s and moved to the Pequot plantation in 1649, where he remained for the rest of his life. Legend has it that his barn was the first *regular* place of worship in the community. *Winthrop Papers*, II, 212*n*; Savage, III, 347. Deane Winthrop (1622–1704) accompanied JWJ to Fishers Island in 1646, but remained in Pequot for little more than a year. Caulkins, pp. 47, 60, 62.

8. *Winthrop Papers*, V, 147–50, 165–66, 168–70, 240–41, 262–65, 279–80; Caulkins, p. 27; Pulsifer, ed., *Recs.* Plymouth Colony, IX, 103; J.H. Trumbull, *et al.*, *Col. Recs. Conn.*, II, 588–89; R.C. Winthrop, *Life and Letters*, II, 386. Amos Richardson (d. 1683) was for two decades a leading Boston merchant, constantly serving various members of the Winthrop family. As will be evident later, he was a particularly close business associate of JWJ. In 1666, he moved to Stonington, Conn. Savage, III, 535; *Winthrop Papers*, V, 281, 310–11, 350–51; *Collections*, Mass. Hist. Soc., Series 5, I, 48*n*; VIII, 243–44; IX, 7–8.

9. *Winthrop Papers*, V, 205–6, 233–34. Pequot, regardless of these economic discouragements, embraced more than forty families by the end of 1648. Mathews, p. 28.

10. Johnston, pp. 216–17; Ellis and Morris, pp. 27, 28 and *n*; *DAB*, XIX, 108–9; J.H. Trumbull, *et al.*, *Col. Recs. Conn.*, I, 65, 94; *Winthrop Papers*, V, 100–1, 111–12; Caulkins, pp. 47, 51 ff.; E.E. Hine, "Fishers Island," *Records and Papers*, New London County Hist. Soc., III, 180–83.

11. Caulkins, pp. 55 ff.; Calder, p. 180; *Winthrop Papers*, V, 161–62, 319; J.H. Trumbull, *et al.*, *Col. Recs. Conn.*, 292*n*.

12. *Winthrop Papers*, V, 127–28, 131, 249–53, 255–59, 263, 267–69, 282–83, 287, 289–90, 309, 313–15, 318, 321–22, 324; *Collections*, Mass. Hist. Soc., Series 3, IX, 280. For Ninegret (or Ninecraft), see Ellis and Morris, p. 38*n*. The Niantics were a subdivision of the Narragansets. As was so often the case with Indians, the lesser part was better organized than the whole.

13. For the circumstances of Peter's departure, see *Winthrop Papers*, V, 93–94, 102, 113, *Collections*, Mass. Hist. Soc., Series 4, VII, 428*n*; Caulkins, pp. 46–47.

14. *Winthrop Papers*, V, 113, 121–22, 133, 159–60, 245–46, 270, 272, 277–78, 378–82; R.C. Winthrop, *Life and Letters*, II, 378; Savage, III, 176–77 (for Matthews); Caulkins, pp. 67–71; *Collections*, Mass. Hist. Soc., Series 4, VI, 76–77, 80–81, 83–84.

15. See "Acts of Commissioners of the United Colonies," Pulsifer, ed., *Recs.* Plymouth Colony, IX, 79; also J.H. Trumbull, *et al.*, *Col. Recs. Conn.*, I, 570, Appendix IV.

16. "Acts," U.C. Commissioners, Pulsifer, ed., *Recs.* Plymouth Colony, IX, 96–97; Winthrop, *Journal*, II, 275; *Winthrop Papers*, V, 99–101.

17. "Acts," U.C. Commissioners, Pulsifer, ed., *Recs.* Plymouth Colony, IX, 79, 83, 96–97; *Winthrop Papers*, V, 156, 189–90, 231*n*; Winthrop, *Journal*, II, 225; Caulkins, p. 63; J.H. Trumbull, *et al.*, *Col. Recs. Conn.*, I, 157–58, 164; *Records and Files*, Essex Quarter Courts, III, 16. The commission was not actually issued until an adjourned session of the court on Wednesday, October 27. The original is in the State Library, Hartford. Its text is in *Collections*, Conn. Hist. Soc., XXIV, 5–6.

18. J.H. Trumbull, *et al.*, *Col. Recs. Conn.*, I, 185–87; Caulkins, pp. 63–64; *Winthrop Papers*, V, 345–46. The original boundaries cited were to lie 4 miles from each side of the (Thames) river and inland 6 miles from the "sea." These were extended in May, 1650, 2 miles to the northward and provisionally far enough to the westward to include the Niantic meadowlands; in May, 1651, the Niantic area was reconfirmed, and in September, 1651, the eastern boundary was reestablished at the Pawcatuck River. J.H. Trumbull, *et al.*, *Col. Recs. Conn.*, I, 208–9, 221–22, 224; II, 557–58.

19. *Ibid.*, I, 310, 313; Caulkins, p. 59; *Winthrop Papers*, V, 315–16, 319–20.

20. Shurtleff, ed., *Recs.* Mass. Bay, II, 229, 242; III, 104, 121, 126, 146; *Winthrop Papers,* V, 199–230, 235, 349 and *n,* 350–51; fragment of Journal of House of Deputies, *Publications,* Col. Soc. Mass., V, 116–32.

21. R.C. Winthrop, *Life and Letters,* II, 362–63, 395–97; Morgan, p. 205; *Winthrop Papers,* I, 325; V, 326–28.

22. *Ibid.,* V, 315–16; J.H. Trumbull, *et al., Col. Recs. Conn.,* I, 179. JWJ was not, however, elected on this occasion.

23. Waters, *Sketch,* p. 43; Shurtleff, ed., *Recs.* Mass. Bay, III, 170 ff., 182; J.H. Trumbull, *et al., Col. Recs. Conn.,* I, 207.

24. *Proceedings,* Mass. Hist. Soc., Series 1, III, 200. Saybrook was as yet the nearest settlement to Pequot which had an organized church.

25. Ms. notes, not necessarily in JWJ's hand, endorsed on back by John Winthrop, F.R.S.: "September 1st 1650 Memo. of Notes of the Town of New London in favor of the Winthrop family." Ms. Win. Paps., 5.9, Mass. Hist. Soc.

26. Caulkins, pp. 58, 66–67, 74–75, 80; *Collections,* Mass. Hist. Soc., Series 3, X, 4–5, 4; VII, 59, 60–64; ms. Win. Paps., 1.123, 5.9, 18.133, Mass. Hist. Soc.; C.A. Browne, "Scientific Notes . . . of John Winthrop, Jr.," *Isis,* XI, 334; Haynes, I, 59 and *n.*

27. Richman, pp. 265, 265*n,* 273–78, 286–88; *Collections,* Mass. Hist. Soc., Series 3, IX, 291–94; Series 4, VII, 280–85. For Elmer, see Savage, II, 115. For his Delaware scheme, see Johnston, pp. 146–47 and *Winthrop Papers,* V, 357–58, 361–62.

28. Stuyvesant (1592–1671/2) is adequately sketched in *DAB,* XVIII, 187–88. JWJ may have been acquainted with Stuyvesant's predecessor, William Kieft, as early as the spring of 1647. *Winthrop Papers,* V, 148, 185. For Baxter and the position of New Netherlands, see *Collections,* Mass. Hist. Soc., Series 5, I, 368*n* and O'Callaghan, *Documentary History of the State of New York,* I, 467.

29. *Collections,* Mass. Hist. Soc., Series 5, I, 370; *Winthrop Papers,* V, 355.

30. Much of it had been left at Ten Hills.

31. For Berkeley and Tanckmarus, see *Winthrop Papers,* V, 229, 232–33, 235, 239–40, 364–68, 370–71; ms. Win. Paps., 5.10, 91, 92, Mass. Hist. Soc. A brief sketch of Dr. Schlegel (1605–53) is in *Winthrop Papers,* V, 364*n.*

32. Morison, *Intellectual Life,* p. 250; C.A. Browne, "Scientific

Notes . . . of John Winthrop, Jr.," *Isis*, XI, 333; Matthews, "Comenius and Harvard College," *Publications*, Col. Soc. Mass., XXI, 146–90, esp. 176; *Winthrop Papers*, V, 98n, 184, 241–42; Sibley, *et al.*, I, 131–37; Ronald Sterne Wilkinson, "George Starkey, Physician and Alchemist," *Ambix*, XI (October, 1963), 121–52.

33. R.S. Wilkinson, "The Problem of the Identity of Eirenaeus Philalethes," *Ambix*, XII (February, 1964), 36; G.L. Kittredge, "Robert Child the Remonstrant," *Publications*, Col. Soc. Mass., XXI, 113–46.

34. R.S. Wilkinson, "The Alchemical Library of John Winthrop, Jr. (1606–1676) and his Descendants in Colonial America," *Ambix*, Vol. XI (February, 1963) and "The Problem of the Identity of Eirenaeus Philalethes," *Ambix*, XII (February, 1964), 24–43.

35. J.W. Hamilton-Jones to author, September 19, 1964, enclosing copy of memorandum to *Ambix*; R.S. Wilkinson, "The Problem . . . ," *Ambix*, XII (February, 1964), 37; see also *ibid.*, XIII, No. 1 (February, 1965).

36. *Winthrop Papers*, I, 285; *Collections*, Mass. Hist. Soc., Series 5, VIII, 212–13.

37. This affair is treated, with obvious but forgivable embellishments, in Anya Seton's novel *The Winthrop Woman*. See also R.C. Winthrop, *Life and Letters*, II, 379; *Winthrop Papers*, V, 213–16, 224–28, 238–39, 298–301, 321–24, 338–39, 342, 345–46, 348, 355–56, 363; and J.H. Trumbull, *et al.*, *Col. Recs. Conn.*, I, 186. Also ms. Win. Paps. 13.167, Mass. Hist. Soc. William Hallett is discussed in Savage, II, 340.

38. J.H. Trumbull, *et al.*, *Col. Recs. Conn.*, I, 186–87, 190–92; ms. Win. Paps., 2.118, 3.128, 5.181, Mass. Hist. Soc.

39. J.H. Trumbull, *et al.*, *Col. Recs. Conn.*, I, 200, 216–18; Palmer and Palmer, pp. 12–13; Savage, I, 374 (for Cheesebrooke); Caulkins, p. 83.

40. *Winthrop Papers*, V, 326–28, 343–44, 346, 352–53, 359–61; ms. Win. Paps., 5.181, Mass. Hist. Soc.; *Collections*, Mass. Hist Soc., Series 3, IX, 289–91; Series 4, VI, 283–84; Series 5, VIII, 42. Humphrey Atherton is in Savage, I, 72–73. The well-known Atherton Land Company, in which JWJ became deeply involved, grew ultimately from this situation. It will be treated later.

41. Ms. Win. Paps., 17.117, 20.75; *Collections*, Mass. Hist. Soc., Series 5, VIII, 211–12. JWS had married a young widow, Mrs. Martha

Coytmore, in early 1648. She bore him a son, Joshua, in December, 1648. Joshua died in January 1650/1. R.C. Winthrop, *Life and Letters*, II, 381.

42. *Winthrop Papers*, V, 292–93, 303–4, 306–8; J.H. Trumbull, *et al.*, *Col. Recs. Conn.*, I, 233.

43. *Collections*, Mass. Hist. Soc., Series 4, VI, 279–81; VII, 399; Series 5, I, 369–70. The Whitfield house survives.

44. J.H. Trumbull, *et al.*, *Col. Recs. Conn.*, I, 218, 222–23; rough draft of license, ms. Win. Paps., 5.204, Mass. Hist. Soc.

CHAPTER 12

Life & Politics in a Wilderness Colony

1. J.H. Trumbull, *et al.*, *Col. Recs. Conn.*, I, 218–40 *passim*. *Collections*, Mass. Hist. Soc., Series 4, VI, 78–79, 460–61; VII, 455, 467.

2. *Ibid.*, VI, 48; VII, 462; J.H. Trumbull, *et al.*, *Col. Recs. Conn.*, I, 240–56 *passim*, 265

3. *Collections*, Mass. Hist. Soc., Series 4, VI, 361–63; VII, 453, 458–59; ms. Win. Paps. 5.163. Matthew Allyn (d. 1670) is sketched in Stiles, II, 27–29; also *Winthrop Papers*, III, 249*n*. John Allyn (d. 1696) is discussed in Stiles, *Windsor*, II, 29 ff.; in Johnston, pp. 160–61; in *Collections*, Conn. Hist. Soc., XXIV, 19*n*; and in Ellis and Morris, p. 97*n*. His beautiful penmanship may be examined in ms. Win. Paps., Vol. 18, Mass. Hist. Soc. John Talcott the elder (d. 1659/60) may be found in Savage, IV, 250; the younger (d. 1688) is in Ellis and Morris, p. 237*n*.

4. Andrews, II, 86–89, 102–10, 117, 302; Henry Bronson, "Early Government of Connecticut," *Papers*, New Haven Colony Hist. Soc., III, 313; J.H. Trumbull, *et al.*, *Col. Recs. Conn.*, I, 119; Palfrey, II, 637–38.

5. J.H. Trumbull, *et al.*, *Col. Recs. Conn.*, I, 266–75 *passim*, 318, 327–29; Johnston, p. 119; Fenwick to Sir Gilbert Garrett and Sir Wm. Marsham, November 10, 1643, Egerton Mss., 2648, fol. 1, British Museum; Andrews, II, 121–22; *Collections*, Mass. Hist. Soc., Series 5, I, 418–20 and *nn*.

6. For the Treaty of Hartford, see Bowen, pp. 17–18; Calder, pp.

63, 189–93; also Johnston, pp. 147–49; "Acts," U.C. Commissioners, Pulsifer, ed., *Recs.* Plymouth Colony, IX, 161, 171, 174, 178, 187, 188–90; XII, 171–86; O'Callaghan *et al.*, eds., *Documents Relative to the Colonial History of New York* (hereafter referred to as *N.Y. Col. Docs.*), I, 459, 611–12. The treaty was finally approved by the Dutch States General in February, 1656. Significantly, it was never ratified in England.

7. The text of the R.I. Charter of 1643/4 is in Bartlett, ed., *Records of the Colony of Rhode Island and Providence Plantations in New England* (hereafter referred to as *Col. Recs., R.I.*), I, 143–46.

8. Johnston, pp. 116–17, 207–8; Bowen, p. 19; Constance Green McLaughlin, "New England Confederation," in Hart, ed., I, 238–40; J.H. Trumbull, *et al.*, *Col. Recs. Conn.*, I, 189–90.

9. *Ibid.*, I, 509n, 509–63. See also J.M. Taylor, *Roger Ludlow*, pp. 98–101.

10. Winthrop's feet were considerably larger than the contemporary average. He wore a size 11 shoe, which in the seventeenth century indicated a foot about 12⅓ inches long. *Winthrop Papers*, V, 242; G.L. Huiskamp, "Boot and Shoe Industry," *Encyclopedia Britannica* (1962 ed.), III, 885; inventory of Robert Turner, 1651, Suffolk County Probate Records, quoted in Dow, appendix.

11. J.H. Trumbull, *et al.*, *Col. Recs. Conn.*, I, 240–80 *passim; Collections*, Mass. Hist. Soc., Series 3, X, 8–11; Series 4, VI, 48, 83–84; *Proceedings*, Mass. Hist. Soc., Series 2, IV, 274.

12. Ms. in Mass. Hist. Soc.; photostat in Conn. Hist. Soc.

13. J.H. Trumbull, *et al.*, *Col. Recs. Conn.*, I, 251, 257, 260n, 261n; *Collections*, Mass. Hist. Soc., Series 3, X, 405; Series 4, VI, 286–92; VII, 416–18; *Proceedings*, Mass. Hist. Soc., XVI, 401 and n, 402; Order of U.C. Commissioners, New Haven, September 12, 1651, ms. Win. Paps., 5.6, Mass. Hist. Soc. For Matthew Griswold (1618–98/9), see *Collections*, Mass. Hist. Soc., Series 4, VII, 405 and n.

14. J.H. Trumbull, *et al.*, *Col. Recs. Conn.*, I, 241–45, 248n, 251; "A Brief description of New England," etc., Egerton Mss. 2395, fol. 409, British Museum; Johnston, pp. 151–54; J.M. Taylor, *Roger Ludlow*, pp. 117–19, 129–31; Calder, pp. 196–98; Osgood, I, 404–6.

15. Samuel Desborough, who had returned to England from Guilford in 1651, Calder, pp. 198, 208–9.

16. J.H. Trumbull, *et al.*, *Col. Recs. Conn.*, I, 240–56 *passim;* Stuyvesant to Endecott and JWJ, February 25, 1652/3 (o.s.), mss. in N.-Y. Hist. Soc. Library; *Collections*, Mass. Hist. Soc., Series 4, VI, 154–55, 523–24; VII, 418, 421. JWJ, however, did operate a kind of "prize court" in New London during the summer of 1653. Testimony of William Baker, *Records and Files*, Essex Quarter Courts, I, 316–17.

17. J.H. Trumbull, *et al.*, *Col. Recs. Conn.*, I, 256–80 *passim.*

18. Weeden, I, 193; *Proceedings*, Mass. Hist. Soc., Series 2, IV, 271–74; J.H. Trumbull, *et al.*, *Col. Recs. Conn.*, I, 243, 246; *Collections*, Mass. Hist. Soc., Series 4, VI, 80–83; VII, 4–5, 446–47; Series 5, I, 378 ff.; Series 6, III, 312, 313*n*; *Collections*, Conn. Hist. Soc., XXII, 129–30, 145–50; JWJ to John Talcott, January 10, 1654/5, copy in ms. Win. Paps., 5.11, Mass. Hist. Soc.

19. Shryock, p. 51; Haynes, I, 91; letter, R.S. Wilkinson to the author, April 7, 1963; C.A. Browne, "Scientific Notes . . . of John Winthrop, Jr.," *Isis*, XI, 335; JWJ's Prescription Records, ms. Win. Paps., 20 a. and 20 b., Mass. Hist. Soc.

20. Walter R. Steiner, M.D., "Governor John Winthrop, Jr., of Connecticut as a Physician," *The Connecticut Magazine*, IX, 34; *Collections*, Mass. Hist. Soc., Series 3, X, 15–18; undated notes of JWJ, ms. Win. Paps., 5.205, Mass. Hist. Soc.

21. Prescription records, ms. Win. Paps., 20 a. and 20 b., Mass. Hist. Soc.; Egerton Mss., 2395, fol. 522, British Museum; Mathews, p. 56; ms. Win. Paps., 5.12, 168, Mass. Hist. Soc.; Mayo, p. 56; *Proceedings*, Mass. Hist. Soc., XLVII, 26; *Collections*, Mass. Hist. Soc., Series 5, VIII, 242; Series 6, V, 337*n*.

22. By far the best treatment to date of Fitz-John Winthrop (1638–1707) and Wait Winthrop (1642–1717) is provided in Dunn, pp. 191 ff.

23. *Collections*, Mass. Hist. Soc., Series 4, VII, 465–67; ms. Win. Paps., 5.169 (fair copy), 5.166 (rough draft), Mass. Hist. Soc. More worldly admonitions are presented in JWJ to Fitz W., February 8, 1655/6, *Collections*, Mass. Hist. Soc., Series 5, VIII, 43. JWJ's handwriting was not a thing of beauty. It constantly reflected a fast-racing mind which usually was well in advance of the words being written. Even his formal correspondence was far from painstaking. Like many of his contemporaries, he was in the habit of writing a rough draft first and

preserving it as a "file copy." Too often this is almost indecipherable, and too often his irregular calligraphy was rendered still worse by a failure to sharpen his quill.

24. *Collections,* Mass. Hist. Soc., Series 6, III, 424–26, 424n; "Chesholme's Stewards Book," *Publications,* Col. Soc. Mass., XXXI, 264n, 264–65; Elizabeth R.W. to Fitz W., August 29, 1658, ms. Win. Paps., 5.16, Mass. Hist. Soc.; JWJ to Fitz W., November 7, 1659, *ibid.,* 5.19; JWJ to Wait W., December 12, 1659, *ibid.,* 5.20; Morison, *Harvard College,* I, 54. "Head" of the class signified topmost *social* rank. (Dudley was the son of JWJ's sister Mary.)

25. *Collections,* Mass. Hist. Soc., Series 3, X, 5–6, 15–18; Series 4, VII, 129–30; Series 5, VIII, 244–46, 251, 252, 253–54; Muskett, p. 28; *Proceedings,* Mass. Hist. Soc., Series 2, VIII, 287–88; T.G. Wright, *Literary Culture in Early New England,* pp. 42, 43, 67; Petersson, p. 243.

26. *Collections,* Mass. Hist. Soc., Series 3, IX, 294–95; Series 4, VI, 290–92; VII, 419–20; Calder, pp. 208–9; Andrews, II, 171–74.

27. The appeals of New Haven comprise a considerable literature. They may be examined in *Collections,* Mass. Hist. Soc., Series 3, IX, 297–99; X, 7–15; Series 4, VII, 469–77, 488, 538; Dexter, I, 235; also Theophilus Eaton to JWJ, September 28, 1654, ms. Win. Paps., 5.11, Mass. Hist. Soc.; John Davenport to JWJ, November 22, 1655, photostat in Conn. Hist. Soc.

28. J.H. Trumbull, *et al., Col. Recs. Conn.,* I, 258, 276–77, 285, 292; Weeden, I, 186, 198; Dunn, pp. 84–85; Shurtleff, ed., *Recs.* Mass. Bay III, 400; *Collections,* Mass. Hist. Soc., Series 4, VII, 403, 421; *Proceedings,* Mass. Hist. Soc., Series 2, III, 193–96.

29. *Collections,* Mass. Hist. Soc., Series 4, VII, 400. John Higginson (1616–1708) is in *DAB,* IX, 13–14

30. *Collections,* Mass. Hist. Soc., Series 3, X, 8–10, 12–14; Series 4, VII, 25; Dexter, I, 235; *Proceedings,* Mass. Hist. Soc., Series 2, III, 192; Conn. Soc., *Vital Records of New Haven,* I, 16.

31. Dexter, ed., I, 241, 305–6, 313–14, 316, 318–19, 412–13; Van Dusen, p. 51; Calder, pp. 157–60; E.N. Hartley, *Ironworks,* pp. 15, 280–83; Andrews, II, 182. The ore bog and furnace lay close to Branford.

32. Weeden, I, 223; Andrews, II, 180.

33. Dunn, p. 77 and *n; Collections,* Mass. Hist. Soc., Series 4, VI, 348*n;* VII, 72–77, 81–83, 589; Series 5, VIII, 217–18, 243–44; J.H. Trumbull, *et al., Col. Recs. Conn.,* I, 293; Calder, pp. 159–60; E.N. Hartley, *Ironworks,* p. 284.

34. J.H. Trumbull, *et al., Col. Recs. Conn.,* I, 297, 298.

CHAPTER 13

His Worship, the Governor

1. *Collections,* Mass. Hist. Soc., Series 4, VII, 421–22; J.H. Trumbull, *et al., Col. Recs. Conn.,* I, 297–308 *passim.*

2. *Collections,* Conn. Hist. Soc., XXII, 183–85; J.H. Trumbull, *et al., Col. Recs. Conn.,* I, 308.

3. *Collections,* Mass. Hist. Soc., Series 3, X, 23–25, 31–33; Series 4, VII, 405–7, 492–94, 495–98, 512; Bailyn, p. 71; Calder, p. 160; and E.N. Hartley, *Ironworks,* pp. 284–89. See also Francis Newman to Clarke and Payne, March 7, 1658/9, ms. Win. Paps., 15.103, Mass. Hist. Soc.; and Dexter, ed., I, 330–31, 412–13, 446. William Payne (c. 1598–1660), one of the wealthiest and most active businessmen in Boston, is sketched in Savage, III, 337–38, and in *Publications,* Col. Soc. Mass., XVIII, 177*n.*

4. Hartford's surviving records, municipal and ecclesiastical, contain no reference to his participation in town meetings, or to membership in a church. *Collections,* Conn. Hist. Soc., Vol. VI; *Historical Catalogue of the First Church in Hartford, 1633–1885,* pp. 10–14. A surviving bill for "Caster" (beaver) and felt (some of it cut for hats), covering purchases from May 4, 1655, to May 7, 1658, is addressed to JWJ at "Peaquit." Ms. Win. Paps., 5.10, Mass. Hist. Soc.

5. J.H. Trumbull, *et al., Col. Recs. Conn.,* I, 301; *Collections,* Conn. Hist. Soc., XIV, 3–5; Love, p. 120 (map); *Collections,* Mass. Hist. Soc., Series 4, VII, 512. An observer of the early 1660s described Hartford as "a gallant town, and many rich men in it." "A Briefe discription of New England," etc., Egerton Mss. 2395, fol. 407, British Museum.

6. Ernest Caulfield, M.D., "Some Common Diseases of Colonial Children," *Publications,* Col. Soc. Mass., XXXV, 5; JWJ to Wait W.,

January 15, 1657/8, ms. Win. Paps., 5.13, Mass. Hist. Soc.; *Collections*, Mass. Hist. Soc., Series 5, VIII, 45–49. Fitz-John appears to have arrived in England before the winter of 1657/8. See *ibid.*, I, 44.

7. JWJ to Stuyvesant, copy in ms. Win. Paps., 5.208, Mass. Hist. Soc.; *Collections*, Conn. Hist. Soc., II, 52; XXII, 185–88. Dunn, p. 78, indicates the Church controversy was over conditions of "membership." This is very likely; not so certain is the suggestion that Winthrop was brought in as governor because he was a neutral outsider.

8. *Collections*, Conn. Hist. Soc., II, 82–86 and *nn*; J.H. Trumbull, *et al.*, *Col. Recs. Conn.*, I, 313, 314, 317, 333–34, 339–40, 343; *Collections*, Mass. Hist. Soc., Series 5, I, 383–85; Burpee, I, 102–5; *Historical Catalogue of the First Church in Hartford*, p. 15.

9. The Garlick trial is in J.H. Trumbull, *et al.*, *Col. Recs. Conn.*, I, 572–73, and *Collections*, Conn. Hist. Soc., XXII, 188–89. The articles of "Union" between Easthampton and Connecticut are in O'Callaghan, *et al.*, *N.Y. Col. Docs.*, III, 27–29.

10. Wait W. was on the bench during the celebrated "Salem" witch trials of 1692. *Collections*, Mass. Hist. Soc., Series 5, VIII, xvi; Dunn, pp. 265–67. More than twenty witchcraft cases are recorded from seventeenth-century Connecticut, and at least ten persons were hanged in consequence, Andrews, II, 116 and *n*. Curiously, no one was executed in New Haven. Calder, p. 91.

11. J.H. Trumbull, *et al.*, *Col. Recs. Conn.*, I, 314–34 *passim*; *Collections*, Mass. Hist. Soc., Series 3, X, 19–20, 21–23; Series 4, VI, 87; VII, 492, 540, 541; Series 5, I, 48–49; *Collections*, Conn. Hist. Soc., XXII, 191, 195–96, 197–99.

12. J.H. Trumbull, *et al.*, *Col. Recs. Conn.*, I, 293, 300; *Collections*, Mass. Hist. Soc., Series 4, VI, 83*n*, 84–87, and 87*n*; Amos Richardson to Fitz W., September 13, 1659, ms. Win. Paps., 5.11, Mass. Hist. Soc.; Palmer, pp. 13–14.

13. J.H. Trumbull, *et al.*, *Col. Recs. Conn.*, I, 314–17, 571–72; Pulsifer, ed., *Recs.* Plymouth Colony, X, 207.

14. J.H. Trumbull, *et al.*, *Col. Recs. Conn.*, I, 315; *Collections*, Mass. Hist. Soc., Series 5, VIII, 45–49; Pulsifer, ed., *Recs.* Plymouth Colony, X, 197. Thomas Prince (1601–73) is sketched in *Collections*, Mass. Hist. Soc., Series 5, I, 392*n*; Josiah Winslow (1629–80) is in *DAB*, XX, 400. Newman (d. 1660) had replaced the recently deceased Theophilus Eaton as governor of New Haven; see Jacobus, *Officials of Connecticut Colony*, p. 40. William Leete is sketched in *Collections*,

Mass. Hist. Soc., Series 4, VII, 538*n* and 570*n;* also in Perry, ed., pp. 113 ff.

15. "Acts," U.C., Pulsifer, ed., *Recs.* Plymouth Colony, X, 197–209, 211. J.H. Trumbull, *et. al., Col. Recs. Conn.,* I, 335, 570 (Appendix IV), 572; II, 26; Palmer, p. 15; Johnston, pp. 209–10.

16. L.B. Wright, *Cultural Life,* p. 82; Dexter, ed., II, 238–40; J.H. Trumbull, *et al., Col. Recs Conn.,* I, 303, 324; *Collections,* Mass. Hist. Soc., Series 3, X, 26–29. New Haven's performance was not quite so brutal as its statutes indicated; moreover, Friends were permitted *temporary* visits to transact business. Calder, p. 97.

17. "Acts," U.C., Pulsifer, ed., *Recs.* Plymouth Colony, X, 212.

18. Examples of this kind of pressure are to be found in *Proceedings,* Mass. Hist. Soc., Series 2, IV, 275–81; *Collections,* Mass. Hist. Soc., Series 4, VII, 186–87, 289, 291; Series 5, I, 96–97.

19. JWJ to Coddington, September 6, 1672, copy in ms. Win. Paps., 5.75, Mass. Hist. Soc. JWJ doubtless had reference to II Peter, 2:20–21 (King James Bible): "Knowing this first, that no prophecy of the scripture is of any private interpretation. For the prophecy came not in old time by the will of man: but holy men of God spake as they were moved by the Holy Ghost." Hebrews, 1:1–2 reads: "God, who at sundry times and in divers manners spake in time past unto the fathers by the prophets, hath in these last days spoken unto us by his Son, whom he hath appointed heir of all things, by whom also he made the worlds."

20. *Proceedings,* Mass. Hist. Soc., Series 2, IV, 277; Savage, IV, 98–99, and Benton, pp. 34–35 (for Sylvester); *Collections,* Mass. Hist. Soc., Series 3, X, 26–29; Series 4, VII, 289; Jones, *et al.,* p. 89*n.* Mary Dyer, on her critical third visit to Massachusetts, was apprehended, tried, and hung.

21. Ms. Win. Paps., 1.161, Mass. Hist. Soc.

22. For Fitz's military fortunes, see *Collections,* Mass. Hist. Soc., Series 4, VII, 281; Series 5, VIII, 229; Series 6, III, 426–29; R.C. Winthrop, *Life and Letters,* II, 355, 360, 384–86; Muskett, pp. 157–59, 164.

23. *Collections,* Mass. Hist. Soc., Series 5, VIII, 45–46.

24. Weis, p. 149; Essex Inst., *Vital Records of Wenham, Mass.,* pp. 63–149; Allen, pp. 158–61; Mayo, p. 56; *Collections,* Mass. Hist. Soc., Series 5, VIII, 45–49, 382–83; ms. Win. Paps. 5.16, 19, 15.101, Mass. Hist. Soc.; *Records and Files,* Essex Quarter Courts, VI, 244.

25. "Acts," U.C., Pulsifer, ed., *Recs.* Plymouth Colony, X, 212;

Collections, Mass. Hist. Soc., Series 5, VIII, 53; Essex Inst., *Vital Records of Wenham,* pp. 63–149 *passim.*

26. *Collections,* Mass. Hist. Soc., Series 4, VII, 404–5, 407–10; Series 5, VIII, 49–52; also George H. Hayes, "The Tale of the Tantiusques," *Proceedings,* American Antiquarian Society, new series, XIV, 472–95.

27. J.H. Trumbull, *et al., Col. Recs. Conn.,* I, 153–54, 289–91, 330–31, 333, 357; Calder, pp. 99–101; Johnston, p. 227; ms. Win. Paps., 5.200, Mass. Hist. Soc.; J.H. Trumbull, ed., *Memorial History of Hartford County,* I, 280; II, 441; Stiles, *Wethersfield,* I, 164–65. For John Hollister (1612–65), see *ibid.,* I, 163; also Case, pp. 19–27. The Wethersfield problem demanded the attention of the General Court —and Winthrop—as late as March, 1660/1. Stiles, *Wethersfield,* I, 164–65; ms. Win. Paps., 5.170, Mass. Hist. Soc.; *Publications,* Narragansett Club, VI, 314–15.

28. *Collections,* Conn. Hist. Soc., XXII, 195–96; J.H. Trumbull, *et al., Col. Recs. Conn.,* I, 336, 341 and *n,* 343; G.W. Allen, "The Case of Captain Penny," *Proceedings,* Mass. Hist. Soc., XLVIII, 117–30; *Collections,* Mass. Hist. Soc., Series 3, X, 29–30; Series 4, VI, 585; VII, 183–84, 193–94, 511–13, 541–43; Series 5, I, 385–87; VIII, 54–57; IX, 13–16; ms. Win. Paps., 5.22, 23, 167, Mass. Hist. Soc.; JWJ to Fitz W., September 9, 1659, *ibid.,* 5.18,; Amos Richardson to JWJ, September 13, 1659, *ibid.,* 5.11; Pulsifer, ed., *Recs.* Plymouth Colony, X, 213–37.

29. Ms. Win. Paps., 5.18, Mass. Hist. Soc.

30. *Collections,* Conn. Hist. Soc., XXII, 195–205; J.H. Trumbull, *et al., Col. Recs. Conn.,* I, 314–35 *passim.*

31. *Collections,* Mass. Hist. Soc., Series 5, VIII, 58; J.H. Trumbull, *et al., Col. Recs. Conn.,* I, 346.

32. *Ibid.,* I, 347–48, 351.

33. *Collections,* Mass. Hist. Soc., Series 4, VII, 62, 132–33; Series 5, VIII, 59. He was definitely absent from the quarter courts of May 15 and June 7, 1660. *Collections,* Conn. Hist. Soc., XXII, 210–11. JWJ's illness had been preceded by deep concern for the condition of his wife, who had been grievously affected by the news of the death of her first grandchild. *Collections,* Mass. Hist. Soc., Series 5, VIII, 58.

34. *Ibid.,* VIII, 60.

Backgrounds for Crises

1. For the Hartlib correspondence, see *Proceedings*, Mass. Hist. Soc., LXXII, 36–67. See also Ronald Sterne Wilkinson, "John Winthrop, Jr., and America's First Telescopes," *New England Quarterly*, XXXV, 520–23. JWJ wrote Hartlib in October, 1660, that his telescope "doth shew little of Saterne"; this was chiefly because the famous rings were presented edge-on. On the other hand, JWJ in 1664 was using another instrument of only 3½-foot length, while in 1668 he was endeavoring to *construct* one of "8 or 10 foot." *Collections*, Mass. Hist. Soc., Series 5, VIII, 93–95; JWJ to Henry Oldenburg (?), c. July, 1668, copy in ms. Win. Paps., 5.172, Mass. Hist. Soc. Winthrop supported, at a time and place wherein it was by no means universally accepted, the Copernican System. Morison, "The Harvard School of Astronomy in the Seventeenth Century," *New England Quarterly*, VII, 9–13.

2. Dr. Benjamin Worsley (fl. 1650–74) was a London physician who had become interested in overseas fauna and flora as bases for the pharmacopoeia. He soon became known as a colonial expert and was employed as such by both the Protectorate and the government of Charles II. He had much to do with the drawing up of the Navigation Act of 1660. Andrews, IV, 11, 41*n*, 58–60. William Brereton (3d Baron Brereton of Leighlin, 1631–79/80) will be treated later.

3. William Potter (fl. 1656) is in *DNB*, XLVI, 223–24. Winthrop's copy of his *Key of Wealth, or a new way of improving Trade* (London, 1650), has survived as Title No. 202 in the Winthrop Collection, New York Society Library. Curiously, it is bare of marginal notes and appears not to have been much handled. Winthrop's ideas upon money are treated at some length in Weeden, I, 318–24. See also L.B. Wright, *Cultural Life*, p. 222, and *Proceedings*, American Antiquarian Society, new series, III, 267–73.

4. *Collections*, Mass. Hist. Soc., Series 4, VII, 218*n*, 231–50; Series 5, VIII, 68–71, 247–49, 262–64; Bailyn, p. 55; ms. Win. Paps., 5.18, 26 and 27, Mass. Hist. Soc.; *Proceedings*, Mass. Hist. Soc., LXXII, 36–40.

5. Win. Paps., 5.209, Mass. Hist. Soc.; see also Caulkins, p. 233.

6. A particularly interesting discussion of the Atherton question is in Richard S. Dunn, "John Winthrop, Jr., and the Narragansett Country," *William and Mary Quarterly*, 3d Series, XIII, 68–86.

7. Arnold, ed., *The Records of the Proprietors of the Narragansett, otherwise called the Fones Record* (hereafter referred to as *Fones Record*), pp. 4–5. Atherton (d. 1661) is in Savage, I, 72–73; for his itch for real estate, see *Winthrop Papers*, V, 273–74. The Richard Smiths are in *Collections*, R.I. Hist. Soc., III, 166–67. Hudson (1619–81) is in Savage, II, 489. See also *Collections*, Mass. Hist. Soc., Series 5, IX, 7–8.

8. Bartlett, ed., *Col. Recs. R.I.*, III, 227, 464; *Collections*, Mass. Hist. Soc., Series 5, IX, 7–8; Richman, p. 502; Bailyn, p. 117.

9. Richman, p. 501; *Collections*, Mass. Hist. Soc., Series 5, IX, 10–12; ms. Win. Paps., 5.18, Mass. Hist. Soc.; "Acts," U.C., Pulsifer, ed., *Recs.* Plymouth Colony, X, 213–37.

10. Arnold, ed., *Fones Record*, pp. 4–5. Hutchinson (1613?–75) was the eldest son of the famous Anne H. and by this time a representative citizen of Boston. He was killed in King Philip's War. Hutchinson, I, 169 and *n*.

11. "Acts," U.C., Pulsifer, ed., *Recs.* Plymouth Colony, X, 213–53; J.H. Trumbull, *et al.*, *Col. Recs. Conn.*, I, 576–77; JWJ to Fitz W., September 9, 1659, ms. Win. Paps. 5.18, Mass. Hist. Soc., Richman, *Rhode Island*, p. 501. Major Mason had just moved from Saybrook to Mohegan (Norwich) in 1659. "Journal of Simon Bradstreet," *New England Historical and Genealogical Register*, VIII (1854), 327.

12. J.H. Trumbull, *et al.*, *Col. Recs. Conn.*, I, 576; *Collections*, Mass. Hist. Soc., Series 5, I, 387–89.

13. "Acts," U.C., Pulsifer, ed., *Recs.*, Plymouth Colony, X, 247 ff.; *Collections*, Mass. Hist. Soc., Series 3, X, 39; Series 5, VIII, 62–63; J.H. Trumbull, *et al.*, *Col. Recs. Conn.*, I, 577.

14. *Collections*, Mass. Hist. Soc., Series 5, IX, 12–13; ms. Win. Paps., 5.26, Mass. Hist. Soc.; ms. copy of mortgage, Conn. State Library, Hartford. The mortgage is printed in *Collections*, Mass. Hist. Soc., Series 5, IX, 25–26.

15. Arnold, ed., *Fones Record*, pp. 12–15; Bartlett, ed., *Col. Recs. R.I.*, I, 465; receipt to Capt. Hutchinson, copy in ms. Win. Paps., 5.26, Mass. Hist. Soc.; *Collections*, Mass. Hist. Soc., Series 5, IX, 12–13.

16. *Ibid.*, Series 6, III, 428–29.

17. *Proceedings*, Mass. Hist. Soc., Series 2, VII, 362–64.

18. This letter, dated at Westminister on March 24, 1659/60, is of major historical value and has been much quoted; it is printed in *Collections*, Mass. Hist. Soc., Series 3, I, 185–93. For John Maidstone, Jr., see Muskett, p. 144, and Metcalfe, ed., *Visitations*, I, 447.

19. Correspondence, Davenport and JWJ, 1659–1660, *Collections*, Mass. Hist. Soc., Series 3, X, 29–34.

20. For Breeden, see Andrews, I, 461*n*, 514, and II, 63*n*. He appears to have been a distant "kinsman" of JWJ; see JWJ to Breeden, July 4, 1664, copy in ms. Win. Paps., 5.186, Mass. Hist. Soc. Breeden's criticisms are in *Collections*, N.-Y. Hist. Soc. (1869), 16–19. The Mason, Gorges, and ironworks petitions are in *Calendar of State Papers, Colonial, Am. and W. Indies, 1661–1668*, pp. 12–32 *passim*; also mss. in P.R.O., C.O. 1:15, no. 31, p. 57. The Stirling matter is discussed in *DAH*, III, 298, and Bowen, p. 27. Lord Stirling's petition of 1661 is in P.R.O., C.O. 1:15, no. 31, p. 11, and is also in *Calendar of State Papers, Colonial Am. and W. Indies, 1661–1668*, p. 34, item 98.

21. "Clarendon Papers," *Collections*, N.-Y. Hist. Soc. (1869), pp. 21–22, 25–27, 45–50. Maverick (c. 1602–70) is in *DAB*, XII, 432–33; the estimated date of his death given therein (c. 1676) is in error; see JWJ to Richard Nicolls, October 27, 1670, copy in ms. Win. Paps., 5.92, Mass. Hist. Soc.

22. Egerton Mss. 2395, fols. 407–9, British Museum.

23. Ms. Register Books in P.R.O.: P.C. 2:55, pp. II and III; P.C. 2:56, pp. 68, 216, 222, 281. See also W.L. Grant, *et al.*, *Acts, P.C. (Colonial)*, I, xii ff., 295, 297–98, 308; *Calendar of State ¡Papers, Colonial, Am. and W. Indies, 1661–1668*, p. 30, item 88; also P.R.O., C.O. 5:903, pp. 1–2.

24. Notes of First Secretary of State Edward Nicholas, May 17, 1661, *ibid.*, 1:15, p. 53; see also *Calendar of State Papers (Colonial), 1661–1668*, p. 30, items 87 and 88; W.L. Grant, *et al.*, *Acts, P.C. (Colonial)*, I, 312; *Collections*, N.-Y. Hist. Soc. (1869), pp. 31–32. An English historian considers that the appeasement of New England was a specific Restoration policy. A.P. Thornton, "Charles II and the American Colonies," *History Today*, VI (January, 1956), 6.

25. Calder, p. 22; Welles, p. 28; J.H. Trumbull, *et al.*, *Col. Recs. Conn.*, I, 353–58; Shurtleff, ed., *Recs. Mass. Bay*, IV (Part I), 448–56.

26. *Collections,* Conn. Hist. Soc., XXIV, 6; J.H. Trumbull, *et al.,* *Col. Recs. Conn.,* I, 361–62.

27. *Ibid.,* I, 359–64; *Collections,* Mass. Hist. Soc., Series 5, VIII, 73–74; JWJ to Edward Rawson, April 9, 1661, copy in ms. Win. Paps., 5.27, Mass. Hist. Soc.; JWJ to John Underhill, June 18, 1661, copy *ibid.,* 5.29.

28. *Collections,* Mass. Hist. Soc., Series 5, VIII, 68–72, 250.

29. The known facts are chiefly based upon the following mss.: John Endecott to JWJ *et al.,* with enclosure, May 7, 1661, P.R.O., C.O. 1:15, nos. 48 and 49 (see also *Calendar of State Papers, Colonial, Am. and W. Indies, 1661–1668,* pp. 27–28, item 81); report of Thomas Kellond and Thomas Kirke to Endecott, May 29, 1661, with appended deposition of Samuel Martyn, June 4, 1661, P.R.O., C.O. 1:15, no. 59 (see also *Calendar of State Papers, Colonial, Am. and W. Indies, 1661–1668,* p. 33, item 96); John Davenport to Colonel Thomas Temple, August 10, 1661, P.R.O., C.O. 1:15, no. 81 (also *Calendar of State Papers, Colonial, Am. and W.I., 1661–1668,* pp. 53–54, item 160); Endecott to Sir Edward Nicholas and Sir William Morrice, n.d., P.R.O., C.O. 1:15, no. 83 (also *Calendar of State Papers, Colonial, Am. and W.I., 1661–1668,* p. 54, item 162); JWJ to John Leverett, May 28, 1661, copy in ms. Win. Paps., 5.28, Mass. Hist. Soc. The details thereafter fall away into hearsay and legend. See Calder, pp. 221–26; also Welles's *The History of the Regicides in New England.*

30. J.H. Trumbull, *et al., Col. Recs. Conn.,* I, 364–65, 582–83; Johnston, p. 169.

31. J.H. Trumbull, *et al., Col. Recs. Conn.,* I, 367–68.

CHAPTER 15

The Charter Journey

1. *Collections,* Conn. Hist. Soc., XXII, 234–36; JWJ to William Leete, May 24, 1661, copy in ms. Win. Paps., 5.28, Mass Hist. Soc.; J.H. Trumbull, *et al., Col. Recs. Conn.,* I, 369–70. Additional business on June 8 was of a strictly internal nature.

2. The petition of June 7, 1661, is printed in B.B. Trumbull, *History of Connecticut,* I, 511–12.

3. *Ibid.*, I, 513–14, 579–81, 584–85; Bates, pp. 12 ff., 581*n*; J.H. Trumbull, *et al.*, *Col. Recs. Conn.*, I, 369. Edward Montagu, 2d Earl of Manchester (1602–71), is in *DNB*, XXXVIII, 227–31.

4. J.H. Trumbull, *et al.*, *Col. Recs. Conn.*, I, 362, 369–70. Talcott's letter of credit, dated June 16, 1661, is in the Connecticut Archives, Conn. State Library; it is printed in *Collections*, Conn. Hist. Soc., XXIV, 7. The £500 was to be over and above Winthrop's personal salary for 1661–62, which was £80.

5. Ms. in P.R.O., C.O. 1:15, 61; also *Calendar State Papers, Colonial, Am. and W.I., 1661–1668*, pp. 35–36, item 102. An effort in 1644 to secure a New Haven charter from the Long Parliament came to naught because of the loss of the well-known "phantom ship." Andrews, II, 155.

6. Calder, pp. 217–19.

7. Dexter, ed., II, 13; Andrews, II, 190–91; Dunn, pp. 123–24; testimony of William Greene and John Meigs, January 1, 1663/4, ms. Win. Paps., 15.59, Mass. Hist. Soc.; Calder, pp. 220–21; William Hooke to John Davenport, March 2, 1662–3, P.R.O., State Papers, Domestic, Charles II, Vol. XLIX; JWJ to Leete, May 24, 1661, ms. Win. Paps., 5.24, Mass. Hist. Soc.; *Collections*, Mass. Hist. Soc., Series 4, VII, 520; Dexter, ed., II, 13. The often cited allegations in a later (1663/4) statement of Davenport and Nicholas Street bear little resemblance to Winthrop's reported letters to Davenport of July, 1661. See Andrews, II, 190–91.

8. Arnold, ed., *Fones Record*, p. 19.

9. *Collections*, Mass. Hist. Soc., Series 5, I, 391, 396–97; VIII, 73. See also Cornell, pp. 241–45.

10. Prescription Records, ms. Win. Paps., 20 a. and 20 b., Mass. Hist. Soc.; lease deed, JWJ to Thos. Clarke and John Payne, June 20, 1661, *ibid.*, 5.29; undated copy of letter, JWJ to Clarke, *ibid.*, 5.171; ms. power of attorney, July 3, 1661, photostat in Conn. Hist. Soc. The power was utilized by Elizabeth R.W. as early as July 5, a good indication that JWJ had already gone. Lease of Fishers Island, ms. Win. Paps., 5.30, Mass. Hist. Soc.

11. Wait was with JWJ in London in the late autumn; see *ibid.*, 5.30. Stone is mentioned in the *Haerlemse Saterdaeghse Courant* for September 17 (N.S.), 1661, as accompanying JWJ as an agent to the king of England! *Collections*, N.-Y. Hist. Soc., Series 2, I, 456. For the

evasion of Leete, see *Collections*, Mass. Hist. Soc., Series 4, VII, 548–50.

12. O'Callaghan, *et al.*, *N.Y. Col. Docs.*, II, 73, 460.

13. Samuel Symonds to JWJ (no date), *Collections*, Mass. Hist. Soc., Series 4, VII, 135; Series 5, I, 53; fragment of "Journal of my voyage from Manhatoes," in JWJ's hand, ms. Win. Paps., 5.29, Mass. Hist. Soc. Winthrop's dating, of the "Old Style," has been followed here, though Holland itself used the "New Style" Gregorian Calendar.

14. O'Callaghan, ed., *Calendar Hist. Mss.*, I, 297.

15. A satisfactory sketch of Downing is in O'Callaghan, *et al.*, *N.Y. Col. Docs.*, II, 415–18 *nn*. See also Downing and Wilberforce, pp. 15–16. The details of JWJ's movements, to his arrival at Harwich on September 15, are contained in his ms. "Journal," cited in note 13.

16. Ms. Win. Paps., 11.21, Mass. Hist. Soc.

17. Bryant, p. 166; Carritt, pp. 58–66.

18. *Collections*, Mass. Hist. Soc., Series 4, VII, 102, 305 ff.; Bates, p. 14; Andrews, II, 145–47, 146*n*; memorandum in ms. Win. Paps., 5.173, Mass. Hist. Soc.; Stow, I, 284.

19. James Richards (d. 1680) was almost certainly a brother of John Richards (d. 1694) who had married the widow of JWJ's brother Adam. Later (in 1692) John married JWJ's daughter Anne. See sketch by A.C. Goodell, Jr., *Proceedings*, Mass. Hist. Soc., Series 2, X, 547–48. See also Savage, III, 532–33.

20. JWJ to Fitz W., December 6, 1661, ms. Win. Paps., 5.31; *Collections*, Mass. Hist. Soc., Series 5, I, 394; Bates, pp. 14–18, 24–25; *Collections*, Conn. Hist. Soc., XXI, 350–51; "The copye of the (Warwick) Patent," ms. in Conn. Archives, Conn. State Library. Bates's suggestion that JWJ found an *original* as well as a "copy of a copy" of the Warwick Patent does not, upon the evidence, ring quite true.

21. *Collections*, Mass. Hist. Soc., Series 1, V, 241; Series 4, VII, 548–50; Series 5, I, 392–93; IX, 30–31; Arnold, ed., pp. *Fones Record*, pp. 19–21.

22. Andrews, II, 58–60, 134; *Proceedings*, Mass. Hist. Soc., XVI, 215–16; JWJ to Worsley, October 27, 1670, copy in ms. Win. Paps., 5.94, Mass. Hist. Soc

23. They were at Hughes (now Huish's) Court, near the river bank in Black Friars. *Proceedings*, Mass. Hist. Soc., XVI, 215–16.

24. Warrant of Attorney, ms. Win. Paps., 5.32, Mass. Hist. Soc.;

Elizabeth R.W. to JWJ, September 24, 1661, *ibid.*, 5.30 (letter, *including signature*, by an amanuensis). Palmes is briefly sketched in Bailyn, pp. 136, 139.

25. *Collections*, Mass. Hist. Soc., Series 4, VII, 134–36; ms. Win. Paps., 16.43, 44, 45. John Payne (c. 1631–c. 1675) was the son of William Payne, who had died in October, 1660. Savage, III, 333, 337–38.

26. Copy in ms. Win. Paps., 5.29, Mass. Hist. Soc. This letter poses a problem in that it is addressed to "Mary, Mat & An." All other evidence (admittedly uncertain) points to Mary's death in 1653.

27. Fitz's attitudes and activities during this period are clear from JWJ's correspondence *ibid.*, 5.30, 31; also in *Proceedings*, Mass. Hist. Soc., XXI, 125–26; *Collections*, Mass. Hist. Soc., Series 5, VIII, 368–70; Series 6, III, 431. Especially perceptive comments concerning this young man are in Dunn, pp. 197–200.

28. A list of JWJ's correspondents is cited in Cromwell Mortimer's dedication to John Winthrop, F.R.S., *Philosophical Transactions*, Vol. XL (August, 1741).

29. *Proceedings*, Mass. Hist. Soc. XVI, 215; JWJ to Fitz W., November 29, 1661, ms. Win. Paps., 5.30, Mass. Hist. Soc. Brereton (1631–79/80) became 3d Baron Brereton in 1664. See Cokayne, *Complete Peerage*, II, 301 and *n.*

30. For a brief popular discussion, see Meyrick H. Carré, "The Formation of the Royal Society," *History Today*, X (1960), 564–71, which includes a bibliography of the standard works upon the subject.

31. Bryant, p. 160.

32. All these individuals are treated in *DNB*. Their portraits, save that of Moray, are reproduced in Meyrick H. Carré, see note 30. For additional information upon Moray, see H. Hartley, ed., *The Royal Society*, pp. 239–50.

33. Ms. Journal Book, Royal Society Library; Raymond Phineas Stearns, "Colonial Fellows of the Royal Society of London, 1661–1788," *Notes and Records of the Royal Society of London*, VIII, 196; "Extracts from the Journal of the Royal Society," Additional Mss. 4447, fol. 25, British Museum.

34. Egerton Mss., fol. 218, British Museum; Stearns, "Colonial Fellows of the Royal Society," p. 196.

CHAPTER 16

The Connecticut Charter

1. Ms. Win. Paps., 5.31; Nicholas, p. 297.

2. Bourne (c. 1611–91) is in *DAB*, II, 485–86, and *DNB*, VI, 31. Middleton (d. December, 1672) has had no biographer. References to him may be found in O'Callaghan, *et al.*, *N.Y. Col. Docs.*, II, 588–89; *Calendar of State Papers (Colonial), 1574–1660*, pp. 379, 432; *Calendar of State Papers, Colonial, Am. & W.I., 1661–1668*, pp. 1–2, 14– 15, 450; *1669–1674*, pp. 141, 164; W.L. Grant, *et al.*, *Acts, P.C. (Colonial)*, I, 418, 426, 475, 531, 535–37; also Pepys's diary entries for December 19, 1667, and March 28, 29 and May 20, 1669, and *New England Historical and Genealogical Register*, XLIX, 271–72. Scott's recent biographer bends over backward to present him as a much maligned victim of power and circumstance. See Lilian T. Mowrer's *The Indomitable John Scott, Citizen of Long Island, 1632–1704*. John Scott was, in 1662, repeatedly referred to as "captain" and was in Eng- land between the end of 1660 and the late summer of 1662. *Collections, N.-Y. Hist. Soc.* (1869), pp. 46–48; *Collections*, Mass. Hist. Soc., Series 5, IX, 40–43.

3. *Ibid.*, Series 4, VII, 304–5.

4. Rawlinson Mss., A175, Bodleian Library, Oxford. *Signatures*, save that of a secretary of state, were not deemed proper on such a docu- ment. See Andrews, II, 132*n*.

5. P.R.O., C.O. 1:16, 36. The third petition was somewhat less care- less with its assertions relative to the Warwick Patent. It is notable that both Winthrop's revisions called for an eastern limit at Narragansett Bay, *not* Plymouth Colony, as per his instructions. Dunn, p. 133, points out that he also adjusted the original list of patentees so as to include residents of *Long Island*.

6. Bates, pp. 5 ff.

7. For John Clarke (1609–76), see Andrews, II, 39–42; T.G. Wright, *Literary Culture*, p. 70 and *n*; and *DAB*, IV, 154–56. His appointment as agent is in Bartlett, ed., *Col. Recs. R.I.*, I, 432–35. His "addresses" are in the P.R.O., C.O. 1:15, 4, 6, 8, 9. See also *Calendar*

of State Papers, Colonial, Am. & W.I., 1661–1668, pp. 4, 5. Thomas (as of July 7, 1662, Sir Thomas) Temple is in Savage, IV, 267, and *DNB*, LVI, 40. His effort to secure Acadia has left a considerable residue in the Public Record Office. For the Massachusetts efforts, see P.R.O., C.O. 1:15, 13 and 14; Hutchinson, I, 186–88.

8. B.B. Trumbull, *A Complete History of Connecticut*, I, 248. This seems to be based upon Cotton Mather's *Magnalia Christi Americana,* a work which always must be treated with caution.

9. P.R.O., C.O. 1:16, 36, 165.

10. Endorsement, February 26, 1661/2, of Colonel Temple's petition, P.R.O., C.O. 1:16, 45; "Entry Book of Papers Relating to New England," *ibid.*, 5:903, also pp. 5–6. Ms. copy of warrant, *ibid.*, 1:16, 21. (It is curious that the warrant does not appear in the Indices of the Privy Seal or Signet. P.R.O., Index 6751 and Index 6814.) For the "Norrogancet Bay" matter see *Collections*, Mass. Hist. Soc., Series 5, IX, 33–34.

11. *Ibid.*, Series 4, VII, 305–6, 520–21; VIII, 189–90. Bates, pp. 5–8.

12. For John, Baron Robartes of Truro (1606–1685), see Cokayne, *Complete Peerage*, X, 712–13 and *nn*.

13. *Collections*, Conn. Hist. Soc., I, 52*n*; JWJ to S. Willys, May 14, 1662, ms. in Boston Atheneum, photostat in Conn. State Library; Bates, pp. 25–26; Andrews, II, 135.

14. *Proceedings*, Mass. Hist. Soc., Series 2, V, 291; JWJ to S. Willys, see note 13; J.H. Trumbull, *et al.*, *Col. Recs. Conn.*, I, 385; Cowse and Maskelyne to JWJ, July 23, 1664, ms. Win. Paps., 15.21; *Collections*, Conn. Hist. Soc., I, 52–53, 54, 55.

15. JWJ to S. Willys, see note 13; J.H. Trumbull, *et al., Col. Recs. Conn.*, II, 3–11. The charter signature "Howard" is that of the dramatist Sir Robert Howard, clerk of the Patents in Chancery from 1660 to 1664. The subscription of his surname alone would normally indicate a peer and is in this case unusual and even pretentious. H.J. Oliver, p. 39.

16. JWJ to Willys, May 14, 1662, see note 13.

17. Bartlett, ed., *Col. Recs. R.I.*, I, 432–35; *Collections*, Mass. Hist. Soc., Series 4, VIII, 189–90; Series 5, VIII, 75. For a time JWJ wondered if Samuel Maverick were not Rhode Island's real agent. *Ibid.*, Series 5, IX, 33–34.

18. Dunn, p. 132.

19. Petitions of John Clarke, May 14 and 16, 1662, Clarendon Mss., 76, fols. 255 and 272, Bodleian Library; *Collections*, N.-Y. Hist. Soc. (1869); JWJ to Clarendon, June 7, 1662, *Collections*, Mass. Hist. Soc., Series 5, VIII, 75; T.G. Wright, *Literary Culture*, p. 70 and *n*.

20. JWJ to Willys, May 14, 1662, see note 13. One of these "enrolled" copies is in P.R.O., C. 66:3013, No. 10.

21. *Collections*, Mass. Hist. Soc., Series 4, VI, 543–44; Series 5, VIII, 75–76; IX, 33–34; JWJ to Thirsby, copy in JWJ's hand, ms. Win. Paps., 5. 196, Mass. Hist. Soc.

22. *DNB*, II, 181; P.R.O., C.O. 5:903, 2–3, 5–6; P.C. 2:55, 33, 201, 217, 321; W.L. Grant, *et al.*, *Acts, P.C. (Colonial)*, I, 300, 306–9, 316. The United Colonies commissioners continued to act *ex officio* as agents of the Society for the Propagation of the Gospel in New England.

23. This loan, plus subsequent small credits, totaled £384/02/00. Unpaid interest charges had increased this by May, 1667, to £484/02/00. Ashurst to JWJ, May 8, 1667, ms. Win. Paps., 18.89.

24. Andrews, I, 400; memo. by JWJ, ms. Win. Paps., 1.160, Mass. Hist. Soc.; Thos. Willys to S. Willys, July 19, 1662, *ibid.*, 20.66; Henry Willys to JWJ, July 26, 1664, *ibid.*, 20.49; statement of Thos. Willys, January 16, 1662/3, *ibid.*, 20.66.

25. *Collections*, Mass. Hist. Soc., Series 5, VIII, 75–76; copy of agreement, no date, ms. Win. Paps., 18.30, Mass. Hist. Soc.; Dunn, p. 138; Clarke to R.I., August 8, 1662, ms. Win. Paps., 11.160, Mass. Hist. Soc.

26. JWJ to Thirsby (n.d.), fragment of copy, *ibid.*, 5.196. JWJ to (almost certainly) Thirsby, fragment of copy in JWJ's hand, *ibid.*, 5.196. (This disproves A.C. Bates's assertion that the charter was carried by the Massachusetts agents, Bradstreet and Norton.) See also S. Willys to JWJ, September 17, 1661, *ibid.*, 20.50.

27. *Collections*, Mass. Hist. Soc., Series 5, VIII, 75–76; *Collections*, N.-Y. Hist. Soc. (1869), p. 47.

28. *Collections*, Mass. Hist. Soc., Series 5, VIII, 75–76; IX, 33–34.

29. JWJ to Thirsby (obviously), summer, 1662, fragment of copy in JWJ's hand, ms. Win. Paps., 5.196, Mass. Hist. Soc. Winthrop indicates that he did not care to risk sending *both* originals aboard a single vessel. See also Secretary Daniel Clark to JWJ, November 17, 1662, *Proceedings*, Mass. Hist. Soc., XI, 344–45. Clark informed Winthrop

that "we have receaved the Charter, the duplicate and the old Coppy of the former Charter [Warwick Patent]." I do not agree with A.C. Bates's conclusion (pp. 14–18, 24–25) that the "duplicate" was of the Warwick Patent; Clark's meaning appears otherwise. Nevertheless, the problem of the "second original" may never be fully resolved. On August 19, 1663, the Connecticut Assembly asked *Winthrop*, who in the meantime had returned to New England, to deliver the "duplicate" of the Charter to "those Freinds" who had been entrusted with the first original. J.H. Trumbull, *et al.*, *Col. Recs. Conn.*, I, 407. But more than two decades later, in a letter to William Whiting, then Connecticut agent in England, the Connecticut assembly indicated that the "duplicate" had been *left by Winthrop in London* in the hands of James Porter (a City merchant with Connecticut ties) and had remained there ever since! *Ibid.*, III, 369. On the face of it, such inconsistencies defy reconciliation. Yet it appears incredible that one of the charter originals should have remained so long in Porter's possession. Furthermore the arrival of the second original in Connecticut by November, 1662, seems not unreasonable. It could easily have been in Winthrop's possession in the summer of 1663, which would account for the assembly's request of August 19.

30. JWJ's copy of Rhode Island petition, ms. Win. Paps., 12.24.

31. P.R.O., ms. Entries of Papers Relating to New England, C.O. 5.903, 39–40; P.C. 2:56, 74, 78; also *Calendar of State Papers, Colonial, Am. & W.I., 1661–1668*, p. 110, item 370, and W.L. Grant, *et al., Acts, P.C. (Colonial)*, I, 337.

32. Royal Society Register Book (copy), I, 209–11, Royal Society Library; "Extracts," Royal Society Journals, Add. Mss. 4447, fol. 31, British Museum.

CHAPTER 17

Avocation, Evasion, & Arbitration

1. *Collections*, Mass. Hist. Soc., Series 5, VIII, 77–80.

2. Register Book of the Royal Society (copy), I, 182–87, 209–11, 292–305, Royal Society Library; "Extracts," Royal Society Journals, Add. Mss. 4447, fols. 28, 31, 36, British Museum; de Beer, III, 326–27; Boyle Letters, 5.197–202, Royal Society Library; ms. Win. Paps.,

5.208, Mass. Hist. Soc.; Fulmer Mood, "John Winthrop, Jr., on Indian Corn," *New England Quarterly*, X (1937), 121–33; *Proceedings*, Mass. Hist. Soc., XVI, 211; *Collections*, Mass. Hist. Soc., Series 5, VIII, 86–88.

3. Wertenbaker, p. 261; *Collections*, Mass. Hist Soc., Series 2, I, 220–22; *Proceedings*, Mass. Hist. Soc., XVI, 215n.

4. Frederick L. Weis, "The New England Company," *Publications*, Col. Soc. Mass., XXXVIII, 212; Kellaway, pp. 49, 108; *Collections*, Mass. Hist. Soc., Series 5, IX, 45–47.

5. JWJ to Fitz W., February 16, 1662/3, ms. Win. Paps., Vol. V; Wm. Constable to JWJ, March 18, 1665/6, *ibid.*, 12.36; R.S. Wilkinson, "George Starkey, Physician and Alchemist," *Ambix*, Vol. XI (October, 1963). In an admirable paper upon the Philalethes Tracts, *Ambix*, Vol. XII (February, 1964), Wilkinson suggests that Winthrop, as the author of these confidential materials, became piqued when Stirk, or Starkey, put one of them into print.

6. *Collections*, Mass. Hist. Soc., Series 4, VIII, 183; Nicholas, p. 304.

7. *Collections*, Mass. Hist. Soc., Series 4, VII, 522–23; "Acts," U.C., Pulsifer, ed., *Recs.* Plymouth Colony, X, 286–87.

8. S. Willys to JWJ, September 17, 1662, ms. Win. Paps., 20.5, Mass. Hist. Soc.; John Allyn to JWJ, December 1, 1662, *ibid.*, 10.17; Calder, pp. 232–35; J.H. Trumbull, *et al.*, *Col. Recs. Conn.*, I, 387n, 387–88, 390; *Collections*, Conn. Hist. Soc., XXIV, 8–9.

9. Andrews, II, 187–88; Calder, pp. 232–35; B.B. Trumbull, *History of Connecticut*, I, 442–44.

10. *Proceedings*, Mass. Hist. Soc., XI, 344–45; John Allyn to JWJ, December 12, 1662, ms. Win. Paps., 10.18, Mass. Hist. Soc.

11. *Collections*, Mass. Hist. Soc., Series 5, VIII, 77–81. Wm. Hooke to John Davenport, March 2, 1662/3, P.R.O., State Papers, Domestic, Charles II, Vol. XIX; Calder, pp. 236–37.

12. For Hooke (1601–77/8) see Sprague, I, 104–6. Major Robert Thompson may be the "Maj. Thomson" referred to in Pepys's diary for January 6, 1662/3, as formerly of the Navy and strong for liberty of conscience. He received a handsome bequest in Edward Hopkins's will. See *New England Historical & Genealogical Register*, XXXVIII, 315–16.

13. *Collections*, Mass. Hist. Soc., Series 5, VIII, 77–81.

14. Dexter, ed., II, 522–23; B.B. Trumbull, *History of Connecticut*, I, 447–48.

15. *Collections,* Mass. Hist. Soc., Series 5, VIII, 77–81. (Winthrop had been reelected governor *in absentia* on May 15, 1662. He had again been reelected, this time on the basis of the charter, on October 9. J.H. Trumbull, *et al., Col. Recs. Conn.,* I, 378–79, 384.)

16. JWJ to Edward Hutchinson, Jr., September 2, 1662, *Collections,* Mass. Hist. Soc., Series 5, IX, 33–34, 37, 38–45; also *Proceedings,* Mass. Hist. Soc., V, 403, and Mowrer, p. 89.

17. *Collections,* Mass. Hist. Soc., Series 5, IX, 34–36, 70–71.

18. *Ibid.,* Series 5, VIII, 77–80; JWJ to Fitz W., February 16, 1662/3, ms. Win. Paps., Vol. V.

19. Ms. Winthrop Deeds, pp. 48 and 58, and ms. Win. Paps., 5.34, Mass. Hist. Soc. For John Harwood see Savage, II, 371.

20. Ms. Win. Paps., 5.35, Mass. Hist. Soc.; *Collections,* Conn. Hist. Soc., XXI, 144–45; Andrews, II, 45 ff. Deane had taken a mortgage on Clarke's property at Newport. A Captain John Brookhaven, master of the *Ann and Elizabeth,* took a shipload of Puritans to Old Providence Island in the spring of 1635. *New England Historical & Genealogical Register,* XIV, 351.

21. Working notes, partly in JWJ's hand, ms. Win. Paps., 12.25, Mass. Hist. Soc. It is just possible that these were used before the Council for Plantations in September, 1662, but JWJ's public disavowal of personal bias would seem to date them after March 17, 1662/3. See note 20.

22. This agreement may be examined in several places, viz., ms. Win. Paps., 15.35; *Collections,* Mass. Hist. Soc., Series 5, VIII, 82–83; Bartlett, ed., *Col. Recs. R.I.,* pp. 518–19; ms. parchment original, Conn. Archives, Conn. State Library; and copy of agreement (probably for the information of the Crown), P.R.O., C.O. 1:17 49 and 50. There is some slight variation in text. Most versions indicate J. Beane and Wm. Potter as witnesses to Winthrop's and Clarke's signatures; the Connecticut parchment original shows Thompson and Worsley. (Query: Was Wm. Potter the monetary theorist?)

23. O'Callaghan, *et al., N.Y. Col. Docs.,* III, 55; Andrews, II, 46.

24. Scott to Hutchinson, etc., April 29, 1663, copy in ms. Win. Paps., 18.28; *Collections,* Mass. Hist. Soc., Series 5, IX, 53.

25. P.R.O., P.C. 2:56, 196; W.L. Grant, *et al., Acts, P.C. Colonial,* I, 349; *Proceedings,* Mass. Hist. Soc., Series 2, XIII, 455; O'Callaghan, *et al., N.Y. Col. Docs.,* III, 55. For the salt and potash, see *Collections,* Mass. Hist. Soc., Series 3, X, 49 ff.

26. P.R.O., P.C. 2:56, 196; W.L. Grant, *et al.*, *Acts*, *P.C. Colonial*, I, 349; P.R.O., C.O. 1:17, 115, 116, 117.

27. *Collections*, Mass. Hist. Soc., Series 5, I, 58; VIII, 86–88; JWJ to Wm. Hooke, "intended" but not sent, ms. Win. Paps., 5.200, Mass. Hist. Soc.

28. *Collections*, Mass. Hist. Soc., Series 5, VIII, 86–88; also JWJ notes, ms. Win. Paps., 5.160, Mass. Hist. Soc.

29. JWJ arrived at Boston on June 4 at the latest. *Proceedings*, Mass. Hist. Soc., XVI, 216; see also Mathew Allyn *et al.* to JWJ, June 6, 1663, ms. Win. Paps., 10.18, Mass. Hist. Soc.

CHAPTER 18

Studies in Aggression

1. A letter from Director Stuyvesant, dated New Amsterdam, June 9, 1663, awaited him and was marked by JWJ as received on June 17. *Collections*, Mass. Hist. Soc., Series 4, VII, 287–90.

2. J.H. Trumbull, *et al.*, *Col. Recs. Conn.*, I, 399; JWJ to Conn. Council, June 30, 1663, rough draft in ms. Win. Paps., 5.37.

3. Calder, pp. 99–101; J.H. Trumbull, *et al.*, *Col. Recs. Conn.*, I, 437–41; Glenn Weaver, "Anglican-Congregational Tensions in Pre-Revolutionary Connecticut," *Historical Magazine of the Protestant Episcopal Church*, XXVI (September, 1957), 270–72.

4. JWJ to Henry Ashurst, October 20, 1663, ms. Win. Paps., 5.38, Mass. Hist. Soc.; *Proceedings*, Mass. Hist. Soc., V, 376–77; JWJ to Boyle, September 25, 1664, copy in ms. Win. Paps., 5.43; *Collections*, Mass. Hist. Soc., Series 5, I, 409.

5. *Ibid.*, Series 4, VI, 521–24, 534–35.

6. Andrews, II, 189; *Collections*, Mass. Hist. Soc., Series 4, VII, 552–553; J.H. Trumbull, *et al.*, *Col. Recs. Conn.*, I, 396; Calder, p. 235; B.B. Trumbull, *History of Connecticut*, I, 444–47.

7. *Collections*, Mass. Hist. Soc., Series 4, VII, 550–551.

8. *Ibid.*, VII, 552–53.

9. JWJ to Davenport, August 6, 1663, copy in ms. Win. Paps., 5.36, Mass. Hist. Soc.; J.H. Trumbull, *et al.*, *Col Recs. Conn.*, I, 406.

10. "Acts," U.C., Pulsifer, ed., *Recs.* Plymouth Colony, IX, 4, 6.

11. *Ibid.*, X, 308.

12. *Ibid.*, X, 309.

13. Andrews, II, 189; Dunn, p. 145; also note 12, above.

14. *Records and Files*, Essex Quarter Courts, III, 168*n*; J.H. Trumbull, *et al.*, *Col. Recs. Conn.*, I, 414, 415.

15. JWJ to Wm. Wells, October 15, 1663, ms. Win. Paps., 5.38, Mass. Hist. Soc.; JWJ to "the honored General assembly of the Colony of Connecticut," copy in *ibid.*, 5.39.

16. Dexter, ed., II, 499–500; Calder, pp. 239–41.

17. JWJ to Leete, February 9, 1663/4, copy in ms. Win. Paps., 5.37, Mass. Hist. Soc.; Dexter, ed., II, 512*n*, 515–17; *Collections*, Conn. Hist. Soc., XXI, 149–50; JWJ to Robt. Chapman, April 27, 1664, copy in ms. Win. Paps., 5.40, Mass. Hist. Soc., JWJ to Leete, December 29, 1663, copy, *ibid.*; depositions of John Meigs and Wm. Greene, *ibid.*, 15.59.

18. Andrews, II, 192; Calder, pp. 249–52; J.H. Trumbull, *et al.*, *Col. Recs. Conn.*, I, 437; "Acts," U.C., Pulsifer, ed., *Recs.* Plymouth Colony, X, 318–19, 322.

19. *Collections*, Mass. Hist. Soc., Series 4, VII, 424–25; JWJ to John Davenport, Jr., September 23, 1664, copy in ms. Win. Paps., 5.41, Mass. Hist. Soc.; JWJ to Leete, February 17, 1664/5, copy, *ibid.*, 5.48 and 49; JWJ to John Davenport, June 17, 1665, *ibid.*, 5.51.

20. *Collections*, Mass. Hist. Soc., Series 5, LX, 53; ms. Win. Paps., 18.28.

21. Williamson (1633–1701) was an original Fellow (1663) of the Royal Society and became its president in 1677. He was made a principal secretary of state in 1674. *DNB*, LXII, 2–7. See also Mowrer, p. 72. Thomas (1600–66) and William (1602–88) Chiffinch are in *DNB*, X, 237–39. See also Bailyn, p. 117.

22. See note 20; also Charles II to Massachusetts, Plymouth, New Haven, and Connecticut, June 21, 1663, over signature of Henry Bennet, copy in "Entry of Papers relating to New England," P.R.O., C.O. 5:903, 22–23, and *Proceedings*, Mass. Hist. Soc., X, 391–92.

23. Charles II to Massachusetts, Plymouth, New Haven, and Connecticut, June 21, 1663, see note 22; charter of Rhode Island, July 8, 1663, Bartlett, ed., *Col. Recs. R.I.*, II, 1–21.

24. J.H. Trumbull, *et al.*, *Col. Recs. Conn.*, I, 390; John Allyn to JWJ, December 1, 1622, ms. Win. Paps., 10.17, Mass. Hist. Soc.; *Collections*, Conn. Hist. Soc., XXI, 144–45.

25. J.H. Trumbull, *et al., Col. Recs. Conn.*, I, 407.

26. *Ibid.*, I, 389–90, 411, 433–34; II, 36, 36*n*, 62–63; JWJ to Worsley, December 7, 1663, copy in ms. Win. Paps., 5.40, Mass. Hist. Soc.

27. Bartlett, ed., *Col. Recs. R.I.*, II, 34–36; JWJ to Arnold and Brenton, undated copy in ms. Win. Paps., 5.166, Mass. Hist. Soc. This letter may never have been received. See Bartlett, ed., *Col. Recs. R.I.*, II, 65–67.

28. *Collections*, Mass. Hist. Soc., Series 5, IX, 59–62.

29. *Ibid.*, Series 4, VI, 295–97; Bowen, p. 34.

30. Calder, pp. 243–44; Mowrer, pp. 97, 99; Scott to Williamson, December 14, 1663, ms. in P.R.O., C.O. 1:17, No. 102; copy in handwriting of Conn. Secretary, John Allyn, ms. Win. Paps., 18.28, Mass. Hist. Soc. See also *Collections*, Mass. Hist. Soc., Series 5, I, 397–99.

31. O'Callaghan, *et al., N.Y. Col. Docs.*, II, 406; Mowrer, pp. 106–17; O'Callaghan, *et al., N.Y. Col. Docs.*, II, 367.

32. *Ibid.*, II, 396, 399, 400–5, 501; R.C. Winthrop Collection, I, No. 6, Conn. Archives, Conn. State Library; Mowrer, pp. 120–21; O'Callaghan, *History of New Netherland*, II, 578.

33. *Collections*, Conn. Hist. Soc., XXI, 150–52; XXIV, 10–11; see also Mowrer, pp. 121–22; O'Callaghan, *et al., N.Y. Col. Docs.*, II, 407.

34. Mowrer, p. 122, implies that the March 1663/4 meeting was called specifically for the purpose of ruining Scott, but this was not so. Its date had been set the previous October. See also J.H. Trumbull, *et al., Col. Recs. Conn.*, I, 416, 420–22.

35. *Collections*, Conn. Hist. Soc., XXI, 152–54; Scott to JWJ, March 21, 1663/4, ms. Win. Paps., 18.29, Mass. Hist. Soc.

36. *Collections*, Conn. Hist. Soc., XXI, 155, 156–58; information of Jacob Milbourn, January 6, 1679/80, Rawlinson Mss. 175, fol. 83, Bodleian Library; *Collections*, Mass. Hist. Soc., Series 4, VII, 525–26, 553–55, 596–97. See also Mowrer, pp. 133 ff.

37. *Collections*, Conn. Hist. Soc., XXI, 156; JWJ to Robert Chapman, April 27, 1664, copy in ms. Win. Paps., 5.46, Mass. Hist. Soc.; Milbourn information, note 36; *Collections*, Mass. Hist. Soc., Series 5, I, 100–1; permit to "this bearer" to visit Scott (in JWJ's hand), April 22, 1664, ms. Win. Paps., 5.40, Mass. Hist. Soc.

38. Milbourn information, see note 36; Calder, pp. 245–46; Mow-

rer, pp. 137–38; J.H. Trumbull, *et al.*, *Col. Recs. Conn.*, II, 16*n*. Mrs. Mowrer's charge that Scott's property was confiscated prior to his trial is not quite fair. It was sequestered, which is not the same thing, by the General Assembly on May 20, under Winthrop's own presidency. J.H. Trumbull, *et al.*, *Col. Recs. Conn.*, I, 430. Scott's lands were not sold to pay his fine until May of 1665. *Ibid.*, II, 16, 16*n*.

39. Milbourn information, note 36.

CHAPTER 19

Benevolent Conquest

1. J.H. Trumbull, *et al.*, *Col Recs. Conn.*, I, 405; *Collections*, Mass. Hist. Soc., Series 4, VI, 526.

2. J.H. Trumbull, *et al.*, *Col. Recs. Conn.*, I, 406–7; *Collections*, Mass. Hist. Soc., Series 5, V, 395–97.

3. *Ibid.*, IX, 55–58.

4. "Acts," U.C., Pulsifer, ed., *Recs.*, Plymouth Colony, X, 299–301; O'Callaghan, *et al.*, *N.Y. Col. Docs.*, II, 385.

5. "Acts," U.C., Pulsifer, ed., *Recs.*, Plymouth Colony, X, 301–4; O'Callaghan, *et al.*, *N.Y. Col. Docs.*, II, 385; *Collections*, N.-Y. Hist. Soc., Series 2, II, 376–77.

6. The details of this episode are derived from "Journal of the Dutch Delegates to the General Assembly at Hartford," October, 1663, O'Callaghan, *et al.*, *N.Y. Col. Docs.*, II, 385–93.

7. Jacobus, *Officials of Connecticut Colony*, p. 20; Love, pp. 236–37, 287*n*.

8. Ms. Win. Paps., 5.39, Mass. Hist. Soc.

9. O'Callaghan, *et al.*, *N.Y. Col. Docs.*, II, 485–86; J.H. Trumbull, *et al.*, *Col Recs. Conn.*, I, 411, 416.

10. *Ibid.*, I, 423–24, 426–27, 431.

11. *Ibid.*, I, 427; *Collections*, Mass. Hist. Soc., Series 4, VII, 187–89; O'Callaghan, *et al.*, *N.Y. Col. Docs.*, II, 368, 407–9. For a rather unfriendly portrayal of Winthrop's bluntness, see O'Callaghan, *History of New Netherland*, II, 512–14.

12. Original in Long Island Historical Society, Brooklyn; see also *Proceedings*, Mass. Hist. Soc., Series 2, V, 305–6; *Records of the Town*

of Brookhaven, A, xiv–xv, 10; "Plan of Mannor of Groton Hall," ms. in Long Island Hist. Soc.; JWJ to Fitz W., August 28, 1665, ms. Min. Paps., 5.52; JWJ to Wait W., April 2, 1672, *ibid.,* 5.70.

13. *Collections,* Mass. Hist. Soc., Series 4, VII, 189.

14. JWJ to Captain Thomas Breeden, July 4, 1664, copy in ms. Win. Paps., 5.186, Mass. Hist. Soc.; Cornell, p. 245; *Collections,* Mass. Hist. Soc., Series 2, VIII, 92; JWJ to Robt. Boyle, September 25, 1664, copy in ms. Win. Paps., 5.43, Mass. Hist. Soc.

15. *DAB,* III, 299; Paul, ed., VIII, 181–82; Instructions to Council of Trade, P.R.O., C.O. 324:1, 191–93; O'Callaghan, *et al., N.Y. Col. Docs.,* II, 295–98; *Proceedings,* Mass. Hist. Soc., X, 382–88; Francis Newton Thorpe, ed., *The Federal and State Constitutions, Colonial Charters, and Other Organic Laws of* [*the U.S.*] (7 vols., Washington, D.C., 1909), III, 1637–40.

16. Privy Council Register, P.R.O., P.C. 2:57, 34, 75; *Proceedings,* Mass. Hist. Soc., X, 388; "Duke of York's Instructions," 1662–66, P.R.O., Adm. 2:1733; also C.O. 324:4, 41–42; O'Callaghan, *et al., N.Y. Col Docs.,* III, 51–54, 57–61, 64–65.

17. Nicolls (1624–72) is sketched in *DAB,* XIII, 515–16.

18. *Visitation of the county of Nottingham, 1569 and 1614* (Harleian Society, IV, 1871), cited in de Beers, III, 581*n*, 581–82; *New England Historical and Genealogical Register,* XXIV, 187; XXXVIII, 72; *Calendar of State Papers, Colonial, Am. & W.I., 1661–1668,* item 115; *Proceedings,* Mass. Hist. Soc., X, 381–82.

19. *Ibid.,* X, 387–88; W.B. Rowbotham, commander, R.N., ed., "Pepys' List of Ships and Officers, 1660–1668," typescript (1957) in P.R.O.; Oppenheim, pp. 330, 332; Clowes, *et al.,* II, 109; "an Establishment of a proportion of gunns," etc., P.R.O., Adm. 2:1725; W.L. Grant, *et al., Acts P.C.* (*Colonial*), I, 463, 504; O'Callaghan, *History of New Netherland,* II, 520; Stuyvesant, who could be expected to exaggerate the English strength, indicated a total of at least 110 guns. O'Callaghan, *et al., N.Y. Col. Docs.,* II, 445–556; Calder, pp. 247–48.

20. O'Callaghan, *et al., N.Y. Col. Docs.,* III, 65; Stokes, IV, 216, 239; *Collections,* Mass. Hist. Soc., Series 2, VIII, 93; Univ. of N.Y. *State Library Bulletin, Hist. No. 2,* p. 73.

21. *Collections,* Mass. Hist. Soc., Series 2, VIII, 92–95; O'Callaghan, *et al., N.Y. Col. Docs.,* III, 84–85; Stokes, IV, 239.

22. William Hubbard, "General History of New England," *Collections*, Mass. Hist. Soc., Series 2, VI, 721–22; Series 5, VIII, 90–91; *Proceedings*, Mass. Hist. Soc., XVI, 222–23, 224–25. Moray and Nicolls were close friends; the former addressed the latter as "Dick," while Nicolls left his reputation at court—a thing seriously to worry about—in Moray's hands during his absence in America. *Ibid.*, XVI, 225–26.

23. *Collections*, Mass. Hist. Soc., Series 5, I, 399–400; VIII, 88–90; O'Callaghan, *et al.*, *N.Y. Col. Docs.*, II, 372–73; Stokes, IV, 238, 239, 240; ms. Win. Paps., 16.140, Mass. Hist. Soc.

24. JWJ to Edward Rainsborough, October 20, 1664, ms. Win. Paps., 5.43, Mass. Hist. Soc.; Stokes, IV, 239, 242; JWJ prescription, August 7, 1664, ms. Win. Paps., 20b.570; ms. Win. Paps., 20.15, Mass. Hist. Soc.; O'Callaghan, *et al.*, *N.Y. Col. Docs.*, II, 372.

25. *Ibid.*, II, 372; Stokes, IV, 240.

26. Mathews, p. 34; O'Callaghan, *et al.*, *N.Y. Col. Docs.*, II, 372; *Proceedings*, Mass. Hist. Soc., V, 376–77; JWJ to Boyle, September 25, 1664, copy in ms. Win. Paps., 5.43, Mass. Hist. Soc.

27. Thompson, p. 491; "A narrative of the proceedings," etc., ms. in Conn. Archives, Conn. State Library.

28. Stokes, IV, 240; O'Callaghan, *History of New Netherland*, II, 520–22; O'Callaghan, *et al.*, *N.Y. Col. Docs.*, II, 410–11.

29. Nicolls to JWJ, ms. Win. Paps., 5.187, Mass. Hist. Soc.; O'Callaghan, *History of New Netherland*, II, 523 and *n*; *Collections*, Mass. Hist. Soc., Series 4, VI, 527–29.

30. O'Callaghan, *et al.*, *N.Y. Col. Docs.*, II, 248–50, 411–12, 444–45; *Collections*, Mass. Hist. Soc., Series 4, VI, 527–29; Series 5, VIII, 252; Stokes, IV, 240. O'Callaghan, *et al.*, *N.Y. Col. Docs.*, II, 411, is in error in mentioning "Colonel George Carteret"; Sir George Carteret never visited America.

31. O'Callaghan, *History of New Netherland*, II, 525 ff.; Stokes, IV, 240; Calder, p. 249; O'Callaghan, *et al.*, *N.Y. Col. Docs.*, II, 414.

32. *Collections*, N.-Y. Hist. Soc., 1869, II, 333–36; O'Callaghan, *History of New Netherland*, II, 525–32, 535*n*; Stokes, IV, 242; O'Callaghan, *et al.*, *N.Y. Col. Docs.*, II, 414; III, 103, 250–53. The "free trade" article (VI) was greatly restricted by the English Privy Council on October 23, 1667; W.L. Grant, *et al.*, *Acts, P.C. (Colonial)*, I, 444.

33. O'Callaghan, *et al.*, *N.Y. Col. Docs.*, II, 415, 445–46; O'Callaghan, *History of New Netherland*, II, 536; Stokes, IV, 233–34.

CHAPTER 20

Connecticut, Winthrop, & the Royal Commission

1. JWJ to Robt. Boyle, September 25, 1664, copy in ms. Win. Paps., 5.43, Mass. Hist. Soc.; "Acts," U.C., Pulsifer, ed., *Recs.* Plymouth Colony, X, 312–22; J.H. Trumbull, *et al.*, *Col. Recs. Conn.*, I, 430. Winthrop compounded a medical prescription on September 11, which would almost certainly place him in Hartford. Ms. Win. Paps., 20b, 570. Mass. Hist. Soc.

2. *Ibid.*, 5.51; *Collections*, N.-Y. Hist. Soc. (1869), p. 58.

3. Nicolls, in a letter to JWJ on October 12, 1664, remarked that he would not "resigne up his Majesties graunt to the Duke for a foot of the Limitts, except in such a way as hath beene formerly discoursed betweene yourself and mee." Ms. Win. Paps., 16.19, Mass. Hist. Soc.

4. *Ibid.*; J.H. Trumbull, *et al.*, *Col. Recs. Conn.*, I, 435.

5. JWJ to Captain Thos. Breeden, no date, but obviously late September, 1664, copy in ms. Win. Paps., 5.164, Mass. Hist. Soc.; J.H. Trumbull, *et al.*, *Col. Recs. Conn.*, I, 433; *Collections*, Mass. Hist. Soc., Series 4, VII, 309–11; JWJ to John Cotton, November 10, 1664, copy in ms. Win. Paps., 5.46, Mass. Hist. Soc.; JWJ to Cartwright (not dated, not sent), copy, *ibid.*, 5.44; JWJ to (obviously) Nicolls, late November, 1664, copy, *ibid.*; Stokes, IV, 247–49; O'Callaghan, *et al.*, *N.Y. Col. Docs.*, III, 68–69.

6. *Collections*, Mass. Hist. Soc., Series 5, VIII, 93–95; B.B. Trumbull, *History of Connecticut*, I, 451–52; JWJ to Sackville, February 14, 1664/5, copy in ms. Win. Paps., 5.48, Mass. Hist. Soc.

7. Dunn, p. 156; Johnston, pp. 205–7; B.B. Trumbull, *History of Connecticut*, I, 451–52; Stokes, IV, 251; J.H. Trumbull, *et al.*, *Col. Recs. Conn.*, II, 15*n*; Nicolls to JWJ, February 14, 1664/5, copy in ms. Win. Paps., 16.23, Mass. Hist. Soc.; Paullin, p. 75, and plate 97 E; Bowen, pp. 19–20.

8. Stokes, IV, 252–53; *Collections,* Mass. Hist. Soc., Series 5, I, 410–12; O'Callaghan, *et al., N.Y. Col. Docs.,* III, 106.

9. *Records and Papers,* New London County Hist. Soc., III, 183; *Collections,* Mass. Hist. Soc., Series 6, III, 461*n;* Stokes, IV, 252–53.

10. Egerton Mss. 2395, fol. 396, British Museum; Order in Council, April 22, 1664, P.R.O., P.C. Register, P.C. 2:42, 57; Ms. copy in P.R.O., C.O. 324:1, 238–43; ms. original, with seal, Egerton Mss. 2395, fols. 393–95, British Museum; O'Callaghan, *et al., N.Y. Col. Docs.,* III, 55–61.

11. *Proceedings,* Mass. Hist. Soc., V, 376–77.

12. *Collections,* Mass. Hist. Soc., Series 4, VII, 190–91; Series 5, VIII, 92; *Proceedings,* Mass. Hist. Soc., Series 2, XIII, 455–56; Series 5, IX, 64; Mowrer, p. 165; O'Callaghan, *et al., N.Y. Col. Docs.,* III, 86; Charles II to governor and council of Conn., April 23, 1664, ms. copy in P.R.O., C.O. 324:1, 245–46; Conn. Council to Charles II, July 15, 1665, *Collections,* Conn. Hist. Soc., XXIV, 11–12; Conn. Assembly to Sir Henry Bennet, copy in ms. Win. Paps., 5.203, Mass. Hist. Soc.

13. *Collections,* Mass. Hist. Soc., Series 5, IX, 72–73.

14. J.H. Trumbull, *et al., Col. Recs. Conn.,* I, 389, 417–18, 439–40; *Proceedings,* Mass. Hist. Soc., XIII, 233.

15. Stokes, IV, 248; Nicolls to JWJ, October 22, 1664, ms. Win. Paps., 15.1, Mass. Hist. Soc.; JWJ to Nicolls, November 10, 1664, copy, *ibid.,* 5.46

16. JWJ to Nicolls, January 18, 1664/5, *ibid.,* 5.47; JWJ to Benedict Arnold, February 11, 1664/5, copy, *ibid.;* JWJ to Nicolls, March 9, 1664/5, *ibid.,* 5.49; *Collections,* Mass. Hist. Soc., Series 2, VI, 723–30; Series 4, VI, 529–32; O'Callaghan, *et al., N.Y. Col. Docs.,* III, 84–85, 93; JWJ to Carr, March 9, 1664/5, copy in ms. Win. Paps., 5.49, Mass. Hist. Soc.

17. John Allyn to JWJ, March 18, 1664/5, *ibid.,* 10.18; *Collections,* Mass. Hist. Soc., Series 5, IX, 66; JWJ to commissioners, copy in ms. Win. Paps., 5.96, Mass. Hist. Soc.

18. *Collections,* Mass. Hist. Soc., Series 2, VII, 91–94; VIII, 92–93; Series 5, IX, 54–55, 63, 67; "Acts," U.C. Pulsifer, ed., *Recs.* Plymouth Colony, X, 320–21; Report of Royal Commissioners, 1665 (Rhode Island), Egerton Mss. 2395, fols. 429–31, British Museum; Bartlett, ed., *Col. Recs. R.I.,* II, 93–94.

19. *Ibid.*, II, 94, 95; O'Callaghan, *et al.*, *N.Y. Col. Docs.*, III, 158.
20. *Collections*, Mass. Hist. Soc., Series 5, IX, 72–73.
21. *Ibid.*; also B.B. Trumbull, *History of Connecticut*, I, 450–51.
22. J.H. Trumbull, *et al.*, *Col. Recs. Conn.*, I, 441; B.B. Trumbull, *History of Connecticut*, I, 456–58.
23. Bowen, pp. 21–23.
24. Privy Council to Royal Commissioners, September 14, 1664, P.R.O., P.C. 2.57, 116, 122; *Proceedings*, Mass. Hist. Soc., Series 2, XIII, 455–56; JWJ to Clarendon, no date, ms. Win. Paps., 5.206, Mass. Hist. Soc. Dunn, p. 161, emphasizes Winthrop's dislike of outside interference with Connecticut justice.
25. Reports of Royal Commissioners, Egerton Mss. 2395, fol. 432, British Museum; Stokes, IV, 259.
26. Nicolls to JWJ, May 4, 1665, ms. Win. Paps., 15.165, Mass. Hist. Soc.; Andrews, III, 64*n*; O'Callaghan, *et al.*, *N.Y. Col. Docs.*, III, 161; JWJ to Sir Wm. Morrice, no date, copy in ms. Win. Paps., 5.63, Mass. Hist. Soc.; royal letter to Royal Commissioners, April 20, 1666, attested true copy (by Nicolls) in Egerton Mss. 2395, fol. 442, British Museum; *Collections*, Conn. Hist. Soc., XXI, 162–63; *Collections*, Mass. Hist. Soc., Series 4, VII, 312.

CHAPTER 21

The Art of Gentle Politics

1. The Valentine's Manual reproduction of "The Dukes Plan," J. Clarence Davies Collection, Museum of the City of New York.
2. JWJ to magistrates of Springfield, Hadley, and Northampton, January 30, 1664/5, copy in ms. Win. Paps., 5.47, Mass. Hist. Soc.; JWJ to Nicolls, copy, *ibid.*, 5.172; JWJ to Captain Manning, date obliterated and May 17, 1665, copies, *ibid.*, 5.50; JWJ to John Harwood, no date, copy, *ibid.*, 5.177.
3. JWJ to "Right Honble." (Nicolls), no date, copy, *ibid.*, 5.96; J.H. Trumbull, *et al.*, *Col. Recs. Conn.*, I, 440–41; II, 13–19; *Collections*, Mass. Hist. Soc., Series 5, VIII, 96–97.
4. Stokes, IV, 256; *Collections*, Mass. Hist. Soc., Series 5, VIII, 96–99; J.H. Trumbull, *et al.*, *Col. Recs. Conn.*, II, 19–21, and 21*n*.

5. *Ibid.; Collections*, Mass. Hist. Soc., Series 3, X, 54–55, 56–57; JWJ to Fitz W., August 28, 1665, ms. Win. Paps., 5.52, Mass. Hist. Soc.; JWJ to Nicolls, rough draft, *ibid.*; JWJ to Nicolls, September 13, 1665, copy, *ibid.*; JWJ to Nicolls, November 23, 1665, copy, *ibid.*, 5.53; O'Callaghan, *et al.*, *N.Y. Col. Docs.*, III, 114–15.

6. Nicolls to JWJ, February 17, 1665/6; also bill of John Baker and "severall men," ms. Win. Paps., 5.54, Mass. Hist. Soc.; JWJ to Nicolls, April 9, 1666, *ibid.*, 5.55; J.H. Trumbull, *et al.*, *Col. Recs. Conn.*, II, 30–43; Nicolls to JWJ, May 23, 1666, ms. Win. Paps., 16.3, Mass. Hist. Soc.

7. *Proceedings*, Mass. Hist. Soc., Series 1, X, 390; JWJ to Nicolls, June 25, 1666, copy in ms. Win. Paps., 5.57; J.H. Trumbull, *et al.*, *Col. Recs. Conn.*, II, 514; O'Callaghan, *et al.*, *N.Y. Col. Docs.*, III, 120–21.

8. *Ibid.; Collections*, Mass. Hist. Soc., Series 5, VIII, 99–101; JWJ to Nicolls, ms. Win. Paps., 5.173, Mass. Hist. Soc. JWJ to John Harwood, c. spring, 1666, copy, *ibid.*, 5.177.

9. *Collections*, Mass. Hist. Soc., Series 3, X, 63–64; Series 5, VIII, 102–3; J.H. Trumbull, *et al.*, *Col. Recs. Conn.*, II, 43–46; JWJ to Nicolls, July 30, 1666, ms. Win. Paps., 5.60, Mass. Hist. Soc.; August 17, 1666, copy, *ibid.*, 5.58.

10. Nicolls to JWJ, August 22, 1666?, *ibid.*, 16.19.

11. JWJ to "Capt. Winthrop" (probably Fitz), October 10, 1666, *ibid.*, 5.60; *Collections*, Mass. Hist. Soc., Series 5, VIII, 102–3, 105.

12. *Ibid.*, Series 3, X, 66–67; Series 5, VIII, 107–11; 115–16.

13. *Ibid.*, VIII, 117–19; rough draft in JWJ's hand, ms. Win. Paps., 5.205, Mass. Hist. Soc.; JWJ to Nicolls, March 26, 1667, *ibid.*, 5.65; rough draft in JWJ's hand, *ibid.*, 5.66.

14. JWJ to Nicolls, May 15, 1667, *ibid.*, 5.67; *Collections*, Mass. Hist. Soc., Series 5, VIII, 120; J.H. Trumbull, *et al.*, *Col. Recs. Conn.*, II, 36–37, 57, 62, 64; JWJ draft notes in ms. Win. Paps., 5.67, 5.208.

15. JWJ to Nicolls, May 15, July 15, September 8, and 18, 1667, *ibid.*, 5.67, 5.68; J.H. Trumbull, *et al.*, *Col. Recs. Conn.*, II, 57–58; O'Callaghan, *et al.*, *N.Y. Col. Docs.*, II, 522–23.

16. Ashurst to JWJ, May 8, 1667, ms. Win. Paps., 18.89, Mass. Hist. Soc.; JWJ to Ashurst, September 23, 1668, copy, *ibid.*, 5.82; J.H. Trumbull, *et al.*, *Col. Recs. Conn.*, II, 23, 24, 29–30, 37; *Collections*, Mass. Hist. Soc., Series 3, X, 49–53; Series 5, I, 416; VIII,

271–72, 273–74; ms. Win. Paps., 5.56 Mass. Hist. Soc.; F.E. Hines, "Fishers Island," *Records and Papers*, New London County Hist. Soc., III, 185, 187; orders and bills in ms. Win. Paps., 5.53, 5.62, also 18.143, Mass. Hist. Soc.

17. *Ibid.*, 5.81.

18. JWJ to Brenton, April 20, 1667, drafts and copy, *ibid.*, 5.66.

19. J.H. Trumbull, *et al.*, *Col. Recs. Conn.*, II, 80–81, 90–92, 95, 95*n*, 96, 101–2, 103, 121–22, 531–33, 543; Andrews, II, 52–54.

20. JWJ to Nicolls, August 26, 1668, copy in ms. Win. Paps., 5.81, Mass. Hist. Soc.; see also September 24, 1670, *ibid.*, 5.92; October 27, 1670, *ibid.*; J.H. Trumbull, *et al.*, *Col. Recs. Conn.*, II, 134–35, 534, 545–46; rough draft in JWJ's hand, ms. Win. Paps., 5.90, Mass. Hist. Soc.

21. JWJ to Wait W., June 17, 1670, *ibid.*, 5.90; J.H. Trumbull, *et al.*, *Col. Recs. Conn.*, II, 534, 551–52.

22. *Ibid.*, II, 137–38, 553–54.

23. *Collections*, Mass. Hist. Soc., Series 5, IX, 78–79.

24. *Ibid.*; also copy of resignation July—, 1670, ms. Win. Paps., 5.91, Mass. Hist. Soc.

25. Andrews, II, 54.

26. J.H. Trumbull, *et al.*, *Col. Recs. Conn.*, II, 53–55.

27. *Collections*, Mass. Hist. Soc., Series 3, X, 58–62. It is likely that Winthrop even went to New Haven in person in an effort to appease the stubborn old Puritan. *Ibid.*, Series 4, VII, 558; also JWJ to FJW, May 3, 1666, ms. Win. Paps., 5.55, Mass. Hist. Soc.

28. J.H. Trumbull, *et al.*, *Col. Recs. Conn.*, II, 53–55, 67; *Collections*, Mass. Hist. Soc., Series 4, VII, 529–31; JWJ to John Davenport, Jr., June 3, 1667, ms. Win. Paps., 5.66, Mass. Hist. Soc.; JWJ to Nicolls, no date, *ibid.*, 5.175; July 15, 1667, *ibid.*, 5.68.

29. J.H. Trumbull *et al.*, *Col. Recs. Conn.*, II, 67–70, 84, 99–100, 109, 120, 124; *Collections*, Conn. Hist. Soc., XXI, 168–70; XXIV, 14–15, *nn*; Johnston, pp. 228–29.

30. *Collections*, Conn. Hist. Soc., XXIV, 14–15, *nn*; J.H. Trumbull, *et al.*, *Col. Recs. Conn.*, II, 120; JWJ to the Rev. John Whiting, January 21, 1670/1, copy in ms. Win. Paps., 5.89, Mass. Hist. Soc.; *Collections*, Mass. Hist. Soc., Series 4, VII, 568.

31. Andrews, II, 113–14; J.H. Trumbull, *et al.*, *Col. Recs. Conn.*, II, 29, 34–35, 61, 64, 67, 91, 110.

32. Estimates based upon "Lists of Families with Quantity of Grain in Possession of Each" (March, 1670), *Collections*, Conn. Hist. Soc., XXI, 190n. If accurate, these figures indicate a higher ratio of voters to population than in 1910.

33. "Acts," U.C., Pulsifer, ed., *Recs.* Plymouth Colony, X, 17; *Collections*, Mass. Hist. Soc., Series 3, III, 209–10; Shurtleff, ed., *Recs.* Mass. Bay, IV, 443; J.H. Trumbull, *et al.*, *Col. Recs. Conn.*, II, 121.

34. *Ibid.*, II, 132, 132n.

CHAPTER 22

Scientific Observer

1. JWJ to Oldenburg, October 20, 1663, copy in ms. Win. Paps., Mass. Hist. Soc.; *Collections*, Mass. Hist. Soc., Series 5, VIII, 90–91; *Proceedings*, Mass. Hist. Soc., XVI, 218–19; Morison, *Harvard College*, I, 354–55.

2. Frank Zabriskie (Wesleyan University) to author, February 16, 1961; John W. Streeter, "John Winthrop, Junior, and the Fifth Satellite of Jupiter," *Isis*, XXXIX, 159–63; *Collections*, Mass. Hist. Soc., Series 5, VIII, 93–95; JWJ to Benj. Worsley, October 27, 1670, copy in ms. Win. Paps., 5.94, Mass. Hist. Soc. There is no evidence of the original letter to Moray in the records of the Royal Society.

3. Mayall and Mayall, pp. 440, 445; Frank Zabriskie to author, see note 2; Streeter, "John Winthrop, Junior," *Isis*, XXXIX, 159–63. This star is denoted Piazzi 225 in Norton's atlas and elsewhere.

4. Chambers, I, 516–17; Oliver, p. 10; JWJ to Oldenburg, c. February 16, 1664/5, copy in ms. Win. Paps., 5.173, Mass. Hist. Soc.; JWJ to Nicolls, January 18, 1664/5, *ibid.*, 5.47; see also JWJ to Theodore Haak, c. July, 1668, copy, *ibid.*, 5.163.

5. Chambers, I, 516–17; JWJ to Nicolls, March 5, 1667/8, ms. Win. Paps., 5.65, Mass. Hist. Soc.; JWJ to Theodore Haak, c. July, 1668, copy, *ibid.*, 5.163.

6. Chambers, I, 516–517; *Collections*, Mass. Hist. Soc., Series 5, VIII, 388–90; Henry Oldenburg to JWJ, March 10, 1671/2, ms. Win. Paps., 16.40; JWJ to Fitz W., c. March 12, 1671/2, *ibid.*, 5.108; JWJ to Wait W., April 29, 1672, *ibid.*, 5.70; JWJ to Henry Olden-

burg, September 25, 1672, Letter Book W3, Royal Society Library. The date of the final letter is inaccurately transcribed as *1673;* it may have been delayed by the Dutch.

7. JWJ to Oldenburg, c. 1664/5, copy in ms. Win. Paps., 5.173, Mass. Hist. Soc.; JWJ to Oldenburg, November 12, 1668, Letter Book W3, No. 21, Royal Society Library; *Collections,* Mass. Hist. Soc., Series 3, X, 47–48; R. Grant, *History of Physical Astronomy,* p. 417; JWJ to Oldenburg, November 12, 1668, Letter Book W3, No. 21, Royal Society Library; see also draft of similar letter in JWJ's hand, ms. Win. Paps., 5.87, Mass. Hist. Soc. R.S. Wilkinson, "John Winthrop, Jr., and America's First Telescopes," *New England Quarterly,* XXXV (December, 1962), 520–23; JWJ to Oldenburg?, c. July, 1668, incomplete copy in ms. Win. Paps., 5.172, Mass. Hist. Soc.; *Proceedings,* Mass. Hist. Soc., Series 2, IV, 265–67; Samuel Eliot Morison, "Astronomy at Harvard," *New England Quarterly,* VII (1934), 19; JWJ to Wait W., April 29, 1672, ms. Win. Paps., 5.70, Mass. Hist. Soc.

8. JWJ to Gov. Bellingham, July 24, 1672, copy in ms. Win. Paps., Mass. Hist. Soc.; *Proceedings,* Mass. Hist. Soc., XIII, 235–36; Secy. Rawson to JWJ, October 8, 1672, ms. in Conn. Archives, Conn. State Library; Morison, *Harvard College,* I, 31–34.

9. *Collections,* Mass. Hist. Soc., Series 5, VIII, 140–43; JWJ to Moray, August 18, 1668, Letter Book W3, No. 20, Royal Society Library. (This letter was sealed with Winthrop's sealing ring.) Also JWJ to Oldenburg, November 12, 1668, *ibid.,* No. 21; draft in ms. Win. Paps., 5.87, Mass. Hist. Soc.

10. *Proceedings,* Mass. Hist. Soc., XVI, 229–30.

11. *Ibid.,* XVI, 239, 244, 245, 248, 251; ms. Win. Paps., 5.87, Mass. Hist. Soc., T.G. Wright, *Literary Culture,* pp. 110–11; Oldenburg to JWJ, March 26, 1670, copy in Royal Society Letter Book (copy) III, 388–90, Royal Society Library. In a letter of October 29, 1667, Theodore Haak suggested that Stuyvesant and Winthrop undertake cooperative reports. *Proceedings,* Mass. Hist. Soc., XVI, 230–31.

12. JWJ to Theodore Haak, c. 1668, copy in ms. Win. Paps., 5.163, Mass. Hist. Soc.

13. Oldenburg to JWJ, March 26, 1670, copy in Royal Society Letter Book (copy) III, 388–90, Royal Society Library; JWJ to Oldenburg, August 26, 1670, Letter Book W3, No. 23, Royal Society Library. (JWJ's *very* rough draft is in ms. Win. Paps., 8.92, Mass. Hist.

Soc.; see also JWJ to Oldenburg, c. 1671, copy, *ibid.*, 5.159. Unsharpened quills were a constant Winthrop minor vice.) JWJ to Oldenburg, October 4, 1669, Letter Book W3, No. 22, Royal Society Library.

14. JWJ to Oldenburg, September, 1671, copy in ms. Win. Paps., 5.159, Mass. Hist. Soc.; JWJ to Oldenburg, October 4, 1669, Letter Book W3, No. 22, Royal Society Library; also JWJ notes in ms. Win. Paps., 5.169, Mass. Hist. Soc.; JWJ to Oldenburg, October 4, 1669, Letter Book W3, No. 22, Royal Society Library; *Proceedings*, Mass. Hist. Soc., XXVI, 244–45; JWJ to Oldenburg, October 11 and 26, 1670, Letter Book W3, Nos. 25 and 26, Royal Society Library, also draft in ms. Win. Paps., 5.89, Mass. Hist. Soc.; Oldenburg to JWJ, April 11, 1671, Royal Society Letter Book (copy) IV, 265–67, Royal Society Library; *Proceedings*, Mass. Hist. Soc., XVI, 249–50; JWJ to Oldenburg, September, 1671, ms. Win. Paps., 5.100, Mass. Hist. Soc. An engraving of the "stellar fish" was published, with Winthrop's comments, in March, 1670/1, in the Royal Society *Transactions*, Vol. V, No. 1.

15. *Proceedings*, Mass. Hist. Soc., XVI, 247–48; *Collections*, Mass. Hist. Soc., Series 5, I, 403–8; JWJ to Oldenburg, August 26, 1670, Letter Book W3, No. 23, Royal Society Library; JWJ to Oldenburg, September, 1671. copy in ms. Win. Paps., 5.100, Mass. Hist. Soc.; JWJ to Boyle, September 27, 1670, copy, *ibid.*, 5.92.

16. JWJ to Wait W., April 30, 1673, *ibid.*, 5.106; JWJ to Oldenburg?, October 20, 1671, copy, *ibid.*, 5.100; JWJ to Lord Brereton, October 11, 1670, copy in Letter Book W3, No. 24, Royal Society Library, also *Collections*, Mass. Hist. Soc., Series 3, X, 124–26.

17. JWJ to Oldenburg, July 24, 1668, *ibid.*, Series 5, VIII, 121–25, and November 12, 1668, Letter Book W3, No. 21, Royal Society Library (an incomplete version is in *Collections*, Mass. Hist. Soc., Series 5, VIII, 129–37); JWJ to Nicolls, September 24, 1670, copy in ms. Win. Paps., 5.92, Mass. Hist. Soc.; JWJ to Oldenburg, c. February, 1664/5, copy, *ibid.*, 5.173, and July 25, 1668, *Collections*, Mass. Hist. Soc., Series 5, VIII, 121–25.

18. JWJ to Oldenburg, October 4, 1669, Letter Book W3, No. 22, Royal Society Library; *ibid.*, No. 22a; also c. July, 1668, copy in ms. Win. Paps., 5.172, Mass. Hist. Soc., and November 12, 1668, Letter Book W3, No. 21, Royal Society Library.

19. *Proceedings*, Mass. Hist. Soc., XVI, 245–46; JWJ to Moray,

October 11, 1670, draft in ms. Win. Paps., 5.94, Mass. Hist. Soc.; also August 18, 1668 (postscript August 26), Letter Book W3, No. 20a, Royal Society Library; JWJ to Benj. Worsley, October 27, 1670, copy in ms. Win. Paps., 5.94, Mass. Hist. Soc.

20. *Proceedings*, Mass. Hist. Soc., XVI, 239–42; JWJ to Worsley, October 27, 1670, copy in ms. Win. Paps., 5.94, Mass. Hist. Soc.

21. JWJ to Moray, August 18, 1668, Letter Book W3, No. 21, Royal Society Library; letters to Moray and Oldenburg, *ibid.*, Nos. 21, 22, and 22a; see also letter to Oldenburg in Royal Society Letter Book (copy), III, 388–90. References to Pell are in *Proceedings*, Mass. Hist. Soc., XVI, 245–47, 249–50, and in ms. Win. Paps., 5.92, 5.94, and 5.95. Colwell is mentioned in JWJ to Wait W., October, 1671, *ibid.*, 5.100.

22. Especially the retained drafts in the ms. Win. Paps., Mass. Hist. Soc., Boston, and the surviving material in the Royal Society Library, London.

23. JWJ to Wait W., March 22, 1670/1, August 9, 1671, October, 1671, August 6, 1672, and October 2, 1672, ms. Win. Paps., 5.74, 5.77, 5.90, 5.99, 5.100, Mass. Hist. Soc.; JWJ to ?, November 14, 1674, ms. in R.I. Hist. Soc., photostat in Conn. State Library. See also ms. Win. Paps., 18.60.

24. John Allyn to JWJ, August 28, 1671, *ibid.*, 10.20.

25. A sketch of Lederer is provided in Cumming, pp. viii–x, see also pp. 53–56, 58–59.

26. Correspondence, *ibid.*, pp. 60–67.

CHAPTER 23

Uncomfortable Old *Age*

1. Lovelace (c. 1621–75) is treated in *DAB*, XI, 436–37.

2. Stokes, IV, 267, also ms. Win. Paps., 16.17, Mass. Hist. Soc.; Lovelace and Nicolls to JWJ, March 20, 1667/8, *ibid.*, 16.21; JWJ to Nicolls, April 15, 1668, copy, *ibid.*, 5.80. Nicolls's popularity in New York is attested to in a letter from JWJ to Sir Robert Moray, August 18, 1668, Letter Book W3, No. 20, Royal Society Library.

3. JWJ to Nicolls, April 15?, 1668, ms. Win. Paps., 5.80, Mass.

Hist. Soc.; Nicolls to JWJ, June 16, July 1, and August 2, 1668, *ibid.*, 16.17, 18; JWJ to Moray, see note 2; Moray to JWJ, *Proceedings*, Mass. Hist. Soc., Series 1, XVI, 243.

4. Matthias Nicolls (1626–c.1688) is in *DAB*, XIII, 514–15. His personality and career can be further followed in *Calendar Council Minutes*, New York, pp. 7–58 *passim*, and *Collections*, Mass. Hist. Soc., Series 3, X, 19–115 *passim*. The *Encyclopedia Americana* (1951 ed.), XX, 329, gives his dates, c. 1630–December 22, 1687.

5. JWJ to Lovelace, November 19, 1669, copy in ms. Win. Paps., 5.88, Mass. Hist Soc.; JWJ to Robert Boyle, September 27, 1670, copy, *ibid.*, 5.92; *Collections*, Mass. Hist. Soc., Series 3, X, 80–82; JWJ to Alexander Bryan, December 28, 1670, copy in ms. Win. Paps., 5.96, Mass. Hist Soc.; JWJ to Wait W., February 6, 1670, *ibid.*, 5.89. For Alexander Bryan, see Savage, I, 281–82.

6. Examples of his routine correspondence with Lovelace are in ms. Win. Paps., 5.84 and 10.19, Mass. Hist. Soc. The 1671 visit to Plymouth is in Pulsifer, ed., *Recs.* Plymouth Colony, V, 78–80, also J.H. Trumbull, *et al.*, *Col. Recs. Conn.*, II, 162, 162*n*. For the New York–Boston post, see *Collections*, Mass. Hist. Soc., Series 5, IX, 83–86; JWJ to Wait W., February 6 and 16, 1672/3, ms. Win. Paps., 5.77; and Stokes, IV, 286–87.

7. JWJ to Wait W., April 7, 1672, ms. Win. Paps., 5.70, Mass. Hist. Soc., J.H. Trumbull, *et al.*, *Col. Recs. Conn.*, II, 180, 180*n*, 181–83, 559–61; JWJ to Lovelace, July 16, 1672, copy in ms. Win. Paps., 5.73; also JWJ memo, *ibid.*, 5.164; report of Conn. Assembly to "Lords of the Committee of Colonies," July 15, 1680, *Collections*, Mass. Hist. Soc., Series 1, IV, 220–22. Fitz was also a deputy from New London by October 1671. Jacobus, *Officials of Connecticut Colony*, p. 63.

8. J.H. Trumbull, *et al.*, *Col. Recs. Conn.*, II, 160, 182, 183, 185–86; JWJ to Elizabeth R.W., August 26 and September 11, 1672, ms. Win. Paps., 5.75, Mass. Hist. Soc.; "Acts," U.C., Pulsifer, ed., *Recs.* Plymouth Colony, X, 351.

9. Report of assembly, see note 7.

10. J.H. Trumbull, *et al.*, *Col. Recs. Conn.*, II, 133–34, 141–42, 153, 160, 190; *Collections*, Mass. Hist. Soc., Series 5, I, 420–21; Andrews, II, 138.

11. J.H. Trumbull, *et al.*, *Col. Recs. Conn.*, II, 164, 174, 201–3, 213, 558–59; Caulkins, pp. 48–50. It was not customary for marriages

to be performed by the *clergy* in early Puritan New England. Lyme was not yet constituted from Saybrook at the time of the incident.

12. J.H. Trumbull, *et al.*, *Col. Recs. Conn.*, II, 176, 184, 184*n*, 189; see also records of Court of Assistants, Conn. Archives, Conn. State Library.

13. J.H. Trumbull, *et al.*, *Col. Recs. Conn.*, II, 144, 154, 165; Van Dusen, p. 344; JWJ to Henry Bull, September 6, 1672, copy in ms. Win. Paps., 5.75, Mass. Hist. Soc.; JWJ to Wait W., May 12 and August 9, 1671, *ibid.*, 5.98, 99.

14. *Publications*, Narragansett Club (First Series) VI, 333–51; J.H. Trumbull, *et al.*, *Col. Recs. Conn.*, II, 156–57, 166–67, 174–75, 198, 231, 231*n*; and Bowen, pp. 37–38. For Rhode Island, see petition of October 26, 1670, ms. in P.R.O., C.O. 1:25, No. 82, petitions of Randall Holden and John Green, 1670, *ibid.*, No. 99, and W.L. Grant, *et al.*, *Acts P.C.* (*Colonial*), I, 785. See also *Collections*, Mass. Hist. Soc., Series 2, VII, 109–10; Bartlett, ed., *Col. Recs. R.I.*, II, 451, 477–78; *Proceedings*, Mass. Hist. Soc., Series 2, III, 258–59; "Acts," U.C., Pulsifer, ed., *Recs.* Plymouth Colony, X, 353; Andrews, II, 64.

15. *Collections*, Mass. Hist. Soc., Series 5, I, 102–3; VIII, 137; Dunn, p. 168; J.H. Trumbull, *et al.*, *Col. Recs. Conn.*, II, 145 and 153–54*n*; JWJ to Wait W., c. November 1670, ms. Win. Paps., 5.96, Mass. Hist. Soc. By way of comparison, Leete's salary as deputy governor was set in October, 1671, at £20 per year. J.H. Trumbull, *et al.*, *Col. Recs. Conn.*, II, 163.

16. *Ibid.*, II, 160–61, 161*n*, 174–75, 231, 231*n*, 525; *Collections*, Mass. Hist. Soc., Series 3, X, 82–84; Series 4, VII, 572–74; Series 5, IX, 81–82; Bowen, p. 38; Bartlett, ed., *Col. Recs. R.I.*, II, 517.

17. JWJ to Wait W., November 27, 1671, ms. Win. Paps., 5.102, Mass. Hist. Soc.; *Collections*, Mass. Hist. Soc., Series 5, VIII, 143.

18. *Ibid.*, Series 5, VIII, 144–46 386–94, 406; also ms. Win. Paps., 5.72, 74, Mass. Hist. Soc.

19. JWJ to Priscilla Reade, September 24, 1674, *Collections*, Mass. Hist. Soc., Series 5, VIII, 163–64; Series 6, III, 321; *New England Historical and Genealogical Register*, VIII, 328; JWJ to Elizabeth W. Newman, January 22, 1672/3, ms. Win. Paps., 5.77, Mass. Hist. Soc.

20. *Ibid.*; JWJ to Priscilla Reade, September 22, 1674, draft, *ibid.*, 5.133; *Collections*, Mass. Hist. Soc., Series 5, VIII, 146–47.

21. JWJ to Wait W., February 16, 1672/3, ms. Win. Paps., 5.77,

Mass. Hist. Soc.; JWJ to Fitz W., April 15, 1673, *ibid.*, 5.106; J.H. Trumbull, *et al.*, *Col. Recs. Conn.*, II, 191–92; JWJ to Wait W., June 2 and 10, 1673, ms. Win. Paps., 5.108, 109, Mass. Hist. Soc.

22. Deed of conveyance, May 25, 1674, attested true copy, *ibid.*, 5.134.

23. *Collections*, Mass. Hist. Soc., Series 3, X, 84–85; Series 6, III, 434–35; JWJ to Sir George Carteret, July 2, 1673, copy in ms. Win. Paps., 5.108, Mass. Hist. Soc.

24. *Collections*, Mass. Hist. Soc., Series 5, VIII, 150; 6, III, 434–35; Lovelace to JWJ, July 31, 1673, P.R.O., C.O. 389:5, 143.

25. *Ibid.*, 389.5, 143–50; *Calendar of State Paps., Colonial, Am. and W. Indies, 1669–1674*, pp. 520–22; *Collections*, Mass. Hist. Soc., Series 5, IX, 88–91; Series 6, III, 436–44; Stokes, IV, 288, 289. Matthias Nicolls escaped, but lost three of his children by shipwreck in Long Island Sound. JWJ to Wait W., November 10, 1673, ms. Win. Paps., Mass. Hist. Soc.

26. W.L. Grant, *et al.*, *Acts, P.C. (Colonial)*, I, 579–80.

27. *Collections*, Mass. Hist. Soc., Series 4, VII, 292–93; Series 5, VIII, 150–51; J.H. Trumbull, *et al.*, *Col. Recs. Conn.*, II, 203*n*, 203–8.

28. *Ibid.*, II, 206, 561; *Collections*, Mass. Hist. Soc., Series 3, X, 86–88; Series 5, IX, 91–92; O'Callaghan, *et al.*, *N.Y. Col. Docs.*, II, 583, 585.

29. J.H. Trumbull, *et al.*, *Col. Recs. Conn.*, II, 561–62; Stokes, IV, 290; Lamb, I, 261; "Acts," U.C., Pulsifer, ed., *Recs.* Plymouth Colony, X, 386–89.

30. JWJ to Leverett, August 27, 1673, copy in ms. Win. Paps., 5.111, Mass. Hist. Soc.; letters from Long Island towns, August 7, 15, and 29, 1673, mss. in "Winthrop Papers," Conn. State Library; Thos. Danforth, Wm. Stoughton, and Thos. Hinckley to JWJ, August 27–28, 1673, ms. copy inserted among "Acts," U.C., Pulsifer, ed., *Recs.* Plymouth Colony, X, 466, copy in Conn. Hist. Soc.

31. Shurtleff, ed., *Recs.* Mass. Bay, IV (Part II), 560–62; *Collections*, Mass. Hist. Soc., Series 5, VIII, 151–52; JWJ to John Pynchon, September 10, 1673, copy in ms. Win. Paps., 5.112, Mass. Hist. Soc.; JWJ to John Pynchon?, undated, copy, *ibid.*, 5.204.

32. O'Callaghan, *et al.*, *N.Y. Col. Docs.*, II, 620, 622, 626, 639–41, 642, 645, 647; Thompson, pp. 119 ff.

33. *Collections*, Mass. Hist. Soc., Series 6, III, 444–45; J.H. Trumbull, *et al., Col. Recs. Conn.*, II, 208–16 and *nn*, 563–65; *Collections*, Conn. Hist. Soc., XXIV, 16–17; JWJ to Wait W., October 20, 1673, ms. Win. Paps., 5.114, Mass. Hist. Soc. A few emergency levies from New Haven and Saybrook went to Long Island in October, but remained there for only a few days. JWJ to Wait W., November 10, 1673, *ibid.*, 5.116.

34. *Ibid.*, 5.159; *Collections*, Mass. Hist. Soc., Series 5, VIII, 158–60; O'Callaghan, *et al., N.Y. Col. Docs.*, II, 648, 652 654–58, 660–61.

35. Ms. address (October 30, 1673) and commission (November 13, 1673) in Conn. State Library; JWJ to Wait W., November 10, 1673, ms. Win. Paps., 5.116, Mass. Hist. Soc.; also draft of commission, *ibid.*, 5.165; *Collections*, Mass. Hist. Soc., Series 5, VIII, 272–73, 397; IX, 95–96, 96*n*; J.H. Trumbull, *et al., Col. Recs. Conn.*, II, 565; E. Palmes to JWJ, November 20, 1673, ms. Win. Paps., 16.58; Lamb, I, 259–60.

36. JWJ to Fitz W., November 14, 1673, ms. Win. Paps., 5.117, Mass. Hist. Soc.; JWJ to Wait W., December 16, 1673, and February 23, 1673/4, *ibid.*, 5.118, 5.104; JWJ to Willys and "the other Gentlemen of the Councell," copy, *ibid.*, 5.192; *Collections*, Mass. Hist. Soc., Series 3, X, 96–97.

37. J.H. Trumbull, *et al., Col. Recs. Conn.*, II, 566–67; *Collections*, Mass. Hist. Soc., Series 3, X, 91–94.

38. *Ibid.*, Series 3, X, 95, 97–101; Series 5, VIII, 274–77; JWJ to Fitz W., March 10, 1673/4, ms. Win. Paps., 5.105, Mass. Hist. Soc.; Shurtleff, ed., *Recs.*, Mass. Bay, IV (Part 2), 576–77; Thompson, pp. 119–22; JWJ to Leverett, May 1, 1674, copy in ms. Win. Paps., 5.125, Mass. Hist. Soc.; E. Palmes to Fitz W., April 12, 1674, *ibid.*, 16.62.

39. *Collections*, Mass. Hist. Soc., Series 3, X, 104–10; J.H. Trumbull, *et al., Col. Recs. Conn.*, II, 220–35 *passim*; O'Callaghan, *et al., N.Y. Col. Docs.*, II, 715–16, 726–27.

40. *Collections*, Mass. Hist. Soc., Series 3, X, 110–11; ms. Win. Paps., 5.121 and 157, Mass. Hist. Soc.; Cumming, pp. 52–53; JWJ to Fitz W., October 20 and November 2, 1674, ms. Win. Paps., 5.136, Mass. Hist. Soc.

41. Andros to JWJ, November 3, 1674, *ibid.*, 10.67, also Stokes,

IV, 303; JWJ to Fitz W., November 25 and December 1, 1674, ms. Win. Paps., 5.136, 137; *Collections*, Mass. Hist. Soc., Series 6, III, 446; JWJ to Wait W., January 25, 1674/5, ms. Win. Paps., 5.121; letter of welcome, JWJ to Andros, initial draft, *ibid.*, 5.124; JWJ to Fitz W., February 8, 1674/5, *ibid.*, 5.122; instructions to Fitz W. and Willys, *ibid.*, 5.197; JWJ to Andros, c. January 25, 1674/5, *ibid.*, 5.162; N. Sylvester to JWJ, May 3, 1675, *Proceedings*, Mass. Hist. Soc., Series 2, IV, 282–83. Fitz's disinclination to the mission was appeased by the inclusion in his party of John Hale of Glastonbury, Conn., a young man renowned for his love of standard pleasures. Fitz W. to JWJ, *Collections*, Mass. Hist. Soc., Series 5, VIII, 277–78; see also Jacobus and Waterman, *Hale, House and Related Families*, pp. 20–21.

CHAPTER 24

Conclusion in Crisis

1. JWJ to Wait W., August 30, 1674, ms. Win. Paps., 5.131, Mass. Hist. Soc.

2. JWJ to Harwood, January 13, 1674/5, copies, *ibid.*, 5.120, 129; JWJ to Priscilla and Samuel Reade, September 2 and 22, and October 15, 1674, copies, *ibid.*, 5.133, 134; JWJ to Fitz W., August 17, September 14 and 19, and October 29, 1674, *ibid.*, 5.130, 132, 135, 202; agreement with Wm. Parks, May 21, 1675, *ibid.*, 5.143; JWJ to Fitz W., October 19, 1674, *ibid.*, 5.135, and February 8 and March 3, 1674/5, *ibid.*, 5.122; JWJ to Wait W., March 22, 1674/5, *ibid.*, 5.124.

3. J.H. Trumbull, *et al.*, *Col. Recs. Conn.*, II, 250–52, 255–59; *Collections*, Mass. Hist. Soc., Series 5, I, 430–31; VIII, 168–69, 170, 171, also ms. Win. Paps., 5.146, Mass. Hist. Soc.; power of attorney to Richard Smith, Sr., of Smithfield, Long Island, copy, *ibid.*, 5.150.

4. P.R.O., C.O. 391:1, 1, 22, 44–45, 55, 69–70, 162–63, and *ibid.*, 324:4, 7–8, 9–10, 22–25, 31–39, copies in Manuscripts Division, Library of Congress, Washington, D.C.; Egerton Mss. 2395, fols. 522 and 573, British Museum.

5. Bowen, pp. 70–71; J.H. Trumbull, *et al.*, *Col. Recs. Conn.*, II, 569.

6. Andros is treated in both *DNB* and *DAB*. See also notes in *Collections*, Mass. Hist. Soc., Series 6, III, 453, and O'Callaghan, *et al.*, *N.Y. Col. Docs.*, II, 740–42.

7. *Collections*, Mass. Hist. Soc., Series 3, X, 116–17; Series 5, VIII, 161–66; *Proceedings*, Mass. Hist. Soc., Series 2, VII, 16–17; E. Palmes to JWJ, May 24, 1675, ms. Win. Paps., 16.25, Mass. Hist. Soc.; JWJ to Fitz W., August 1, 1674, copy, *ibid.*, 5.128; JWJ to Wait W., August 5, 1674, *ibid.*, 5.129; J.H. Trumbull, *et al.*, *Col. Recs. Conn.*, II, 569; O'Callaghan, *et al.*, *N.Y. Col. Docs.*, III, 230–31.

8. Winthrop's draft, ms. Win. Paps., 5.207, Mass. Hist. Soc.; J.H. Trumbull, *et al.*, *Col. Recs. Conn.*, II, 252, 570–71.

9. *Ibid.*, II, 250 ff., 571–73, 580*n*; *Collections*, Mass. Hist. Soc., Series 5, VIII, 166–67; Univ. of N.Y., *Calendar Council Minutes New York*, p. 22.

10. JWJ to Andros, June 9, 1675, ms. Win. Paps., 5.145, Mass. Hist. Soc.; Univ. of N.Y. *Calendar Council Minutes New York*, p. 22.

11. J.H. Trumbull, *et al.*, *Col. Recs. Conn.*, II, 573–74; Univ. of N.Y., *Calendar Council Minutes New York*, p. 22; *Collections*, Conn. Hist. Soc., C.H.S., XXI, 207–9.

12. Ellis and Morris, p. 56; Leach, p. 242. The latter is the most recent and satisfactory general study of the conflict.

13. Egerton Mss. 2395, fol. 522, British Museum; Ellis and Morris, pp. 116, 131–34.

14. The details are best presented in Leach, pp. 30–49.

15. *Collections*, Mass. Hist. Soc., Series 3, X, 118–19; Series 4, VI, 297–304.

16. *Ibid.*, Series 3, X, 118–19.

17. J.H. Trumbull, *et al.*, *Col. Recs. Conn.*, II, 331–32, 579; Ms. Winthrop Deeds, Commissions, &c., fol. 56, Mass. Hist. Soc.; JWJ to Fitz W., also JWJ resignation, July 1, 1675, ms. Win. Paps., 5.146, Mass. Hist. Soc.

18. J.H. Trumbull, *et al.*, *Col. Recs. Conn.*, II, 260–64, 332–35.

19. *Ibid.*, II, 578–79; Univ. of N.Y., *Calendar Council Minutes New York*, p. 22.

20. The Podunk is an inconsiderable tributary of the Connecticut River a short distance to the northeast of Hartford and was then the locale of inconsiderable groups of Indians. It possibly is the inspiration of the well-known generic name for an inconsiderable rural commuity.

21. J.H. Trumbull, *et. al., Col. Recs. Conn.,* II, 333; *Collections,* Conn. Hist. Soc., XXI, 209.

22. J.H. Trumbull, *et al., Col. Recs. Conn.,* II, 334–35, 578–80.

23. *Ibid.,* II, 334–35.

24. Dunn, pp. 183–84; J.H. Trumbull, *et al., Col. Recs. Conn.,* II, 580–81; O'Callaghan, *et al., N.Y. Col. Docs.,* III, 235.

25. J.H. Trumbull, *et al., Col. Recs. Conn.,* II, 263–64; *Collections,* Conn. Hist. Soc., XXI, 214–15.

26. *Ibid.,* XXI, 209–11, 217–18; J.H. Trumbull, *et al., Col. Recs. Conn.,* II, 263, 335n, 338n, 581n; *Collections,* Mass. Hist. Soc., Series 5, VIII, 279; Series 6, V, 3–4.

27. *Ibid.,* Series 5, VIII, 171–74; JWJ to Wait W., July 9, 1675, ms. Win. Paps., 5.147, Mass. Hist. Soc. (a printed version, *Collections,* Mass. Hist. Soc., Series 5, VIII, 170–71, erroneously cites the addressee as Fitz); JWJ to Wait W., July 19, 1675, *ibid.,* 5.149; J.H. Trumbull, *et al., Col. Recs. Conn.,* II, 338n; *Collections,* Conn. Hist. Soc., XXI, 216–17.

28. J.H. Trumbull, *et al., Col. Recs. Conn.,* II, 261, 344, 345 ff.; also *Collections,* Conn. Hist. Soc., XXI, 221–22; XXIV, 18.

29. J.H. Trumbull, *et al., Col. Recs. Conn.,* II, 345 ff.; *Collections,* Conn. Hist. Soc., XXI, 213–14, 221–22; XXIV, 18; Ellis and Morris, pp. 83, 99.

30. The "Rev. Simon Bradstreet's Journal," *New England Historical and Genealogical Register,* VIII (1854), 329; *Collections,* Mass. Hist. Soc., Series 4, VII, 576; J.H. Trumbull, *et al., Col. Recs. Conn.,* II, 351–52; JWJ to Andros, August 27, 1675, draft in ms. Win. Paps., 5.150, Mass. Hist. Soc.

31. Richard Smith to JWJ, September 1 and 17, 1675, *ibid.,* 18.10, 111; "Acts," U.C., Pulsifer, ed., *Recs.* Plymouth Colony, X, 362–65. For the presence of his daughters, see M. Nicolls to JWJ, no date, ms. Win. Paps., 15.154.

32. "Acts," U.C., Pulsifer, ed., *Recs.* Plymouth Colony, X, 362; Hutchinson, I, 55n; *Collections,* Mass. Hist. Soc., Series 5, I, 409n, 424n.

33. "Acts," U.C., Pulsifer, ed., *Recs.* Plymouth Colony, X, 362–65.

34. *Proceedings,* Mass. Hist. Soc., Series 2, XIII, 352; *Collections,* Mass. Hist. Soc., Series 4, VII, 577–78; "Acts," U.C., Pulsifer, ed., *Recs.* Plymouth Colony, X, 365 (ms. insert in Conn. Hist. Soc. copy),

456; *Collections,* Conn. Hist. Soc., XXI, 227–28; Ellis and Morris, p. 129; JWJ to Fitz W., October 4 and 5, 1675, ms. Win. Paps., 5.152, Mass. Hist. Soc.; JWJ to Richards, November 15, 1675, copy, *ibid.,* 5.154.

35. JWJ to Conn. council, draft (no date), *ibid.,* 5.199; *Collections,* Mass. Hist. Soc., Series 4, VI, 305–7; Series 5, IX, 99, 90*n*, 100; "Acts," U.C., Pulsifer, ed., *Recs.* Plymouth Colony, X, 360–61, 456–57; Leach, p. 118. Wait W. was accepted by the commissioners in Richards's place shortly after November 8. JWJ to Leete, November 15, 1675, copy in ms. Win. Paps., Mass. Hist. Soc.

36. "Acts," U.C., Pulsifer, ed., *Recs.* Plymouth Colony, X, 467, plus ms. copy of covering letter in Conn. Hist. Soc. copy; JWJ to Fitz W. and Leete, November 12, 1675, ms. Win. Paps., 5.153, 154, Mass. Hist. Soc.; JWJ to Fitz W., November 4, 1675, *ibid.,* 5.152; JWJ to Treat, December 18, 1675, *Collections,* Mass. Hist. Soc., Series 5, VIII, 174–75.

37. Leach, p. 143; Willys to JWJ, February 18, 1675/6, ms. Win. Paps., 20.53, Mass. Hist. Soc.

38. Samuel Sewell diary, *Collections,* Mass. Hist. Soc., Series 5, V, 11; JWJ to Robert Boyle, December, 1675, incomplete copy in ms. Win. Paps., 5.157. In this, his last surviving letter to Boyle, JWJ asked for help against the territorial claims of the Duke of York.

39. *Collections,* Mass. Hist. Soc., Series 5, VIII, 175–76; see also ms. Win. Paps., 5.139, Mass. Hist. Soc.

40. Thos. Danforth to Leete, January 6, 1675/6, ms. copy inserted in Pulsifer, ed., *Recs.* Plymouth Colony, Vol. X, copy in Conn. Hist. Soc.; commissioners to Josiah Winslow, January 11, 1675/6, copy in JWJ's hand, ms. Win. Paps., 5.138, Mass. Hist. Soc.; *Collections,* Mass. Hist. Soc., Series 5, VIII, 176–77. Connecticut's dissatisfaction is indicated, *ibid.,* Series 4, VII, 582–84; John Allyn to JWJ, January 12, 1675/6, ms. Win. Paps., 10.30; Allyn to commissioners, February 16, 1675/6, *ibid.,* 10.31; Conn. council to JWJ, February 18, 1675/6; *Proceedings,* Mass. Hist. Soc., XIII, 234–35. Winthrop's moderation is evident in JWJ to Fitz W., March 21, 1675–6, ms. Win. Paps., 5.141, and Samuel Willys to Fitz W., April 23, 1676, *ibid.,* 20.54.

41. JWJ to John Harwood, December 27, 1675, copy, *ibid.,* 5.156; JWJ to Samuel Reade, copy, *ibid.;* JWJ to Samuel Reade, March 14, 1675/6, copy, *ibid.,* 5.141. Reade was the son of Priscilla Reade; he was

not really Winthrop's cousin, but a nephew by marriage. The Harwood liabilities were settled, at a discount, by Fitz and Wait in September, 1677. Ms. Winthrop Deeds, Commissions, &c., fol. 54, Mass. Hist. Soc.

42. "Diary of Increase Mather," *Proceedings*, Mass. Hist. Soc., Series 2, XIII, 362–63; *Collections*, Mass. Hist. Soc., Series 5, VIII, 404–5; U.C. commissioners to Leete and the Connecticut council, April 5, 1676, ms. copy inserted in Pulsifer, ed., *Recs.* Plymouth Colony, X, blank page 468, copy in Conn. Hist. Soc. Winthrop's will would prove an unpleasant bone of contention for decades.

43. U.C. commissioners to Leete and the Conn. council, April 5, 1676, see note 42; J.H. Trumbull, *et al.*, *Col. Recs. Conn.*, II, 432–33, 452–53; Morison, *Intellectual Life*, p. 244; Samuel Sewell diary, quoted in *Proceedings*, American Antiquarian Society, new series, VII, 383*n*; "Diary of Increase Mather," *Proceedings*, Mass. Hist. Soc., Series 2, XIII, 363; Bridgman, p. 309.

44. Harold S. Jantz, "The First Century of New England Verse," *Proceedings*, American Antiquarian Society, new series, LIII, 403, 407, 445, 482.

45. Mather, I, 159; L.B. Wright, *Cultural Life*, pp. 152, 222; Walter R. Steiner, M.D., "Governor John Winthrop, Jr., of Connecticut as a Physician," *The Connecticut Magazine*, XI (1907), 27; Waters, *Sketch*, p. 62; Palfrey, III, 233–38; Morison, *Builders*, pp. 269, 288; T.G. Wright, *Literary Culture*, p. 152.

46. Ms. Win. Paps., 16.40, Mass. Hist. Soc.

Bibliography

PRESENTED here is no more than a classified list of the sources and works which appear in the several citations accompanying each chapter. (The classification, as is inevitable with such things, is quite arbitrary.) Appropriate comments will be found among the citations, but no bibliographic critique is attempted here. It will be noted that, thanks to the labors of numerous individuals and organizations over the years, many of the sources relative to John Winthrop, Jr., and his times are available in print. Only one who actually has delved in this particular garden can possibly understand what this means in terms of convenience.

MANUSCRIPT SOURCES

Additional Manuscripts, British Museum.
Clarendon Manuscripts, Bodleian Library.
Connecticut Archives, Connecticut State Library.
Egerton Manuscripts, British Museum.
Manuscript Documents in Public Record Office, London, including those of Privy Council (P.C.), and Colonial Office (C.O.). Also Chancery (C.) and Close Rolls.
Ms. Letter Books of the Royal Society, Royal Society Library.
Manuscript Notes Relative to New York, New-York Historical Society.
Ms. Parish Register, St. Katherine's Church, Wickford, Essex.
Manuscript Parish Register, St. Mary's Church, Great Stambridge, Essex.
Ms. Register Book of the Royal Society (Copy), Royal Society Library.

Ms. Winthrop Deeds, &c., Massachusetts Historical Society.
Manuscript Winthrop Papers, Massachusetts Historical Society.
Rawlinson Manuscripts, Bodleian Library.

PRINTED SOURCES

Arnold, James N., ed. *The Records of the Proprietors of the Narragansett, Otherwise Called the Fones Record.* Vol. I of *Rhode Island Colonial Gleanings.* Providence, R.I., 1894.

Bannerman, A.M. Bruce, ed. *The Register of St. Matthew, Friday Street, London, 1583–1812 and the United Parishes of St. Matthew and St. Peter Cheap, Marriages 1754–1812.* Vol. LXIII of *Harleian Society Registers.* London, 1933.

Bartlett, J.R., ed. *Records of the Colony of Rhode Island and Providence Plantations in New England.* 7 vols. Providence, R.I., 1856–62.

Calendar of State Papers, Colonial Series, America and West Indies. Great Britain.

Collections of the Connecticut Historical Society.

Collections of the Massachusetts Historical Society.

Collections of the New-York Historical Society.

Collections of the Rhode Island Historical Society.

The Connecticut Society of the Order of the Founders and Patriots of America. *Vital Records of New Haven, 1649–1850.* 2 vols., Hartford, Conn., 1917.

de Beer, E.S., ed. *Diary of John Evelyn.* 6 vols., Oxford, 1955.

Dexter, Franklin Bowditch, ed. *New Haven Town Records, 1662–1684.* Vols. I and II of Ancient Town Records, published by New Haven Colony Historical Society. New Haven, Conn., 1919.

Diary of Samuel Pepys. No special edition cited; indications are given by date.

The Essex Institute. *Vital Records of Wenham, Massachusetts, to the End of the Year 1849.* Salem, Mass., 1904.

Grant, W.L., *et al.*, eds. *Acts of the Privy Council of England, Colonial Series.* 6 vols. Hereford and London, 1908–12.

Jensen, Merrill, ed. *English Historical Documents, American Colonial Documents to 1776.* New York, 1955.

Bibliography

Notes and Records of the Royal Society of London.

O'Callaghan, E.B., ed. *Calendar of Historical Manuscripts in the Office of the Secretary of State, Albany.* 2 vols., Albany, N.Y., 1865–66.

O'Callaghan, E.B., *et al.*, eds. *Documents Relative to the Colonial History of New York.* 13 vols., Albany, N.Y., 1856–81.

Pulsifer, David, ed. *Records of the Colony of New Plymouth.* 12 vols., Boston, 1855–61.

Records and Files of the Quarterly Courts of Essex County, Massachusetts. 8 vols., Salem, Mass., 1911–21.

Records and Papers of the New London County Historical Society. New London, Conn.

Records of the Town of Brookhaven [1657–1798]. 3 vols., New York, 1930–32.

A Report of the Record Commissioners Containing Boston Births, Baptisms, Marriages, and Deaths, 1630–1699. Boston, 1883.

Shurtleff, Nathaniel B., M.D., ed. *Records of the Governor and Company of the Massachusetts Bay in New England.* 5 vols., Boston, 1854.

Trumbull, J. Hammond, *et al.*, eds. *The Public Records of the Colony of Connecticut.* 15 vols., Hartford, Conn., 1850–90.

University of the State of New York. *Calendar of Council Minutes, 1668–1783.* Bulletin 58, New York State Library, March, 1902, History 6. Albany, N.Y., 1902.

Winthrop, John. *History of New England (Journal).* James Kendall Hosmer, ed. 2 vols., New York, 1908.

Winthrop Papers, 1498–1649. Allyn B. Forbes, ed. 5 vols., Boston, 1929–47.

SECONDARY WORKS

Abbott, Wilbur Cortez. *The Writings and Speeches of Oliver Cromwell.* 2 vols., Cambridge, Mass., 1939.

Acton, Lord, *et al.*, eds. *The Cambridge Modern History.* 8 vols., New York, 1902–11.

Allen, Myron O., M.D. *The History of Wenham, Civil and Ecclesiastical, From Its Settlement in 1639 to 1860.* Boston, 1860.

Ambix (the journal of the Society for the Study of Alchemy and Early Chemistry).

The American Historical Review.

American Literature.

Andrews, Charles M. *The Colonial Period of American History*. 4 vols., New Haven, Conn., 1934–38.

Bailyn, Bernard. *The New England Merchants in the Seventeenth Century*. Cambridge, Mass., 1955.

Banks, Charles Edward. *The Planters of the Commonwealth, 1620–1640: A Study of the Emigrants and Emigration in Colonial Times*. Boston, 1930.

Bates, Albert Carlos. *The Charter of Connecticut, a Study*. Hartford, Conn., 1932.

Battis, Emery. *Saints and Sectaries: Anne Hutchinson and the Antinomian Controversy in the Massachusetts Bay Colony*. Chapel Hill, N.C., 1962.

Bell, Walter George. *Fleet Street in Seven Centuries*. London, 1912.

Bell, Whitfield J., Jr. *Early American Science, Needs and Opportunities for Study*. Williamsburg, Va., 1955.

Bellot, Hugh H.L. *The Inner and Middle Temple: Legal, Literary, and Historic Associations*. London and New York, 1902.

Benton, Charles E. *Ezra Reed and Esther Edgerton, Their Life and Ancestry*. Poughkeepsie, N.Y., 1912.

Bernhard, Hubert J., Dorothy A. Bennett, and Hugh S. Rice. *New Handbook of the Heavens*. New York, 1954.

Bowen, Clarence Winthrop. *The Boundary Disputes of Connecticut*. Boston, 1882.

Boynton, John Farnam, and Caroline Harriman Boynton. *The Boynton Family*. Privately printed, 1897.

Bradford, William. *History of Plymouth Plantation*. Wm. T. Davis, ed. New York, 1908.

Bridgman, Thomas. *Memorials of the Dead in Boston*. . . . Boston, 1853.

Bryant, Arthur. *The England of Charles II*. London and New York, 1935.

Burke, Sir Bernard, and P. Ashworth. *A Genealogical and Heraldic History of the Peerage and Baronetage*. London and New York, 1913.

Burpee, Charles W. *History of Hartford County, Connecticut, 1633–1928*. 3 vols., Chicago, Hartford, Conn., and Boston, 1928.

Butler, H.B., C.R.L. Fletcher, and Emery Walker. *Historical Portraits, 1600–1700.* Oxford, 1911.

Calder, Isabel MacBeath. *The New Haven Colony.* New Haven, Conn., 1934.

Carritt, E.F. *A Calendar of British Taste from 1600 to 1800.* London, c. 1948.

Case, Lafayette Wallace, M.D., comp. *The Hollister Family in America.* Chicago, 1886.

Caulkins, Frances Manwaring. *History of New London, Connecticut.* New London, Conn., 1852.

Chambers, George F. *A Handbook of Descriptive and Practical Astronomy.* 4th ed. 3 vols., Oxford, 1889–90.

Chitwood, O.P. *A History of Colonial America.* 2d ed. New York, 1948.

Clowes, William Laird, *et. al. The Royal Navy, A History from the Earliest Times to the Present.* 5 vols., Boston and London, 1898.

The Connecticut Magazine.

C(okayne), G.E., ed. *Complete Baronetage.* 5 vols. Exeter, 1900–6.

Cokayne, G.E., *et al. The Complete Peerage of England, Scotland, Ireland, Great Britain, and the United Kingdom, Extant, Extinct, or Dormant.* 13 vols. London, 1910–59.

Cooley, La Verne C. *A Short Biography of the Rev. John Cotton of Boston and a Cotton Genealogy of His Descendants.* Batavia, N.Y., 1945.

Cornell, Thomas C. *Captain Thomas Willett.* . . . Poughkeepsie, N.Y., 1890.

Cumming, William P. *The Discoveries of John Lederer, with Unpublished Letters by and about Lederer to Governor John Winthrop, Jr., and an Essay on the Indians of Lederer's Discoveries by Douglas L. Rights and William P. Cumming.* Charlottesville, Va., 1958.

Dale, T.C., ed. *The Inhabitants of London in 1638.* 2 vols., London, 1931.

Dictionary of American Biography (DAB).

Dictionary of National Biography (DNB).

Dow, George Francis. *Everyday Life in the Massachusetts Bay Colony.* Boston, 1935.

Downing, W.C., and R. Wilberforce. *Genealogy of the Downing Family and Immediate Collateral Relations: with Biographical and Historical References and Notes, 1509–1901.* Philadelphia, 1901.

Dunn, Richard S. *Puritans and Yankees, The Winthrop Dynasty of New England, 1630–1717.* Princeton, N.J., 1962.

Ellis, George W., and John E. Morris. *King Philip's War.* New York, 1906.

The Essex Antiquarian.

Felt, Joseph B. *History of Ipswich, Essex and Hamilton.* Cambridge, Mass., 1834.

Ferguson, Henry L. *Fishers Island, N.Y., 1614–1925.* New York, privately printed, 1925.

Fiske, John. *The Beginning of New England, or the Puritan Theocracy in Its Relations to Civil and Religious Liberty.* Tercentenary ed. Boston and New York, 1930.

Gardiner, Samuel R. *History of England from the Accession of James I to the Outbreak of the Civil War, 1603–1642.* 10 vols., London, 1884.

Goodwin, George, and John Britton. *The Churches of London, a History and Description of the Ecclesiastical Edifices of the Metropolis.* 2 vols., London, 1839.

Grant, Robert. *History of Physical Astronomy from the Earliest Ages to the Middle of the Nineteenth Century.* London, 1852.

Hart, Albert Bushnell, ed. *The Commonwealth History of Massachusetts.* 5 vols., New York, 1927–28.

Hartley, E.N. *Ironworks on the Saugus: The Lynn and Braintree Ventures of the Company of Undertakers of the Ironworks in New England.* Norman, Okla., 1957.

Hartley, Sir Harold, F.R.S., ed. *The Royal Society: Its Origins and Founders.* London, 1960.

Haydn, Joseph, and Horace Ockerby, comps. *The Book of Dignities.* 3d ed. London, 1894.

Haynes, Williams. *American Chemical Industry, a History.* 6 vols., New York, 1945–54.

Hervey, S.H.A. *Biographical List of Boys Educated at King Edward VI Free Grammar School, Bury St. Edmunds, from 1550–1900.* Bury St. Edmunds, Suffolk, 1908.

Historical Catalogue of the First Church in Hartford, 1633–1885. Hartford, Conn., 1885.

Historical Magazine of the Protestant Episcopal Church.

History Today.

Bibliography

Hosmer, James K. *The Life of Sir Henry Vane, Governor of Massachusetts Bay and Leader of the Long Parliament.* Boston and New York, 1888.

Hutchinson, Thomas. *The History of the Colony and Province of Massachusetts Bay.* Lawrence Shaw Mayo, ed. 3 vols., Cambridge, Mass., 1936.

Isis (Quarterly Organ of the History of Science Society).

Jacobus, Donald Lines. *List of Officials, Civil, Military and Ecclesiastical, of Connecticut Colony from March 1636 Through 11 October 1677, and of New Haven Colony Throughout Its Separate Existence.* New Haven, Conn., 1935.

Jacobus, Donald Lines, and Edgar Francis Waterman. *Hale, House and Related Families, mainly of the Connecticut River Valley.* Hartford, Conn., 1952.

Jenkinson, Wilberforce. *London Churches before the Great Fire.* London, 1917.

Johnston, Alexander. *Connecticut, A Study of a Commonwealth-Democracy.* Boston and New York, 1887.

Jones, Rufus M., et al. *The Quakers in the American Colonies.* London, 1911.

Kellaway, William. *The New England Company, 1649–1776, Missionary Society to the American Indians.* London, 1961.

Kent, William, ed. *An Encyclopedia of London.* London, 1937.

Lamb, Martha J. *History of the City of New York, its Origin, Rise and Progress.* 2 vols., New York, 1877–80.

Leach, Douglas Edward. *Flintlock and Tomahawk, New England in King Philip's War.* New York, 1958.

Leder, Lawrence H. *Robert Livingston, 1654–1728, and the Politics of New York.* Chapel Hill, N.C., 1961.

London County Council. *No. 17 Fleet Street.* London, 1951.

Love, William DeLoss. *Colonial History of Hartford.* Hartford, Conn., 1935.

Mather, Cotton. *Magnalia Christi Americana, or the Ecclesiastical History of New England.* Thomas Robbins, ed. 2 vols., Hartford, Conn., 1855.

Mathews, Lois Kimball. *The Expansion of New England: The Spread of New England Settlement and Institutions to the Mississippi River, 1620–1865.* New York, 1962.

Maxwell, Constantia. *A History of Trinity College, Dublin, 1591–1892.* Dublin, 1946.

Mayall, R. Newton, and Margaret W. Mayall. *Olcott's Field Book of the Skies.* 4th ed. New York, 1954.

Mayo, Lawrence Shaw. *The Winthrop Family in America.* Boston, 1948.

Metcalfe, Walter C. *A Book of Knights.* . . . London, 1885.

—— ed. *The Visitations of Essex.* . . . 2 vols., London, 1878–79.

Miller, Perry. *Orthodoxy in Massachusetts.* 2d ed. Boston, 1959.

Morgan, Edmund S. *The Puritan Dilemma: The Story of John Winthrop.* Boston and Toronto, 1958.

Morison, Samuel Eliot. *Builders of the Bay Colony.* London, 1930.

—— *Harvard College in the Seventeenth Century.* 2 vols., Cambridge, Mass., 1936.

—— *The Intellectual Life of Colonial New England.* Great Seal ed. Ithaca, N.Y., 1960.

Mowrer, Lilian T. *The Indomitable John Scott: Citizen of Long Island, 1632–1704.* New York, 1960.

Muskett, Joseph James, ed. *Evidences of the Winthrops of Groton, Co. Suffolk, England and of Families in and near that County with whom they Intermarried.* Boston, 1894–96.

The New England Historical and Genealogical Register.

The New England Quarterly.

Nicholas, Donald. *Mr. Secretary Nicholas (1593–1669), His Life and Letters.* London, 1955.

Noble, John, and J.F. Cronin, supervisors. *Records of the Court of Assistants of the Colony of the Massachusetts Bay, 1630–1692.* 3 vols., Boston, 1901–28.

Notestein, Wallace. *The English People on the Eve of Colonization, 1603–1630.* New York, 1954.

O'Callaghan, E.B., M.D. *Documentary History of the State of New York.* 4 vols., Albany, N.Y., 1850–51.

—— *History of New Netherland; or, New York under the Dutch.* 2 vols., New York, 1848.

Oliver, H.J. *Sir Robert Howard.* Durham, N.C., 1963.

Olivier, Charles P. *Comets.* Baltimore, Md., 1930.

Oppenheim, M. *A History of the Administration of the Royal Navy and of Merchant Shipping in Relation to the Navy.* Reprint ed. Ann Arbor, Mich., 1961.

Oppolzer, Theodor Ritter von. *Canon der Finsternisse.* Vienna, 1887.

Osgood, Herbert L. *The American Colonies in the Seventeenth Century.* 3 vols., New York, 1904–7.

Page, William, ed. *The Victoria History of the County of Suffolk,* 2 vols., London, 1907.

Palfrey, John Gorham. *History of New England.* 3 vols., Boston, 1858–64.

Palmer, Henry Robinson, and Henry Robinson Palmer, Jr. *Stonington by the Sea.* Republished ed. Stonington, Conn., 1957.

Paul, Sir James Balfour, ed. *The Scots Peerage.* 9 vols., Edinburgh, 1904–14.

Paullin, Charles O. *Atlas of the Historical Geography of the United States.* John K. Wright, ed. Washington, D.C., and New York, 1932.

Perry, Charles Edward, ed. *Founders and Leaders of Connecticut, 1633–1783.* Boston and New York, 1934.

Petersson, R.T. *Sir Kenelm Digby, The Ornament of England, 1603–1665.* Cambridge, Mass., 1956.

Pevsner, Nikolaus. *The Buildings of England; Essex.* London, 1954.

Philosophical Transactions (Royal Society).

Pierce, Frederick Clifton. *Forbes and Forbush Genealogy.* Published for the author, 1892.

Prendergast, John. *The Cromwellian Settlement of Ireland.* Dublin, 1875.

Proceedings of the American Antiquarian Society.

Proceedings of the Massachusetts Historical Society. (In many citations, the differentiation by *series*—twenty volumes in each—has not been followed but by simple volume designation in numerical order, which is begun in the third series, Vol. I of which is Vol. XLI.)

Publications of the Colonial Society of Massachusetts.

Publications of the Narragansett Club.

Richman, Irving Berdine. *Rhode Island, Its Making and Its Meaning.* New York and London, 1908.

Rose, the Reverend Hugh James. *A New General Biographical Dictionary.* 12 vols., London, 1857.

Rose-Troup, Frances. *The Massachusetts Bay Company and its Predecessors.* New York, 1930.

Rutland, Robert Allen. *The Birth of the Bill of Rights, 1776–1791.* Chapel Hill, N.C., 1955.

Savage, James. *A Genealogical Dictionary of the First Settlers of New England.* 4 vols., Boston, 1861.

Shaw, William A. *The Knights of England.* 2 vols., London, 1906.

Shryock, Richardson Harrison. *Medicine and Society in America, 1600–1860.* New York, 1960.

Sibley, John Langdon, *et al. Biographical Sketches of Graduates of Harvard University in Cambridge, Massachusetts.* 10 vols., Cambridge, Mass., 1873–1958.

Sprague, William B. *Annals of the American Pulpit.* 9 vols., New York, 1857–60.

Steiner, Bernard Christian. *A History of the Plantation of Menunkatuck, and of the Original Town of Guilford, Connecticut, Comprising the Present Towns of Guilford and Madison.* Baltimore, Md., 1897.

Stiles, Henry R. *The History and Genealogies of Ancient Windsor, Connecticut; including East Windsor, South Windsor, Bloomfield, Windsor Locks, and Ellington, 1635–1891.* 2 vols., Hartford, Conn., 1892.

——*The History of Ancient Wethersfield, Connecticut. . . .* 2 vols., New York, 1904.

Stokes, Isaac Newton Phelps. *The Iconography of Manhattan Island, 1498–1909.* 6 vols., New York, 1915–28.

Stow, John. *A Survey of London.* Charles L. Kingsford, ed. 2 vols., London, 1908.

Taylor, John M. *Roger Ludlow, The Colonial Lawmaker.* New York and London, 1900.

Taylor, W.B.S. *History of the University of Dublin, its Origin, Progress, and Present Condition, with Biographical Notices of Many Eminent Men Educated Therein.* London, 1945.

Thompson, Benjamin F. *History of Long Island; containing an Account of the Discovery and Settlement; with other important and interesting Matters to the Present Time.* New York, 1839.

Transactions of the American Antiquarian Society.

Trevelyan, George Macaulay. *England Under the Stuarts.* 1st ed. London, 1904.

Trumbull, Benjamin, D.D. *A Complete History of Connecticut, Civil and Ecclesiastical, from the Emigration of its First Planters, from England, in the Year 1630, to the Year 1764; and to the Close of the Indian Wars.* 1st ed. New Haven, Conn., 1818; 2d ed. New

London, Conn., 1898. (Both are 2 vols.; 1898 edition is cited here unless otherwise noted.)

Trumbull, J. Hammond, ed. *Memorial History of Hartford County.* 2 vols., Boston, 1886.

Van Dusen, Albert. *Connecticut.* New York, 1961.

Waters, Thomas Franklin. *A Sketch of the Life of John Winthrop the Younger, Founder of Ipswich, Massachusetts.* Ipswich, Mass., 1900.

—— *Ipswich in the Massachusetts Bay Colony.* Ipswich, Mass., 1905.

Watson, Edward William. *The Church of England.* 2d ed. London and New York, 1944.

Wedgwood, C.V. *The King's War, 1641–1647.* Vol. II of *The Great Rebellion.* London, 1958.

Weeden, William B. *Economic and Social History of New England, 1620–1789.* 2 vols., Boston and New York, 1890.

Weis, Frederick Lewis. *The Colonial Clergy and the Colonial Churches of New England.* Lancaster, Mass., 1936.

Welles, Lemuel A. *The History of the Regicides in New England.* New York, 1927,

Wertenbaker, Thomas Jefferson. *The Puritan Oligarchy.* New York, 1947.

Wheatley, Henry B. *London Past and Present, Its History, Associations, and Traditions.* 3 vols., London, 1891.

Whitehill, Walter Muir. *Boston, A Topographical History.* Cambridge, Mass., 1959.

William and Mary Quarterly.

Williamson, Hugh Ross. *George Villiers, First Duke of Buckingham, Study for a Biography.* London, 1940.

Willson, D. Harris. *King James VI and I.* New York, 1956.

Winthrop, Robert C. *Life and Letters of John Winthrop, Governor of the Massachusetts-Bay Company at their Emigration to New England, 1630.* 2 vols., Boston, 1869.

Winthrop Collection, New York Society Library.

Wright, Louis B. *The Cultural Life of the American Colonies, 1607–1763.* New York, 1957.

Wright, Thomas Goddard. *Literary Culture in Early New England, 1620–1730.* New Haven, Conn., 1920.

Index

Index

"Grammar school," 11–13
Graphite, 124–25
Gravesend, L.I., 160, 268, 274
Great Stambridge (Essex), 2–3, 9, 34, 357
Great Swamp Fight, 353
Green, Samuel, 324
Greenwich, Conn., 141
Gresham College, see Royal Society
Greville, Robert, see Brooke, second **Baron**
Griswold, Matthew, 166
Groton Manor, 3–4, 10, 357, 367; life, 12; sale, 51–52
Guilford, Conn., 141, 160
Gurdon, Brampton, 52, 56, 362
Gurdon, Robert, 24, 362

Haak, Theodore, 314, 422
Hadley, Mass., 181, 189
Hale, John, 429
"Half-Way Covenant," 165, 189, 302
Hallett, William, 158
Halley's comet, 311
Hamburg, 114
Hamilton, second Marquis of, 288
Hamilton, third Duke and Duchess of, 288–89
Hampden, John, 86
Harlakenden, Roger, 107
Harmonia Mundi, de (Georgius), 102
Harris, William, 326
Harrison, Katherine, 306
Hartford, Conn., 97, 139; described, 161; Winthrop's residence, 179–80; religious controversy, 180–81, 189, 302–3, 394; compared to New York, 291; population (*1670*), 305
Hartford, Treaty of, 164, 166, 264, 266, 390
Hartlib, Samuel, 118, 192–93, 213–15, 217, 379
Harvard College, 103, 116, 153; Winthrop's sons, 172; Winthrop's gifts, 233, 311; Indians, 307–8
Harwood, John, 240, 338, 354, 433

Haynes, John, 161–63; Hartford property, 179–80
Hempstead, L.I., 259, 268
Hervey, William, 29
Hesilrige, Sir Arthur, 87
Hewes, Joshua, 256
Hibbins, William, 111, 113
Higginson, Mrs. John, 174
Hilles, Thomasine, 6
Hilton, William, 70–71
Hinckley, Thomas, 351
Holland, Cornelius, 117
Hollister, John, 189
Hooke, the Rev. William, 237
Hopkins, Edward, 88, 149, 151, 161, 163, 213, 237
Hopkins, Mrs. Edward, 149
"House of Hope," 92
Housing, construction, 58–59, 316
Howell, John, 281–82
Howes, Edward, 27, 56, 60, 70; quoted, 65
Howes, Henry, 87
Hoyle, Joshua, 21, 79, 362
Hudson, William, 195, 257, 286
Hudson River, 291
Hudson Valley, 280
Humphrey, John, 49, 56, 107
Huntington, L.I., 333
Hurricanes, 138–39, 350
Hutchinson, Anne, 100, 105–6, 384
Hutchinson, Edward, 122, 196, 239, 256–57, 300, 398

Île de Ré, 31–32
Incest, 325
Indians: trade, 71, 96; Winthrop's attitudes, 95, 139, 321–22, 349; internecine warfare, 97, 134–36, 158–59, 196; hostilities, 97–99, 144–47, 166, 196–97, 343–57; land transactions, 125, 196–98, 240, 287; displacement, 137–38; sales of firearms, 158; missionary work, 228, 233–34, 247; intertribal agreements, 292, 294–95, 321–22; Harvard College, 307–8;

Winthrop, Anna, 7, 11

Winthrop, Anne, 56, 58

Winthrop, Anne (daughter), 329, 351, 402

Winthrop, Anne Brown, 40

Winthrop, Deane, 88, 143, 368, 385

Winthrop, Elizabeth ("Betty"), 100, 138, 180; marriage, 187–88

Winthrop, Elizabeth Fones, 12, 25, 40, 46, 56, 157–58, 363

Winthrop, Elizabeth Reade, 88, 94, 99, 373; marriage, 83–84; at Ipswich, 100–1; at Ten Hills, 112, 119, 132; to Fishers Island, 138; preference for New Haven, 179, illnesses, 182, 318, 328; Betty's marriage, 187; Lucy's marriage, 216; death, 329

Winthrop, Fitz-John, 138, 274, 276, 281; schooling, 171–72; in England, 180, 187, 198, 216, 219, 394; Betty's marriage, 187–88; transfer of Narragansett holdings, 241; returns to New England, 244; at Fort Albany, 293; incursion into Rhode Island, 301; commands New London militia, 323; engages Dutch on Long Island, 334–36; in New York, 337, 429; proposed marriage, 338; regard for Andros, 340; illness, 346; birthplace, 376; settlement of Harwood debt, **433**

Winthrop, Forth, 26, 51, 359

Winthrop, Henry, 7, 40, 48, 51, 364–65

Winthrop, John, Jr.: youth and education, 1–2, 12–15, 18–27, 362; birth, 7; landholdings, 9, 34, 71–72, 119, 132, 151, 168, 194, 330, 365; appearance, 15; character and personality, 15, 22, 68–69, 98–99, 124, 157–59, 232, 354; attitude toward war, 32–33, 113, 167–68, 193, 297–298; agent for Bay Colony, 45–51, 78–81, 111–13, 118–19; library, 55, 60, 88, 93, 102, 155, 157, 377, 387; Bay Court of Assistants, 62 ff.; political education, 64–66, 72, 85, 107–8;

governor of Warwick domain, 86–87, 92–99; financial difficulties, 159, 194, 224–25, 227–28, 240–41, 298, 338, 354; governor of Connecticut, 177 ff.; advice to Fitz-John, quoted, 171, 187; obtains new Connecticut charter, 204 ff.; advice to daughters, quoted, 216; death, 354–55; handwriting, 391–92

Winthrop, John, Sr.: birth, 4; "Confirmation of Arms," 4–5; education, 5; marriage to Mary Forth, 5–7; "experienca," 8, 9, 11, 12, 357; Puritanism, 8–9, 10; landholdings, 9, 17, 64, 361, 365; marriage to Thomasine Clopton, 11–12; marriage to Margaret Tyndal, 13; financial difficulties, 18, 364; attitude toward John, Jr., 21–22, 23, 27, 31, 133, 362; attorney, 26, 34; political attitudes, 26, 34–35; sale of property, 34, 51–52; formation of Massachusetts Bay Company, 43–45; chosen governor of Bay Company, 45; emigration to America, 47–48; journal, quoted, 58; governorship, 62–63, 67, 72–74, 105; land grants, 64; quarrels with Dudley, 64–65; Indians, 146, 149; death, 151; marriage to Martha Coytmore, 159, 388–89

Winthrop, Joshua, 389

Winthrop, Lucy, 216, 330

Winthrop, Margaret Tyndal, 13, 47, 56, 151

Winthrop, Martha, 329, 351

Winthrop, Martha Fones, 12, 25, 46–47, 79, 82; marriage, 47, 52–54, 367; emigration to New England, 56; at Agawam, 69–71; death, 74–75

Winthrop, Mary (daughter of Adam, III), 7

Winthrop, Mary (Winthrop's sister), 56

Winthrop, Mary (Winthrop's daughter), 132; death, 171

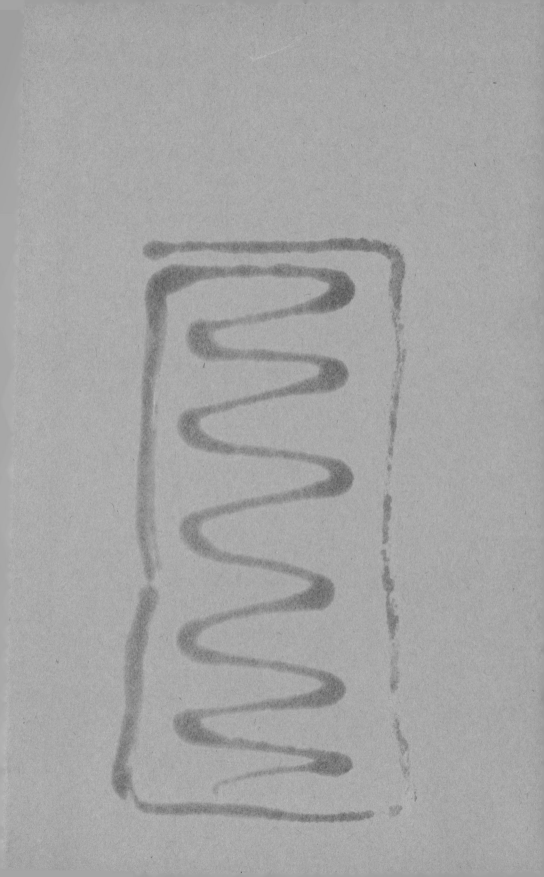